LEGENDS
OF THE
SAMURAI

LEGENDS
OF THE
SAMURAI

Hiroaki Sato

THE OVERLOOK PRESS
WOODSTOCK • NEW YORK

First published in 1995 by
The Overlook Press
Lewis Hollow Road
Woodstock, New York 12498

Library of Congress Cataloging-in-Publication Data

Sato, Hiroaki
Legends of the samurai / Hiroaki Sato.
p. cm.
1. Samurai—History. 2. Samurai—Conduct of life. 3. Ethics, Japanese.
4. Japan—History. 5. Martial arts—Japan—History.
6. Philosophy, Oriental. I. Title.
DS827.S3S36 1995
952-dc20 95-18058 CIP
The excerpt from *They Came to Japan* on pp.244-245 is quoted
by permission of Michael Cooper

Manufactured in the United States of America
Book design by Bernard Schleifer

ISBN: 0-87951-619-4
7 9 8 6

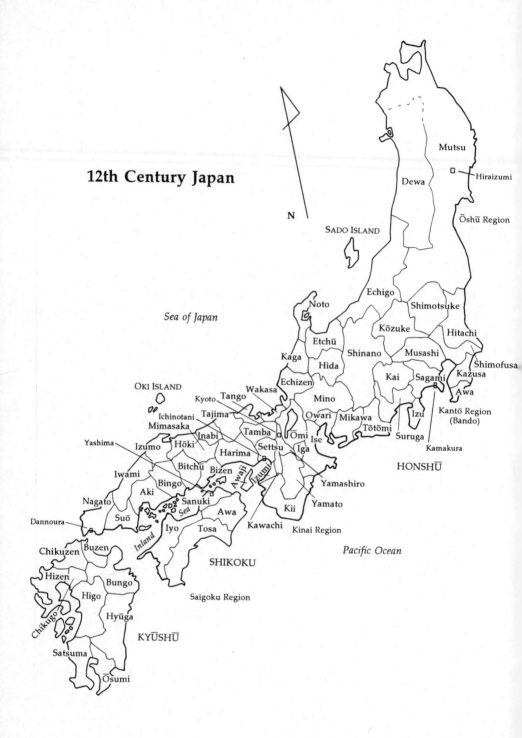

12th Century Japan

N

Mutsu

Hiraizumi

Dewa

Ōshū Region

SADO ISLAND

Sea of Japan

Noto

Echigo

Shimotsuke

Kōzuke

Hitachi

Etchū

Kaga

Shinano

Musashi

Hida

Shimofusa

OKI ISLAND

Echizen

Kai

Sagami

Kazusa

Kyoto

Tango

Wakasa

Mino

Awa

Ichinotani

Tajima

Owari

Mikawa

Izu

Kantō Region
(Bando)

Mimasaka

Tamba

Ōmi

Tōtōmi

Yashima

Inabi

Ise

Suruga

Izumo

Hōki

Settsu

Iga

Kamakura

Harima

Iwami

Bitchū

Bizen

Izumi

Yamashiro

HONSHŪ

Bingo

Aki

Sanuki

Yamato

Nagato

Suō

Awa

Kii

Dannoura

Iyo

Tosa

Kawachi

Kinai Region

Chikuzen

Buzen

Inland Sea

Pacific Ocean

Hizen

Bungo

Higo

Chikugo

Hyūga

Saigoku Region

Satsuma

KYŪSHŪ

Ōsumi

SHIKOKU

CONTENTS

Part One: Samurai Prowess

ACKNOWLEDGMENTS
AND NOTES

"The Abe Family" first saw print in the Fall-Winter 1977 issue of *St. Andrews Review*. I wish to thank Ron Bayes, founder and editor of *SAR*, a gallant magazine which fulfilled its mission and folded in late 1991.

Part of the Introduction and the section on Oda Nobunaga were originally a speech entitled "The Samurai and Poetry," given on February 19, 1992, at Cornell University.

For the English translations of official titles I generally followed Ivan Morris in *The Pillow Book of Sei Shōnagon*, vol. 2. But where I found his equivalent unacceptable, as in calling the second-ranking officer in the Imperial Police "assistant director," I devised my own. For different translations of certain titles, see Karl Friday's book on the early samurai, *Hired Swords*.

Of many such titles that appear in the accounts, "governor" (*kami*) must be viewed with the most caution. At first designating someone appointed to head a province, governorship was a position of substantial revenues and prestige perhaps until the early twelfth century. Thereafter the title gradually lost substance and became nominal until, with sporadic exceptions, it all but lost the original sense of governance. The reader should not be surprised to see "governor" attached to some of the men working for warlords.

Many of the stories, accounts, and arguments cited in this book are accompanied by running commentary, as well as notes. Some historical facts and other background information, such as the birth and death dates of the people concerned, are repeated so as to make each context easy to understand.

In most instances brackets indicate that the information given in them—be it date, name, or note—is supplied by me.

In giving dates before the mid-nineteenth century I have followed the custom of rendering the lunar calendar in English—for example, "the first month" rather than "January" as in the solar calendar. I have given Japanese and Chinese names as they are given in Japan and China, family name first.

In the old days Japanese of rank and status usually had more than one name. At times any of the personal names and the family name were used interchangeably, without gaining or losing respectability, as in the case of Kusunoki Masashige, who is sometimes called by the family name, Kusunoki, sometimes by his personal name, Masashige.

I wish to thank Kinoshita Tetsuo, Hirata Takako, Fujii Sadakazu, and Fujii Misako for acquiring necessary texts and books, and Deborah Baker and Jessika Hegewisch, my earlier editors on this book at The Overlook Press, for reading initial sections of the manuscript. Nancy Rossiter read the manuscript as it was completed chapter by chapter. She also prepared the maps on the basis of one of the maps in *Hired Swords*, with permission of Stanford University Press. Kyoko Selden read the finished manuscript and gave me helpful comments; so did my meticulous editor friend, Eleanor Wolff.

I thank Murakami Tamotsu for preparing the picture depicting Kusunoki Masashige for the cover and six illustrations.

Above all, Robert Fagan spent many days and nights on the manuscript for a period stretching over eight years. I am grateful that he never gave up.

INTRODUCTION

A samurai with a deep, wide-brimmed hat is walking through an apparently deserted field. Suddenly, more than a dozen bandits with drawn swords spring out of the surrounding grass, encircle him, and demand prompt surrender of his swords and other valuables, or else. The samurai indicates compliance and starts to take off his *haori*, the outer jacket, and the bandits relax a little. That instant he draws his sword and cuts down ten or so of them with lightning speed. The remaining few run away, screaming for their lives. The samurai takes out a tissue from his breast, wipes the blood off his sword, puts the sword back into its sheath, and resumes his walk as if nothing has happened.

Or—

A famous swordsman visits a daimyo at his mansion. A *rōnin*, a masterless samurai, who happens to be staying there, is confident of his own swordsmanship; upon learning who the visitor is, he asks him to "teach" him some fighting techniques. "Teaching" is a euphemism for a serious match. The swordsman declines. But the daimyo shows interest, and at his urging the swordsman finally agrees to fight with wooden swords. Out in the garden the two men face each other and a moment later strike—with their wooden swords hitting each other's body, apparently simultaneously.

The swordsman says, "Did you get that?"

The rōnin says, "It was a draw," looking exceedingly pleased that he's had a draw with a famous swordsman.

But the swordsman calmly says, "No, *I* won."

Upset and angered, the rōnin asks for a rematch. He gets it, and exactly the same thing happens. The two men's blows appear simultaneous.

Exactly the same exchange occurs again: The rōnin says it was a draw, and the swordsman says he won.

The rōnin becomes outraged. And the daimyo shows greater interest, half disbelieving what the swordsman has said. The rōnin now insists on another match — this time with real, steel swords. The swordsman declines but is again overruled by the daimyo. But as soon as the two men face each other, the fight is over — with the rōnin keeling over, his head split in two. The swordsman walks up to the daimyo and shows that part of his body which the rōnin's sword seemed to have struck. Part of his outer jacket is slightly cut, but not the clothes underneath, let alone his flesh.

Such may be your images of the samurai: a fantastic killing machine or a preternatural user of the sword. They are, indeed, typical of the stories of samurai endlessly spun in modern Japan as well, albeit of a particular period. I cite them at the outset, however, to make two things clear.

First, this book, *Legends of the Samurai,* aims to show the changing ethos of the Japanese warrior from a variety of angles, so it does more than assemble tales of samurai demonstrating their martial skills. Such tales, in fact, make up a minor portion of the volume, mostly collected in Part One.

Second, for such stories and some of the others, I have tried to select those versions given in the times as close to the actual incidents as possible, rather than modern retellings. Still, difficulties remain. Even if we are to lay aside the case of one mythical hero, Yamato Takeru, †[1] the time gap is often great. For example, in recounting the story of Yorozu, † a would-be "shield of the emperor," the compilers of the *Nihon Shoki* (History of Japan) were recalling, in 720, an incident of nearly 140 years earlier. There is also the urge, which seems to exist in every age, to turn a man or his actions into a legend, either to fulfill narrative convention or out of the weakness to yield to fantasy. This may at times obscure what really happened and how contemporaries viewed it.

---

1. The dagger shows the person so marked plays a notable role in this book.

The two vignettes cited above, both concerning the swordsman Yagyū Jūbē Mitsuyoshi (1607–1650), may illustrate the point. Mitsuyoshi's reputation as a swashbuckler probably began to stir imaginations of the popular story-telling variety not long after his death, yet the stories are already clearly exaggerated. The modern fiction writer Kaionji Chōgorō, while retelling the second anecdote in an essay entitled *Heihōsha* (Martial-Arts Experts),[2] makes an interesting case about swordsmen as killers. A swordsman during the Tokugawa Period (1603–1868), he says, had only four compelling reasons to be engaged in killing: when ordered by his lord, the shogun in particular, to kill a criminal or someone marked as a danger; for revenge; in a quarrel; and when he ran into a robber or bandit with murderous intent.

Of these situations, quarrels may not be worth our contemplation, Kaionji says. A good swordsman would have studiously avoided any argument that might lead to sword-brandishing. Most robbers and bandits were likely to be poor swordsmen, so that if a real swordsman ran into one or two of them, he would probably have subdued them without killing them. As for acts of vengeance, few great swordsmen are known to have been involved in them. Finally, government orders to kill someone were issued to swordsmen only in the early part of the Tokugawa Period. This explains why most of the famous swordsmen are known not to have killed a single person, Kaionji concludes.[3]

THE BOW BEFORE THE SWORD

I started this Introduction with anecdotes of a swordsman, but the swordsman is not synonymous with the samurai. The sword was a vital weapon for him from the very beginning, of course. Yet, until the fourteenth and fifteenth centuries when foot soldiers began to eclipse horsemen in battles and swordsmanship began to be pursued as a skill, the bow and arrow were the samurai's primary weapon. In a telling episode in *Heike Monogatari* (The Tale of the Heike), Japan's greatest military narrative that took its final shape in the fourteenth century, Commander in Chief Minamoto no Kurō Yoshitsune† (1159–89), during the shore battle at Yashima in early 1185, drops his bow in the water

---

2. Kaionji Chōgorō, *Shidan to Shiron*, pp. 286–305.
3. *Ibid.*, pp. 297–298.

and struggles to retrieve it even as the enemy soldiers on the boats try to strike him off his horse and his own men urge him to abandon it. When he finally retrieves it and returns to the beach, some veteran warriors openly complain:

> "That was a terrible thing to do, sir. Your bow may be worth a thousand, even ten thousands of gold, but how could it be worth risking your life?"
>
> "It isn't that I didn't want to lose the bow itself," Yoshitsune replied. "If my bow were like my uncle Tametomo's and required two or three men for the stringing, I even might have deliberately dropped it for the enemy to take. But mine is weak and feeble. If the enemy had taken it, he would have jeered at me, saying, 'See, this is Minamoto General Kurō Yoshitsune's bow!' I wouldn't have liked that. That's why I risked my life to get it back."

In *Hōgen Monogatari* (The Tale of the Hōgen Era), an account of a military clash in 1156, Yoshitsune's uncle, Tametomo (1139–70), is depicted as a bowman so powerful that after his capture his arms were dislocated at the shoulders "with a chisel," lest he use his bow again. Indeed, "bowman" (*yumitori*) continued to be used as an honorary title for a distinguished warrior long after the sword superseded the bow. The warlord Imagawa Yoshimoto† (1519–60), who was called "The Number One Bowman of the Eastern Sea," is one such example.

THE SAMURAI AND HIS ORIGINS

The word *samurai* derives from the verb *saburau*, "to wait on, serve," and in an early legal usage it meant a personal attendant. It isn't clear exactly when its meaning narrowed to designate mainly an armed attendant, then a certain type of warrior. Still, by emphasizing the original meaning of "attendant" or "servant," one can note the singular fate of the samurai as warrior: Even after he became the de facto ruler of Japan in the twelfth century, de jure he remained subordinate to the supreme civilian, the emperor. The highest position he could aspire to, *sei-i tai-shōgun*, "commander in chief to subjugate the barbarians," or shogun, was indeed technically no more than the emperor's military deputy and an emergency position at that.

As in most countries, warriors had existed in Japan since time immemorial. But the type of warrior that would go on to found a government separate from the imperial court is thought to have come into being after the efforts to establish a centralized governing body were made in the seventh and eighth centuries and the governmental system of T'ang China was adopted.

One of the eight ministries set up in the process was *Hyōbu Shō*, the Ministry of Military Affairs. Copying the Chinese example, a great many local military units were also created. Unlike China, however, Japan, far smaller and a congregation of islands, had only a few groups that were potentially threatening to the central government. At the same time, the burden imposed on anyone drafted was considerable. He was unable to engage in productive activity during his service. The soldierly gear specified by law to be acquired and carried by each man at his own expense, of course, made a long list. "One man taken, one household lost" was the saying.

In time the numbers of defense outposts and the soldiers manning them were reduced, with the men relieved of duty allowed to return to farming. In their place men from relatively well-to-do families, who were adept at using bows and riding horses, were selected. These men were each provided by the government with two footmen and adequate provisions, and required to hone their martial skills whenever possible. Although there were more institutional changes made along the way, these gentleman-soldiers, so to speak, are said to have become the main ancestors of the samurai warriors.

By the tenth century some gentleman-soldiers had formed near-autonomous local groups. Several won notoriety as outlaws, one, Taira no Masakado (d. 940), going so far as to declare himself Emperor. Some others—such as Minamoto no Mitsunaka† (913–997), whose conversion to Buddhism is described with a comic touch elsewhere in this book—created their own spheres of influence and wealth but maintained close ties with the central government, often serving as provincial governors. In either case, they were on the whole centrally oriented. Masakado turned against the imperial court and established his own, it is said, because he could not get a post he wanted in the imperial police as a means of furthering himself in the government. He was killed by warriors sent by the court.

As may be expected, within each such group close master-servant relationships developed. Protection of land holdings was a major factor. Equally important was the fierce loyalty born through shared experiences of life and death. Of special significance in this regard were the Former Nine-Year War (1051–62) and the Latter Three-Year War (1083–87), both fought to subjugate the powerful clans in the northern regions of Mutsu and Dewa. Mainly through these wars the Minamoto clan, also called Genji in Sinified form, consolidated its power and established itself as leader of the eastern region, the Kantō. Through a series of similar though less spectacular achievements, the Taira clan, also called Heiji or Heike in Sinified form, would establish itself as the prevailing force in the western region, the Saigoku or Saikai. Both clans traced their origins to the imperial house.

THE ASCENDANCE OF
THE SAMURAI

As noted, samurai status changed in the second half of the twelfth century. The change came in two stages.

First, in 1156, then in 1159, there were brief armed clashes in Kyoto, the seat of government. They were the direct results of power struggles within the imperial house. Both Minamoto and Taira warriors took part in them, with members of the clans divided in intermingling webs of alliances. In the end the Taira clan, led by Kiyomori (1118–81), emerged victorious, and the rival Minamoto clan was vanquished.

But the military outcome of the clashes was a lesser part of the story. In 1160, the year after the second conflict, Kiyomori was appointed *sangi,* "imperial advisor," a position in the Great Council of State and the first such honor accorded to a warrior.

This had historic import: The admittance of a warrior to the highest circle of governance signaled the end of the status of the samurai as the court aristocrats' mercenaries or, in Karl Friday's catchy phrase, "hired swords."[4] Kiyomori would go on to become the prime minister in 1167 and wield enormous power in other ways as well.

The next stage of the shift in samurai status was the consequence of another military confrontation, again between the Minamoto and Taira clans, but this time prolonged and nationwide. In 1180 the Minamoto clan, led by Yoritomo† (1147–99), who was then in exile near Kamakura, raised an army against the Taira and defeated them in 1185. This war was also fought in the name of a variety of imperial orders

---

4. Karl Friday, *Hired Swords: The Rise of Private Warrior Power in Early Japan.*

and for court-mandated causes. But Yoritomo was different from Kiyomori. Kiyomori accumulated and exercised power at the center of the government. Yoritomo, in contrast, generally stayed aloof from imperial polity. It was toward the end of 1190, more than five years after the destruction of the Taira clan, that he visited Kyoto to have an audience with the emperor, Gotoba (1180–1239), and the retired emperor, Goshirakawa (1127–92). During the visit he was appointed *gondainagon*, "acting major councilor," as well as *taishō*, "major captain"—the highest rank—of the Inner Palace Guards, Right Division. But he resigned from both posts the next month. In 1192 he was appointed shogun but resigned from it two years later. Evidently his interest lay in creating, as he did, his own government.

The government he established would later be called the Kamakura Bakufu—*bakufu* being a word which originally meant the field headquarters of a general in war. Thereafter, until the imperial restoration in 1868, this form of "government within the government" would be the real power, with the court, in Kyoto, relegated to being "the source of honors and the seat of national ceremony and ritual."[5]

THE AGE OF
WARRING STATES

The Kamakura Bakufu lasted until 1333 when Emperor Godaigo† (1288–1339), advocating absolute imperial authority, briefly won the day. More than a century earlier, in 1220, the feisty Emperor Gotoba had entertained a similar notion and raised an army against Kamakura, but his troops were trounced and he was exiled. Godaigo was luckier. Though arrested and exiled at the early stage of his attempt to regain his authority, he was able to return from exile, destroy the Kamakura government, and become, rightfully, "the Supreme One." But his mismanagement—in particular his rewarding court nobles far more sumptuously than warriors—bred discontent in no time. Ashikaga Takauji† (1305–58), who had turned traitor to the Kamakura and joined Godaigo's cause, soon rebelled. In a series of battles, he defeated Godaigo's commanders, among them the ablest and the most dedicated soldier Kusunoki Masashige† (1294–1336). He elected a man

5. George Sansom, *A History of Japan to 1333*, p. 331.

of his choice emperor and forced Godaigo to surrender the imperial symbols, "the three divine treasures": mirror, sword, and jewel. In 1338 he had himself appointed shogun.

The shogunate started by Takauji was headquartered in Kyoto, and continued for fifteen generations, until the time of Yoshiaki (1537–97). But from start to end this administration was wracked by dissension and revolts. Three main reasons may be advanced for this.

For one, Godaigo, not exiled the second time but allowed to escape, established his own court in Yoshino, in present-day Nara. This "Southern" court, which existed in parallel with the "Northern" court, in Kyoto, until 1392, helped fuel the schisms in and outside the Ashikaga Shogunate, not only during its existence but for a long time after its demise as well. For another, the placement, in Kamakura, of the shogunate deputy for the Eastern region, called the *Kantō kubō*, created similar problems: It encouraged suspicions, invited rivalries, and promoted shifting allegiances. Finally, the organization of the central administration emphasized deputization and group decision-making. Such an arrangement might work if the leader had firm authority or economic backing. Ashikaga shoguns often lacked both.

The decade-long civil strife called the Ōnin War (1467–77) was touched off when the eighth shogun, Yoshimasa (1435–90), disagreed with his wife, Hino Tomiko (1440–96), on his successor and the several clans designated to serve as shogunate deputies took strong partisan positions. The war dragged most of the governors and other local men of power into taking sides with one or the other of the two antagonists at the center, but it was only the first clear breakdown of the Ashikaga shogunate. By strengthening already manifest local assertiveness and independence, it directly led to the second, larger round of chaos: Japan's *sengoku jidai*, the "age of warring states," when men with means or talent openly fought among themselves for control or expansion of territory.

Well over a century of battles for local hegemony tore Japan. Brutalities perpetrated during the period were astonishing at times, no doubt. At the same time, however, the country remained on the whole fluid and open, rather than static and closed, and occasionally produced unconventional, rationalist attitudes. Asakura Takakage (also Toshikage: 1426–82), a small landowner-samurai who became the governor of a domain and who is therefore regarded as a forerunner of the age of warring states, left a "house law." Here are some of its articles:

ITEM: In the Asakura family no such position as senior administrator shall be created. Choose men on their ability and loyalty.

ITEM: Don't make an incompetent a general or a commissioner simply because the position has been handed down from generation to generation.

ITEM: Don't yearn too much for a sword made by a famous smith. This is because even if you give a man a sword worth ten thousand coppers, he won't be able to beat a hundred men each holding a spear worth a hundred coppers.

ITEM: Be good to a brave man even if he's ugly in appearance. Also, even someone timid can be useful as your attendant if he has presentable looks.

ITEM: When there is a battle you can win or a castle you can scale, it's regrettable to miss the opportunity trying to select an auspicious day or to put yourself in the right direction. No matter how auspicious the day may be, you aren't showing good judgment if you launch a ship in a hurricane or if you, with few men, dash into battle with an overwhelming force.

Cited in full elsewhere in this book are similar but somewhat more down-to-earth "house lessons" left by Hōjō Sōun† (1432–1519). Sōun was not unlike Takakage: Originally a rōnin, he rose to become an illustrious warlord.

THE SAMURAI
UNDER THE TOKUGAWA

Chaos eventually seeks unity. With as many as 150 warlords in place by the mid-sixteenth century, the desire to become the overlord of them all was inevitable. Oda Nobunaga† (1534–82) was the first to pursue the desire in earnest and achieve notable success. When he was assassinated in the midst of his work, one of his generals, Toyotomi Hideyoshi (1536–98), took over and completed the task. Tokugawa Ieyasu (1542–1616), one of Hideyoshi's five commissioners at his death, made the unification his own by, among other things, having himself appointed shogun and founding his bakufu in Edo, present-day Tokyo, in 1603.

The shogunate that Ieyasu founded lasted for a quarter of a millennium, the longest of the three military governments. The system collapsed in the end as internal economic stresses mounted and foreign pressures to break its isolationist policy, adopted early in the seventeenth century, proved impossible to resist. Nonetheless, the period is distinguished by a singular lack of military strife. Two administrative measures helped achieve this peace: hostage-taking on a vast scale and codification of hierarchy and behavior.

The hostage-taking system, called *sankin kōtai*, "serving the lord in shifts," required daimyo—lords with holdings or annual revenues of 10,000 *koku* or about 50,000 bushels of rice or more—and Tokugawa vassals with the rank of *hatamoto*, "aide-de-camp," to spend every other year or half of each year in Edo, under the direct supervision of the central government. Asano Naganori† (1667–1701) was fulfilling his Edo-residence requirement when he acted in a manner that would touch off what was to become the most famous vendetta in Japanese history. (It may be added, as a reminder of the status of the imperial court at the time, that the incident occurred while Naganori was a member of the committee to receive the purely ceremonial annual messengers from Kyoto.)

The division of the entire population into four classes—samurai, farmers, craftsmen, and merchants, in that order—and the detailed ranking, set and made largely hereditary within the samurai class, was not always enforced as rigidly as is often assumed. The merchants, the lowest rung of the ladder, in no time took the upper hand of the samurai, the highest, in economic life. Within the samurai class, too, there was a good deal of freedom, as witness Arai Hakuseki† (1657–1725): A man from a samurai family working for a small local lord, he rose to the exalted position of shogunate counselor. Still, the class system and the hereditary ranking arrangements blocked social mobility and, shall we say, unrest, to a remarkable degree.

The lack of military action came with the creation of civilian bureaucracies, and both peace and civilian life forced the samurai to justify himself as warrior. The Confucian scholar Nakae Tōjū (1608–48) made an early attempt to provide the samurai with philosophical underpinnings for his existence. In his treatise *Okina Mondō* (Questions and Answers with an Old Man), he has two imaginary men engage in the following Socratic discourse:

> Someone asked: "They often say that literary and martial skills are like the two wheels of a cart, the two wings of a bird. Does this mean that 'literary' and 'martial' are two different things? How do you define 'literary' and 'martial' in this context?"

The Master replied: "Ordinary people have a great misunderstanding about 'literary' and 'martial.' By 'literary' they mean the ability to compose poems in Japanese and make verses in Chinese, the ability to write well, and being mild and delicate in temperament, whereas by 'martial' they mean training in and knowledge of the bow and horse, martial arts, and military strategy, and being rough and stern in temperament. They seem right, but they are utterly wrong.

"By nature, literary and martial skills are a single virtue, and they are not separate from each other. Just as the creation of heaven and earth, completed in a single breath, has two elements of yin and yang, so human nature, made of a single virtue, has two elements of 'literary' and 'martial.' This means that having literary skills without having martial skills is not truly being literary, and having martial skills without having literary skills is not truly being martial. Just as yin is the root of yang, and yang the root of yin, literary skills are the root of martial skills, and martial skills the root of literary skills.

"To rule the nation well and correctly follow the five ethical principles,[6] with heaven as warp and earth as woof, is the 'literary' task. If, however, there appears someone who is not afraid of heaven's order and commits evil, cruel, immoral acts and thereby blocks the 'literary' path, it will be necessary to punish him with a penalty or raise an army against him and subjugate him, so that the nation may be governed in unified peace. That is the 'martial' task. This is why the Chinese character for *bu* (*wu*, martial, military) is made by combining the two characters of *hoko* (*ko*, halberd, weapons) and *yamuru* (*chih*, stop block).[7]

Arguments such as this, stressing the essentially civilian nature of military rule, were powerful and became the backbone of the Tokugawa government. This was not adequate for individual samurai, however, and they had to devise a code of conduct for themselves. The centuries-old notion that honor was of ultimate importance for the samurai and that to uphold this honor he had to be prepared to die was fine-tuned in the Edo Period. So was born the proposition enunciated by Yamamoto Tsunetomo† (1659–1721): "The way of the warrior, I've found, is to die."

---

6. According to the Chinese philosopher Mencius, the "five ethical principles" are affection between father and son, righteousness between ruler and subject, separate functions for husband and wife, proper order between old and young, and trust between friends.

7. The observation on the Chinese character *wu* goes back to China's "oldest narrative history," *The Tso Chuan.* In Burton Watson's translation, see p. 99.

DECAPITATION AND
DISEMBOWELMENT

Two practices are likely to attract the attention of anyone reading samurai accounts: beheading and disembowelment. The Japanese practice of decapitating an enemy soldier was probably copied from early warfare in China where a soldier was rewarded with promotion by a single rank for taking the head of a worthy enemy in battle. The expression *shukyū o ageru*, "take a head and raise a rank," derived from that reward system.

The origins of disembowelment remain obscure, though a number of instances are reported in China and elsewhere. One curious thing is that the earliest extant Japanese document referring to disembowelment attributes the act to a female deity. Explaining the name Harasaki ("Belly-tearing") Swamp, the *Harima no Kuni Fudoki* (Topographical Reports on Harima Province), compiled in the early eighth century, says it is so called because "the Deity of Hananami's wife, the Deity of Ōmi, pursuing her husband, reached this place, but finally becoming resentful and incensed, tore her own belly with a sword and submerged herself in the swamp."

Whether or not they knew that the first to perform the act was a female deity, by the eleventh century the samurai had adopted belly-cutting as a means of showing courage or avoiding the disgrace of submitting themselves to indignities in the hands of their enemies. The practice appears to have become widespread in the fourteenth century. Disembowelment was also used to follow one's lord in death. In the seventeenth century the Tokugawa government took it up as a form of penalty for a disgraced samurai—a way for a samurai to honorably dispatch himself.

Slitting open one's belly in itself seldom brings immediate death, and failure to die from self-inflicted wounds can be excruciating and messy. In recognition of this a prescription at one time dictated cutting the belly horizontally, then vertically, followed by a *coup de grâce*: stabbing or cutting the neck. General Nogi Maresuke (1849–1912), who committed suicide on the day of the funeral of Emperor Meiji (1852–1912), is believed to have followed this procedure.

But to carry the three steps to the necessary end requires uncommon fortitude. This led to the arrangement of having or providing a second, *kaishaku* or *kaishakunin*, whose role is to cut the head off at one of two points.

In one approach the kaishaku performed decapitation at the very moment the condemned samurai, seated, craned his neck as he leaned forward to take the short sword or dirk placed on a ceremonial tray a few feet in front; this procedure did not entail actual disembowelment. In the most stylized form of this approach worked out during the Tokugawa period, a fan was often substituted for the short sword.

In the other approach the kaishaku waited until the man he was to help completed the first or the second of the three steps. This was the approach that a samurai named Taki Zenzaburō chose for his own disembowelment on March 2, 1868, graphically described by Sir Ernest Mason Satow (1843–1929), Secretary of the British Legation in Edo:

> After we had sat quietly thus for about ten minutes footsteps were heard approaching along the verandah. The condemned man, a tall Japanese of gentleman-like bearing and aspect, entered on the left side, accompanied by his *kai-shaku* or best men, and followed by two others, apparently holding the same office. Taki was dressed in blue *kami-shimo* of hempen cloth; the *kai-shaku* wore war surcoats (*jimbaori*). Coming before the Japanese witnesses they prostrated themselves, the bow being returned, and then the same ceremony was exchanged with us. Then the condemned man was led to a red sheet of felt-cloth laid on the dais before the altar; on this he squatted, after performing two bows, one at a distance, the other close to the altar. With the calmest deliberation he took his seat on the red felt, choosing the position which would afford him the greatest convenience for falling forward. A man dressed in black with a light grey hempen mantle then brought in the dirk wrapped in paper on a small unpainted wooden stand, and with a bow placed it in front of him. He took it up in both hands, raised it to his forehead and laid it down again with a bow. This is the ordinary Japanese gesture of thankful reception of a gift. Then in a distinct voice, very much broken, not by fear or emotion, but as it seemed reluctance to acknowledge an act of which he was ashamed—declared that he alone was the person who on the fourth of February had outrageously at Kōbé ordered fire to be opened on foreigners as they were trying to escape, that for having committed this offense he was going to rip up his bowels, and requested all present to be witnesses. He next divested himself of his upper garments by withdrawing his arms from the sleeves, the long ends of which he tucked under his legs to prevent his body from falling backward. The body was thus quite naked to below

the navel. He then took the dirk in his right hand, grasping it just close to the point, and after stroking down the front of his chest and belly inserted the point as far down as possible and drew it across to the right side, the position of his clothes still fastened by the girth preventing our seeing the wound. Having done this he with great deliberation bent his body forward, throwing the head back so as to render the neck a fair object for the sword. The one *kai-shaku* who had accompanied him round the two rows of witnesses to make his bows to them, had been crouching on his left hand a little behind him with drawn sword poised in the air from the moment the operation commenced. He now sprang up suddenly and delivered a blow the sound of which was like thunder.[8]

It is said that the writer Mishima Yukio (1925–70) was determined to follow the same approach, but as he cut deeply into his belly his muscles tensed and he bucked up and his kaishaku was unable to cut his head off with a single stroke as planned.

THE SAMURAI
AND POETRY

Ancient and classical tales of samurai, like some other Japanese narratives, are sprinkled with verses. Incorporating verses into narratives is a notable feature of Buddhist scriptures, and ancient Chinese historians and other writers liked to place them at strategic points of their stories. The chroniclers and storytellers of ancient Japan were familiar with both and may well have picked up the rhetorical device from them. In later periods, the ability to compose poems became part of a gentleman's education, and the custom of writing a verse in preparation for death developed. As a result of all this, the relationship between the samurai and poetry writing became nearly inseparable.

---

8. *A Diplomat in Japan*, pp. 345–346. Satow, referring to an English newspaper's accusation that "it was disgraceful for Christians to have attended the execution," goes on to observe, "I was proud to feel that I had not shrunk from witnessing a punishment which I did my best to bring about. It was no disgusting exhibition, but a most decent and decorous ceremony, and far more respectable than what our own countrymen were in the habit of producing for the entertainment of the public in the front of Newgate prison." Satow's friend at the British Legation, A. B. Mitford (Lord Redesdale), was also a witness and wrote his own account of the same execution; it is included in Nitobe Inazō's *Bushidō, The Soul of Japan*, reprinted in *Bushido: The Warrior's Code*, pp. 76–78. It originally appeared in Mitford's book, *Tales of Old Japan*.

In the seventh century—some scholars say even earlier—the two units of five and seven syllables became the basis of Japanese versification. At first, long verses were written by repeating the 5-7-syllable combination indefinitely, but the *tanka*, "short song," made up of 5-7-5-7-7 syllables, became the most widely used poetic form by the ninth century.

Not long after it became standard in versification, the tanka developed a tendency to break up into two hemistiches or sections of 5-7-5 and 7-7, and poets, in pairs, began to compose the two separately and "link" them, often reversing the order of the sections, composing 7-7 first, 5-7-5 second. So was born the poetic form of *renga*, "linked verse." Later, the linking of the 5-7-5- and 7-7–combination would be repeated up to fifty times to make a sequence consisting of a hundred verse sections. Often as many as a dozen people took part in composing a single such sequence.

One way of understanding renga, in its minimal combination of two sections, might be to imagine yourself and a friend of yours composing something similar to a children's riddle but in a poetically sophisticated form, say, a heroic couplet: One of you will say the first line, the other promptly completing the poem by saying the second. Puns are essential. Let us look at an example.

In the *Heike Monogatari* there is a story about the poet-warrior Minamoto no Yorimasa† (1104–80) shooting down a fantastic beast that comes to the roof of the Imperial Palace in a dark cloud and gives the emperor nightmares.[9] Grateful for Yorimasa's bowmanship, the emperor rewards him with a sword. Taking the sword to hand it over to Yorimasa, Minister of the Left Fujiwara no Yorinaga (1120–56) steps down the stairs. At that moment, up in the sky a cuckoo, a prized bird of summer, calls a couple of times. Thereupon the minister comes up with the following 5-7-5:

Hototogisu na o mo kumoi ni aguru kana

A cuckoo makes himself known above the clouds

Yorimasa, respectfully kneeling at the bottom of the staircase, responds with a 7-7:

---

9. The same warrior shoots down a monstrous bird called *nue* in the same tale. The *nue* story is told differently in the Kō no Moronao section in the *Taiheiki* and appears in this book on pp. 189–190.

yumiharizuki no iru ni makasete

as the crescent moon is eclipsed

If composed by one poet, this would be a tanka, and a pretty good one at that. The fact that two composed it turns it into a renga, and the use of puns makes it a worthy one. In Yorinaga's hemistich, *na o aguru* means both "to call" and "to establish one's reputation," and *kumoi*, both "clouds, where clouds are" and "the Imperial Palace." So the 5-7-5, though seemingly an impromptu description of a natural phenomenon, is also a great compliment paid to Yorimasa meaning, "You, our trusty warrior, have established your reputation even with your Sovereign."

Similarly, in Yorimasa's completing hemistich, *yumiharizuki*, "moon arched like a bow," means the moon at any time between the new and full moons but, in particular, the crescent moon; it also puns on "a drawn bow"; *iru* means both "to be eclipsed" and "to shoot"; finally, *makasete* indicates the process of something happening as well as the state of no effort exerted. So the 7-7, again seemingly innocuous, is also a self-deprecating response meaning, "Sir, I just drew the bow and shot, no more."

Composing longer renga sequences became the rage among samurai during the fourteenth century and, even though they came with complicated rules, their popularity continued throughout the "age of warring states." The warlord Hosokawa Fujitaka (later Yūsai: 1534–1610), who was a learned scholar and poet, recalled how his fellow warlord and poet Miyoshi Chōkei (1523–64) would act in a renga session:

> [Chōkei] would sit like a statue, keeping a fan placed by his knees, slightly aslant. If it was extremely hot, he would very quietly pick up the fan with his right hand, open it deftly by four or five ribs with his left hand, and use it close to himself lest he make noise. He then would close it, again with his left hand, and place it back where it was. He would do it so precisely that the fan would not be off its original position even by the breadth of a single straw of the tatami.[10]

---

10. The description appears in *Taion Ki* (Record of the People to Whom I Am Greatly Indebted) by the poet and educator Matsunaga Teitoku (1571–1653).

It may be amusing to note that Chōkei was one of the more notable hustlers among the warlords and did quite well as a result of his hustling.

This admiring portrayal of Chōkei tells us one important thing about classical verse composition in Japan. Renga, as a group game, placed the utmost value on the participants' observance of protocol, etiquette, and rules. A large part of the enjoyment lay, apparently, in the sense of participation, both in a given group and in tradition as a whole. As far as we can tell from actual compositions, the content was of secondary value or it was of primary value only insofar as the poet was able to display his grasp of traditional dictates.

The sense of tradition was no less vital in the composition of renga's parent, the 5–7–5–7–7–syllable tanka. I shall cite three examples.

In the seventh month of 1183, the Taira clan abandoned the capital and fled west in the face of a large Minamoto army advancing from the east, taking with them the young emperor, Antoku (1178–1185), and setting fire to houses in their retreat. However, one of the top Taira commanders, Tadanori (1144–1184), rode back to pay a farewell call to his teacher of poetry, Fujiwara no Shunzei (1114–1204). As the *Heike Monogatari* tells the story, when he was admitted into Shunzei's room, he said:

> "You have kindly guided me, sir, in the way of poetry for many years, and I have never regarded it as less than most important. Yet, for the last few years there has been turmoil in Kyoto, and the country has been torn, the whole affair involving the fate of our house. In consequence, even while I did not want to neglect my study, I was unable to come to you every time. His Majesty has already left the capital. Our clan is now doomed.
>
> "I had heard there would be an anthology and thought that should you extend your indulgence to me and include perhaps a single verse of mine, that would be the greatest honor of my lifetime. But soon the world was thrown into chaos, and when I learned the compilation was suspended, I was greatly aggrieved. When the world calms down, sir, you are likely to resume the compilation of the imperial anthology. Should you find anything appropriate in the scroll I've brought here with me and be indulgent enough to include just one verse, I would rejoice in my grave and would protect you into the distant future."

When he had left, he had taken with him a scroll in which he had assembled and written 100-odd poems that he thought were good from among the ones he had composed over the years. Now he took it out of the joining of the body plates of his armor and reverentially gave it to Lord Shunzei.

Shunzei, the supreme arbiter of poetry of his day, had indeed received, in the second month of the same year, a command from Retired Emperor Goshirakawa to compile the seventh imperial anthology of Japanese poetry. The *Heike* goes on to say that he did include one of Tadanori's poems in *Senzai Shū*, the anthology he finished after the world calmed down, but listed it as "poet unknown," because Tadanori, by then dead, was an enemy of the imperial court.[11] So what was the poem like? Did it describe an aspect of a warrior's life? Confusion of a powerful clan whose fortune was suddenly reversed? Sufferings of people caught in military strife? No. It went:

Sazanami ya Shiga no miyako wa arenishi o
mukashi nagara no yama-zakura kana

The capital of Shiga of rippling waves has turned wild
but mountain cherries remain as of old

In 667 Emperor Tenji (626–671) had moved the nation's capital to Ōtsu, in Shiga, on the west bank of Lake Biwa, but it was abandoned a year after his death. By Shunzei's time Shiga had long become an *utamakura*, "poetic place name," and the poem, composed on the set topic of "Blossoms in My Home Town," is a typical one combining imagined nostalgia for an abandoned capital and the contrasting beauty of unchanging cherry blossoms. Indeed, it is safe to assume that none of the 100-odd poems Tadanori assembled with care went beyond the topics and diction deemed proper by the dictates of court poetry.

Another example comes from Hosokawa Fujitaka, and it may have been intended to be his farewell to the world:

---

11. Some texts of the *Heike* attribute another anonymous poem in *Senzai Shū* to Tadanori; if his poems in later anthologies, where he is identified by name, are added, he has a total of ten (or eleven) of his pieces included in imperial compendiums—a respectable accomplishment. The *Heike* quotes one more poem by Tadanori, which is said to have been found in his helmet when he was beheaded. The *Senzai* lists four poems by three other Taira men as anonymous.

Inishie mo ima mo kawaranu yo no naka ni
  kokoro no tane o nokosu koto no ha

In the world that today remains unchanged from ancient times
  leaves that are words retain seeds in the human heart

This Fujitaka wrote in 1600, when his castle was surrounded by an overwhelming enemy. He sent it to the imperial court, along with a record of what he had learned as "secret transmissions" about the first imperial anthology of Japanese poetry, *Kokin Shū*, compiled in the early tenth century. By that time the tradition of handing down certain interpretations of obscure words and phrases in the anthology had been firmly established, and no one at the time had a greater grasp of such transmissions than Fujitaka, warrior though he was. Emperor Goyōzei (1571–1617), known for his keen interest in learning, was aggrieved at the prospect of losing such a scholar; he at once took steps to save the man, which in the end succeeded, even though Fujitaka initially refused to submit himself to such an unwarrior-like surrender.

As written in such circumstances, this poem has no hint of military overtones or the suggestion that it was composed by a samurai driven up against the wall. Instead, it is characterized by an obvious allusion to the *Kokin Shū*: the opening phrases, *inishie mo ima mo,* refer to the title of the anthology where *kokin* is a Sinified way of saying *inishie,* "ancient times," and *ima,* "now," while the second half of the poem directly refers to the opening sentence in the preface to the anthology: "Japanese poetry has its seeds in the human heart, and takes form in the countless leaves that are words."

A far more recent tanka, written by a latter-day samurai, again shows the importance of poetic tradition. On March 17, 1945, Lieutenant General Kuribayashi Tadamichi, commander of the Japanese forces defending Iwo Jima, telegraphed three tanka to the General Headquarters before charging into the enemy with the 800 soldiers remaining under his command. This is one of the three:

Ada utade nobe ni wa kuchiji
  ware wa mata natabi umarete hoko wo toramuzo

Foe unvanquished, I won't perish in the field;
  I'll be born again, to take up the halberd seven more times!

The 70,000-man U.S. assault on Iwo Jima began on February 16. During the 36-day battle that followed, all but a thousand out of the 21,000 Japanese defenders of the island were killed, while the American forces suffered a total of 25,851 casualties, "of whom 6,821 were killed, died of wounds, or were missing in action."[12]

General Kuribayashi's verse alludes to the words of the warrior Kusunoki Masashige's brother, Masasue, before the two stabbed each other to death: the words expressing the hope to be reborn seven times to avenge the emperor, which had long become a nationalist slogan.[13] It may be said that the general's sentiment, along with the poetic form and diction he chose, was hopelessly anachronistic: Just imagine all those modern weapons of destruction used in that battle, and he was talking about "taking up a halberd"! But there is no doubt that in the act of composing the poem, Kuribayashi was expressing his desire to be part of Japan's age-old tradition.

I should also mention verse written in Chinese in accordance with Chinese prosody, called *kanshi*. My examples will be two of the better-known ones composed by Nogi Maresuke, a general mentioned earlier as having committed disembowelment on the day of an emperor's funeral.

Nogi commanded an army in both the Sino-Japanese War (1894-95) and the Russo-Japanese War (1904–05). In both wars he was ordered to attack Lüshun, which, in those days, was called Port Arthur in the West. He wrote one of the two poems in early June 1904, when, leading the Third Army to Lüshun he passed through Nanshan, where a great battle had just been fought and Katsuyori, one of his two sons, had been killed. It reads:

Mountain and river, grass and tree, grow more barren;
for ten miles winds smell of blood in the fresh battlefield.
Conquering horses do not advance nor do men talk;
outside Jinzhou Castle, I stand in the setting sun.

When he wrote this poem Nogi had no way of knowing that he would shortly plunge into a prolonged series of savage battles. Even

---

12. Bill D. Ross, *Iwo Jima: Legacy of Valor*, p. xiii.
13. See p. 187 of this book. Commander Hirose Takeo (1868–1904), of the Imperial Navy, for example, used the pledge in several of his poems, most notably in one extolling loyalty to the emperor and one sent to his relatives before leading a commando in Luxu, at the beginning of the Russo-Japanese War, in which he was directly hit by an artillery shell.

though in the war ten years earlier he had taken Luxu in a single day, subduing the Russian fortress at the same place would take him more than four months. In the end the Russian and Japanese armies threw a combined total of 145,000 soldiers into the battles, of whom 78,000 became casualties, 18,000 killed. Nogi wrote the following poem toward the end of 1905 as he and his army prepared to return to Japan.

> Emperor's army, a million, conquered the powerful foe;
> field battles and fort assaults made mountains of corpses.
> Ashamed—how can I face their fathers, grandfathers?
> We triumph today, but how many return?[14]

TRANSLATION

A translator of old Japanese chronicles, tales, and records faces several vexing problems, most of which converge in a single question: whether to try to preserve the nuances of the original writings or ignore them for readability. I have elected to take the former course because my aim is to reproduce the original writings in English, rather than to retell them—unless of course the act of translation itself is thought to be the retelling process.

Among the more obvious problems are the old custom of one man changing his name several times in his lifetime, as happens, for example, with the warlords Takeda Shingen† (1521–73) and Uesugi Kenshin† (1530–78), and the custom of referring to a single man by changing official titles, as happens most notably with Minamoto no Kurō Yoshitsune. Calling Shingen and Kenshin by their mature names throughout the English translation will misrepresent not only the original accounts used but also their lives, in which name-changes played significant roles. In a similar way, calling Yoshitsune uniformly

---

14. In a small book entitled *Nogi*, published in 1913, the American journalist Stanley Washburn lovingly describes how his colleague, Richard Barry, of *Collier's Weekly*, attempted to translate some of Nogi's poems into English with the poet himself, agonizing over "whether the meters of Shakespeare or those of Swinburne [are] the more worthy to carry the ideas of the General."

It must be noted that, even though Nogi emerged from the war as an international hero, during the last phase of the assault on Port Arthur General Kodama Gentarō (1852–1906), deputy chief of staff of Japan's Manchurian forces, replaced him as de facto commander and led the siege to Japanese victory. This was done with Nogi's consent but without public knowledge, and Kodama returned to his headquarters as soon as victory was secured. Kodama died the following year, it is said, because of the anxiety and exhaustion he had to go through during the war.

by his name when he is referred to by changing titles will violate the delicate sense of development and change, thereby doing injustice to the remarkable military commander and those who meticulously tried to record his moves.

Though with no direct bearing on translation, two other aspects may prove rough going for some readers: the listing of names that occasionally appears and, related to it, assumption of knowledge on the reader's part.

First, about name listing, it may well be remembered that for the warriors participation or nonparticipation in a given military action determined their reputation and rewards. This explains why old military chronicles and narratives accord as a matter of fact a prominent position to *soroe*, the "lineup," of the participants. A prime example in Western literature is found in Book Two of the *Iliad*. In writing a biography of his former lord, Oda Nobunaga, Ōta Gyūichi (1527–1610?) even used a new paragraph when he listed more than a certain number of people who engaged in a military action.

Second, a vital part of any enumeration of names is the enumerator's sure knowledge that someone who finds the listing of value will recognize some of the names listed and the context in which they appear or that the reader, at the least, will know a good deal about the principal figures in a given sequence of events described. This assumption loses much of its validity with time and, of course, when the account is translated into a foreign language. However, if you find bewildering the excerpts from the *Azuma Kagami* (History of the East) describing the movements of Yoshitsune or those from the *Nihon Gaishi* (An Unofficial History of Japan) describing countless battles of Shingen and Kenshin, I hope you will remember that one purpose of *Legends of the Samurai* is to give a variety of *styles* of narration.

THE MAKEUP OF THIS BOOK

This book has four parts.

PART ONE, "Samurai Prowess," is mainly a collection of tales of men accomplished in some martial skills. The majority of stories are selected from the *Konjaku Monogatari Shū* (A Collection of Tales of Times Now Past), a compendium of more than a thousand stories put together in the twelfth century. The section ends with a tale of a samurai in the early thirteenth century.

PART TWO, "Battles Joined," is an assemblage of stories of distinguished warrior-commanders and warlords and their battles. The sources for this section range from a government chronicle, to grand Chinese-style narratives, to contemporary accounts. The section brings the story up to the sixteenth century.

PART THREE, "The Way of the Warrior," is designed to present views written by the samurai themselves, although some of those whose writings are quoted in translation are not so much warriors as men of letters. Among the latter are Arai Hakuseki, who has left a memorable portrait of his father, and Confucian scholars who argued the merits and demerits of the vendetta carried out by forty-seven samurai. This section takes the story forward to the first half of the eighteenth century.

PART FOUR, "A Modern Retelling," consists of a single fictionalized "modern" recounting of a series of incidents that took place in the mid-seventeenth century, with the focus of the narrative on a samurai who elected to commit disembowelment without his lord's permission. The reteller is Mori Ōgai (1862–1922), an outstanding man of letters who rose to the rank of surgeon general in the Japanese Imperial Army. Ōgai was trained in Western medicine and versed in Western values, but when his friend, General Nogi Maresuke, committed suicide by disembowelment, he decided to reexamine Japan's past, searched out old documents, and wrote a series of historical stories. The one selected here, "The Abe Family," was the second in the series. Admired for faithfully recreating the samurai ethos of the time described, as seen, of course, by a man of wide knowledge, the story is, I hope, a fitting end to *Legends of the Samurai*.

CHRONOLOGY

587: During the Soga-Mononobe clash, warrior Yorozu killed.

Nara Period: 710–794

712: *Kojiki* (Record of Ancient Matters) compiled.

720: *Nihon Shoki* (History of Japan) compiled.

749: Ōtomo no Yakamochi writes a poem on the discovery of gold.

End of the eighth century: *Man'yō Shū* (Collection of Ten Thousand Leaves) compiled.

Heian Period: 794–1185

940: The rebel Taira no Masakado, who declared himself Emperor, killed.

Mid-tenth century: Minamoto no Mitsuru and Taira no Yoshifumi engage in an equestrian duel.

999?: Minamoto no Yorinobu subdues an armed burglar.

Early eleventh century: Sei Shōnagon writes *Makura no Sōshi* (The Pillow Book).

1051–62: Former Nine-Year War. Minamoto no Yoriyoshi commands government forces. *Mutsu Waki* (The Story of Mutsu), an account of the war, written.

1083–87: Latter Three-Year War. Minamoto no Yoshiie commands government forces.

1098: Yoshiie allowed to enter imperial court.

1156: Hōgen Disturbance.

1159: Heiji Disturbance. Taira no Kiyomori emerges victorious, with leaders of the Minamoto clan, including Yoshitomo, killed.

1160: Kiyomori admitted to imperial court.

1180: Minamoto no Yoritomo raises an army against the Taira.

1183: During the Taira's retreat from Kyoto, Tadanori rides back to entrust his poems with Fujiwara no Shunzei.

Kamakura Period: 1185–1333

1185: The Taira vanquished.

1189: Minamoto no Yoshitsune killed.

1192: Yoritomo appointed shogun (but resigns two years later).

Twelfth century: *Konjaku Monogatari Shū* (A Collection of Tales of Times Now Past) compiled.

Around 1200: *Uji Shūi Monogatari* (Tales Gleaned from Uji) compiled.

1219–1222?: *Hōgen Monogatari* (The Tale of the Hōgen Era) and *Heiji Monogatari* (The Tale of the Heiji Era) completed.

1254: Tachibana no Narisue compiles *Kokon Chomon Jū* (A Collection of Ancient and Modern Tales That I've Heard).

Early fourteenth century: *Azuma Kagami* (History of the East), describing the first ninety years of the Kamakura government, compiled.

1333: Emperor Godaigo briefly restores imperial rule.

Namboku-chō (Northern-Southern Court) Period: 1336–1392

1336: Kusunoki Masashige killed in the battle of the Minato River. Ashikaga Takauji helps install Kōmyō as Emperor (Northern Court). Godaigo takes his court to Yoshino (Southern Court).

1338: Takauji appointed shogun.

1349: *Baishō Ron* (On the Plums and Pines), a chronicle of the early years of the Ashikaga Shogunate, completed.

1371: Akashi no Kakuichi, who is thought to have given the final shape to the *Heike Monogatari* (The Tale of the Heike), dies.

1370–72?: Monk Kojima and others enlarge and complete *Taiheiki* (Chronicle of Great Peace).

Ashikaga (Muromachi) and Momoyama Periods: 1392–1603

1392: Ashikaga Period begins as Emperor Gokomatsu, of the Southern Court, receives the "three treasures" from Emperor Gokameyama, of the Northern Court.

1467–77: Ōnin War. Beginning of the "Age of Warring States."

1519: Hōjō Sōun, who wrote "21 House Lessons," dies.

1543?: A Portuguese ship brings a harquebus to Tanegashima, Japan.

1555: The biggest clash between Takeda Shingen and Uesugi Kenshin at Kawanakajima.

1560: Oda Nobunaga defeats Imagawa Yoshimoto in the battle of Okehazama.

1565: Thirteenth Ashikaga shogun Yoshiteru dies fighting with sword.

1573: Nobunaga drives the fifteenth Ashikaga shogun Yoshiaki out of Kyoto. Shingen dies.

1575: Nobunaga defeats Shingen's son, Katsuyori, by deploying 3,000 harquebuses. The first strategic use of guns in Japan.

1578: Kenshin dies.

1582: Nobunaga assassinated by Akechi Mitsuhide. Mitsuhide defeated by Toyotomi Hideyoshi and killed.

1590: Hideyoshi completes the unification of Japan.

1592: Hideyoshi sends armies to Korea with the aim of conquering China.

1597: Hideyoshi sends armies to Korea for the second time.

1598: Hideyoshi dies.

1600: Most warlords divide into two camps, East and West, and clash at Sekigahara. Tokugawa Ieyasu, leader of the Eastern camp, emerges victorious.

Tokugawa (Edo) Period: 1603–1868

Early seventeenth century: Obata Kanbē Kagenori compiles *Kōyō Gunkan* (A Military History of the Great Men of Kai).

1603: Ieyasu becomes shogun.

1610?: Ōta Gyūichi, who wrote *Shinchō-kō Ki* (Biography of Lord Nobunaga), dies.

1614–15: Ieyasu destroys the remnants of Hideyoshi supporters in two battles in Osaka.

1639: The last of a string of isolationist edicts issued as the entry of Portuguese into Japan is prohibited. Such edicts began with Hideyoshi's execution of twenty-six Christian missionaries and converts in 1597.

1640: Oze Hoan, who wrote *Shinchō Ki* (Biography of Nobunaga), dies.

1642: Swordsman Miyamoto Musashi completes his tract on martial arts and strategy, *Gorin no Sho* (Book of Five Elements). The Hosokawa house, of which Musashi is a guest, annihilates the Abe family.

1661: The Nabeshima house proscribes disembowelment to follow one's master in death.

1663: Tokugawa government proscribes disembowelment to follow one's master in death.

1701: Asano Naganori attempts to kill Kira Yoshinaka in Edo Castle and is ordered to commit suicide by disembowelment.

1702: Forty-seven samurai avenge their lord, Naganori. Early in the following year all of them disembowel themselves by government decree.

1721: Yamamoto Tsunetomo, whose observations on samurai ethos were collected in *Hagakure* (Hidden in Leaves), dies.

1725: Arai Hakuseki, who wrote his autobiography *Oritaku Shiba no Ki* (Breaking and Burning Firewood), dies.

1832: Rai San'yō, who wrote *Nihon Gaishi* (Unofficial History of Japan), dies.

1868: Sir Ernest Mason Satow, of the British Legation, witnesses Taki Zenzaburō's disembowelment.

Modern Period: 1868–present

1894–95: Sino-Japanese War. General Nogi Maresuke commands an army to attack Luxu (Port Arthur).

1904–05: Russo-Japanese War. Nogi commands an army to attack Luxu, now a Russian fortress, and sustains enormous casualties.

1912: Nogi commits suicide by disembowelment on the day of Emperor Meiji's funeral.

1913: Mori Ōgai publishes "The Abe Family."

1941: Japan attacks Pearl Harbor.

1945: General Kuribayashi Tadamichi killed in a death charge on Iwo Jima. Japan surrenders.

1970: Mishima Yukio commits suicide by disembowelment.

GENEALOGY OF THE MINAMOTO CLAN

(Line does not always show direct father-son relationship)

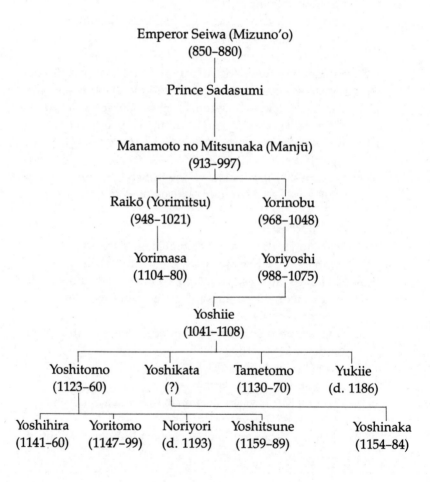

Emperor Seiwa (Mizuno'o)
(850–880)

Prince Sadasumi

Manamoto no Mitsunaka (Manjū)
(913–997)

Raikō (Yorimitsu)   Yorinobu
(948–1021)   (968–1048)

Yorimasa   Yoriyoshi
(1104–80)   (988–1075)

Yoshiie
(1041–1108)

Yoshitomo   Yoshikata   Tametomo   Yukiie
(1123–60)   (?)   (1130–70)   (d. 1186)

Yoshihira   Yoritomo   Noriyori   Yoshitsune   Yoshinaka
(1141–60)   (1147–99)   (d. 1193)   (1159–89)   (1154–84)

PART ONE

Samurai Prowess

YAMATO TAKERU:
LOSER AS HERO

IT WAS BRILLIANT OF Ivan Morris to describe Yamato Takeru, Yamato the Brave, as the archetype of the "Japanese heroic parabola" in his book, *The Nobility of Failure: Tragic Heroes in the History of Japan*. Yamato Takeru, most likely a composite mythological figure, accomplished a great deal in the early part of his life but died a "poignant, lonely" death without being accorded due recognition or reward. Japanese history abounds with such failed heroes.

Every country has a special place for similar figures. In the United States, for example, men like Jesse James, George Armstrong Custer, and Robert E. Lee have been and continue to be extolled because they were valiant losers. The endless fascination with the South as a whole accrues from the simple fact that it was the loser in a war that tore the nation apart. What might make Japan somewhat different is that the losers, mythical or historical, have provoked a far greater amount of sympathy, adulation, and exaltation than the winners. Yamato Takeru stands out among them because he is the earliest such figure who is fully described, and because Yamato, which initially appears to have designated a small corner of Nara, in time became a symbolic name of all Japan. (Many imperial sons and daughters in the mythological and semi-mythological periods are given the name Yamato, but this particular prince outshines them all.)

Yamato Takeru appears in both of the two earliest official histories of Japan: the semi-mythological *Kojiki* (Record of Ancient Matters), compiled in 712, which is the oldest extant book in the country, and *Nihon Shoki* (History of Japan), compiled in 720.

Yamato Takeru was one of the many sons of the twelfth emperor Keikō, who, unlike his better-known offspring, may have actually existed in the fourth century. His initial name was Ousu, "Small Mortar"—as in a mortar and a pestle—and he had a brother by the name of Ōusu, "Big Mortar." The *Nihon Shoki* says: "Both Prince Ōusu and Prince Ousu were born of the same placenta as twins in one day. The emperor, exasperated, warned the mortar. Therefore, he named the two princes Big Mortar and Small Mortar."

Keikō's puzzling behavior as regards a mortar has been explained by some scholars by referring to the folk custom that requires the husband to carry a heavy mortar around the house when his wife is having difficult labor. Keikō, whose official name was Ōtarashi-hiko-oshiro-wake, uttered his warning to the mortar because, we are told, it took so long for the second of the twins to be born. At any rate, the son so born "grew to be ten feet tall and strong enough to lift with ease a large ritual vessel made of copper," as the *Nihon Shoki* puts it with a bit of Chinese hyperbole. (The *Nihon Shoki* was written in Chinese as Chinese was the official language of the day.) Hyperbolic or not, the language used to describe Yamato Takeru is equal to that reserved for the emperor, and his consorts are called empresses. In at least one ancient text he himself is called emperor.

In the *Kojiki*, from which the rest of the story will be taken, Ousu, our hero, begins his career by murdering his twin brother in a rather unceremonious fashion. From the description of his hairdo, he was at best an adolescent at the time.

The emperor said to Prince Ousu, "Why is it that your big brother doesn't come to our meals in the mornings and in the evenings? You go to him yourself and persuade him."

After he said this, five days passed, but Prince Ōusu still hadn't shown up. So the emperor asked Prince Ousu, "Why is it that your big brother hasn't come in so long? Haven't you talked to him yet?" The prince replied, "I've already persuaded him." The emperor said, "How did you do that?"

The prince replied, "When he entered the privy at daybreak, I waylaid him, grabbed and squashed him to death. Then I tore off his limbs, wrapped them up in straw mats, and threw them away."

When he heard this, the emperor became terrified of his own son's brave, wild mind and told him, "Toward the west there are two braves in Kumaso. They are rebellious people who refuse to surrender to me. Go and kill them."

He then sent him away. At the time the prince still had his hair done up on his forehead.

Prince Ousu received from his aunt, Princess Yamato, a robe and a trouser-skirt, put a dagger in his breast, and set out.

When he arrived at the house of the Kumaso Braves, he saw that it was surrounded by three cordons of soldiers and that a pit-dwelling had just been built. People were talking and moving about as they prepared a feast to celebrate the pit-dwelling and laid out food. The prince went near the dwelling and walked about as he waited for the feast day.

When the feast day came, he combed down his hair like a girl and put on the robe and the trouser-skirt his aunt had given him. So disguised as a girl, he mixed with the women, slipped into the pit-dwelling, and sat down. When the Kumaso Braves, two brothers, the older and the younger, saw him, they were taken with his maidenly beauty, let him sit between them, and made merry.

At the height of the feast, the prince pulled out his dagger from his breast, grabbed the older brother by the lapel, and stabbed him through the chest.

The younger brother was terrified to see this, and ran. The prince sprang after him and, at the foot of the staircase, took hold of him at the back, and stabbed him through the ass. At this the younger Kumaso Brave said, "Don't move the dagger. I have something to say."

So the prince held him down for a while. The Brave said, "Who are you?"

The prince said, "I am a son of Emperor Ōtarashi-hiko-oshiro-wake, who, seated at the Hishiro Palace in Makimuku, rules the Great Eight Islands, and my name is Boy Prince Yamato. His Majesty heard that you two Kumaso Braves haven't surrendered or paid your respects, so he sent me here to kill you."

When he heard this, the Kumaso Brave said, "That's quite correct. In the west there's no other Brave, no strong man other than the two of us. But in the Great Country of Yamato is a man far braver than we are. May I give you a new name? From now on you should call yourself Prince Yamato Takeru."

As soon as this was said, the prince killed him by splitting him like a ripe melon. From then on people honored the prince by calling him Prince Yamato Takeru. On his way back he subdued and pacified all the mountain deities, river deities, and the deities of straits.

When he entered Izumo Country,[1] he decided to kill the Izumo Brave. So he became friends with him. He secretly made a sword out

---

1. *Kuni*, the word which I have translated "country" here, will be translated "province" elsewhere in this book. The sense of tribal independence was probably much stronger in the semi-mythological period covered here than in the later periods.

of oak and flaunted it as a regular sword as he went to bathe in the Hi River with the Izumo Brave. He came out of the water first, picked up the sword that the Izumo Brave had untied and left, and said, "Let's exchange our swords."

Later, when the Izumo Brave came up from the river and put on Yamato Takeru's sword, the prince challenged him, saying, "Let's cross our swords."

When each tried to draw his sword, the Izumo Brave couldn't draw his. But the prince drew his and struck and killed the Izumo Brave. He then sang this song:

> *Yatsume sasu Izumo Takeru ga hakeru tachi*
> *tsuzura sawa-maki sa-mi nashi aware*

> The Brave of Izumo where eightfold clouds rise wears a sword,
>   bound many times with black vines it has no blade, what a
>   pity!

Having so swept and conquered the country, he returned and gave a report.[2]

The emperor again said to Prince Yamato Takeru, "Subdue and pacify the wild deities and the people who haven't surrendered to us in the twelve countries to the east." When he sent him off with the ancestor of Kibi no Omi, whose name was Misuki-tomo-mimi-take-hiko, as second in command, he gave him a long spear made of holly.

When so ordered and on his way, the prince stopped by the Great Shrine of Ise, offered prayers at the Seat of the Goddess, and said to his aunt, Princess Yamato: "His Majesty must wish I were dead. Otherwise, why should he send me away, without many soldiers, to subdue the evil people of the twelve countries to the east, when not much time has passed since I returned from the mission to strike down the evil people to the west? When I think of all this, I'm convinced he wishes I were dead."

He prepared to leave, troubled and weeping, when Princess Yamato gave him the Grass-Laying Sword, as well as a bag, saying, "When you find yourself in an emergency, untie the string and open the bag."

---

2. So far Yamato Takeru's actions are characterized by what may be called biblical crudities. But when ordered to take up at once a new campaign to the east, he fathoms his imperial father's true intent and sheds his boyish and brutal singlemindedness.

When he reached Owari Country, he entered the house of Princess Miyazu, the ancestor of the Governor of Owari. He wanted to marry her at once. But deciding to do so on his way back, he went on to the countries to the east and subdued and pacified all the wild deities of mountains and rivers as well as the people who had not surrendered.

When he reached Sagamu Country, the governor there lied and said to him, "There's a large swamp in the middle of this plain. The deity who lives in the swamp is a terribly unruly one."

To see the deity, the prince went into the field. Then the governor set the field afire. Realizing that he had been deceived, the prince opened the bag his aunt had given him, and found flint stones in it. So he first mowed away the grass with his sword. Then he struck the flints and set a counterfire which burned away from him. When he came out of the field, he cut the governor and his men to death, and set fire to them and burned them. This is why the place is now called Yaizu, "Burning Ford."

When he went out of the country and tried to cross the sea called Running Water, the deity of the strait stirred up the waves and turned his ship round and round, so the prince could not make any headway. When she saw this, his empress,[3] whose name was Princess Oto-tachibana, said, "I'll go into the sea in your place. You, milord, must complete your mission and report to His Majesty."

She then had eight reed mattresses, eight leather mattresses, and eight silk mattresses laid on the waves, and went down to sit on them. The rough waves quieted down on their own, and the prince's ship could now proceed. The empress sang:

> *Sanesashi Sagamu no ono ni moyuru hi no*
> *honaka ni tachite tohishi kimi wa mo*

The flames burning the field of Sagamu where the hills rise
    nearby,
    standing in their midst, you asked for me!

Seven days later her comb was washed up on the shore. They picked it up, built a tomb, and placed the comb in it.

---

3. The sudden appearance of Yamato Takeru's wife suggests the composite nature of this story.

When he went out of the country, subdued all the wild *emishi*[4] and pacified the wild deities of mountains and rivers, and was on his way back, the prince reached the slope leading to Mt. Ashigara. He was eating dried rice there, when the deity of the slope transformed himself into a white deer and stood near him. The prince picked up one end of the *hiru* plant he hadn't finished eating, and struck the deer with it. He hit it in the eye and killed it. So he climbed up the slope, stood at the top, heaved a sigh three times, and said, "My wife!" This is why that country was named Azuma, "My Wife."

He went overland out of the country and came out of it to Kai. When he was at the Sakaori Palace, he sang:

Niibari Tsukuba o sugite ikuyo ka netsuru

Since passing Niibari and Tsukuba, how many nights have we slept?

An old torch-lighter followed the song with:

kaga-nabete yo niwa kokonoka hi niwa tōka o

Add up the days, and of nights there are nine nights, of days, ten days.[5]

When he went overland from that country to Shinano Country, the prince quickly subdued the deity of the Slope of Shinano and returned to Owari Country where he went to stay with Princess Miyazu, with whom he had made a pledge at an earlier date. When she dedicated a large banquet to him, the princess also dedicated a large sake cup to him. She had a stain of menstrual blood on the hem of her outer garment. When he saw the menstrual blood, the prince sang:

Across boundless heavenly Mount Kagu
sickle-necked swans fly—
your arm as slim, as pliant,

---

4. Thought to be the Ainu.
5. The exchange is made in the form of *sedōka*, "repeat song," so called because it was made up of two 5-7-7-syllable *katauta*, "half-songs." Traditionally, this duet has been regarded as the origin of the poetic form of *renga*, "linked verse."

I had wanted to use as a pillow,
I had thought of sleeping with you,
but on the hem of the outer garment you wear
    the moon has risen.

Princess Miyazu sang in reply:

Our Prince of the high-shining sun,
our Sovereign familiar with the eight corners,
as each year, with a new resolve, passed,
so has each month, with a new resolve, passed.
Sir, sir, I couldn't wait for you any more,
and on the hem of the outer garment I wear
    there the moon has risen.

There and then he married her and, leaving his Grass-Laying Sword with her, went to kill the deity of Mt. Ibuki.

There he said, "I'll take on the deity of this mountain empty-handed, face to face." When he climbed the mountain, he ran into a white boar. It was as large as an ox. When he saw it he made a forbidden assertion,[6] saying, "This thing in the guise of a white boar must be the messenger of the deity. I won't kill it now, but I will on my way back." He then continued to climb. Seeing this, the deity let loose a great rainfall and completely dazed Prince Yamato Takeru. So he went back down. As he reached Shimizu, "Clear Water," of Tama-kurabe, and rested, he gradually came to his senses. This is why the clear water there was named and is called Isame no Shimizu, "Clear Water Where He Came to His Senses."

When he left that place and came near Tagino, the prince said, "I've always thought I could fly through the sky. But now I can hardly walk, my legs tottering." This is why the place was named and is called Tagi, "Totter."

When he went a little farther from the place, exhaustion overtook him, so he walked slowly with a stick. This is why the place was named and is called Tsuetsuki-zaka, "Slope with a Walking Stick."

As he reached the lone pine at the cape of Otsu, there was still the sword he had forgotten when he'd had a meal there before. Seeing it, he sang:

---

6. *Kotoage shite*, "raise up words." It appears that it was a taboo to assert oneself in certain circumstances.

Facing Owari directly,
lone pine there at the cape of Otsu, o brother!
Lone pine, if you were human,
I'd let you wear a sword, wear a robe,
  lone pine, o brother!

When he went out of the place and reached Mie Village, he said again, "My feet are crooked threefold and are quite fatigued." This is why the place was named and is called Mie, "Threefold." When he went out of the place and reached Nobono, he longed for his own country and sang:

Yamato wa kuni no mahoroba
tatanazuku oakaki
yama-gomoreru Yamato shi uruwashi

Yamato is prominent in the country.
In layers of blue fences,
secluded in mountains, Yamato is beautiful.

He sang again:

Inochi no matakemu hito wa
Heguri no yama no kumakashi ga ha o
uzu ni sase sonoko

Those of you full of life,
wear on your hair, all of you, large oak leaves
of woven-mat Heguri Mountain!

This is a country-longing song. He sang again:

Hashikeyashi wagihe no kata yo kumoi tachikumo

How lovely! From the direction of my house, clouds rise!

This is a *katauta*, "half-song." At that moment his illness suddenly worsened. He sang:

Otome no tokonobe ni

waga okishi tsurugi no tachi
sono tachi waya

The sword-blade I left
next to my maiden's bed,
that blade!

As soon as he finished singing, he passed away. This news was taken to the emperor by horse relay.

The prince's empresses and children who were in Yamato came down in various groups and built a tomb. Then they crawled about in the adjoining paddies and, weeping, sang:

Nazuki no ta no inagara ni
inagara ni hahi motohorō toko-kazura

Among the rice stalks in the adjoining paddies,
among the rice stalks crawl the vines of wild yam.

At this the prince turned into a large white bird, flew up into the sky, then toward the beach. His empresses and children followed, bruising and tearing their feet on the stumps of bamboo grass, but forgetting their pain as they wept. They sang:

Asaji no hara koshi nazumu
sora wa ikazu oshi yo ikuna

The bamboo grass field hampers our waists.
We can't move through the sky, though our feet move.

They then waded into the sea and, as their movements were hampered, sang:

Umi ga ikeba koshi nazumu
ō-kawara no uegusa
umiga ha isayou

The seagoing hampers our waists.
Like grasses grown in a large river,
we can't move forward or back in the sea.

When the bird flew again and rested on the shore, they sang:

Hamatsu chidori hama yowa ikazu iso-zutau

Beach plovers don't move along the beach but along the shore.

They sang these four songs at the prince's funeral. This is why they have been sung at every emperor's funeral ever since.[7]

---

7. These four songs were indeed sung until quite recently, the last occasion being the funeral of Emperor Meiji (1852–1912). The meanings of these, as well as some of the other poems cited in this narrative, are obscure.

YOROZU:
"I WANTED TO
SHOW MY BRAVERY!"

T HE YEAR IS 587. Politics at the imperial court is, as it has been for some years, at the mercy of the two dominant families, the Soga and the Mononobe. Umako, the leader of the Soga, carries the title of ō'omi, "chief administrator," which puts him in charge of the imperial bureaucracy; Moriya, the leader of the Mononobe, carries the title of ōmuraji, "great chieftain," which makes him the representative of all the "clans" (or professional corporations) as set up by imperial decree. The two are equals at the court. Naturally, each tries very hard to overpower the other. An obvious and traditional way of taking control is to install a man of one's choice among the imperial offspring as emperor. In the fourth month of 587 the thirty-first emperor, Yōmei, dies, and at once succession intrigues are set in motion. The Mononobe try to promote a prince by the name of Anahobe. The secret move comes to light, and Umako immediately has Anahobe and his close brother, Yakabe, assassinated. Then he decides to vanquish the Mononobe once and for all. The Mononobe family, as its name "armed division" suggests, is by occupational designation a military clan, with the authority of police added. But as serious clashes occur, their power to control the clans proves unexpectedly weak; without gaining much support from those who are supposed to provide it, they are destroyed within days. In the eighth month Prince Hatsusebe, who was on the Soga side during the military upheaval, is installed as the thirty-second emperor, Sushun. Five years later, Soga no Umako, hearing that Emperor Sushun resents him, has him assassinated, then has the assassin killed as well. The story of Yorozu is told in the section on Emperor Sushun in the *Nihon Shoki*.

Great Chieftain Mononobe no Moriya's servant, Yorozu, of the bird-catchers' division, who led a hundred men, was guarding his master's houses in Naniwa. When he heard that the great chieftan had been destroyed, he escaped by horse during the night and headed toward Arimaka Village in Chinu. He passed by his wife's house and hid himself on a nearby hill.

The imperial court took up the matter and declared:

"Yorozu harbors rebellious intentions. That is why he has hidden himself on the hill. Destroy his kinfolk at once. No failure shall be tolerated."

Yorozu came out alone, on his own; his clothes were tattered and dirty, his face emaciated, but he held a bow and wore a sword. The commander in charge dispatched several hundred soldiers and had them surround Yorozu. Alarmed, Yorozu hid himself in a bamboo thicket. He tied some ropes to bamboos and, by tugging and moving them, confused his enemies as to where he was. The soldiers were indeed deceived, and rushed toward the swaying bamboos, shouting, "There's Yorozu!" Yorozu shot at them. Not a single arrow missed. The soldiers were terrified and did not dare go near him.

Yorozu then unhooked the string from the bow and, with the bow under his arm, ran toward the hill. The soldiers shot at him across a river. There was not a single hit. Thereupon, one soldier ran fast and ahead of Yorozu, crouched near the river, put an arrow on his bow, and shot at him. It hit his knee. Yorozu pulled the arrow out of his knee. He put the string back in his bow and started shooting. He then lay on the ground and called out: "I am a shield for the emperor and wanted to show my bravery, and his majesty never called upon me to do so. Instead, I've been pressed into this extreme position. Someone who can speak to me, come! I must know whether you intend to kill or capture me."

Thereupon, the soldiers competed in shooting at Yorozu. Yorozu swept aside the flying arrows and killed more than thirty men in short order. He then cut his bow into three with his sword, bent the sword and threw it into the river. Then he stabbed himself through the neck with his dagger and died.

The Governor of Kauchi submitted to the imperial court a report on the way Yorozu died. The court issued an order:

"Hack the man's corpse into eight pieces, skewer and display them on high in the eight provinces."

When, following this order, the Governor of Kauchi tried to hack and skewer Yorozu's corpse, there were thunderclaps, and torrential rains fell.

There was a white dog that Yorozu kept. He trotted around his master's hacked body, looking up and down, and barking. Finally he picked up the master's head and put it in an old grave. He then lay alongside the pillow end of it and starved himself to death.

The Governor of Kauchi made inquiries about the dog and, mystified, sent a report to the imperial court. The court expressed pity and issued a complimentary order, which said:

"The dog has done something we rarely hear of in the world. Make him an example for the future. Allow Yorozu's kinfolk to make a tomb and to bury him."

Accordingly, Yorozu's kinfolk built two tombs side by side in Arimaka Village and buried him and his dog.

ŌTOMO NO YAKAMOCHI:
TO DIE BY OUR
SOVEREIGN'S SIDE

THE ŌTOMO WERE AN early hereditary military clan, even though some of their more prominent members are known to us almost exclusively as poets. Yakamochi (716?–785), the last shining star in the declining years of the distinguished clan, is a prime example. We now think of him as a major poet of the earliest periods and as a probable editor of the great poetic anthology, *Man'yō Shū* (Collection of Ten Thousand Leaves), which was compiled in the second half of the eighth century. Yet true to his clan's hereditary role he held a round of military posts, culminating in a position called *jisetsu seitō shōgun*, which may be given as "commander-in-chief-at-large to subjugate the East." The clan's normal duty was guarding the gates of the Imperial Palace.

Like most of the other poets in the *Man'yō Shū*, Yakamochi writes lyrics. But, perhaps because he has the greatest number of poems preserved in the anthology, his poetry shows a range and variety rare in others. One unusual poem (no. 4049) expresses the Ōtomo clan's resolve to remain loyal to the throne. The occasion for its composition was the imperial proclamation, made public on the first day of the fourth month, 749, that gold had been found for the first time in the Japanese domain. The news merited the emperor's public expression of gratitude because the Great Buddha of Nara, whose casting had begun two years earlier, required vast quantities of copper and gold.

What directly led Yakamochi to compose this verse appears to have been not so much the discovery of gold as the citation of his clan and the closely affiliated Saeki clan, as exemplars of loyalty to the emperor. The proclamation, which was displayed in front of the giant Buddha under construction, specifically cited one of the Ōtomo's traditional public vows, which begins with the phrase, "When seagoing." Yakamochi incorporated it with two others in his poem with a slight change. This particular vow, as revised by Yakamochi, was set to music in 1880 to be used as a ceremonial song by the Imperial Japanese Navy.

The poem is written in *chōka* (long-song) form, which repeats the 5–7–syllable pattern three or more times and normally ends, as here, with a 7-syllable unit; a chōka is usually followed, again as here, by one or more envoys in tanka (short-poem) form. Yakamochi's title for the poem is: "Celebrating the Imperial Proclamation that Gold has been Found in Michinoku."

This country of reed plains, of fresh rice stalks,
which descendants of Heaven have ruled
for generations since the Imperial Ancestor,
God's Prince, came down from Heaven
and ruled it—this country, in its four directions,
that one Imperial Generation after another has governed
has mountains and rivers so wide, so abundant
the products and treasures brought as tributes
are numberless, inexhaustible.
Nonetheless, ever since Our Sovereign
persuaded various people
and began this Auspicious Work,
he had wondered, privately worried,
if there certainly would be gold,
when in the mountain called Oda, in Michinoku,
in the country to the east where roosters crow,
there was gold, the report said.
His Majesty's mind was now clear.
"With the gods of Heaven and Earth complimenting,
with the spirits of Our Imperial Ancestors assisting,
something that happened in the distant past
has been revealed again to Our Generation,[1]
showing Our country will prosper,"
thought His Majesty, god as he is.
He makes his countless officers
follow his orders at will,

---

1. This is interpreted as a reference to the discovery of copper in 708, when to celebrate the occasion the name of the era was changed to Wadō, "Japanese Copper." Some scholars note, however, that Yakamochi may have been referring to the discovery of gold on Tsushima Island, in 701, which apparently proved false. On that occasion the name of the era was changed to Taihō, "Great Treasure," and Yakamochi's great-uncle, Miyuki, then Minister of the Right, was rewarded.

caresses and administers to
the old, the women, and the young
to each and everyone's heart's content.
This is what especially ennobles him,
what makes us rejoice all the more.
The Ōtomo's distant ancestor
held an office serving the Emperor
bearing the title called Chief Ōkume.
"When seagoing, we might become watery corpses,
mountain-going, corpses for grasses to grow from.
Our wish is to die by our Sovereign's side
with no looking back." This vow made,
our ancestors have passed from ancient days
to us children of the present
their manly, unsullied name.
The Ōtomo and Saeki clans
hold an office with a vow passed down,
a vow their ancestors made,
that we their children, following our Sovereign,
will not let their name die.
"As I hold a catalpa bow in my hand,
wear a sword and dagger on my hip,
stand guard in the morning,
stand guard in the evening,
guarding our Sovereign's imperial gates,
I can be bested by no one,"
we vow again and double our resolve,
hearing the praise in our Sovereign's word,
　　　so ennobling.

Envoys

I think of a man's mind, hearing the praise in our Sovereign's
　　word, so ennobling

Place a clear marker on the grave of the Ōtomo's distant ancestor,
　　so the people may know

So His Majesty's generation may prosper, on a Michinoku
　　mountain to the east, gold has bloomed

MINAMOTO NO MITSURU
AND TAIRA NO YOSHIFUMI:
THE DUEL

BATTLES OF ANY AGE, in any place, are mostly messy affairs. But in the old idealized form, in Japan and elsewhere, the two commanders of the opposing armies would sometimes engage in combat to decide the outcome of the battle between themselves. The following story, from the *Konjaku Monogatari Shū* (A Collection of Tales of Times Now Past; vol. 25, sec. 3) is the oldest full account of such a battle known in Japan.

The exact birth and death dates of the two men in the story are unknown. However, it is known that Taira no Yoshifumi was a nephew of Masakado (d. 940), the rebel warrior who proclaimed himself emperor.

In the brief but fascinating passage describing the exchange of messengers before battle a lacuna in the original text leaves us unsure what the messengers do or don't do with their horses. I have opted for the possibility that they don't break into a gallop, rather than that they don't ride their horses.

In the East there were once two warriors, Minamoto no Mitsuru and Taira no Yoshifumi. Mitsuru was commonly known as Minota no Genni and Yoshifumi as Muraoka no Gorō.

Both worked hard at the way of the warrior. But as they did so, they grew resentful of each other. This was because some men were busybodies and told one boss what the other said about him. Some would tell Yoshifumi, "Mitsuru is saying about you, sir, 'He can't challenge me, but contradicts me in everything. That's disgusting.' "

Hearing this, Yoshifumi would say, "How can he say something like that? I know quite well his ability, his way of thinking, everything.

I say to him, 'If that's what you really think of me, come out onto a suitable field to fight me.' " Such a remark would duly be conveyed to Mitsuru.

Even though the two men had stout minds and were wise, as some people kept egging them on, they eventually erupted in anger and sent word to each other: "We can't go on saying such things about each other. We will set a date, go onto a suitably large field, and fight each other to see who is the better." So by letter they picked a field and set a date. From then on, each man's army prepared for battle.

When the promised day arrived, each army marched to the specified field around ten in the morning. Each army had five to six hundred soldiers, every one of them ready to give up his life and working up his nerve. The two sides were about a hundred yards apart, each with shields lined up at the front.

Soon each side sent out to the other a warrior to carry a formal letter declaring war. As the warrior returned to his camp, the other side, as set by the rule, shot arrows at him. Not to bolt at that moment or turn to look but to return calmly to his camp was valued as a sign of bravery.

After this the two sides moved their shields forward and were readying themselves to shoot, when Yoshifumi had his side tell Mitsuru: "In today's battle it wouldn't be interesting if we had our armies shoot at each other. You and I simply wanted to know what each has to show the other, did we not? If that's the case, we won't allow your army and mine to engage in shooting matches. Instead, I think only the two of us should run out and shoot at each other to the best of our abilities. What do you think?"

When he heard this, Mitsuru sent this word out: "That's exactly what I had wanted. I will come out at once."

He then detached himself from the shields, alone on horseback, and stood, with a fork-tipped arrow ready on his bow.

Yoshifumi was pleased with this response and told his soldiers, "I want to have a shooting match with him, alone, using all the skills I have. Leave the matter to me and watch. If I get shot down, then retrieve my body and bury me."

He then walked his horse out past the shields, alone.

The two men started galloping toward each other, arrows ready on their bows, and made the first shots. Hoping to shoot the enemy down with the second arrow, each drew the string and shot as they galloped past each other. When they had run past each other, they turned their horses around and galloped back.

Again each drew his string but this time they galloped back toward each other without shooting. When they had run past each other, they again turned their horses around and galloped back. Again they drew the strings and took aim. Yoshifumi took aim at the center of Mitsuru's body and shot. But because Mitsuru jerked himself sidewise, almost falling off his horse, to avoid the shot, the arrow hit the cover of his sword hilt.

Mitsuru himself turned back and shot at the center of Yoshifumi's body, but Yoshifumi twisted himself to avoid the shot and the arrow hit his sword belt.

When the two of them galloped toward each other, Yoshifumi called out to Mitsuru, "Both of us shoot at the center of the body. We now know what we have to show to each other, and it isn't too bad. As you know, we are not old enemies, so now let's stop. We simply wanted to challenge each other. We didn't want to kill each other, did we?"

"I agree," Mitsuru said. "We've seen what we have to show each other. It's a good thing to stop now. I'll pull back my army."

And each did pull back his army.

The soldiers on each side were gripped with terror each time their masters were galloping toward each other and shot, thinking, Now he's going to be shot down! Now he's going to be shot down! Indeed, they felt it harder to bear to see their masters fight than they would have if they themselves had shot at each other. So, the turn of events puzzled them at first, but when they heard the whole story, they rejoiced among themselves.

That's the way warriors used to be in the old days.

After this incident, Mitsuru and Yoshifumi became fast friends who didn't hesitate for a moment to talk to each other about anything.

MINAMOTO NO MITSUNAKA: WARRIOR'S CONVERSION

EELING GUILTY about killing birds and beasts, let alone humans, may not necessarily have required the influence of Buddhism, which was introduced into Japan in the sixth century; but the renunciation of secular life as a result of feeling such guilt certainly did. In the following episode from *Konjaku Monogatari Shū* (vol. 19, sec. 4), the conversion to Buddhism of the warrior Minamoto no Mitsunaka (913–997) is detailed with delightful tongue-in-cheek. Mitsunaka, who achieved social status of a grand scale, is also known as Tada no Manjū because the sinified pronunciation of his name is Manjū and he lived in Tada, Settsu Province. Some official records list him as a poet as well, and he indeed has a poem in the third imperial anthology, *Shūi Shū* (no. 334). It is a reply to a poem of Kiyowara no Motosuke (908–990) upon the latter's departure for Higo Province as governor. The exchange went:

> *Ikabakari omouran tote omouran*
> *oite wakaruru tōki wakare o*

> How much do you think I will think of you,
> as we old men go apart far from each other?

In reply:

> *Kimi wa yoshi ikusue tōshi*
> *tomaru mi no matsu hodo ikaga aran to suran*

> You are all right, having a distance to go;
> I stay here to wait, for how long I don't know

Among the people mentioned in the story, En'yū-in is the sixty-fourth emperor, En'yū (959–991). Emperor Mizuno'o is another name of the fifty-sixth emperor, Seiwa (850–880), whose six sons started the six different Minamoto families, called in Sinified form Genji. Of the six lines, the one that began with Prince Sadasumi flourished as a military clan, his son Tsunemoto (917–961) becoming the commander in chief of the Defense Headquarters. Because of this geneology the Minamoto have been traditionally called Seiwa Genji.

Monk Genken (977–1020), Mitsunaka's third son, started out as a warrior monk of formidable reputation but became a devout Buddhist. He was also a poet and left a small collection of fifty-one poems.

During the reign of En'yū-in, there was a man by the name of Minamoto no Mitsunaka, who was Chief of the Imperial Stables of the Left. He was a son of the Governor of Chikuzen, Tsunemoto. Because he was a peerless warrior, the imperial court treated him with courtesy and the people of nobility, ministers and those of higher ranks, sought him out for employment. His birth was by no means base, either, as he was a close descendant of Emperor Mizuo. As a result of his service to the imperial court for many years, as someone who served as governor of various provinces, Mitsunaka was peerless in influence and achievement. In the end he became the Governor of Settsu. As he faced old age, he built a house in a place called Tada, in the county of Teshima of that province, and confined himself in it.

He had many sons, all of them accomplished in the way of the warrior, except one who was a monk. His name was Genken, A monk on Mt. Hiei,[1] Genken was a disciple of Bishop Jinzen,[2] of Iimuro. He once visited his father in Tada and was greatly troubled by his father's crime of killing living things. When he went back to Yokawa, Genken visited Monk Genshin[3] to pay his respects and said to him:

"I am extremely saddened to see the way my own father behaves. He's already over sixty years old and not many years are left for

---

1. Mt. Hiei, northeast of Kyoto, is where Enryaku Temple, the headquarters of the Tendai Sect of Buddhism, is located.

2. Jinzen (943-990), who served as head of the Tendai Sect, was reputed to be the "most knowledgeable" Buddhist of his day.

3. Genshin (942–1017) was a ranking priest of the Tendai Sect who wrote, in 985, a famous introduction to Buddhism, *Ōjō Yōshū* (Essentials of Deliverance).

him. Still, he keeps forty to fifty hawks in the summer and endlessly kills living things. Keeping hawks in the summer is the best way of taking lives.

"He sets up fish traps in streams and catches a great many fish. He keeps many eagles and feeds them live animals. Every day he has his men drag fish nets through the sea and constantly sends many armed men to the hills to hunt for deer. All this is the killing he does while staying in his own place. When it comes to the things he has killed in remote places, you can't begin to count their number.

"Furthermore, when he comes across anyone who goes against his wishes he has him killed like an insect. If the man's crime is a little tolerable, he has his hands and feet cut off.

"If he continues to pile up so many sins, I keep worrying, How much will he have to suffer in the coming life? This makes me so very sad. I think of inducing him to think, I must become a monk, but I'm too afraid of him and can't find a chance to propose that to him.

"Reverend, would you be kind enough to work to induce him to enter the priesthood? As I have indicated, he has a mind like a demon's, but it seems to me he will take the words of a distinguished holy man like you seriously."

"That's an extremely admirable thing you have said," Monk Genshin replied. "If we succeed in persuading someone like your father to enter the priesthood, that alone will be a virtuous accomplishment. In addition, because it will prevent him from killing many more living things, such an act will produce countless other virtuous accomplishments. I will certainly give it a try.

"But it will be difficult for me to work it out alone. This is something I should work out with people like Kaku'un and Ingen.[4] You go on ahead to Tada and stay there. Later I will come along with these two men, pretending that we happen to have decided to visit you while traveling as part of our religious discipline. When you see us, make a lot of fuss and say to your father, 'Distinguished holy men, so-and-so, have come to ask me religious questions during their pilgrimage.'

---

4. Ingen (954–1028), the twenty-sixth head of the Tendai Sect. He appears in the diary of Murasaki Shikibu, the author of *Genji Monogatari* (The Tale of Genji), as one of the monks who came to the court to offer prayers when Shōshi, Emperor Ichijō's consort, was preparing to give birth in 1008. In her entry on the eleventh of the ninth month, Murasaki reports that the prayers Ingen wrote and recited were "moving, ennobling, and stirring."

"Now, your father may have a mind like a demon's, but he has certainly heard about us. If he shows any alarm and awe at what you say, tell him, 'These holy men don't easily come down the mountain even when summoned by the emperor. A visit like this during a pilgrimage is something that rarely happens.' Then urge him, 'So, please use this opportunity to do something virtuous and ask them to give some sermons. If you listen to their sermons, your sins may be reduced somewhat and your life prolonged.' If we have the chance to give sermons, we will try to persuade him to enter the priesthood. Even in casual conversation we'll do our best to make him realize what his situation is like."

Rejoicing, Genken went away to return to Tada.

Monk Genshin met the two men in question and said, "I'm going to the Province of Settsu to work out such-and-such a scheme. Come with me." The two men's response was, "That's a very good idea." So the three of them together set out for Settsu.

It was a two-day trip to the province, and by the early afternoon of the following day they had arrived somewhere near Tada. They sent word through a messenger: "So-and-so are coming to see Master Genken. They say they see no reason not to take this opportunity to do so because they have just visited the Holy Mountain of Mino'o."

When Genken heard the messenger, he told him to bring them along right away. Then he ran to his father and said, "Sir, holy men so-and-so have come to visit us from Yokawa!"

"What did you say, son?" said the governor. When he made certain of what he had heard, he said, "I, too, have heard that they are extremely distinguished men of the robe. I will make sure to meet them and pay my respects. This is very gladdening news. Treat them nicely! Put the place in order!"

He himself became instantly restless and ran about making a lot of commotion.

Genken was pleased in his heart. He invited the holy men in and installed them in splendidly, fascinatingly constructed quarters.

The governor sent word to the holy men through Genken: "Although I ought to hurry to visit you in your quarters, I fear it would be rude of me to do so when you must be tired from your travels. Accordingly, may I suggest that you have a good rest for the remainder of the day and perhaps take a bath in the evening. I wish to visit you tomorrow. May I expect to have your thoughts on this, sirs?"

"We are on our way back from Mt. Mino'o where we went to pay our respects, and we plan to return to our temple today. Because of your generous words, however, we would like to meet you before doing so."

When Genken brought this reply, the governor said he was very pleased.

"These three men we have here today," said Genken, "don't come to the emperor even when His Majesty summons them. But they happened to come to us like this, so unexpectedly. May I suggest that you take this opportunity to present them with some Buddhist sutras?"

"What you say is quite wonderful," the governor said. "I certainly will do that."

At once he had a picture of the Amida Buddha painted and presented it to the holy men. He then had copying work begun of the Sutra of the Lotus Flower and sent word to the holy men: "I have decided to take this opportunity to do things like this. May I plead with you that you will stay at least until tomorrow to give some rest to your feet?"

"Having come thus far, we will gratefully follow your suggestion and shall leave tomorrow," was the holy men's reply.

The governor had water heated for their bathing that night. The bath water was prepared so exquisitely and was so clean that it would have been impossible to exhaust the things to be said in praise of it. The holy men spent the night, leisurely bathing.

By noon of the next day the Buddhist sutra was all ready. Also, the life-size statues of the Sakyamuni, which the governor had been unable so far to complete for dedication, busy as he was in his criminal doings, were now ready, all erected neatly. Early in the afternoon the governor had the sutra hung on the south side of the Shinden Building and had a messenger convey to the holy men that he was now ready for them.

All three holy men came over and held a memorial service with Ingen as chief officiator. Perhaps the time had come for the governor to take Buddhist vows: During Ingen's sermon he wept aloud. He was not the only one. All the men of his mansion, warriors with demonic hearts though they were, also wept.

When the sermon was finished, the governor walked up to the holy men and, meeting them formally, said, "By some karma you happened to visit me so suddenly and preached on virtuous deeds.

This may be an indication that the time has come for me. Years have passed and I am old. I have piled up countless numbers of sins. Now I'd like to become a monk. Would you be gracious enough to stay with me for two more days so that I may enter the way of the Buddha?"

"That is an extremely admirable thing to say, governor," said Monk Genshin. "We'd certainly be glad to do what you have requested. However, tomorrow is a felicitous day. So it will be best for you to enter the priesthood tomorrow. After tomorrow, there won't be another felicitous day for quite a while."

Genshin said this probably because in his heart he thought, A man like this is prone to feel pious right after hearing a sermon and say something like that. But he's sure to change his mind if we allow several days to slip by.

"In that case, would you hurry and make me a monk today?" the governor said.

"This is not a propitious day to enter the priesthood," said the monk. "Wait just one more day and take Buddhist vows early tomorrow morning."

The governor said, "I'll be more than happy to do that."

Then, rubbing his hands in happiness, he went back to his quarters, summoned his principal soldiers, and said, "I'm going to take Buddhist vows tomorrow. All these years I've done nothing remiss in the way of the warrior. But I will remain in the way of the warrior only through tonight. Keep that in mind, and give me good protection throughout the night."

When they heard this the retainers went away, everyone in tears.

Later, equipped with bow and arrow and wearing armor, four to five hundred men surrounded the governor's mansion three to four rows deep. They kept up bonfires burning throughout the night, while making several groups of men walk around the area. They provided protection without any laxity, not even allowing a fly to get in.

The governor felt more and more uncertain of himself as the night progressed. As soon as the day broke, he quickly took a bath and asked the holy men to hold the service to allow him to enter the priesthood. The three men gladly complied. In the meantime, the many hawks in the hawk cage were set free after their foot tethers were cut; they flew away like released crows. Men were sent to the fish traps placed in various places to destroy them. All the eagles in the eagle cage were released. Men were sent out to get all the large fish nets, which were then cut to shreds in front of the mansion. All the armor, bows and arrows, and army canes stored in the warehouses were taken out, stacked up, and burned.

About fifty close retainers who had served the governor over the years took Buddhist vows at the same time. Their wives and children wept among themselves endlessly.

Even though the act of taking Buddhist vows is significant under any circumstances, this particular one was an occasion for rejoicing. Because the holy men taught him even more ennobling teachings as readily understandable stories after he took the vows, the governor rubbed his hands even more vigorously with joy and wept.

We've succeeded in telling him some virtuous things, the holy men thought. But before we leave, we might as well make him a little more religious.

So they said, "May we stay here another day? We'd like to leave the day after tomorrow."

Overjoyed by this, the new convert returned to his quarters. That day came to an end.

The following day the holy men told one another, "We've stirred up some religious sentiments in him. If we put him in a state of frenzy now, we might stir up some more."

In case the governor were to be converted, the holy men had brought along a bodhisattva costume and about ten other accessories. Now they hired some people who could play the flutes and shō[5] and, in some hidden place, put one of them in the bodhisattva costume.

"When the new convert comes to us," the holy men instructed them, "we'll tell him religious things. At that time you will start playing the flutes and the shō behind the mound to the west of the pond, then come out playing some intriguing music."

When they did as they were told, the new convert was mystified and asked, "What music is that?"

The holy men pretended not to know a thing about it, and said, "We wonder about that, too. Perhaps they have sent messengers to welcome you to Paradise. Let us pray."

The holy men and about ten of their disciples offered prayers in a chorus of stirring voices. The new convert's rubbing of his hands in joy

---

5. The musical instrument called shō may be described as the Oriental counterpart to the bagpipe, at least in appearance. The Chinese version had thirteen to nineteen bamboo tubes, the Japanese one seventeen, arranged on a pot, which is much smaller than the bag of the bagpipe. In Japan the instrument is still used in the court dance called gagaku.

seemed to know no end. Then someone slid open the papered door of the room where the new convert was. And behold, the golden bodhisattva, holding a golden lotus, was walking toward him. When he saw this, the new convert, weeping loudly, tumbled down the verandah to the ground and prayed. The holy men also offered prayers reverently. After a while the bodhisattva left with the accompanying musicians.

When he climbed back to the verandah, the new convert said, "You have shown me such extraordinarily virtuous things. I'm someone who has killed an immeasurable number of living things. I'd like to atone for these sins. By building a Buddhist hall I will stop committing any more crimes and save the lives of living things."

At once he set out to build a hall. The holy men left Tada early next morning to go back to their mountain. Afterward, when the hall was completed, a memorial service was held. What is now known as Tada Temple is a cluster of halls that began to be built with this one.

FUJIWARA NO YASUMASA
AND HAKAMADARE:
PRESENCE OF MIND

THE BELIEF THAT A great man can affect other people without using a word or making a gesture is conveyed well in an episode from *Konjaku Monogatari Shū* (vol. 25, sec. 7), where a nobleman overpowers a famous robber with sheer force of mind.

About the robber Hakamadare ("Drooping Trouser-Skirt") little that is certain is known. Fujiwara no Yasumasa (958–1036), on the other hand, appears in official records as an aristocrat of distinction who held a round of governorships. For a while he was married to the great poet and lover of many men, Lady Izumi (b. ca. 976), whose amorous liaisons were considered scandalous even in an age when sexual standards were far more tolerant. Characteristically, Izumi's poem which in its heading mentions Yasumasa (*Shiika Shū*, no. 239) is addressed to a different lover.

Yasumasa himself has a poem in another imperial anthology, *Go-Shūi Shū* (no. 448). But as a poet he was evidently no match for Izumi, even though he was more than a match for the greatest robber of his day. He also appears to have been a tough administrator, for in 1028, while he was Governor of Yamato, a priest filed a complaint accusing him of imposing unnecessarily harsh measures in governing the province.

It is a curious fact that Yasumasa's brother, Yasusuke, was also a notorious robber who used ignominious means to entrap and murder vendors of arms, cloth, and other valuable commodities. A story in *Uji Shūi Monogatari* (Tales Gleaned from Uji, sec. 125) says he got away scot-free, but an official record says he committed suicide when he was arrested and imprisoned.

His father, Munetada, who is mentioned at the end, is known to have shot a governor's son and his soldier servants to death in the eighth month of 999. When the chief of Imperial Police came to question him, he freely admitted what he had done and was exiled to Sado Island.

There was once a man who may be called the "generalissimo" of robbers and who went by the name of Hakamadare. He had a strong mind and a powerful build. He was swift of foot, quick with his hands, wise in thinking and plotting. Altogether there was no one who could compare with him. His business was to rob people of their possessions when they were off guard.

Once, around the tenth month of a year, he needed clothing and decided to get hold of some. He went to prospective spots and walked about, looking. About midnight when people had gone to sleep and were quiet, under a somewhat blurry moon he saw a man dressed in abundant clothes sauntering about on a boulevard. The man, with his trouser-skirt tucked up with strings perhaps and in a formal hunting robe which gently covered his body, was playing the flute, alone, apparently in no hurry to go to any particular place.

Wow, here's a fellow who's shown up just to give me his clothes, Hakamadare thought. Normally he would have gleefully run up and beaten his quarry down and robbed him of his clothes. But this time, unaccountably, he felt something fearsome about the man, so he followed him for a couple of hundred yards. The man himself didn't seem to think, Somebody's following me. On the contrary, he continued to play the flute with what appeared to be greater calm.

Give him a try, Hakamadare said to himself, and ran up close to the man, making as much clatter as he could with his feet. The man, however, looked not the least disturbed. He simply turned to look, still playing the flute. It wasn't possible to jump on him. Hakamadare ran off.

Hakamadare tried similar approaches a number of times, but the man remained utterly unperturbed. Hakamadare recognized that he was dealing with an unusual fellow. When they had covered about a thousand yards, though, Hakamadare decided he couldn't continue like this, drew his sword, and ran up to him. This time the man stopped playing the flute and, turning, said, "What in the world are you doing?"

Hakamadare couldn't have been struck with greater fear even if a demon or a god had run up to attack him when he was walking alone. For some unaccountable reason he lost both heart and courage. Overcome with deathly fear and despite himself, he fell on his knees and hands.

Hakamadare and Yasumasa

"What are you doing?" the man repeated. Hakamadare felt he couldn't escape even if he tried. "I'm trying to rob you," he blurted out. "My name is Hakamadare."

"I've heard there's a man about with that name, yes. A dangerous, unusual fellow, I'm told," the man said. Then he simply said to Hakamadare, "Come with me," and continued on his way, playing the flute again.

Terrified that he was dealing with no ordinary human being, and as if possessed by a demon or a god, Hakamadare followed the man, completely mystified. Eventually the man walked into a gate behind which was a large house. He stepped inside from the verandah after removing his shoes. While Hakamadare was thinking, He must be the master of this house, the man came back and summoned him. As he gave him a robe made of thick cotton cloth, he said, "If you need something like this in the future, just come and tell me. If you jump on somebody who doesn't know your intentions, you may get hurt."

Afterward it occurred to Hakamadare that the house belonged to Governor of Settsu Fujiwara no Yasumasa. Later, when he was arrested, he is known to have observed, "He was such an unusually weird, terrifying man!"

Yasumasa was not a warrior by family tradition because he was a son of Munetada. Yet he was not the least inferior to anyone who was a warrior by family tradition. He had a strong mind, was quick with his hands, and had tremendous strength. He was also subtle in thinking and plotting. So even the imperial court did not feel insecure in employing him in the way of the warrior. As a result, the whole world greatly feared him and felt intimidated by him. Some people said he didn't have any offspring because he behaved like a warrior though not from a military house.

MURAOKA NO GORŌ AND
HAKAMADARE:
TO KNOW WHEN TO BE ALERT

ASAMURAI MUST KNOW WHEN he must be alert and when he need not be. This lesson is illustrated by another episode about the great robber Hakamadare in *Konjaku Monogatari Shū* (vol. 29. sec. 19).

Some scholars think Muraoka no Gorō, whose official name was Taira no Sadamichi, may be the same as Taira no Yoshifumi who appears in "The Duel," pp. 19–21.

Ōsaka Barrier is a checkpoint on Mt. Ōsaka between present-day Shiga and Kyoto. It is said to have been built in 646 and abolished in 814. While in existence it was regarded as the "entrance" to Kyoto from the East. By the time of this story it had become a mere name, though famous as an *uta-makura*, "poetic place name." The best-known poem about the barrier, attributed to Semimaru, a legendary player of a lute-like instrument, the *biwa*, is included in the second imperial anthology, *Gosen Shū* (no. 1090). It puns on Ōsaka, which means "meeting slope":

> *Kore ya kono yuku mo kaeru mo wakarete wa*
> *shiru mo shiranu mo Ōsaka no seki*

So this is it: both those who go and those who return do
    part,
    both friends and strangers meet at Ōsaka Barrier!

Because his business was robbery, the robber Hakamadare was once arrested and imprisoned. But at the time of an imperial pardon he was kicked out. He had no place to stop at and stay and couldn't think of anything to do. So he went to Ōsaka Barrier, stripped himself completely naked, and laid himself by the roadside, pretending to be dead.

Passersby who saw him gathered around him and made a lot of commotion, saying, "How on earth did he die? He doesn't have a wound or anything!"

A warrior armed with bow and arrow and riding a fine horse came from the direction of Kyoto, accompanied by many armed men and servants. When he saw the many people gathering in one spot and looking at something, he stopped his horse, summoned an attendant, and told him to find out what they were looking at. The attendant came back soon and said, "There's a dead man there, sir, without a wound or anything!"

He had hardly finished saying that when the warrior called his men to order, readjusted his bow and arrow, kicked his horse ahead, and passed by, warily glancing at the dead man.

The people who saw this clapped their hands and laughed, saying, "A warrior accompanied by so many soldiers and servants runs into a dead man and gets scared! What a great warrior he is!" They continued to deride him and laugh at him until he was out of sight.

Not long afterward, when all the people had dispersed, leaving no one around the dead man, another warrior on horseback came by. This one didn't have any soldiers or servants, but was simply armed with bow and arrow. He rode up carelessly to the dead man.

"What a pitiful fellow! How on earth did he die? He's got no wound or anything," he said, and poked at him with the tip of his bow. Suddenly the dead man grabbed the bow, jumped up, and pulled the man off his horse.

"This is how you'd avenge your ancestors!" he cried, drew the sword the warrior wore, and stabbed him to death.

He then stripped the warrior of the trouser-skirt he wore, put it on, hoisted the bow and quiver on himself, climbed upon the horse, and headed eastward as swiftly as if flying. In the end, as planned, he joined ten to twenty naked men who had been similarly kicked out of prison. By robbing every man he met on the road of his trouser-skirt, horse, bow, arrows, army staff, and all, he clothed and equipped his men. As he and these twenty to thirty men rode away from Kyoto, he didn't meet a single worthy opponent he couldn't handle.

A man like Hakamadare could do that sort of thing to you if you were off your guard even slightly. If you didn't know better but went near enough for him to touch you, how could he not grab at you?

When people inquired about the first rider who had passed by in all alertness, he turned out to be no less than Muraoka no Gorō, more officially known as Taira no Sadamichi. People then understood why he had acted the way he had. He had many armed men and servants, but he knew what he knew, and didn't allow himself to be off guard. That was wise of him.

In contrast, the warrior without a soldier or servant who got too close and was killed was stupid. Thus people praised the one while criticizing the other.

TAIRA NO KOREMOCHI, A.K.A. GENERAL YOGO: "DID YOU BRING HIS HEAD?"

I N THE FOLLOWING EPISODE from *Konjaku Monogatari Shū* (vol. 25, sec. 5) the man mentioned at the outset, Fujiwara no Sanekata (d. 998), was of blue-blood aristocratic stock and his appointment as Governor of Mutsu, in 995, was totally "unexpected," according to another story in *Konjaku* (vol. 24, sec. 37). Mutsu to the Japanese in the central government of Kyoto in those days was what Arizona or South Dakota might have been to the Easterners in the United States a hundred years ago: It was remote, vaguely defined, and barbarous. And the reaction of an aristocrat to his appointment as governor of that province may have resembled to some degree that of a Supreme Court justice of New England stock working as a circuit court judge in a Western state in America during the nineteenth century, even though a provincial governorship at the time entailed more than legal adjudication. That may explain why Sanekata's appointment spawned some stories.

It is said that Sanekata's temporary removal from the court—which was what was apparently intended though he died in his governor's post—was a result of his hot-tempered behavior. One day he started to argue with a fellow aristocrat, Fujiwara no Yukinari (972–1027), snatched Yukinari's headgear from his head, threw it into the courtyard, and stomped away. Yukinari, who would become known as one of the three greatest calligraphers of his period, had an attendant pick up his headgear. As he calmly dusted it and put it on, he muttered, "A nobleman with such terrible manners!"

Emperor Ichijō (980–1011), who watched all this from his seat behind a see-through blind that set him apart, decided to promote Yukinari to Chief of the Imperial Secretariat, while appointing Sanekata Governor of Mutsu. He explained that Sanekata might acquire a touch of courtly refinement by being stationed in Mutsu because its euphonious alternative name, Michinoku, was an *uta-makura*, "poetic place name." For a fifteen-year old emperor it was an explanation full of sophistication and irony. Many of the place names used as *uta-makura* were far-away places which were poetic only in the poet's imaginings. Here is, in any event, one of the most famous poems incorporating that place name:

> *Michinoku no shinobu-mojizuri*
> *tare yue ni midaresomenishi ware naranakuni*

> The dye with hare's-foot-fern, of Michinoku–
> who else would have made me feel as disturbed?[1]

About Fujiwara no Morotō little is known other than that some records list him as "General Yogo's enemy." However, his grandfather, Fujiwara no Hidesato, also known as Tawara no Tōta, is famous for slaughtering a monstrous centipede and, more factually, for killing the rebel Taira no Masakado. Legend has it that when Hidesato went to see Masakado, pretending to be willing to become his ally, an overjoyed Masakado held a feast to welcome him. During the feast, though, Masakado carelessly wiped away the rice he had spilled on his trouser-skirt, rather than make his attendant do the job. When Hidesato saw this, he decided that Masakado was not destined to be a great leader.

But now to the story.

When Middle Captain Sanekata became Governor of Mutsu and went to the assigned province, because he was a gentleman of noble birth all the distinguished soldiers there feasted him and served him closely at his mansion day and night as they had never done with any of his predecessors.

In the same province there was a man by the name of Taira no Koremochi. He was the first son of Kanetada, Governor of Kazusa, who was a son of Shigenari, Acting Governor of Musashi, who was, in turn, the younger brother of the warrior Taira no Sadamori, Governor of Tamba. When his grand-uncle, Sadamori, adopted all of his nephews and their sons as his sons, Koremochi was especially young

---

1. By Minamoto no Tōru (822–895), who is known for constructing in his garden a replica of Shiogama, another *uta-makura* in Mutsu. The poem, which appears in *Kokin Shū* (no. 724), is based on a conceit that dye-patterns made with hare's-foot-fern are irregular and therefore "disturbed." What is implied is "who else but you."

and became the fifteenth boy to be adopted, so his nickname became Master Yogo.[2]

There was also a man by the name of Fujiwara no Morotō. He was a grandson of the warrior Tawara no Tōta Hidesato. His nickname was Sawamata no Shirō.

These two men, who had a quarrel over the ownership of some negligible fields and paddies, appealed to the governor, each with his own justification. Because each man's justification seemed reasonable and because both were distinguished men, the governor was unable to decide the case, when, after just three years in his post, he died. The two men's worries and anger did not cease, however, and they continued to regard each other with unease. Then, too, there were busybodies who kept telling one about the other in an improper sort of way, saying terrible things. As a result, even though they were initially good friends, their relationship simply went on worsening as each kept saying more and more frequently, "So he says that about me," or "How could he say that about me?" In the end, they issued an ultimatum—a serious matter.

It was decided that both would line up their soldiers and do battle. They sent a note to each other to set the date and agreed to meet in a particular field. Koremochi assembled about 3,000 soldiers, but Morotō managed only a little over 1,000, an incomparably inferior force in number. Thereupon, Morotō canceled the battle and moved over to the Province of Hitachi. When he heard this, Koremochi said, "That's the way it should be. He couldn't possibly have put up a fight against me." He remained somewhat boastful for several days, though he kept his soldiers alert for a while. As many days passed, however, they started going home, each saying, "I have something to do."

Also, some of the busybodies, especially those who wanted to go home without any mishap, tried to comfort Yogo, saying things like:

"Master Sawamata wouldn't have wanted to carry out a useless battle because of what busybodies said. Besides, the number of his soldiers was no match for yours."

"The whole argument between the two of you was groundless, if we may say so, sir."

"People are saying, 'Master Sawamata is going about in Hitachi and Shimotsuke.'"

---

2. Fifteen was also counted as "ten plus five" and that "plus five" was pronounced *yogo*.

Finding these words persuasive, Yogo let all his soldiers go home and relaxed his guard.

But on the first of the tenth month, about two o'clock in the morning, Yogo was startled out of his sleep by the sudden commotion of the waterfowl in the large pond in front of his house. Yogo immediately called out to his soldier-servants:

"The enemy soldiers must have come! The birds are making a lot of noise!

"Men, put on your bows and arrows!

"Saddle the horses!

"Send someone up the lookout tower!"

Then he put a man on a horse and said, "Run ahead and see what's going on!"

The man galloped back almost at once. "Sir, in the field to the south, I can't tell how many, but black figures of soldiers are scattered all about for four or five hundred yards!"

Yogo said, "This surprise attack means I'm finished, but I'll make my last stand."

He made several groups, each consisting of four or five men on horseback, position themselves with their shields up on the road by which the enemies were expected to come. In the house there were altogether only about twenty men equipped with bows and arrows, regardless of their rank.

He must have heard that I'd relaxed my guard, so he's given this surprise attack. There's no way I can survive this, Yogo thought, and sent his wife, a few of the maids, and an infant child to the hill behind the house to hide. The infant grew up to be Saemon no Tayū Shigesada.

Having sent them away, Yogo felt at ease and, running around, gave orders. The enemy soldiers, now near the house, encircled it and attacked. Yogo's men fought back, but there were too few of them to make an effective force.

Sawamata's men set fire to the house to burn it down. When someone came out, a great many men shot at him, so most people stayed put, wriggling like worms.

In time the day broke and everything became visible. Sawamata's men wouldn't allow a single person to escape. They kept everybody in the house and shot some to death, burned others to death. When finally the fire died down, they went inside and counted a total of eighty-odd men and children burned to death. They searched for Yogo's corpse, repeatedly turning over many of the dead bodies, but all the corpses were charred black, some so completely burned that there was little left recognizable as human beings.

Well, Sawamata thought, we killed all of them, without even letting a dog out alive. I'm sure Yogo's dead. Relieved by this thought, he began to withdraw. On his side, too, there were twenty to thirty casualties, some wounded, others killed. Some of them had to be carried back on horseback.

On his way back, he stopped by the house of the man known as Great Prince. A son of Fujiwara no Koremichi, Governor of Noto, Great Prince was a wise, brave warrior who was so considerate and wily that he had no enemy and was respected by everyone. Sawamata, who was married to a sister of Great Prince, stopped by in the hope of feeding his soldiers and giving them sake as they had fought a fierce battle all night.

When Great Prince greeted Sawamata, he spoke: "I'm impressed that you killed Yogo in so brilliant a fashion. He was extremely clever, a man of such energy and ferocity that I wouldn't have expected you to shut him up in his house and kill him. Well, now I trust you made sure to cut off his head and bring it here with you, tied to your saddle. Let me see it."

"You say a silly thing, sir, if I may say such a thing," Sawamata responded. "We forced him to stay within his compound to fight, and he did fight, giving loud orders, running about on his horse. When the day broke, we could easily have seen anybody who'd tried to escape, but we didn't allow a single fly to get away. Some of the survivors we shot to death instantly, the others we shut up in the house and burned. Afterward we burned to death every one of those who even managed to whimper. Why should I have brought with me a burned head, such a disgusting thing to carry? There shouldn't be any doubt that we killed him, sir."

He said this with a triumphant air, his hands ostentatiously placed on his chest.

"Yes, I understand why you say that," Great Prince said. "But the way this old man thinks, I would feel a lot more relaxed about you if you had Yogo's head tied to your saddle just in case it revived. Otherwise you don't know what might happen. I say this because I know very well how his mind works. If you stayed here even for a while, I'd feel terrible. It would be very terrible indeed to have to fight for someone as unreasonable as you at my old age. All these years I've met many people but shrewdly managed not to get involved in a fight like this. And now this! Leave these premises at once!"

With these words Great Prince pitilessly tried to chase Sawamata away. Sawamata was in the habit of deferring to Great Prince as if he were his father, so he prepared to leave as he was told to.

"I'll have everything you need readied at once," said Great Prince. "For now, just leave this place right away. Don't tarry to think of anything."

"Pity. Wise old man he is, indeed," Sawamata said to himself, secretly sneering, but rode away with all his men.

When they had gone several hundred yards, they came upon a hillock in the field with a stream flowing beyond, to the west. They all stopped by the stream and dismounted, saying, "Let's have a rest here."

They were removing their bows, arrows, and everything, when the servants dispatched by Great Prince brought ten large kegs of sake, several tubs of sushi, plus a quantity of carp and birds, everything down to vinegar and salt. So first they heated sake and drank it, each with his own cup. Because they had begun preparing for the fight the previous evening and had fought until late that morning, they were extremely tired. When they drank several cups quickly to slake their thirst and on empty stomachs besides, they all became seriously drunk and lay down to sleep as if dead. Great Prince had also sent a quantity of dry grass, fodder, and soybeans for the horses. So they took down the saddles, removed the bridles, and let the horses free on tethers. The horses, too, ate to painful excess and lay about stretched out.

Yogo had run about in his house till daybreak, giving orders and shooting down many enemies, until he ran out of his arrows and his men were reduced to only a few. He had then decided it would be useless to fight any longer. He ripped an outer garment off a dead woman, put it on, and mussed up his hair to make himself look like a lowly maid. With only his sword held under his clothes, he leapt out in the middle of smoldering smoke into the deep part of the stream to the west. Then he cautiously paddled to a growth of reeds farther off and stayed still, holding onto the roots of a weeping willow.

After his house burned down, Sawamata's soldiers surged into it and counted the number of those who were shot or burned to death. Yogo could hear a fellow asking aloud, "Where the hell is Yogo's head?" and a couple of men saying, "Here it is!" or "No, here it is!" After a while they all left.

When he thought they had gone a couple of miles, thirty to forty of his own soldiers who had been away returned at a gallop. Thinking their master was among those burned to death, they all wept aloud.

When he saw a total of fifty to sixty men on horseback had returned, Yogo cried out, "I'm right here!"

His men tumbled off their horses when they heard this and wept aloud in sheer happiness—no less loudly than they had at first. When he climbed up on land, his men sent their attendants running home—some bringing back clothes, some food, some bows, arrows, and army canes, some horses and saddles.

Yogo put on proper clothes, ate some food, and said, "When I was attacked last night, I first thought of running away into the hills to save my life. But I decided not to leave my name as a fellow who ran away, so I ended up going through all this. Now what do you think is our next step?"

"They have a much greater force, with four to five hundred men," they said. "And we have only fifty to sixty men. With this small number, sir, you wouldn't be able to do anything immediately. You should put together an army at a later date, then go out to fight, sir."

"What you men say is quite right," Yogo said. "But here's what I think. If I had stayed inside the house and been burned to death, I wouldn't be kicking around like this now. Instead, I deliberately fled, so I don't regard myself as quite alive. If I showed myself to you like this for another day, that would be a damnable shame to me. I don't give a damn about my life.

"Now you men get together to make an army and fight later. As for me, I'll go to his house all alone, show him I'm alive when he assumes I was burned to death, and give him at least one shot before I die.

"That's what I think. If I didn't do what I said I would, wouldn't I be a damnable embarrassment to my descendants far into the future? I wouldn't think of raising an army to kill him later—that wouldn't do. If you men don't want to risk your lives, don't come. I'll go alone."

This said, Yogo started riding out, all by himself.

When he did, even those of his men who suggested fighting later said, "He's quite right. There's nothing more to be said about it. Let's follow him right away."

"I can assure you of one thing," Yogo said. "Those bastards are all exhausted after fighting all night and have to be lying dead asleep by a stream or on the sunny side of a hillock or else in some forest of oak trees near here. Their horses, too, must be having a rest, their bridles removed and full of food. The bows must be all unstrung. If we assaulted them with great shouts, even a thousand of them wouldn't be able to do anything. If we don't do it today, there'll be no other day.

"Those of you who don't want to risk your lives, don't hesitate, just stay behind!"

He wore an indigo jacket over a yellow shirt and had on chaps made of summer deer skin and a hunter's hat made of rush. He carried on his back a quiver filled with about thirty battle arrows and adorned with an arrowhead setter and a fork-tipped arrowhead and, in his hand, a thick bow which was partly wrapped in leather. The sword he carried was brand-new, and the horse he rode was a "seven-incher"[3] with a chestnut belly, an excellent steed that could move forward or backward at will.

He counted his men: there were seventy-odd warriors on horseback and thirty-odd on foot, an assembly of more than a hundred. This must have happened because those who lived close by had quickly heard the news and run to this place. Those who lived at a distance hadn't heard the news yet and would come later.

They began tracking down Sawamata, and they pressed forward steadily. When they were passing by Great Prince's house, Yogo sent in a warning: "Taira no Koremochi was attacked last night but managed to escape."

Great Prince, who had thought this a likely possibility, had kept two dozen soldiers in his house, a couple of them on the lookout tower, with the gate bolted tightly. Because he had given the order not to respond, Yogo's messenger simply went away after delivering the warning.

Great Prince called down one of the lookouts and asked, "Tell me what you saw. Did you look carefully?"

"Yes, sir, I did. About a hundred yards out on the road, about a hundred soldiers were hurrying their horses. They practically flew away, sir. One of them was riding a large horse, wearing an indigo jacket over a yellow shirt, with a hunter's hat, and chaps made of summer deer skin. He looked quite outstanding, and I guessed he was the master of the group, sir."

---

3. The standard height of the horse in use in Japan in those days was set at four feet, and a larger horse was expressed by the number of extra inches. So a "seven-incher" means a horse four feet, seven inches high.

"That must be Yogo himself," said Great Prince. "The horse must be the big one he has. I've heard that's an excellent steed. If he attacked riding on that one, who could resist him? Sawamata's going to die a miserable death. He thought what I told him was silly; he clearly showed he thought he'd done just fine. He must be lying somewhere near a hill, exhausted from the fight. If Yogo sets upon him, all his men will be shot to death. You listen—I can assure you of that. Keep the gate bolted tight, and don't you ever, ever make any noise. You just go on back up the tower and watch out for what happens in the distance."

Yogo sent a man running ahead of the group with instructions to check out closely where Sawamata was. The man ran back and said, "In the marshy field on the south side of the hill near here, they're eating or drinking, some lying down, some looking ill."

Yogo was pleased to hear this. Giving the order to attack at once, he galloped ahead as if flying. He rode up the north side of the hill; then from the top he dashed down the steep south slope. Despite the downhill run the field seemed like a riding ground. Shouting at the top of their lungs and whipping their horses as in a *kasagake*,[4] fifty to sixty men charged.

It was at this moment that Sawamata no Shirō and his soldiers rose to their feet and saw this. Some tried to put on their bows and arrows, some their armor. Some tried to bridle their horses. Some stumbled and fell in confusion. Some tried to run, abandoning their bows and arrows. Some grabbed their shields and tried to fight. The horses, alarmed and upset, ran about, whinnying, so no one could get hold of them to put on their bridles. Some horses kicked their attendants and galloped away. During this confusion thirty to forty soldiers were shot to death. Some of the men fled, without even thinking of mounting a horse to fight.

Sawamata was shot and his head was cut off.

Afterward, Yogo led his men to Sawamata's house. Sawamata's people, who thought their master had returned after winning the fight, happily started to bring out food, when Yogo's soldiers forced

---

4. *Kasagake*, "hung hat," is a horseback shooting game in which a target twenty to thirty yards away was shot at from a running horse. The name derives from the fact the stationary target used initially was a hat made of rush. A similar game in which a moving target was used was called *inuoi*, "dog-chase"—obviously because the target was a dog. In both games *hikime* arrows were used. A hikime had a blunt wooden head to prevent damage to the target; it also had several holes in its shaft so that it made a whooping noise when shot. These arrows were used in sports and certain rituals.

themselves in, set fire to the house, and shot anyone who tried to resist. However, Yogo sent in some of his men to bring Sawamata's wife out along with her maid. He then put her on a horse and had her wear an *ichimegasa*[5] so that she might be not be exposed unnecessarily. Her maid was made to attire herself similarly. Both stayed close to Yogo on horseback as he ordered his men to set fire to all the houses.

"Don't touch any woman, high or low," he told his soldiers. "But men—well, shoot to death anyone you see."

This was done as every man was shot on sight. At times, some of the men shot would suddenly jump up and run.

By evening all the houses were burned down and Yogo withdrew. On his way back, he went up close to Great Prince's gate and sent in this message: "I will not come in. However, I have done nothing to embarrass Master Sawamata's lady. In due respect to the fact that she is your honor's sister, I wished to make certain to send her to you."

Great Prince was pleased to hear this, opened the gate, and received his sister, Sawamata's wife. He then sent out word that she was definitely with him. When the messenger came back with this message, Yogo headed toward his own place.

It was probably after this incident that Yogo's reputation rose in the eight provinces of the East and people began to say he was an incomparable warrior. The descendants of his son, Saemon no Tayū Shigesada, now have the honor of serving the government.

---

5. *Ichimegasa*, "market-woman's hat," is a large, deep hat for women, which was made of rush and lacquered. Originally it was used by common women—hence the name; later it was adopted by the ladies of the nobility. It was large and deep enough to hide its wearer's face.

KANETADA AND KOREMOCHI: MEANING OF REVENGE

A S WARRIORS KILLED and were killed, revenge often became an important part of a warrior's life, and so an important subject to contemplate as well. The following episode from *Konjaku Monogatari Shū* (vol. 25, sec. 4), one of the earliest detailed accounts of a vendetta to avenge one's father, is remarkable for the complex reasoning it gives to the appropriate circumstances for punishing the avenger. It may be noted that the idea of avenging one's father as a moral imperative, which originated in China, may not have been prevalent in the period described. General Yogo or Taira no Koremochi has appeared in the story immediately preceding this.

Once the Governor of Kazusa was a man by the name of Taira no Kanetada. He was a son of Shigemochi, the younger brother of the warrior Taira no Tadamori. While Kanetada was stationed in Kazusa Province as governor, General Yogo, or Koremochi, who was his son and was in Mutsu Province, sent him word: "Sir, I haven't seen you for quite a while. Now that you have come down here as Governor of Kazusa, may I come to see you to offer my congratulations?" Kanetada was pleased to hear this. He had preparations made to welcome him and waited. In due time Koremochi's arrival was announced and the people of Kanetada's mansion went about in excitement.

It happens that at the time Kanetada had a cold and, instead of going out to greet Koremochi, was lying inside the outer blind, having a smallish samurai he especially favored massage his hips. While the two of them were on the front verandah, gossiping about various things that had happened during the past years, several of Koremochi's principal soldiers were lined up in the garden in front, all armed with bow and arrow.

The first among them was a man whose common name was Tarōnosuke. About fifty years of age, he was large and plump, with a long beard and a fearsome glower. Apparently he looked like a good soldier. When Kanetada noticed him, he asked the man who was massaging his hips if he recognized him. The man said no, he didn't. Kanetada said, "Well, he is the fellow who killed your father some years ago. You were still an infant at the time. It's quite natural that you don't recognize him."

"People had told me, 'Someone killed your father,' but I didn't know who it was," the man said. "And now I see his face just like this." With this, he rose to his feet and left, tears in his eyes.

By the time Koremochi finished his supper, the sun had set, so he went to separate quarters to rest. After accompanying his master to his place, Tarōnosuke went to his own lodging quarters. There, too, some people were entertaining guests on their own, and they made quite a bit of noise as they carried in a variety of food, fruit, wine, fodder, and hay. It was the end of the ninth month, and torches were erected in some spots on the ground in the dark garden.

After he finished eating a good share of the food, Tarōnosuke lay down to sleep in peace and comfort. He had his brand-new sword near his pillow and laid out next to him were arrows, a quiver, armor, and a helmet. Out in the garden were some of his men, armed with bow and arrow, walking around on watch to protect him. The quarters where he slept were surrounded by two layers of giant cloth curtains, which no arrow could have shot through. The torches erected in the garden made the place as bright as day, and because his men vigilantly walked about there was absolutely nothing to fear. Tired from a long trip and having drunk a good deal of sake, Tarōnosuke was quite relaxed as he slept.

Meanwhile, as for the man who'd heard the governor say, "That man killed your father," then risen to his feet, and left with tears in his eyes, the governor didn't think much about him, assuming that he had just gone away. Afterward, though, the man had gone to the kitchen and repeatedly honed the tip of his dagger. With the dagger in the chest of his jacket, he went to Tarōnosuke's quarters as darkness fell, and boldly watched out for his chance. Then, in the confusion of people bringing in food and things, he nonchalantly mixed in and, pretending to be bringing in a square tray, slipped into the space between the two curtains.

Avenging one's father is something Heaven's Way permits us, he thought to himself. He then prayed, "May Heaven let me carry out without any unexpected mishap what I plan to do as my filial duty tonight."

He remained crouched without anyone noticing him. At last, when the night became deep and he was sure that Tarōnosuke was fast asleep, he suddenly went up to him, slit his throat, and danced out. No one noticed him.

In the morning Tarōnosuke didn't come out for so long that one of his men went in to tell him it was time to eat some porridge and found him lying dead, splattered with blood. He cried out, "Look at this!" In no time the other men were dashing about, some with arrows ready to shoot, others with swords drawn. But it was all useless. First, of course, it was necessary to find out who killed Tarōnosuke. Because he had no close associates other than his men, they were mutually suspicious that there had to be someone among them who knew, but talk in that direction wasn't of much use, either.

"He surely died in a weird sort of way," they said to one another loudly in their flattened voices, excited as popping peas.

"Why didn't he make some noise? We didn't expect him to die so miserably while we served him, trotting ahead of him, running after him, all these years. He may have run out of luck, but this was a terrible way to die."

When he heard the news, Koremochi became very upset.

"This is an embarrassment to me," he said. "Anyone who had any fear of me couldn't have killed one of my men the way he did. The killer did it because he doesn't have an iota of fear of me.

"The timing and the place are particularly inconvenient. It would have been tough enough in my own place, but to have one of my own killed while visiting an unfamiliar place is terribly galling.

"Come to think of it, though," he continued, "Tarōnosuke killed someone years ago. Lord Governor had a smallish samurai who was the son of the one who was killed. That fellow must have done the killing."

With these thoughts, Koremochi went to the governor's mansion.

"Sir," he began when he sat in front of the governor. "Last night someone killed one of the men who accompanied me here. To have one of my own killed like this while traveling is a great embarrassment to me.

"This isn't just anyone's doing. Years ago we had a fellow shot to death who rudely tried to pass before us on horseback. You, sir, have that fellow's son serving you. I am quite certain that it's *his* doing. I think I'd like to summon and question him, sir."

"Without a doubt this must have been that man's doing," the governor said. "Yesterday I saw the man in question in the garden among the men who came here accompanying you. At the time I had some pain in my hips so I was having him massage them. I asked him if he knew the man. He said he didn't. So I said to him, 'Your father was killed by that man. It's a good thing to recognize a man like that by his face. He probably doesn't think anything of you, and that's too bad.' He lowered his eyes, suddenly stood up, and left.

"I haven't seen him since. He's a fellow who never leaves me, waiting on me day and night. So the fact that he hasn't shown up since last evening is strange indeed. Also, here's something that makes me suspicious of him: He was busy honing his sword in the kitchen last night. This I heard while my men were voicing their suspicions this morning.

"Now, you say, 'I'd like to summon and question him.' Do you mean by this that if it was indeed his doing you intend to kill him? I will summon him only after I've heard what your intentions are.

"I, Kanetada, am an unworthy man, and you're a clever one. Still, I'm your father. Suppose someone killed me and one of your men killed him. Suppose then people were critical and nasty about *him*. Would you think that's good? Isn't avenging one's father something Heaven's Way permits? You are such an outstanding warrior that someone who killed me would never be able to rest.

"However, you propose to take to task a man who's just avenged his father, even though he's someone who works for me. That shows you wouldn't even go into mourning for me."

Kanetada said this in a loud voice as he rose to his feet. Koremochi realized he had said something wrong. He, too, rose to his feet, showing as much respect as he could. He then decided there was nothing he could do about it and went back to his province of Mutsu. His men took care of Tarōnosuke's body.

About three days later, the man who had killed Tarōnosuke showed up in black. He came forward before the governor in such dejection, in such obvious trepidation, that both the governor and those in the same room were moved to tears. Afterward people held him in respect and fear. But in no time he fell ill and died. The governor pitied him for that.

Avenging one's father is something rarely done even among outstanding warriors. But this man did it all on his own, boldly, killing the man he wanted to, even though the man was closely guarded by armed men. This showed it was indeed something Heaven's Way permitted, and people praised him for his act.

TACHIBANA NO NORIMITSU:
"WHAT SPLENDID SWORDSMANSHIP!"

WITH A DESCRIPTION OF THE SAME MAN AS VIEWED BY
SEI SHŌNAGON, AUTHOR OF *THE PILLOW BOOK*

THE FOLLOWING VIGNETTE in *Konjaku Monogatari Shū* (vol. 23, sec. 15) details physical movements in sword fights in such a convincing way that the narrator seems to have anticipated such Japanese movie directors as Kurosawa Akira and Okamoto Kihachi.

The man who is said to have felled three sword-brandishing assailants in quick succession is Tachibana no Norimitsu (b. 965?). Norimitsu is also known to have captured a burglar. That was when he was working as household administrator at a major counselor's mansion. At one time or another he was also Assistant Master of Palace Repairs, Lieutenant of the Outer Palace Guards, Left Division, Chief of Imperial Police, Acting Governor of Tōtōmi, and Governor of Noto, Tosa, and Mutsu.

Ichijō (980–1011) was emperor from 986 to 1011.

Former Governor of Mutsu Tachibana no Norimitsu was not from a warrior's house, but he had a stout mind and was wise in plotting and planning. He was also extremely strong, quite good-looking, and well thought of, so people treated him with respect.

When he was young—it was during the reign of Emperor Ichijō—and was a chamberlain also in the employ of the Palace Guards, he once went quietly out of his night duty room in the Inner Palace to meet a woman. It was late at night. Carrying only a sword, on foot, and accompanied by a page boy, he went out of the gate and was walking down Ōmiya Street. As he passed by a tall hedge, he sensed quite a number of people standing around and became deeply apprehensive. The ninth-day moon of the eighth month hung close to the ridge of Mt. Nishi, so the west side of the tall hedge was quite dark and he could barely make out the men standing around.

He then heard one of the men near the hedge say, "You there! Stop! We have noblemen here. You can't pass this place."

Here they come, Norimitsu thought, but he couldn't think of turning back. So he quickened his pace.

"Look, he's ignoring us," somebody cried and sprang toward him. Norimitsu hunkered down and took a good look. He didn't see a bow, but he did see the gleam of a sword. Relieved that it wasn't a bow, he ran forward in a crouched position. When the chaser ran up to him, he thought his head might be split, and quickly stepped aside. The chaser couldn't stop himself immediately but ran past him. That instant Norimitsu stepped behind him, drew his sword, and struck him. His head split in the middle, the chaser fell forward.

A good hit, Norimitsu thought. Then another man cried, "What happened to him?" and ran toward Norimitsu. Norimitsu didn't have the time to put his sword into the sheath. He held it against his side and ran.

"He's a good one," the new chaser said. This was a much faster runner than the first one. Norimitsu decided he couldn't handle this one the way he did the first and, with a sudden change of plan, squatted down. The chaser, running fast, stumbled on him and fell. Norimitsu stood up that instant and, before the man managed to rise to his feet, split his head.

This is it, Norimitsu thought. But there was another. This one cried out, "He's a really good one! I won't let him get away!" He, too, sprang toward him.

"This time I'll be done in! May God and Buddha help me!"

With these prayers, Norimitsu held forward his sword with both hands like a spear and faced the chaser so abruptly that their bodies almost smashed into each other. This chaser also held a sword, and he tried to slash Norimitsu. But they were so close, so suddenly, that he didn't even manage to slash Norimitsu's clothes. On the other hand, Norimitsu's sword, held like a spear, pierced through the chaser's body, and as he twisted out his sword, the man fell backward. That instant Norimitsu struck and lopped off the man's sword-holding arm at the shoulder.

He ran some distance and listened to see if there was yet another one. But there was no sound. So he ran, went inside the middle gate, and, standing close to a column, waited for his page boy. The boy came up Ōmiya Street, weeping. When Norimitsu called out the boy ran up to him. He sent him off to the night duty room for fresh clothes. He then had the boy hide the bloodied jacket and trouser-skirt he was wearing. He also told the boy never to tell anyone anything. Then he carefully washed the blood off the grip of his sword, put on a fresh jacket and trouser-skirt, and, looking as if nothing had happened, returned to the night duty room and went to sleep.

All night he was terribly anxious that it might be found out he did the killings. When morning came, there was a good deal of hubbub:

"Three large men were found dead on Ōmiya Street, near the gate to the imperial kitchen. They were evidently cut down, not far from one another."

"What splendid swordsmanship!"

"Someone thought these men had fought among themselves, but when he looked closely, he found out that they were cut dead with a single stroke."

"Maybe their enemy did it."

"These men looked like robbers, though."

Even some of the ranking courtiers invited each other out to see the murdered men. Norimitsu himself was urged a number of times to go out to see the spectacle. At first he didn't want to, but if he didn't go, people might begin to get suspicious of him, he decided. So, reluctantly, he went out with some of his friends.

There were too many people for the oxcart, so he had to walk alongside it. When the cart was drawn up to the scene, the three men were still as they had been. There was, however, a heavily bearded man about thirty years old. He wore a patternless trouser-skirt, an indigo jacket worn-out from washing, and an equally worn-out yellow shirt. He also had a sword with boar bristles on its sheath. He was in deer-skin shoes. Scratching his side, pointing his finger, looking this way and that, he was talking.

Norimitsu was wondering who in the world he could be, when one of the servants attending the oxcart reported, "He's saying he killed these men, sir, because they were his enemies."

Norimitsu was delighted to hear this. Some of the courtiers on the cart said, "Tell the man to come here. We'd like to find out the details." So the man was summoned.

When he came closer, you could see he had high cheekbones, a jutting jaw, a flat nose, and red hair. His eyes were bloodshot as if rubbed too hard. He knelt on one knee, as he held his sword by the grip.

"What happened?" someone asked.

"Sir, about midnight last night I passed by this place on my way to some place, when three men ran up to me, crying, 'How dare you pass by us!' I thought they were robbers, and cut them down. But when I looked at them this morning, they were the very men I had been looking for all these years. So I thought, I ended up killing my enemies, and was meaning to cut their heads off for proof."

While saying this, he kept pointing his finger, nervously looking up and down. And because the noblemen exclaimed, "My! My!" and kept asking questions, the man became quite worked up and babbled on and on.

Norimitsu found this very amusing. Well, if he wants credit for it, I'm delighted to give it to him, he thought, and kept a straight face.

This is said to be what he told his children when he became quite old.

The Norimitsu described in this story (and in another, in which he catches a burglar) is a man as viewed in a men's world. From a woman's viewpoint, he comes out somewhat differently.

It happens that he was a close friend of Sei Shōnagon (dates uncertain), the author of the famous collection of essays, *Makura no Sōshi* (The Pillow Book). They were such close friends indeed that the ladies and gentlemen of the court teased them by calling him her big brother and her his little sister. Some scholars suspect that they may even have been husband and wife for a while. Perhaps because of their close association, Lady Sei has left a telling description of the man in her book.[1]

The account doesn't concern itself with warriorship, but I have translated it here for contrast.

When I take my days off in a village, people seem to gossip about how senior courtiers come to see me, and so on. Since I have no

---

1. Episode 84; in Ivan Morris's translation, episode 80.

profound reason for my withdrawal, such gossip shouldn't bother anyone. Also, if someone comes to see me day and night, how can I say I'm not home and turn him away embarrassed? Even those who aren't too close to me come to visit.

But all this became so annoying that the last time I left court I didn't tell anyone where I was going to be. The only people who knew were Lord Tsunefusa, Middle Captain of the Inner Palace Guards,[2] and Lord Narimasa.[3]

One day Lieutenant of the Outer Palace Guards, Left Division, Norimitsu came by and was gossiping, when he said, "Yesterday, the Lord Counselor, the Middle Captain,[4] came to me and repeatedly said, 'It's most unlikely that you don't know the whereabouts of your own sister. Just tell me.' I kept telling him I didn't know, but, oh, he was so persistent!

"It's really difficult," he continued, "not to tell what you actually know. I almost broke into a smile. Worse, the Middle Captain of the Left happened to be there, looking so cruelly innocent that I would have burst out laughing if our eyes had met. I was at my wits' end, grabbed the seaweed that happened to be lying on the table, and stuffed and stuffed my face. People must have thought that was an odd thing to eat between meals. But, thank goodness, it saved me from telling him where you are. All that would have been useless if I had smiled. It amuses me that he decided I truly didn't know."

"Please," I said, "never tell him."

Then some days passed.

Very late one night someone knocked on the gate in such a terribly exaggerated fashion that I thought for whatever business it was witless to knock on the gate so loudly, especially because the gate wasn't far from the house. Anyway I sent out a servant. It turned out to be someone from Takiguchi.[5] He had brought a letter, as he put it, "From a lieutenant of the Outer Palace Guards, Left Division." Though everyone was asleep, I had a lamp brought up to me and took a look.

---

2. Minamoto no Tsunefusa (968–1023); he became Middle Captain in the tenth month of 998.

3. Minamoto no Narimasa, whose dates are unknown in part because he did not attain high rank.

4. "Lord Counselor" is Fujiwara no Tadanobu (967–1035), who acquired that position in the fourth month of 996.

5. Where the offices for the Palace Guards were located.

"Tomorrow is the last day of the Sacred Recitations," the letter said. "The Lord Counselor, the Middle Captain, will confine himself for abstinence. If he keeps nagging me, 'Tell me, tell me where your sister is,' I won't be able to pull another trick. I'll never be able to hide it. Shall I tell him what the truth is? What do you think? I'll do whatever you tell me to."

I didn't write a reply. I merely wrapped a small piece of seaweed in paper and sent it back.

Sometime afterward he came by and said, "Because he kept nagging me I spent that whole night taking him to various places which I knew were wrong, of course. He kept asking me so earnestly, and that was a pain.

"My question is, why didn't you send me some kind of reply instead of wrapping a silly piece of seaweed to give to me? That was a wrapped mystery! How could you wrap something like that and send it to someone? Did you make some kind of mistake?"

Seeing that he didn't get the point of it at all, I was a bit upset. Without saying a word, I wrote on the edge of a sheet of paper that was on the inkstone:

Kazuki suru ama no sumika wa soko nari to
    yume iuna to ya me o kuwasekemu

Lest you point to where the diver lives, lest you do,
    I made you eat that seaweed[6]

And I gave it to him. But he exclaimed, "So you wrote a poem! I'll never read it," pushed it back, and ran away.

So, though we used to talk to each other and take care of each other, for some reason our relationship began to cool a little. Then he wrote to me: "Even if something untoward happens, please do not forget what we vowed to each other. I would hope that people will continue to regard me as your brother."

He used to say, "Anyone who loves me shouldn't write a poem to me. I will regard everyone who does as an enemy. Only when you decide it's all finished between us, do that to me."

So, in reply to his letter, I sent him the following:

---

6. The 'diver' is a metaphor for herself—one hiding temporarily from view.

*Kuzureyoru Imo Se no yama no naka nareba
sara ni Yoshino no kawa to dani miji*

Because our friendship has crumbled like Mounts Imo and Se,
you no longer see Yoshino as a stream[7]

Perhaps he no longer did. He didn't even reply to it.

Then he was promoted to the fifth grade and became the Acting Governor of Tōtōmi. And so we parted company while still on unfriendly terms.

Despite his avowed dislike of someone composing a poem to express love or a witty thought, Norimitsu himself is listed as a poet in official records, for a poem of his is included in the fifth imperial anthology, *Kin'yō Shū* (no. 371). The headnote to the poem says he composed it at the Ōsaka Barrier on his way to Mutsu to assume its governorship and that he sent it back to Kyoto. He was appointed Governor of Mutsu in 1006, four years after he was Acting Governor of Tōtōmi, so we must assume the recipient of the poem was not Lady Sei:

*Ware hitori isogu to omoishi Azuma-ji ni
kakine no mume wa sakidachinikeri*

I thought I was the only one hurrying toward the East,
but the plum flowers above the fence were ahead of me

---

7. The Yoshino River flows between Mt. Imo and Mt. Se. The poem suggests that the relationship between Lady Sei and Norimitsu no longer flows as the Yoshino River does, not when it is blocked by landslides from the two mountains.

SAKANOUE NO HARUZUMI: A WARRIOR'S SHAME

A SAMURAI OFF GUARD CAN FACE ignominy—this lesson is poignantly conveyed in a vignette about a man who was active around the year 1000. The episode in *Konjaku Monogatari Shū* (vol. 29, sec. 21) is also notable for the warrior's clearly delineated status in his relation to the court aristocracy which he served directly or indirectly in the earlier periods.

About the warrior, Haruzumi, little else is known. But the governor mentioned here, Koretoki, appears in several records beginning in 988, when a diarist wrote that someone tried to murder him, to 1034. In 994 he is known to have joined a posse of distinguished warriors to hunt a group of bandits.

There was a man by the name of Sakanoue no Haruzumi in the county of Ito in Kii Province. He was never lax in the way of the warrior. He was one of the armed officers who worked for Governor Taira no Koretoki.

Once he came up to Kyoto on business. Because he had some enemies he never let himself be off guard. He went about armed with bow and arrow, and had his men do the same, so that no one could touch him.

Late one night he was on his way to a certain place with his men, when, in lower Kyoto, they came across a group of court nobles on horseback with their vanguard ostentatiously leading the way. The vanguard ran up, shouting, so Haruzumi dismounted. But they further ordered, "Men, lower your bows! Prostrate yourselves!" In some confusion Haruzumi and his men complied, setting aside their bows and arrows.

In the position of prostration, their faces right on the ground, they were wondering to themselves, "The nobles must have passed by now," when they—Haruzumi and everyone in his retinue, his men and servants included—were roughly pushed down by the neck. In consternation Haruzumi twisted his face and looked up. What he had taken to be court nobles were in fact several toughs on horseback, armored and fully equipped. The terrifying men put arrows on their bows and, aiming at Haruzumi, said, "Make a single false move and you'll be shot dead!"

"Dammit, these are bandits and they have played a trick on me!" When he realized this, Haruzumi's sore regrets knew no bounds. But any move would have meant certain death, so he and his men had to leave themselves completely to the mercy of these bastards, allowing themselves to be trampled to the ground, pulled up to their feet, and robbed of everything—their clothes, bows, quivers, horses, saddles, swords, daggers, and even their shoes.

After the incident Haruzumi said, "If I hadn't allowed myself to be off guard, the toughest of those robbers wouldn't have had a chance to shame me like that, unless he had killed me first. I would have fought my best, and might even have captured him. But they sent their vanguard first and made me lie low on the ground to show my respect, and I lost the chance to do anything. All this shows I have no luck in the way of the warrior."

He then stopped acting like a man of arms. Instead, he downgraded himself to the status of a "side-runner."

MINAMOTO NO RAIKŌ:
ALERT AND PENETRATING

I N THE OLD DAYS Minamoto no Raikō (also called Yorimitsu, 948–1021) used to be known to Japanese children mainly as the dignified warrior commanding four strongmen with whom he vanquished a monstrous creature called Shuten Dōji, "Drunken Boy," on Mt. Ōe. Some say Shuten Dōji was a collective name for groups of marauding bandits; if so, Raikō, who held governorships of several provinces, was certainly responsible for controlling such outlaws.

The four strongmen, fancifully known as Raikō's *shiten'nō*, "Four Guardian Kings," are Watanabe no Tsuna (953–1024), Sakata no Kintoki (dates unknown)[1], Usui Sadamitsu (955–1021), and Urabe no Suetake (950–1022). About Suetake a few stories are told elsewhere in this volume.

It is known that while holding governorships Raikō accumulated considerable wealth. In 988, for example, when Fujiwara no Kaneie (929–990), then regent, held a banquet to celebrate his sixtieth year, Raikō presented thirty horses to the invited guests as celebratory gifts. And in 1018 when Fujiwara no Michinaga (966–1027), then chancellor, built a new mansion, Raikō provided all the furniture needed for it. Raikō became one of the few men from the military class to be admitted to the inner court in the earlier periods.

Perhaps because of his court connections Raikō also became one of the first military men to leave a renga in an imperial anthology. The verse, made with his wife, is found in the fifth imperial anthology, *Kin'yō Shū* (nos. 703–704), and comes with a headnote explaining the circumstances of the composition:

---

1. The wonder boy in ancient Japan, reputed to have been born of a "mountain woman" and a red dragon.

When Minamoto no Raikō arrived to take up his post as Governor of Tajima, he saw the Keta River flowing right in front of his mansion. One day he noticed a boat coming from upstream and asked the attendant who had just opened the window about it. The attendant replied that it was harvesting a plant called *tade* (knotweed, smartweed). When he heard this, Raikō simply said:

tade karu fune no suguru narikeri

a boat harvesting smartweed is passing by

His wife took this to be a linked verse to be completed, and said:

asa madaki kararo no oto no kikoyuru wa

I thought I heard someone rowing smartly before dawn[2]

The following story comes from the *Kokon Chomon Jū* (A Collection of Ancient and Modern Tales That I've Heard, sec. 335).

One cold night Raikō was walking back from a certain place, when he realized that he was close to Yorinobu's house. So he sent Kintoki off with the message: "We happen to be passing by. This cold is god-awful. Do you have some good wine?"

Yorinobu happened to be drinking at the moment and was delighted. He told Kintoki: "Tell your master exactly what you see here. We are exceptionally pleased with his inquiry. Do us a favor by coming over to join us." Raikō came at once.

While they were exchanging sake cups, Raikō happened to look in the direction of the stable and saw a boy tied up with a rope. He was puzzled and asked Yorinobu, "Who's that you've tied up over there?"

---

2. This employs a pun: *Kararo*, which means both a "Chinese-style oar" and "must be bitter." Smartweed stalks exude bitter-tasting juices. Raikō's wife was the mother of the famous poet Lady Sagami.

"Kidōmaru,"[3] was the reply.

Raikō was alarmed. "If that's truly Kidōmaru, how could you have him tied up like that? If he did something criminal, I wouldn't treat him as casually as that."

Yorinobu agreed that Raikō was right. He called some of his soldier-servants and had Kidōmaru tied up more tightly. He also had him chained to prevent him from escaping.

When he heard Raikō's words, Kidōmaru fumed and said to himself, "That's a goddamned thing he said. No matter what happens, I'm gonna get revenge on him before the night's over!"

With several bottles emptied, Raikō got drunk and went to bed; so did Yorinobu. When everything quieted down, Kidōmaru, a powerful fellow, tore his rope and chain apart and got away. He then got in through the ventilating window in the gable into the space above the ceiling of the room where Raikō slept.[4] The idea was for him to break through the ceiling and drop right onto Raikō and fight him.

Raikō, however, was no ordinary man. He sensed what Kidōmaru was up to, and decided it would be too dangerous to let him drop onto him. He said, "Something bigger than a weasel and smaller than a marten is making noise up in the ceiling."

He then called out, "Is there anyone there?"

Tsuna identified himself and presented himself.

Raikō said, "We'd like to reach Kurama tomorrow. It's still night, but I'd like to leave right now. Tell this to everybody."

Tsuna replied, "Everyone's ready, sir!"

When he heard this, Kidōmaru decided he wouldn't be able to beat Raikō then and there. He had thought that the man was drunk and fast asleep. Any halfhearted attempt would bring disaster to himself, not to Raikō. So he made up his mind to make a new attempt on his life on the way to Kurama the next day, and got out of the ceiling.

When he reached the field leading directly to Mt. Kurama, he looked around but couldn't find a convenient spot to hide himself. So he picked a particularly large bull from among the many cattle grazing there, killed it, and pulled it up to the roadside. He then tore open the bull's belly, pushed himself into it, and waited, only his eyes showing.

---

3. The name may be freely given as "Demon Boy."
4. The usual traditional Japanese house leaves unused the space between the flat ceiling and the roof, which is often used as an attic in European and American houses.

As expected, Raikō came. He was in a white hunting robe and sported a sword. All of his four men—Tsuna, Kintoki, Sadamitsu, and Suetake—were with him. Raikō stopped his horse and said, "This field looks interesting. There are a lot of cattle, too. Let's do a bull-chase."

The four men gladly raced about, competing with one another, shooting hikime arrows at the cattle. It was quite a spectacle. In the midst of this excitement, though, Tsuna suddenly pulled out a real, sharp arrow and shot at the dead bull.

As everyone looked on in puzzlement, the belly of the dead bull trembled. A large boy jumped out of it, with a drawn sword, and dashed at Raikō. It was Kidōmaru! He was pierced with the arrow but didn't seem to give a damn about it. He simply charged toward his enemy. But Raikō didn't lose a bit of his calm. He drew his sword and beheaded Kidōmaru with a single stroke.

Kidōmaru didn't fall, but kept on charging and managed to stab through Raikō's saddlebow with his sword. And his head flew and bit into the front rope-decoration of the harness. To the very end he was brave and fearsome.

GUARDIAN KINGS AND THE OXCART: A COMIC INTERLUDE,

WITH AN ACCOUNT OF THE ORIGIN OF *HANIWA*

THE JAPANESE WARRIOR USED THE horse from very early times, as is clear from the *haniwa* figures which have been found in great numbers in and around the old giant tombs for ancient emperors and other people of importance; some are horses decked out militarily. There has even been a theory that Japan was overrun by the equestrian tribe of the Tungus of Siberia from the early fourth to the fifth century A.D. This intriguing theory was put forward by the historian Egami Namio during the brief period after the Second World War, when, as another historian, Inoue Mitsusada, puts it, the sense of liberation from the oppressive rule under the militarists and jingoists pervaded the nation. The theory hasn't so far won over the majority.

Yet the Japanese men of war never developed the one type of equipment anyone would first think of in picturing in his mind ancient Greek heroes such as Achilles and Hector and some of the more imposing nation-building warriors of old China: the chariot. This explains the unsoldierly embarrassment experienced by three of Minamoto no Raikō's "Four Guardian Kings," as recounted in the following episode from *Konjaku Monogatari Shū* (vol. 28, sec. 2).

The occasion was the day after the Kamo Festival, held in the fourth month, when the vestal of Kamo Shrines, accompanied by an imperial messenger, returned to her place of residence in Murasakino. The festive procession was most extravagant in those days and attracted huge crowds, including ladies and gentlemen of the aristocracy. The festival, now called Aoi Matsuri and held on May 15, is regarded as one of the three greatest festivals in Japan today.

Like the episode about Sakanoue no Haruzumi, pp. 59–60, this story also shows how completely the samurai in those days subordinated themselves to the aristocracy. In addition, it shows the way the warriors from the East, like these three, were regarded as hicks who spoke a barely intelligible rural dialect.

Among Governor of Settsu Minamoto no Raikō's soldiers were three outstanding men: Taira no Hidemichi, Taira [Urabe] no Suetake, and Sakata no Kintoki. All these men were sparklingly attractive in appearance and quick with their hands. They had strong minds and were wise in thinking and plotting. There was nothing clumsy about them. Their military exploits in the East were numerous, and people feared them as warriors. The Governor of Settsu himself treated them with special regard and kept them in close attendance.

Once, on the day following the Kamo Festival these three warriors discussed how to view the procession.

"All of us could ride our horses to Murasakino, but that would be extremely unsightly," they agreed. "On the other hand, we couldn't walk there, trying to hide our faces. We're dying to see the show, but don't know what to do."

"How about borrowing our monk friend's oxcart?" one of them ventured. "We could see the show riding in it."

"We aren't allowed to ride in an oxcart," said another. "If the guards of the noblemen found out, they'd pull us out and kick us. They might even kill us."

"How about keeping the blinds down, pretending we're women? The third one suggested.

"That's a great idea!" chorused the other two.

At once they borrowed their monk friend's cart and brought it out. Then these three warriors lowered its blinds, put on weird-looking indigo formal jackets, and climbed in. Since they pulled their shoes inside and didn't even let their sleeves out, the carriage looked perfectly like one in which ladies rode.

As the cart rumbled toward Murasakino, however, these men, who had never ridden in a vehicle like this, were tossed about as if shaken in a lidded box. They tumbled against each other, their heads bumped against the side boards, they banged cheek against cheek, or they fell right on their backs. They finally collapsed and rolled on the floorboards. It was unbearable. As they were carried forward like this, besides, the men became very sick. They vomited all over the cart's steps and dropped their headgear in their confusion.

The ox happened to be a superb specimen, though, and didn't let up as it pulled the carriage quickly forward. So the men cried out in their heavy accent, "Not so fast, not so fast!" This mystified the people in the carriages moving near them, as well as the lowly attendants walking behind their carts.

"What kind of people are riding in this ladies' cart? They cry out just like Eastern geese, don't they?" they said to one another in bafflement. "Could it be some daughters of Eastern people are going to see the procession?"

Still, the voices they heard were loud and no doubt men's, so it was all a mystery to them.

They finally arrived in Murasakino and their carriage was parked, with the ox unharnessed. Theirs was among the first carts to get there, and they had plenty of time to wait for the procession. But as though seasick, these men felt extremely ill. Their eyes rolled and everything looked upside down. So in their sickness all three fell asleep, their asses high up in the air.

The procession came and passed. But fast asleep as if dead, they missed all of it. They stirred and awoke only when everything was over and people made a good deal of noise harnessing the oxen back to their carriages. Still feeling ill and realizing they had missed the procession while asleep, they were angry with themselves and bitter.

"If we let our cart fly again on our way back, we are sure to die," they said. "None of us is afraid of dashing into the middle of a thousand enemy soldiers on horseback, for that's all routine for us. But there's no point in putting ourselves at the mercy of a miserable, snotty ox-boy and shaming ourselves like this. If we return on this cart, we can't be sure we'd make it back alive. We'll sit around a while and walk back along the boulevard when everybody's gone."

With this agreement, they came out of their carriage only when people had dispersed. After they sent back the oxcart, they put on their shoes, pulled their headgear low down to their noses, and, hiding their faces with their fans, returned to the mansion of the Governor of Settsu, which was in Ichijō.

Suetake said later: "We are brave warriors, sure. But we have no use for fighting on an oxcart. After that horrible experience, we never even went close to one again."

Here I might as well recount the story of the origin of *haniwa*.

As the portions of the *Nihon Shoki* (History of Japan) translated below tell it, these clay figures, which Picasso once praised for their pristine beauty, began to be made during the reign of the eleventh emperor, Suinin, to substitute for the live human sacrifices buried at the funeral of an important person.

However, the accounts about the practice of burying live human beings given in the *Kojiki* (Record of Ancient Matters) and *Nihon Shoki* conflict with each other. The *Kojiki* says that "human fences" for sacrificial burial began to be built with the death of Prince Yamato Hiko—the very person whose death and the accompanying human burials, the *Nihon Shoki* says, prompted Suinin to consider the discontinuation of the practice. But the *Nihon Shoki* also makes the same emperor describe the practice as "an ancient custom." The conflict may never be resolved because old records describing that period are very limited. If, at any rate, Suinin made such a decision, it was a noble one.

During the winter of the twenty-eighth year [of Suinin's reign], on the fifth of the tenth month, Prince Yamato Hiko, a brother of the Emperor's mother, died.

On the second of the eleventh month, Prince Yamato Hiko was buried at Tsukisaka, in Musa. On that occasion the people who had served him closely were assembled, and all of them were buried alive as they stood along the rim of his tomb. For days they did not die but cried and groaned. When they finally died, they decayed and rotted. Dogs and crows gathered and ate them. The emperor, when he heard them cry and groan, thought it was all too painful. He said to his ranking courtiers, "To force people to follow someone in death because he loved them while he was alive is all too painful. It may be an ancient custom, but there is no reason why we should follow it if it is not a good one. Discuss among yourselves how to discontinue forcing people to follow someone in death. . . ."

During the autumn of the thirty-second year [of his reign], on the sixth of the seventh month, Princess Hibasu, one of his consorts, died. The day of her burial was some time away. The emperor said to his ranking courtiers, "I learned earlier that it was no good to allow people to follow a dead person. What shall we do at the time of the coming funeral?"

Haniwa

"It is not wise to bury living people in the tomb of an imperial person," Nomi no Sukune said. "If we do that, how can we tell the following generations about him? With your permission, I wish to devise a plan and report it to you."

He sent a messenger and summoned one hundred potters from Izumo Province. Then he himself supervised them in obtaining clay and making figures of a variety of people, horses, and other things with it. Bringing the figures so made to the emperor, he said, "From now on these clay figures should be made to substitute for living people by erecting them in the tomb. This should become the rule for future generations."

The emperor was greatly pleased by this. He said to Nomi no Sukune, "Your plan fulfills my wishes perfectly."

And these clay figures were erected for the first time in Princess Hibasu's tomb. . . . Then an imperial edict was issued, which said: "From now on make it a rule to erect clay figures and not to hurt people."

MINAMOTO NO YORINOBU:
"LET YOUR LITTLE KID
BE STABBED TO DEATH!"

NYONE WHO HAS SEEN Kurosawa Akira's movie *Seven Samurai* will remember an early sequence where a warrior confronts a burglar who has taken hostage a peasant's baby.

The scene begins with the warrior, a passerby, readying himself to have his head shaven. Tonsure done by a priest, another passerby, the warrior borrows his robe and puts it on. By then the two rice balls he had asked to be made are brought to him. Carrying these rice balls but not his swords, he approaches the barn in which the robber is threatening the life of the frantically crying infant. The warrior announces he, a priest, merely wants to relieve the robber and the baby of their hunger. Then he throws the rice balls into the barn, one after the other. After throwing in the second rice ball, he dashes into the barn. Moments later, the robber totters out. Evidently mortally wounded, he slowly falls to the ground. The warrior goes on to become the leader of seven samurai who protect a village from marauding bandits.

In my earlier book from this imprint, *The Sword and the Mind*, I noted Kurosawa's scene as based on one of the legendary stories involving the swordsman Kamiizumi Hidetsuna (ca. 1508-88). Now I must amend myself somewhat to say the Hidetsuna story may derive from the first of two stories about Minamoto no Yorinobu (968-1048), which is from *Konjaku Monogatari Shū* (vol. 25, sec. 11).

It goes without saying that during the days when burglars and thieves were "as innumerable as grains of sand on the beach"—attributed to the great robber Ishikawa Goemon (1558-94)—a cornered man taking a child hostage may have been a distressingly common occurrence. The stories recounting the rescue of such a child, therefore, must be legion. Here I will only note that the emphasis in each of the three accounts is somewhat different. In Kurosawa's version it is on the ability to size up a situation and act swiftly, decisively; in the legend about Hidetsuna it's on the calmness of the mind that enables an accomplished swordsman to face unarmed a man brandishing a sword; in Yorinobu's story, it's on the essential requirement for the warrior to live up to his calling.

Yorinobu was a distinguished warrior who held several governorships and became Commander of the Western Defense Headquarters. In popular tales he tends to be outshone by one of his brothers, Raikō, perhaps because Raikō has many entertaining stories created around the four warriors who worked for him. Nevertheless, in the unusually realistic tale about a child rescue that follows, Yorinobu comes out as an admirable man of unflappable common sense and compassion. If factual, the incident took place in 999 or before.

When Governor of Kawachi Minamoto no Yorinobu was in Kō-zuke Province where he was then governor, there was a man called Fujiwara no Chikataka, who was a Lieutenant of the Outer Palace Guards, Right Division, and also the son of Yorinobu's nurse-maid. He was as accomplished a warrior as Yorinobu.

Once while he was in the province of which Yorinobu was governor, Chikataka caught a burglar who came into his house and left him with a guard. Somehow, though, the burglar managed to remove his shackles and tried to escape. But there was no way he could get out of the house. So he took hostage Chikataka's son, a lovely boy of four or five, who happened to be running about. The man then took the boy into an inner storage quarter, held him down with his leg, and threatened to take his life with a drawn sword placed against the boy's belly.

At the time Chikataka was in the governor's office. When a man came running and said, "The burglar's taken your young son hostage," Chikataka, alarmed and blubbering, ran back to his house. And indeed, he saw the burglar holding a sword against his son's belly. Chikataka felt the world go dark. He didn't know what to do. He wanted to jump in and take the boy away, but there was that large glittering sword held against his son's belly, and the burglar shouting, "Don't come near me! If you come near me, I'll stab this boy to death!" If I let him stab my boy to death as he says he would, Chikataka thought, it would be utterly useless to cut this bastard into a hundred, a thousand pieces later. So he told his soldier-servants not to go near the burglar but to watch him from some distance and, saying he would inform the governor, he dashed away.

The governor's office was close by. The governor, alarmed to see his lieutenant run in in frantic agitation, immediately asked, "What's the matter?"

"My boy, my only child, he's been taken hostage by a burglar," Chikataka blurted, crying.

"I understand how you feel," the governor said with a laugh. "But why should you cry like that? One would think you ran into a demon or a god. Don't you think it rather unseemly for you to cry like a crybaby? Let your little kid be stabbed to death, if need be. Only with that attitude could you call yourself a warrior. If you worried about yourself, worried about your wife or your child, you'd accomplish nothing. To be fearless means not to worry about yourself, not to worry about your wife or your child.

"Having said what I had to," the governor continued, "let me come with you to see how things are." He then picked up his sword and went to Chikataka's house.

When the governor stood at the entrance to the inner storage quarter where the burglar was, the burglar saw that the governor himself had come. This time he didn't bluster as he had to Chikataka; instead, he lowered his eyes and pressed the sword closer to the boy, apparently ready to pierce the boy with it if anyone came near. Meanwhile the boy was crying himself hoarse.

The governor spoke to the burglar: "Did you take that boy hostage because you wanted to keep yourself alive, or because you wanted to kill the boy? Tell me what you think in no uncertain terms, you burglar there!"

The burglar said in a voice one could hardly hear: "Why should I want to kill a boy like this, sir? I didn't want to lose my life, I just wanted to live. That's why I took him hostage, just in case."

"I see," said the governor. "If that's the case, throw that sword away. I, Yorinobu, tell you to do that, so you have no choice but to throw it away. You don't think I would let you kill the boy and let it go at that, do you? You must have heard about me, the way I am. Make sure to throw the sword away, you burglar there!"

The burglar thought awhile, and said, "Thank you, sir. I don't think I can refuse to do what you tell me to. I will throw the sword away." He then flung the sword into a far corner, made the boy stand up, and let him go. The boy ran out.

The governor stepped back, summoned his soldier-servants, and said, "Bring that man over here." They grabbed the man by the collar, pulled him out into the courtyard, and made him sit down on the ground. Chikataka wanted to cut the burglar apart, but the governor said, "This man deserves praise for having let his hostage go. He's so destitute that he came into your house as a burglar. Then, because he wanted to keep himself alive, he took your son hostage. There's nothing hateful about him. Besides, when I told him to let your boy go, he followed my request and let him go. He understands how things are. Set this man free at once."

The governor then said to the burglar, "Tell us what you need to have." But the burglar merely cried and cried, unable to say anything.

The governor said, "Give him something to eat. He's done something bad, and someone might end up killing him. Go to the stable, pick a sturdy horse for hay-making, put a cheap saddle on it, and bring it here."

He also sent his men off to get a cheap bow and quiver. When everything was brought together, the governor made the burglar put the quiver on his back and mount the horse in the courtyard. He then put ten days' worth of dried rice in a bag, wrapped the bag in a cloth bag, and tied it around the burglar's waist. This done, he said to the burglar, "Now leave! Run away!" Following his word, the burglar galloped away.

Because he was awestruck by Yorinobu's words, the burglar had let his hostage go. When you think of this you can fully understand Yorinobu's reputation as a warrior.

The boy who was taken hostage entered the priesthood on Mt. Mitake when he grew up. In the end he attained the holy office of *acharya* and assumed the name Myōshū.

In 1046, two years before his death, Yorinobu filed a scroll of written prayers with the Hachiman Shrine at Iwashimizu in which he spelled out the genealogical authenticity and military achievements of his family. In the previous year his son Yoriyoshi had held the coming-of-age rite for his son Yoshiie at the shrine and given him the name, Hachiman Tarō. Hachiman Tarō Yoshiie would go on to be admired by his contemporaries as the greatest warrior. Yorinobu's written prayers made the Minamoto clan's worship of the Hachiman Shrine official. From then on Hachiman became their guardian deity.

Describing his own military exploits in the prayers, Yorinobu stated with what might be called a Chinese flourish:

In recent years, in the fourth year of Emperor Goichijō's Manju Era [1027], a greedy rat, Taira no Tadatsune, Kazusa Province, with an ambition of the worst kind, sprawled himself across the eastern capital, shunted aside the Governor of Bandō, extended his ferocious influence so as to trample upon the carriers of imperial tributes, and rebelled against the regulations of the imperial court. He held government goods as his own and robbed products levied as taxes. He ignored official edicts and resisted imperial messengers, so that the imperial house frequently dispatched its crack troops to destroy him. Nevertheless he managed to escape capture by building impregnable forts and, standing at the outer fringe of the imperial castle, waited for the chance to seize the imperial court, when I, your humble servant, finally had the good fortune of being selected by the court to commit myself and sally forth to subjugate the East, appointed as I was Governor of Kai in the second year of the Chōgen Era [1029]. Without rounding up the local populace for military duty, without expending allocated supplies, without beating the drums, without waving the flags, without drawing bows, without shooting arrows, without hiding and without attacking, I captured the invading bandit by making no move whatsoever.

As it happens, this account is largely factual. The news of the rebellion of Taira no Tadatsune in Kantō (also called Bandō) reached the court in the sixth month of 1028. The court held a session to select the head of a posse comitatus. Yorinobu was highly recommended, but somehow two other men, one famous for his military prowess, were picked and dispatched. They could not make any military progress against Tadatsune, and one of them was dismissed toward the end of 1029. In the spring of 1030 Tadatsune assaulted the governor's headquarters of Awa, and the governor fled. The court appointed a successor to the governorship, but the man selected was engaged in a vicious struggle of his own and had no inclination to accept the appointment.

The ravaging of the farmlands by both the rebels and the government soldiers continued. Finally, in the ninth month of 1030, the court recalled the remaining posse leader and appointed Yorinobu as his replacement. Yorinobu, appointed Governor of Kai in the previous year, was staying in Kyoto and, for some reason, was slow to leave for the East. Then, when he finally arrived at his post in the spring of 1031, a curious thing happened: The notorious rebel Tadatsune surrendered promptly. About a month later Tadatsune fell ill and while traveling to Kyoto to respond to the summons, he died, on the sixth of the sixth month.

Why did Tadatsune surrender so promptly? One reason may lie in his special relationship to Yorinobu, as described in the following tale from *Konjaku Monogatari Shū* (vol. 25, sec. 9), which, if factual, happened in 1012 or earlier.

When Yorinobu became Governor of Hitachi and was staying in that province, there was a warrior by the name of Taira no Tadatsune in the province of Shimofusa. His personal influence was extremely great, and he wandered about as he wished throughout Kazusa and Shimofusa, paying no taxes and otherwise doing nothing officially required. He even ignored the orders of the Governor of Hitachi at times. The governor was greatly incensed by this and was eager to go to Shimofusa and attack Tadatsune.

In the same province, however, there was a man by the name of Taira no Koremoto, an officer of the Outer Palace Guards, Left Division. When he heard about the governor's intentions, he told the governor: "Tadatsune is influential. Furthermore, he lives in a place barely accessible to human beings. All this makes it impossible to attack him with a few men. If you wish to come across the border to this place, do so with a great number of soldiers."

When he heard this, the governor said, "That may be so, but I can't leave it like this." He then set off as he was, and went over to the province of Shimofusa. Koremoto lined up 3,000 soldiers and came to meet him in front of the Kashima Shrine.

On the beach so white and wide and almost 2,000 yards long, because it was daybreak all the bows glistened in the morning sun. The governor had come along with the armed men of his manor and the warriors of his province, about 2,000 in all. As these soldiers stood along the edge of the beach west of Kashima County, they didn't look like men: One saw only their bows glistening like clouds. Popular tales tell of such things, but such masses of armed men have never actually been seen, the amazed people said.

The estuary of the Kinu River was just like the ocean. Kashima was right across the waters in front of Katori, but you could barely make out the faces of the people on the other side. Tadatsune had his residential fort far inside the inlet. If you tried to get there for an attack by going along the edge of the inlet, it would take about seven days. If you went straight across the waters, you could attack him in a single day. Tadatsune, a man of great power, had taken away and hidden all the ferryboats.

With no way of crossing the waters, some of the soldiers standing around the beach were wondering if they ought to go around the edge, when the governor summoned a man by the name of Ōnakatomi no Narihira and put him on a small boat to send him to Tadatsune. His word was: "If he isn't going to fight, come back as quickly as you can. If his decision is to fight and you can't make it back, simply turn the boat downstream. When we see it, we'll make the crossing."

With these instructions Narihira rowed away in the small boat.

Meanwhile Koremoto dismounted and held the governor's horse by the bit. Seeing this, several soldiers also dismounted, making soughing sounds like winds blowing through grasses. The dismounting sound was just like a blowing wind.

At the other end, Narihira turned the boat downstream. Tadatsune had said as his reply to the governor: "The Lord Governor is a great man. I'd be happy to surrender to him. But Koremoto is an enemy of my family. While that fellow is with him, how could I possibly come to kneel before him?" He had added, "Without a single boat for crossing, how could even one man come here?"

When he saw the boat turned downstream, the governor said to the several soldiers around him, "If we go around the edge of this sea for an attack, several days will pass. That's why he isn't running away. Also, the way he's set it up he's apparently inaccessible. If only we could attack him today, that bastard would be surprised out of his wits. But he has hidden all the boats. What do you think we should do?"

The soldiers said, "There's no other way, sir. We should go around for an attack."

"Well," the governor said. "This is the first time I have seen Bandō. So I have no detailed knowledge about this region. But my family has handed down a bit of information about this sea: 'It has a shallow, banklike underwater road, running straight to the other side; it's about ten feet wide and as deep as the height of a horse's stomach.' I should think that road should begin somewhere around here. There has to be someone among you soldiers who knows about it. He will go first. I will follow."

This said, he kicked his horse and started to gallop into the water. At that moment, a man by the name of Makami no Takafumi called out: "Sir, I've crossed this water many times. Let me ride ahead of you, sir!"

Takafumi then had his attendant carry a bundle of reeds and, making him slap his horse's rump with it every now and then, began to cross the inlet. Seeing this, other warriors and their men followed. There were two spots where they had to swim. When several hundred soldiers had gone into the water, the governor followed.

As it turned out, among all the many men there were three who knew about the underwater road. But none of the others had even heard about it.

The governor sees this region for the first time, they thought to themselves. Then how can he know about something even we don't know? He's got to be a warrior far superior to all the rest! The fear of the man increased among them.

While Yorinobu and his men were crossing, Tadatsune was calm, relaxed. He's going to attack me by going around the sea, he thought. I've taken away and hidden the boats, so he won't be able to cross it.

Besides, thought Tadatsune, he couldn't possibly know about the road in the shallows. Only I know about it. In the several days he has to spend going around the sea, I'll escape. Then there will be no way he can attack me.

Having these thoughts, he kept his men at rest.

It was then that a man who worked around the house dashed in, shouting, "The Lord of Hitachi found the shallow road in the sea and is already crossing it with some of his men! What shall we do, sir?!"

He said this in a flattened voice[1] in great consternation. This, of course, was quite contrary to what Tadatsune had expected.

"So I've been attacked! This is it! This is it!" he said. "I'll send him a note of surrender."

At once he wrote down a family register. He stuck it to one end of a letter-holding stick and had an attendant carry it along with a letter of apology by small boat.[2]

---

1. The characterization of the way Tadatsune's servant talked as "flattened" is supposed to be the recorder's jab at the rural accent of the Bandō people.
2. Offering a family register, called *myōbu*, was equal to a pledge of loyalty.

When the boat approached him, the governor took the family register and said, "So he has sent me his family register accompanied by a letter of apology. There's no need for us to attack and kill him now. We will immediately turn back."

This said, he turned his horse around. So did his men.

It must be after this incident that people began to think of him as an indescribably superior warrior and to fear him more than ever before.

RAIKŌ AND OTHERS: TALES OF ARCHERY

BEFORE THE SWORD CAME TO be regarded as "the soul of the samurai," the bow and arrow were the warrior's primary weapons. Here are some stories about the virtuoso performances of some of the warriors in the earlier periods, including a man who deliberately chose to be a target.

The first episode, from *Konjaku Monogatari Shū* (vol. 25, sec. 6), concerns Minamoto no Raikō, who was evidently advanced in age at the time. His father, here referred to as Tada no Manjū, was Minamoto no Mitsunaka (912–997). The great pomp that accompanied Mitsunaka's Buddhist conversion is described in pp. 27–29. Sanjō (976–1017) was emperor from 1011 to 1016.

One day when Emperor Sanjō was Crown Prince and lived in Higashi Sanjō, he was walking by the south front of the Shinden Building, where there were a couple of noblemen in the western colonnade. There he noticed a fox lying under the western eaves of the Buddha's Hall to the southeast.

At the time the Crown Prince's chief military aide was Minamoto no Raikō. Tada no Manjū's son, Raikō was such an accomplished warrior that the imperial court made him serve in a military capacity and the whole world regarded him as fearsome. This same man was among the noblemen there, so the Crown Prince gave him a bow and a hikime arrow and said, "Shoot that fox lying under the southeastern eaves."

"Your Highness, I'm afraid I must excuse myself," Raikō replied. "If it were someone else, there should be no harm in his missing the target. But for me to miss the target would be profoundly embarrassing. Furthermore, Your Highness, it would not be possible for me to hit the target. When I was younger, if I happened to see a deer I would shoot at it even if it was far away and I couldn't see it clearly. But I haven't done anything like that for many years. Now, even in sports shooting, I can't tell where my arrow drops."

Raikō's hope was that if he didn't shoot but talked awhile, the fox would trot away. Unfortunately, though, the fox not only did *not* trot away, but fell sound asleep facing west.

Meanwhile the Crown Prince earnestly kept urging him to shoot. In the end Raikō was unable to excuse himself anymore. He took up the bow and put the hikime to it.

"I might make it if this bow were strong enough, Your Highness," he said. "Besides, a hikime is too heavy to cover this much distance. A battle arrow might, but not a hikime. If the arrow didn't reach the target but dropped on its way, that would be far more embarrassing to me than missing the target. I really don't think I'll make it."

Still, he tucked his jacket in with a string and rolled up his sleeves. He then lowered the tip of his arrow somewhat, pulled the bowstring as far back as the length of the arrow permitted, and shot. He couldn't even see where the arrow was going. But within a second the arrow hit the fox's chest. The fox jerked up its head and tumbled headlong into the pond.

With a weak bow and a heavy arrow, even the most powerful archer's shot wouldn't have reached the target but dropped on its way, thought the Crown Prince and everyone else who was there. But Raikō hit the fox. This is a wonder of wonders!

The fox drowned in the water and died, so a man was sent to pick it up and discard it elsewhere.

Later, to express his great admiration, the Crown Prince gave Raikō a horse selected from the imperial stable. When he was given the horse in the courtyard, Raikō turned to the Crown Prince seated inside the room and said, "That was not my doing, Your Highness. Not to shame my ancestors, my guardian deity helped me in the shooting."

Afterward he would say the same thing to his brothers and relatives, "No, that wasn't the arrow I shot. You must understand that."

When Raikō's words became known, people praised him all the more for it.

Stories about the trick of deliberately becoming a shooting target and avoiding the shot must exist everywhere. The episode below, from *Kokon Chomon Jū* (sec. 347) and notable for its stark rationality, involves one of Minamoto no Raikō's "Four Guardian Kings."

Among the soldiers who served Suetake, Raikō's warrior, was a fellow who excelled in bravery. Suetake himself was a first-class bowman who could shoot a needle hung from a thread.

The man in question one day said to Suetake, "You may be able to shoot a needle hung from a thread, sir, but I bet you won't be able to shoot me if I stand in front of you but a dozen yards away."

That's a damned stupid thing to say, Suetake thought, and, succumbing to the urge to show up the man, he said, "If I miss you, I'll give you anything you want. If I don't miss you, what will you give me?"

"My life, of course, sir," the man replied. That certainly was good enough.

So Suetake agreed to go ahead, and the man, as stated, stood a dozen yards away from him. Suetake knew he was sure to hit him. That would mean losing one of his own subordinates. But accepting that this was the way things had turned out, he stopped thinking about it and carefully shot at him. He missed. The arrow hit a spot under the man's armpit, five inches away from his body. Having lost the bet, Suetake had no choice but to give the man whatever he wanted, as promised. And the man didn't hesitate to accept anything given him.

Later, the man said, "Would you like to try once again, sir?"

This brazenness disquieted Suetake again, and he agreed. The first miss was mysterious, but this time I can't possibly fail, he thought. He kept the string drawn for a while and, aiming at the man's heart, released the arrow. He missed again. The arrow hit a spot under the man's right armpit, five inches away from his body.

"Let me explain why you missed, sir," the man said. "You are an excellent archer, but you don't think enough, if I may say such a thing, sir. A man's body is surely big, but it isn't much larger than a foot in width. You shoot at it, aiming at its center. Suppose I, the target, jump aside as soon as I hear the sound of the string at the release of the arrow. I can miss the arrow by at least five inches. That's how it happened. The next time around, you might shoot with that in mind, sir."

The man's reasoning was so perfect that Suetake had nothing to say.

The following episode, from *Konjaku Monogatari Shū* (vol. 25, sec.12), has to do with another relative of Raikō: his nephew, Yoriyoshi (988–1075). As we will see, Yoriyoshi would go on to become the Governor of Mutsu and fight as commander in the so-called Former Nine-Year War.

Aside from showing an instance of divine skill in archery, this story is also an illustration of a father's exemplary, unstinting generosity toward his son.

When Minamoto no Yorinobu, Governor of Kawachi and warrior, heard that someone in the East had a fine horse, he sent a message politely asking for it. Unable to decline the request, the owner of the horse sent it to Kyoto. On the way a horse thief saw it, desperately wanted it, and decided to steal it by any means. So he followed it secretly. But because the soldiers guarding it remained vigilant, the thief didn't have a chance to steal it before they all reached Kyoto. Upon arriving in the Capital, the horse was first put in Yorinobu's stable.

In no time someone told Yorinobu's son, Yoriyoshi: "A fine horse has arrived at your father's place today from the East." When he heard this, Yoriyoshi thought: It's certain that an unworthy fellow will ask my father for the horse and get it sooner or later. Before that happens I'll go see it, and if it's a really fine horse, I'll ask for it and get it.

So, even though it was pouring that day and it was already evening, Yoriyoshi, dying to see the horse, went to visit his father through the downpour.

"Well, why haven't you come to see me for such a long time?" the father said to his son. Even while saying this, he guessed that his son had heard about the arrival of the horse and came with the thought of asking for it. So, before Yoriyoshi opened his mouth, Yorinobu said, "I've heard that a horse has arrived from the East, but I haven't seen it yet. The fellow who sent it to me says it's a fine horse. It's too dark to see anything now. If you look at it tomorrow morning and like it in any way, it's yours."

Told this before he made the request, Yoriyoshi was greatly pleased. "Well, then, sir," he said, "may I stay overnight, so that I may look at the horse in the morning?"

The two of them spent the evening gossiping. When the night became late and the father retired to sleep in his bedroom, Yoriyoshi followed suit and lay in a room nearby to sleep.

Meanwhile, it continued to rain noisily. Around midnight the thief stole in, mingling with the noise of the rain, led the horse out, and left. Sometime later a cry went up from the direction of the stable: "A thief has taken the horse that arrived last night for the master!"

Yorinobu heard this, though faintly. Without even asking the sleeping Yoriyoshi, "Did you hear that?" he tucked in the hem of his robe, as a lady would, as he rose to his feet. He slung a quiver across his back and ran to the stable. He led out a horse himself and put on it a cheap saddle which was on hand. He then rode out, alone, toward the Ōsaka Barrier to give chase. As he did this, he thought, This thief must be a fellow from the East. He saw it was a fine horse and followed it with the thought of stealing it. But he couldn't do it before reaching Kyoto. Last night he came in by the noise of the rain and got away with it.

Yoriyoshi also had heard the cry. He thought exactly as his father did, and didn't tell him, either. He had gone to sleep in his clothes, so he simply got up, slung a quiver across his back, led out a horse from the stable, and rode out toward the Ōsaka Barrier to give chase, alone.

The father thought, My son is sure to come on this chase.

The son thought, My father is sure to be ahead of me, giving chase. He galloped on. By the time he passed the riverbed, the rain had stopped and the sky had cleared up. He rode on even faster, until he came near the Ōsaka Barrier.

The thief, riding the horse he had stolen, thought he'd gotten away with it. He slowed his hard gallop as he came to the Ōsaka Barrier and had his horse wade into the ample pool of water that had formed next to it. When he heard that wading noise, Yorinobu, as if he had planned it with his son beforehand, and even though it was still dark and he didn't even know his son was there, cried out, "Shoot, he's there!"

He had hardly finished saying this when he heard the sound of a flying arrow. He sensed something was hit. Then he heard the clanking of empty stirrups as the startled horse broke into a gallop without its rider. Yorinobu said, "You've shot the thief down! Run ahead and get hold of the horse!" Then, without waiting, he turned back and headed home.

Yoriyoshi ran ahead of the horse and got hold of it. By then some of Yorinobu's soldiers had caught up, and these met Yoriyoshi on his way back, a few at a time. By the time he reached Kyoto there were twenty to thirty of them with him.

Yorinobu got back to his mansion and, without even thinking of saying this or that, walked to his bedroom and went back to sleep. Yoriyoshi, too, went back to sleep after putting the horse he had brought back in the care of the grooms.

The following morning, Yorinobu called out Yoriyoshi. But instead of evincing any knowledge of his son's extraordinary exploits of shooting and bringing back the horse, he simply ordered that the horse be brought out. When it was, Yoriyoshi looked at it and saw it was a fine horse indeed. He simply said, "I accept your offer, sir," and took the horse.

The only thing is that, though it hadn't been promised the previous night, the horse came with a fine saddle. Yoriyoshi decided it was an award for shooting the thief down.

Mutsu Waki (The Story of Mutsu), an account of the Former Nine-Year War in which Yoriyoshi led the government's forces, describes the man's prowess in archery this way:

"Yoriyoshi invariably took any animal that ran across the field, be it a stag, deer, fox, or rabbit. By his own choice he carried a weak bow, but the arrow he shot never failed to bury itself up to its feathers. Even a furious beast would fall before the power of his string. That's the way he surpassed the others in bowmanship."

The last two episodes also have to do with Raikō, though this time only indirectly: Mutsuru, the protagonist of one story and a bystander in the other—both from *Kokon Chomon Jū* (secs. 348 and 349)—is a brother of Watanabe no Tsuna, one of Raikō's "Four Guardian Kings." Little else is known about him. Ichiin is Emperor Toba (1103–1156); his proscription against taking the lives of fish and fowl may derive from the fact that he had by then taken Buddhist vows.

When Ichiin resided in the Toba Palace, an osprey flew in and caught fish in the pond every day. One day he decided to have it shot, and asked if there was anyone suitable for the job in the Warriors' Office. Mutsuru happened to be there. When summoned, he was given this imperial order:

"An osprey has attached itself to this pond and catches many fish. Shoot it. However, it would be cruel to kill it. His Majesty's wish is to have neither the bird nor the fish killed. Find an appropriate scheme to do the work."

There was no way Mutsuru could decline the order. He left at once and soon returned with a bow and an arrow. The arrow was fork-tipped. Standing near the edge of the pond, he waited for the osprey to come. As expected, it flew in. It caught a carp and was flying up when Mutsuru shot at it with a full-drawn bow. The arrow hit its target but the osprey flew away. The carp dropped to the pond and floated with its white belly up.

When Mutsuru tugged the fish in and offered it for an imperial inspection, it turned out that the osprey's foot clutching the carp had been severed. Its foot was severed, but it didn't die that instant. The fish, too, did not die even though it had been clawed by the bird. In accordance with the order that neither the bird nor the fish be killed, Mutsuru had worked out this scheme.

Lord Ichiin decided it was no ordinary man's feat, and rewarded Mutsuru with a prize.

This same Mutsuru, a Lieutenant of the Outer Palace Guards, Left Division, once wanted to equip some battle arrows with feathers and sought ibis feathers. He couldn't find enough of them, so asked his subordinates if they had any.

When Jōroku Dayū, who was an excellent archer, heard this, he asked his attendants to go out and look for ibises. He soon received the report that some ibises were sighted in the paddies north of the river.

When he came out with a bow and arrows, the ibises had risen and were flying south. Jōroku readied his bow and arrow but didn't shoot right or left. Instead, he asked Mutsuru which bird he especially wanted to have. Mutsuru replied that he wanted the last one in flight, but Jōroku still didn't seem to be in any hurry. Finally, when the birds flew away farther into the distance and seemed to be above the southern bank of the river, he drew the string to the full and shot. The arrow hit the bird.

Greatly impressed but also puzzled, Mutsuru asked Jōroku, "Why did you neglect to shoot when the bird was up close? Why did you shoot it only when it flew farther away?"

"I'm glad you asked," said Jōroku. "If I had shot the bird when it was close, it would have dropped into the river and its feathers would have gotten wet and spoiled. I shot it when it reached the farther shore, not to damage its feathers."

No doubt he was an accomplished archer who could shoot at will.

TAIRA NO MUNETSUNE:
THE SILENT ONE

QUIET BUT EFFICIENT—men endowed with these qualities have always won admiration, but among such men Taira no Munetsune (982–1023) has cast a long shadow because of the following episode in *Konjaku Monogatari Shū* (vol. 23, sec. 14).

Though the episode describes a night escort during which nothing murderous happened, behind it is an age in which men in arms constantly fought with one another. Munetsune's father, Muneyori, when Governor of Mutsu, assaulted Taira no Korehira, another governor and his "competitor in the way of the warrior," and was exiled to the island of Oki. While a lieutenant of the Outer Palace Guards, Left Division, Munetsune himself was charged with the crime of engaging in a private war and was once prosecuted by the Imperial Police for a murder. In his poem included in the sixth imperial anthology, *Shiika Shū* (no. 335), Munetsune expresses gratitude to Archbishop Genkaku for winning a pardon for some imperial offense he had committed.

During the time when the Lord of Uji[1] was in his prime, Myōson,[2] Archbishop of Mii Temple,[3] was once in attendance for all-night prayers at the court. No lighting oil was used.

After a while, without telling anyone what its purpose was, the Lord of Uji thought of an errand and decided to send out Myōson and

---

1. Fujiwara no Yorimichi (992–1074), who served three emperors as regent and chancellor.
2. Myōson (971–1063) held a round of high Buddhist posts.
3. Also known as Onjō-ji, it is the headquarters of the Tendai sect. The temple, in Ōtsu, is some distance from Kyoto.

have him return before the night was over. He had a horse, which was neither nervous nor jumpy but dependable, taken out of the stable and saddled, and asked aloud, "Is there anyone who can escort this gentleman?"

Munetsune, then a lieutenant of the Outer Palace Guards, Left Division, was on duty. "Munetsune is at your service, sir."

"Very good," the lord said, and because Myōson at the time was not an archbishop but a mere monk, he added, "A monk must go to Mii Temple tonight but return before the night is over. As his escort, see to it that he does that."

"I understand, sir."

Munetsune always kept his bow and quiver leaning against a wall of his night duty room and a pair of straw sandals hidden under the floor mat. Also, he had only one man in his service, who was apparently of base stock. So everyone who observed him would say, "What an economical fellow!"

When he was given the escort order, Munetsune immediately tucked up high the hems of his trouser-skirt and tied them. He then took out the straw sandals from where he always kept them, put them on, put the quiver on his back, and came out to the place where the horse was.

The monk asked, "What's your name?"

"Munetsune, sir," was the reply.

"We're going to Mii Temple," said the monk. "How come you're standing around like that as if you were going there on foot? Don't you have a mount?"

"Even if I'm on foot, I'll never be left behind, sir. Let's be on our way," Munetsune said.

The monk wondered to himself, "This is very odd."

When they had gone seven or eight hundred yards, with Munetsune's servant leading the way with a lantern, Myōson was terrified to see, walking straight toward him, two men dressed in black and armed with bows and arrows. However, upon seeing Munetsune, they dropped to their knees and said, "Here's your horse, sir!" Then a few horses trotted out of nowhere. Because it was night the monk couldn't make out the color of the horses, but he saw the men had also brought a pair of riding boots with them. Munetsune put these on over his straw sandals and mounted his horse.

Feeling secure now that he had two mounted men with quivers accompanying him, Myōson continued on his way for another two hundred yards, when two men dressed similarly in black and armed with bows and arrows appeared from the roadside. This time Munetsune didn't say a word. The two at once led out their horses and joined the escort. The monk said to himself, "They are also his men. What a fabulous thing to do!"

They went on another two hundred yards, and two more men showed up in similar fashion and joined the escort. Munetsune said nothing. The men who joined the escort didn't seem to have anything to say among themselves, either. From then on, too, at every one or two hundred yards a new duo joined up, so that by the time they had gone the distance of the riverbed of Kamo, there were thirty-odd men. While he was marveling at the mysterious doings of Munetsune, Myōson arrived at Mii Temple.

Having done what he was instructed to do, he began his trip back before midnight. He traveled as if enveloped before and after by the same men-at-arms, feeling absolutely secure. The men didn't slip away until they reached the riverbed. After they entered Kyoto proper, however, without any word from Munetsune, the men began to disappear two by two at each spot from which they had appeared. By the time they had only a hundred yards to go to the Lord of Uji's mansion, there were only the two men who had appeared first. Munetsune dismounted at the spot where he had mounted his horse, took off the riding boots, and walked off in the straw sandals in which he had come out of the mansion. The two men picked up the boots and, leading the horses on foot, they too walked away to hide themselves. Now only Munetsune and his lowly servant remained, and these two together walked in through the gate in their sandals.

Mystified by the way both men and horses had emerged as if by prior understanding, Myōson went to see Lord Yorimichi, determined to tell him about it. Yorimichi had waited without going to bed. After reporting on the errand he had been told to carry out, Myōson made sure to observe, "Munetsune is a baffling sort of a fellow," adding, "He has quite a group of capable men lined up for himself."

Contrary to his expectations that he would ask for details, Yorimichi somehow didn't follow up Myōson's observations with any questions. The monk was disappointed.

Munetsune was a son of the warrior by the name of Taira no Muneyori. He was brave and, unlike regular men, used very large arrows. So people used to call him the Lieutenant of Big Arrows of the Outer Palace Guards, Left Division.

TAIRA NO SADATSUNA:
WHEN NOT TO RISK YOUR LIFE

THE WARRIOR MUST BE PREPARED to risk his life at any time—but only in the right circumstances. He must also know when not to risk his life, as a brief episode from *Kokon Chomon Jū* (sec. 341) illustrates.

About the protagonist, Taira no Sadatsuna, little is known. A *shirabyōshi*, "white rhythm," was a female dancer who danced in an elegant, courtly costume; she often worked as a prostitute. Wada Yoshimori (1147–1213) was a renowned warrior with a brilliant military record. When Hōjō Yoshitoki (1143–1224), regent of the Kamakura Shogunate and de facto ruler of Japan, had his brother and others murdered, Yoshimori raised an army against him but was defeated and killed. He is an important figure in the upcoming section on Minamoto no Yoshitsune.

When robbers forced themselves into his Kyoto house, Lieutenant of the Outer Palace Guards, Left Division, Taira no Sadatsuna, of Furukōri, was drunk and asleep with the *shirabyōshi* dancer Gyokuju. When the robbers broke into his bedroom, Sadatsuna drew his sword and struck them aside. He then pushed Gyokuju ahead of him, retreated to the backyard, went over the cypress fence into his neighbor's place, and got away along with his companion.

People heard about this incident and said, "So he ran away from robbers. That's terrible!"

When he heard this, Sadatsuna said, "If the same thing happened again, I'd do the same. I don't want to risk my life with robbers.

But if my lord ran into trouble, I would give up my life any number of times."

Sadatsuna kept his word. When Lieutenant of the Outer Palace Guards, Left Division, Wada Yoshimori went into battle, Sadatsuna ran ahead of any troop he led — carrying a scarlet arrow-protector[1] and riding a black steed during the day, and carrying a white arrow-protector and riding a white steed mottled with black during the night. He was a true embodiment of "a warrior worth a thousand men." True to his word, he was gallant and brave.

However, meeting no one willing to accept his challenge for a duel, and his side losing the battle, Sadatsuna committed suicide.

---

1. Or *horo*, a large cloth bag an equestrian warrior used to carry on his back to protect himself from the arrows.

PART TWO

Battles Joined

MINAMOTO NO YOSHIIE: "THE SAMURAI OF THE GREATEST BRAVERY UNDER HEAVEN"

THE LORD OF SHIRAKAWA was once assaulted by a spirit while asleep. Informed that he needed to place an appropriate weapon above his pillow, he summoned Yoshiie. Yoshiie at once offered a bow made of spindletree and lacquered black. The Lord of Shirakawa stopped being tormented by the spirit after placing the bow above his pillow.

Deeply moved, he asked Yoshiie if he had used the bow during the Twelve-Year War. Yoshiie replied he did not remember. That, we hear, increased the lord's admiration.

This brief episode from *Uji Shūi Monogatari* (Tales Gleaned from Uji, sec. 66) illustrates the great respect resembling awe that the imperial court headed by Emperor Shirakawa (1053–1129), here called the Lord of Shirakawa, came to feel for the warrior Minamoto no Yoshiie (1041–1108). By the time of this episode some nobles had called him "the commander of all samurai" and "the samurai of the greatest bravery under heaven." The second designation was used by Fujiwara no Munetada (dates uncertain) in his diary when Yoshiie was permitted to enter Shirakawa's court in 1098. Entering the imperial court was an honor seldom accorded to warriors.

Yoshiie distinguished himself in two civil wars traditionally known as the Former Nine-Year War (1051–1062) and the Latter Three-Year War (1083–1087)[1] – in the first as one of the commanders under his father, Yoriyoshi,

---

1. The wars obviously lasted longer than the designated periods, though sometimes the Former Nine-Year War is said to have begun in 1054. At times the Twelve-Year War refers to the Former Nine-Year War, sometimes to the combination of the two wars.

Governor of Mutsu, and in the second as himself Governor of Mutsu. Both wars were waged to break the power of the clans in the Mutsu region that were influential as leaders of the Ebisu.[2]

The Abe family whose heads were appointed county chiefs in the region, which was the territory of the previously dominant Ebisu, are said to have been themselves Ebisu, and as their autonomy increased they became the real rulers of the region. Furthermore, they were not only popular and powerful among those they ruled; they were cultured as well. The cultural sophistication of the Abe is suggested by the renga exchange which, as narrated in an episode below, is said to have taken place in the heat of a battle between Yoshiie and Abe Sadatō, the leader of the people the Minamoto were fighting. It is said that Munetō, Sadatō's brother who surrendered at the end of the Former Nine-Year War, shamed the Kyoto aristocrats who had assumed his boorish ignorance and tried to make a laughingstock of him. When they pointed at plum blossoms, a routine topic of poetry, and asked if he knew what they were, Munetō promptly responded with a poem:

Waga kuni no mume no hana to wa mitaredomo
Ōmiya-bito wa nan to iuran

In my province I'd see them as plum blossoms;
what, I wonder, do Kyoto nobles call them?

Naturally, fighting the people led by such men, in alien territory with a harsh climate, was grueling for Yoriyoshi and his soldiers. Mutsu was Abe turf; logistics was a constant problem for Yoriyoshi, and many soldiers deserted. Changes of heart among local clan leaders were not infrequent and often crucial. Kiyohara no Tsunekiyo, who was at first on Yoriyoshi's side, switched to the Abe forces and took with him 800 of his private soldiers. It was because of this turncoat act that Yoriyoshi, as told in the following narrative, put Tsunekiyo to slow death when he was captured alive. In the end Yoriyoshi won because Kiyohara no Noritake, a powerful leader of Ebisu in Dewa joined him with 10,000 soldiers. On his own Yoriyoshi had only 3,000 soldiers under his direct command.

---

2. A large, vaguely defined group of people also identified as *emishi*, "barbarians." The view that these people were the same as the ethnic group known today as the Ainu was the dominant one during the Meiji and Taishō eras (1868–1926), but today it is questioned. But no one has turned up definitive evidence to refute the view.

It was in one of the many tough earlier battles that Yoshiie's fame as a great archer was established. *Mutsu Waki,* an account of the Former Nine-Year War, tells the story succinctly.

In the eleventh month of the same year [1057] the commander in chief [Yoriyoshi] led an army of 1,800 soldiers, resolved to destroy Sadatō and his men. Sadatō, leading an army of 4,000 crack troops, turned Kogane no Tameyuki's stockade at Kawasaki into his front-line outpost and put up a defense in Kimoni. The winds and the snow were extremely fierce, and the roads and paths difficult to follow. The government forces ran out of food and both men and horses were exhausted. The rebels galloped into their midst on fresh horses and shot at them as they tottered about on their weakened legs. Not only were the two sides different in spirit, but because one had few soldiers and the other many, they also differed in strength. The government forces were beaten in a great many engagements, with several hundred men killed.

However, Yoshiie, the first son of the commander in chief, far surpassed his fellow commanders in fury and bravery, and was like a god as he shot from his horse. Galloping again and again into the layers of encircling soldiers with glinting swords, he broke out to their left or to their right and, with his longbow and arrows, shot enemy commanders. None of his arrows left his bow in vain, and every target that was hit toppled over dead. He dashed about like lightning and flew like wind, his divine military prowess known to all. The Ebisu people ran about, none with the courage to challenge him. . . .

[Still,] the soldiers guarding the commander in chief were either scattered, killed or wounded, and in the end only six of his officers on horseback were left. These were Yoshiie, Junior Secretary of Palace Repairs Fujiwara no Kagemichi, Ōyake no Mitsutō, Kiyohara no Sadahiro, Fujiwara no Norisue and Noriakira. The 200 horse-riding rebels half-circled and attacked them from the solid left and right wings, shooting arrows like rain. The commander in chief's horse was hit by a stray arrow and dropped dead. Kagemichi obtained a horse and gave it to him. Yoshiie's horse was also shot and killed. Noriakira robbed a rebel of his horse and gave it to Yoshiie. While all this was going on, it was almost impossible to break away. But Yoshiie kept shooting down enemy commanders. Also, Mitsutō and the other men fought with abandon. Finally, the rebels, deciding that these men were gods, retreated, so Yoriyoshi's men were also able to retreat.

Yoshiie was eighteen years old at the time.

Mutsu Waki goes on to tell how during this war Yoshiie's prowess as a bowman impressed so many men that Kiyohara no Noritake, the Ebisu leader who joined the government army, once asked to see the force of his shooting. Yoshiie gladly concurred. Noritake hung three sets of armor from a tree, and Yoshiie shot at them. The arrow easily pierced all three. Amazed, Noritake declared that Yoshiie must indeed be the reincarnation of Hachiman, the deity of the bow and arrow.[3]

In 1062, the last year of the Former Nine-Year War, there were a series of battles. On the fifth of the ninth month, 1062, Sadatō assaulted Yoriyoshi's camp with an army of 8,000 men. Yoriyoshi had 6,500 under his command, but after a ferocious battle lasting several hours forced Sadatō to retreat, then gave chase. That night, while his main troops rested in the camp, Yoriyoshi ordered Noritake to continue the chase. In the dark of the night Noritake led fifty commandos into the enemy camp. Thrown into confusion, Sadatō's forces retreated farther, leaving a trail of bloody casualties, and by the time they reached the castle by the Koromo River they had abandoned two more military outposts.

During the afternoon of the sixth, Yoriyoshi's men attacked the castle in three groups. Noritake, leading one group, had about thirty particularly agile men climb a giant tree whose branches extended almost to the other shore where the castle stood. Using vines and ropes, these men successfully crawled along over large branches, jumped down to the other side, and stole into the enemy quarters and set fires. Thrown into confusion, Sadatō and his men fled out of the castle. It was at that time that the famous exchange of renga between Sadatō and Yoshiie is said to have taken place.

In an episode from *Kokon Chomon Jū* (sec. 336), whose emphasis on details differs from the account given in *Mutsu Waki*, the governorship of Iyo mentioned was awarded Yoriyoshi for his military achievements in this war.

---

3. For Yoshiie's middle name, Hachiman Tarō, see p. 74.

Minamoto no Yoriyoshi, Governor of Iyo, spent twelve springs and autumns in Mutsu warring against Sadatō and Munetō.

On one occasion he left the Defense Headquarters to move his men to Akita Castle. It snowed abundantly and all the men in his army turned cloth-white. Sadatō's castle by the Koromo River rose on a high bank. Yoriyoshi's soldiers built rafts and attacked and fought with their shields raised above their helmets. Finally, Sadatō and his men gave up resistance and escaped from the rear of the castle. Yoriyoshi's first son, Hachiman Tarō, gave hot pursuit along the Koromo River and called out, "Sir, you show your back to your enemy! Aren't you ashamed? Turn around a minute, I have something to tell you."

When Sadatō turned around, Yoshiie said:

Koromo no tate wa hokorobinikeri

Koromo Castle has been destroyed
[The warps of your robe have come undone][4]

Sadatō relaxed his reins somewhat and, turning his helmeted head, followed that with:

toshi o heshi ito no midare no kurushisa ni

over the years its threads became tangled, and this pains me

Upon hearing this, Yoshiie put away the arrow he had readied to shoot, and returned to his camp. In the midst of such a savage battle, that was a gentlemanly thing to do.

One doesn't have to be a historian to note that this could not have been a "historical fact"; commanders of battling armies of several thousand men wouldn't have had the time or inclination to engage in "a battle of poems" like this. Then why was such a legend born? The cultural sophistication of the

---

4. *Koromo*, the place name, also means "robe" or "cloth"; and *tate* means both "castle" and "warp," as in "warp and woof."

衣のたては
ほころびに
けり　義家

年を経し
糸の乱れの
苦しさに
貞任

Yoshiie Exchanging Renga with Sadatō

leaders of the Abe clan was either already known or came to be known later. As Yoshiie's reputation as an outstanding warrior spread and even became legendary, it became necessary to make him more than a man of brawn and bravery—more of an all-around man.

Sadatō continued his retreat, finally reaching his residential stronghold, a stockade rising next to the Kuriya River. By then many of his able and trusted commanders had been killed. Yoriyoshi headed with his army for the stockade on the fourteenth. The following passage from *Mutsu Waki* does not have Yoshiie as its principal player but vividly renders the savagery of war and its aftermath.

[Yoriyoshi's army] arrived on the evening of the fifteenth and surrounded the two stockades—the one by the Kuriya River and the other in Ubato. They were separated from each other by seven or eight hundred yards. The camps, like a bird with its wings spread wide, were in firm defense throughout the night. There was a large marsh to the northwest of the Kuriya Stockade; the front end of the Ubato Stockade was some distance from the river. The riverbank rose about thirty feet from the water like a cliff, and was pathless. The Kuriya Stockade was built on the bank, itself an enforcement. A lookout tower was set up above the stockade, manned by alert soldiers. Between the river and the stockade was a trench, its bottom covered with swords erected upside down; the ground had iron blades planted all over it. The soldiers of the stockade shot at distant enemies with crossbows and threw stones at those nearer. As for those who managed to reach the stockade, they poured boiling water on them or swung sharp swords at them and killed them.

When the government forces arrived, the soldiers on the lookout tower challenged them, calling out, "Come and fight us!" Then fifty to sixty maids climbed the tower and sang songs. The commander in chief was outraged by this and in the early morning of the sixteenth began to attack and fight. All day and all night the crossbows he had gathered together were used in confusing numbers, and the arrows and stones flew like rain. But the defense inside the stockades was solid and could not be overcome. Several hundred men in the government forces were killed.

In the early afternoon of the seventeenth the commander in chief ordered his commanders and their men: "Go to the villages and destroy the houses. Bring the debris and fill the castle trenches. Cut dry reeds and pile them on the riverbank."

So the houses were destroyed and their debris was brought; dry reeds were cut and piled up in no time like mountains. The commander in chief dismounted, turned toward the far-off Imperial Castle and prayed: "Once, when the virtues of the Han Dynasty had not yet deteriorated, a sudden downpour answered the wish of the commander of the Western Defense Headquarters. Now heaven's will is apparent again. May a great wind help this old subject remain loyal. I here supplicate and pray: May the Three Shrines of Hachiman send forth winds and blow on the fire to burn down these stockades!"

Then he himself picked up a torch and, calling it a divine fire, tossed it. At that moment a dove flew over the camp. The commander in chief prayed again. Suddenly a violent wind rose, and the smoke and flames leapt about.[5]

The arrows the government forces had shot before this were stuck in the walls of the stockade and on the roof of the lookout tower like the straws on a straw raincoat. The flying flames followed the wind and reached the feathers of these arrows. The stockade and the tower were instantly engulfed in fire. The thousands of men and women within the castle were stricken with grief and cried in unison. Some rebels, crushed and confused, threw themselves into the blue waters or beheaded themselves with glinting white blades.

The government forces crossed the waters to attack and fight. Thereupon, some several hundred desperate rebels, armored and brandishing swords, broke out of the stockade into the encircling army. They were determined to die, with no wish to live. Many of the government troops were wounded or killed. When he saw this, Takenori ordered his men to open the way for the rebels and let them out. His men opened the way. The rebels suddenly changed their mind, decided to escape, and began to run without fighting. Thereupon the government soldiers struck at them at will and killed all of them.

Tsunekiyo was captured alive. The commander in chief summoned him and accused him harshly: "Your ancestors were all servants of my family. But in recent years you have trampled upon the emperor's wishes and despised your former masters. This is all

---

5. For Minamoto warriors the dove was an embodiment of the Hachiman deity and one flying above their encampment was regarded as an exceptionally good omen.

traitorous and goes against the Way. Do you think you can or cannot use a white sign today?"[6]

Tsunekiyo hung his head, unable to say anything. The commander in chief hated him so much that he had his head cut off slowly with a blunt sword. This was because he wanted to prolong his pain and suffering.

With sword drawn, Sadatō slashed some government soldiers. Government soldiers stabbed him with halberds. Six of them put him on a large shield and brought him to the commander in chief. He was more than six feet tall, the circumference of his waist seven feet and four inches. He had an extraordinary face, his skin was white, and he was fat. The commander in chief accused him of various crimes. Sadatō once tried to face him down before dying. His brother Shigetō was cut to death. But Munetō threw himself into deep mud and managed to get away. Sadatō's son, aged thirteen and called Boy Chiyo, had a beautiful face. Donning his armor, he came out of the stockade and fought well. In fury and bravery he recalled his grandfather. The commander in chief pitied him and wanted to forgive him. But Noritake stepped forward and said, "General, you shouldn't forget that you may bring harm unto yourself later by entertaining a bit of justice now." The commander in chief nodded in assent and in the end had Chiyo cut to death.

Inside the castle fifty or sixty beautiful women, all dressed splendidly and every one wearing a necklace made of gold and jade, wailed in grief in the smoke. They were brought out and given to the soldiers. However, Noritō's wife alone behaved differently; when the stockade was destroyed, holding her three-year-old son, she had said to her husband, "You are about to be killed. I won't be able to live alone. I hope to die before you do." Indeed, holding her infant, she threw herself into a deep abyss and died. We must say she was a woman of admirable courage.

The following two episodes took place after the war. The first one, from *Kokon Chomon Jū* (sec. 338), describes Yoshiie's great fame as a warrior and his exemplary attitude toward Munetō, one of Abe Sadatō's brothers who had survived.

---

6. The meaning of "white sign" is not clear.

In the Twelve-Year War Sadatō was killed. Munetō was treated with gentlemanly courtesy, however, because he had surrendered. He attended Yoriyoshi's first son, Yoshiie, mornings and evenings.

One day Yoshiie went to a certain place with Munetō as his companion. Both the master and his attendant friend were dressed in hunting clothes and carried quivers. While passing through a large field, they saw a fox run. Yoshiie drew a fork-tipped arrow and chased the fox. He thought it would be cruel to kill him, so he shot the arrow in a way it would glance between the fox's ears. Indeed, the arrow struck the ground right in front of the fox. His way blocked, the fox dropped to the ground, seemingly dead.

Munetō dismounted and lifted the fox. "The arrow didn't even touch him," he said, "but he died."

Yoshiie looked at the fox and said, "He was scared and fainted. I didn't want to kill him and deliberately missed him. He'll revive soon. Release him when he does."

When Munetō picked up the arrow and came to him, Yoshiie let him put it in his quiver.

Yoshiie's soldier-servants who saw this happen were critical of Yoshiie, saying, "Heavens, that was dangerous. Munetō surely surrendered, but he's got to have some resentment left in him. How could our master have exposed his flank and let Munetō put back the arrow? That was too dangerous. Suppose Munetō was desperate and wanted to harm him?"

But Yoshiie was a man who was almost like a god. Munetō, on his part, never dreamed of doing anything wrong. That's why, we think, the two men trusted each other so.

Again, one night, Yoshiie went to see a woman with Munetō as his sole companion. The woman's house was old, with the mud fence crumbling, the gate leaning to one side. Yoshiie went in through the door at the end of the oxcart shed and met the woman there. Munetō waited outside, at the middle gate partitioning one corridor.

The fifth-month sky was as dark as if ink had been splashed all over it. It began to rain, and thunder started to roll; it was damnably scary. Munetō knew something would happen that night. Sure enough, a large number of robbers walked in rambunctiously. Just this side of the front gate they made a fire, and, from the reflections,

Munetō could tell there were about thirty of them. He was wondering what to do, when a dog ran from under the floor beneath him, barking. So he took out a hikime arrow and shot it. The dog scampered about, yapping and yelping. Moments later, in like fashion, Munetō quickly shot the dog several times more.

"Who's there?" Yoshiie called out.

"Munetō, sir!"

"You are shooting at the dog too fast. Are you trying to impress someone?"

When they heard these words, the robbers said to themselves, "That's Lord Hachiman, dammit!" and ran away, we hear, in utter confusion.

Munetō was later moved to Iyo, a province on the Island of Shikoku—the governorship of which was given to Yoriyoshi as a reward for his work in the Former Nine-Year War—and afterward to Dazaifu, in Kyūshū, the southernmost military and diplomatic headquarters in those days. The court took these actions probably because it felt that Munetō, as a "barbarous" Ebisu, should not be allowed to live near the Capital.

The following episode is from *Kokon Chomon Jū* (sec. 337). As noted earlier, Yoshiie, as Governor of Mutsu, was the commander in chief.

After the Twelve-Year War, when Yoshiie went to visit the Lord of Uji[7] and told him of various battles, Lord Masafusa,[8] who was there and listened carefully, muttered to himself, "He certainly is a talented and wise warrior. But he doesn't know what the art of war is all about."

---

7. Fujiwara no Michiyori (992–1074), a regent.

8. Ōe no Masafusa (1041–1111), a poet and Chinese scholar. Among the posts Masafusa held was that of acting head (or general) of Dazaifu. This is why at one point he is referred to as General Ōe, although the generalship at Dazaifu was more nominal than real.

One of Yoshiie's soliders happened to overhear this and was indignant that Masafusa should have made such an impertinent observation. So, when General Ōe came out, followed not long afterward by Yoshiie, the soldier told Yoshiie that the general had said such and such about him.

Yoshiie said, "I think he's quite right." He then walked up to the place where Masafusa was preparing to get on his oxcart, and greeted him. Soon he became one of his disciples and diligently pursued his studies, attending Masafusa's sessions every time.

Later, during the War of Eihō,[9] while attacking Kanazawa Castle,[10] he saw a file of geese fly away, then dip toward some harvested paddies. But they were suddenly startled in midflight and flew back, their formation disturbed. Suspicious, the commander in chief held his horse's bridle and said: "Some years ago, General Ōe taught me this: 'When soldiers lie in ambush, flying geese break their formation.'[11] There have to be some enemies lying in ambush."

He then ordered detachments to be sent behind the enemy's rear. His remaining army itself was divided, and the spot in question was encircled from three sides. Sure enough, about 300 men on horses were hiding. The battle that ensued between the two armies was confusing and prolonged. Yet, because the ambush had been discerned beforehand, the commander in chief kept the upper hand and in the end defeated the soldiers of Takehira and others.

"Without this one particular teaching of General Ōe," Yoshiie said, "I might have lost this battle."

Takehira was the first son of Kiyohara no Takenori, an Ebisu leader who, it may be recalled, in the earlier war joined the government forces commanded by Yoshiie's father, Yoriyoshi. In reward for his exploits, Takenori had been appointed commanding general of the Defense Headquarters set up to keep the Ebisu people under control. In other words, an Ebisu leader who did not work for the central government in Kyoto was put in a position directly responsible for controling the Ebisu people. This seemingly curious measure

---

9. The Latter Three-Year War. So referred to here because it started during the Eihō era (1081–1084).

10. Formerly Sadatō's residential stronghold, destroyed in the earlier war.

11. Rephrasing of a sentence in *Sun Tzu*: "Birds rising in flight is a sign that the enemy is lying in ambush," in Griffith's translation.

may have been taken in part because, unlike the Abe, the Kiyohara were not Ebisu themselves but descendants of a government officer.

The Latter Three-Year War began as a squabble among the members of the Kiyohara family. Yoshiie was a bystander who was forced to take sides. As it turned out, this war proved as grueling as the previous one, and Yoshiie won it only by laying siege to Kanazawa Castle, completely cutting off their food supplies. Still, the court regarded Yoshiie's war as a private, not government, affair, and did not give him any reward after the war. When this happened, Yoshiie rewarded his men out of his own holdings. That was not something customarily done, and Yoshiie's generosity is said to have helped generate unprecedented loyalty to the Minamoto clan in the Kantō region.

When the Latter Three-Year War was over, Yoshiie was in his late forties. The last episode to be cited, from *Kokon Chomon Jū* (sec. 339), describes the warrior when he was much younger—perhaps not long after returning to Kyoto from the previous war.

When he was in his youthful prime, Yoshiie used to meet secretly with a certain monk's wife. The woman's house was near where Nijō Boulevard and Ikuma Street crossed. It had a viewing tower built above the mud fence and a moat dug in front of it, with thorny thickets planted at its end. The monk himself was known as exceptionally capable in the way of arms, and was careful in laying out such things.

Yoshiie would come late at night when he knew the monk was away. He would park his oxcart at the outer end of the moat, the woman would pull up the window on the viewing tower and lift the blind, and he would jump right in from the thills of the oxcart. The moat itself was quite wide, and to be able to leap up like that was something no ordinary man could hope to do.

Their meetings were repeated so many times that the monk finally learned about them and tormented his wife for information. When she told him exactly how it was, he said, "Well, then, next time pretend I'm not here, and let the fellow in." She had no way of getting out of this, and agreed to do what she was told.

The monk planned to cut the man down as he jumped in. So he stood a thick go board like a shield at the spot where the man would come in, the idea being to make him stumble. And he waited, sword drawn.

As expected, the oxcart was parked, and the woman did what she had done at other times. From the thills the man jumped in, like a flying bird, but as he did so he drew his short sword held close to his side, cut in midflight several inches off the top of the go board, and landed safely.

Dumbfounded by the thought that this was no human being, the monk couldn't think of any move to make. Then, seized with terror, he fell off of the tower in confusion and ran away.

Later, when he made further inquiries, he learned that the man was no less than Hachiman Tarō Yoshiie. His fear simply increased.

Some readers may be puzzled to hear about a monk who had a wife and was "exceptionally capable in the way of arms." The secularization—or degradation and corruption, if you will—of Buddhist monks began early in Japan. The direct cause is traced to the relaxation of government rules on certification and ordination of monks in the ninth century that became necessary as a great many temples were built and thousands of monks had to be created and maintained. Because a Buddhist monk was exempted from certain taxes and labor, everyone wanted to become one. In 914 the Confucian scholar Miyoshi no Kiyotsura (847–918) reported to the emperor some of the social ills of the time and said:

> So many people these days shave their heads by themselves and put on priestly robes that two thirds of the people under heaven have tonsured heads. The monks all keep wives and children in their homes and eat meat. In appearance they may look like Buddhist monks; in reality they are the same as butchers.

As celibacy and the rule against the eating of sentient beings were violated, carrying weapons and fighting became prevalent among monks. In 970 Ryōgen (912–985), the chief abbot of the Enryaku Temple, on Mt. Hiei, issued strictures on the conduct within the mountain compounds and said that the monks who carried swords, bows, and arrows and "indulged in harming others were no different from butchers."

To return to Minamoto no Yoshiie, what is historically notable about him is that despite the high regard in which the aristocracy held him as a warrior, he remained, in the eye of the ruling class, a *samurai* in the original sense of the word: an armed servant with few privileges of a court noble. This was vividly illustrated in 1081 when Yoshiie was still in Kyoto, before heading for Mutsu as governor and becoming embroiled in what would be called the Latter Three-Year War.

That year the armed monks of Enryaku and Onjō Temples clashed, so the court dispatched Yoshiie and the chief of the Imperial Police to the Onjō Temple to arrest the leaders of the armed monks (called *akusō*, "evil or tough monks"). In the following month, when the emperor went to visit the Hachiman Shrine at Iwashimizu, Yoshiie and his brother Yoshitsuna were ordered to accompany his majesty as guards in case of the monks' reprisal. But because they did not have proper court titles that would have allowed them to guard the emperor, they were appointed "forerunners" *(sengu* or *maegake)* of the regent, who accompanied his majesty, and their armed soldiers were made to follow the procession.

When the procession returned to Kyoto that night, Yoshiie was asked to stay next to the imperial carriage as a guard, in an informal hunting outfit and carrying a bow and arrow. A mere warrior allowed to be so close to the emperor, a noble who observed this noted in his diary, was an "unheard of" arrangement.

In the twelfth month of the same year, the emperor went to visit the Kasuga Shrine, in Nara. At that time, too, Yoshiie was ordered to guard the procession. That he did, fully armed, but again as the regent's guard, not the emperor's, and he and his men, numbering more than a hundred, were made to stay far behind the imperial procession.

The relationship between the samurai and the imperial court would greatly change a century later.

MINAMOTO NO YOSHITSUNE:
A HERO HOUNDED

Twenty-first day, tenth month [1180]. Today a young man, alone, stood outside Lord Kamakura's quarters, asking for an audience with him. [Toi] Sanehira, [Tsuchiya] Munetō, and [Okazaki] Yoshizane became suspicious about this and were unwilling to relay the request. Time passed by until the commander himself heard about it and said, "Considering his age, he may be Kurō, from Ōshū. Let me see him right away." And so Sanehira summoned the man. Sure enough, he was Yoshitsune. At once he was allowed to proceed to where his lordship was, and the two of them reminisced about the events of long ago and shed tears over their pasts.[1]

This dramatic appearance in history of Minamoto no Kurō Yoshitsune (1159–89) is recorded in the *Azuma Kagami* (History of the East), an official account of events related to the first half of the Kamakura Bakufu, the military government established by his older brother Yoritomo (1149–99), here called Lord Kamakura and the "commander" (*bue* or *buei*). The *Azuma Kagami* is judged to be reliable on the whole, though it does show obvious bias toward Yoritomo and those who worked to maintain the power structure he created. The military title given Yoritomo here is a case in point. Even though at age twelve he had been granted the rank of Acting Commander (*gon no suke*) of the Outer Palace Guards, Right Division, of which *bue* or *buei* is the Chinese name

---

1. In the sections from the *Azuma Kagami* translated here, most of the bracketed descriptions are in the original text, although the bracketed personal names are provided by the annotator I used. A few are my additions.

(pronounced the Japanese way), by the time this encounter with his brother took place, he had long since lost that title; worse, he was now, in the view of the Kyoto court, a rebel leader. He would be restored to the rank of commander only two years later. For that matter, he would not publicly be recognized as the Master of Kamakura and called Lord Kamakura until two months afterward.

The drama of the encounter derives from what had happened before the meeting and what would unfold in the years ahead.

Minamoto no Yoshitomo (1123–60), the two brothers' father and Yoshiie's great-grandson, was heavily involved in the armed strife that twice ensued from the power struggles within the imperial household: the Hōgen Disturbance, in 1156, and the Heiji Disturbance, in 1159. In the first Yoshitomo was on the winning side but was forced to behead a dozen of his relatives, among them his own father and nine of his own brothers. In the second he was on the losing side and while trying to escape was assassinated – in the bathroom of the house of a man he thought he could trust. As a result, Taira no Kiyomori (1118–81), the leader of the other military clan who was on Yoshitomo's side in the first clash but his opponent in the second, gained further ascendancy and soon took the upper hand in controlling the aristocracy, thereby starting the historic role reversal between aristocratic master and warrior-servant.

Following Yoshitomo's vanquishment, his eight sons were hunted down for execution as a matter of course. Indeed, his first son, Yoshihira, was captured and beheaded. By singular luck, though, most of the seven others fared better. Yoritomo was captured but allowed to go into exile because Kiyomori's stepmother, when she saw the captured boy, said he looked exactly like her late son and pleaded with Kiyomori for clemency. Yoshitsune, still a suckling baby, was also allowed to live because his mother, different from Yoritomo's and an extraordinary beauty, agreed to become Kiyomori's mistress in exchange for the lives of her three sons. Needless to say, the surviving sons of the vanquished leader of a military clan were constant security risks, and Yoritomo, Yoshitsune, and others had to lie low. Still, it appears that Yoritomo, in his place of exile, Izu, and Yoshitsune, first at a temple on Mt. Kurama, north of Kyoto, then in the Ōshū (north of Shimotsuke, on the Pacific side), had considerable freedom of movement.

During the ensuing decades Kiyomori's tyranny mounted to the point where it was said, "Anyone who isn't a member of our [Taira] clan has to be a nonhuman." Discontent also mounted – not only among the usurped aristocrats and members of non-Taira clans, but also among the general populace. Finally, in the fourth month, 1180, Prince Mochihito, unable to contain his frustration and anger, sent Yoritomo an imperial order (*ryōji*), which began:

To the members of the Minamoto clan in the provinces of the three regions of the Tōkai, Tōsan, and Hokuriku, as well as their soldiers:

It is ordered that Lay Priest Kiyomori[2] and the rebellious cohorts who follow him be pursued and destroyed at the earliest time possible.

At first Yoritomo was cautious. But then the news reached him that in the following month Prince Mochihito's action had been exposed and he had been killed in battle, along with Minamoto no Yorimasa, who had encouraged him to revolt.[3] Kiyomori was bound soon to dispatch a punitive army against Yoritomo or otherwise try to destroy him. Time was running out. So in the eighth month he raised an army against the Taira. But his first battle with local clans, on Mt. Ishibashi, ended in disaster, and Yoritomo was almost captured and killed.

Luck was with him again, however: He was able to regroup quickly, the sending of Kiyomori's army from Kyoto was delayed because of a squabble between its commander in chief and his chief of staff, and the army that finally faced Yoritomo's troops across the Fuji River, on the twentieth of the tenth month, was puny and bedraggled. When a detachment of Yoritomo's army feigned an attack to the rear of the Taira forces, a vast number of waterfowl suddenly took to wing from a large marsh nearby, terribly confounding the Taira men. Deciding that all the local clans in the Eastern provinces were on Yoritomo's side, the Taira commanders vied with one another, it is said, in fleeing back to Kyoto. Yoritomo wanted to pursue them, but some of the powerful clan leaders who were with him strongly counseled against it, advising instead further consolidation of his power in the Kantō region before engaging in another battle – the counsel that Yoritomo accepted. It was on the following day that Yoshitsune turned up to meet him.

There is no evidence that the two had met during the twenty years after their father's defeat and death, and there is little known about Yoshitsune during the same period except what has been noted above. He probably spent his early years at a temple near Kyoto because Kiyomori ordered him, along with Tokiwa's two other sons, to become a monk, but in his adolescence escaped to the north to seek the protection of Fujiwara no Hidehira (d. 1187), the overlord of the vast region of Ōshū.[4] There is not much recorded about him following his reunion with Yoritomo, either, except that during a period

---

2. Kiyomori had taken Buddhist vows in 1167.

3. For episodes about Yorimasa, see the Introduction, pp. xxvii–xxviii and the section on Kō no Moronao, pp. 189–190.

4. With Yoshiie's help and encouragement, Fujiwara no Kiyohira (1056–1128) established himself as successor of the Abe clan and created a formidable power base and a flourishing culture. The third-generation family head Hidehira further strengthened the family's hold on the region, turning it into a "kingdom" unto itself.

of a little over a year, from the first month of 1184 to the third month of 1185, he would prove himself to be one of the greatest military commanders in Japanese history and then would be hounded by his brother, eventually to death.

The relationship that was to develop between the two brothers is adumbrated in the passage where Yoshitsune appears for the second time in the *Azuma Kagami*. On the twentieth of the seventh month, 1181, when the construction of the treasure hall of the new Tsurugaoka Hachiman Shrine was finished, Yoritomo came to attend the completion ceremony and presented the carpenters with horses. It seems that a horse presented as a gift was led on decorative reins by two or more men walking on both sides.

Accordingly his lordship told Master Kurō to lead out the horses, to which Kurō replied, "At the moment there's no one to do the leading with me." His lordship repeated his order and said, "When we have right here with us Hatakeyama Jirō, Sanuki Shirō, and others, how dare you say there's no one to do it with you? Am I to understand you think this function is too lowly for you and that's why by saying such a thing you're indicating you don't want to do it?"

Master Kurō was struck with great fear, and at once left his seat and led two horses.

On such ceremonial occasions, "leading a horse" was an act expressing obeisance to one's master, and this incident is interpreted as Yoritomo's attempt to impress upon Yoshitsune that he was merely one of his subordinates.

Through this year the *Azuma Kagami* has only one other entry on Yoshitsune: On the fifth of the eleventh month, he, along with the leaders of several clans, wanted to take their forces to Tōtōmi Province to defend a friendly leader, but gave up on the plan when another clan leader counseled against the move. For the year of 1182 no entry is found on Yoshitsune, and for 1183 the document's entries are missing. Following these two blank years things pick up for Yoshitsune early in 1184.

Meanwhile, even though Yoritomo himself was more interested in consolidating his power than sending out forces to fight the Taira, there was a good deal of military action. In particular, Minamoto no Yoshinaka (1154–84),

Yoritomo and Yoshitsune's cousin,[5] who had also raised an army against the Taira in response to Prince Mochihito's command, made his own attempt to reach Kyoto and won a string of battles.

Yoshinaka's most important battle took place not far from the capital, on the eleventh of the fifth month, 1183, at Kurikara Pass, on the border of Kaga and Etchū; in it he destroyed the bulk of the Taira clan's central forces. Two months later, on the twenty-second of the seventh month, he reached Mt. Hiei, which overlooks Kyoto from the northeast. With other Minamoto armies pressing in, the Taira men decamped from the capital and fled westward three days later, taking with them the young emperor, Antoku (1178–85). On the twenty-eighth Yoshinaka entered and occupied Kyoto. Retired Emperor Goshirakawa (1127–92) then issued him a formal command to destroy the Taira clan.

The political alliance between Yoshinaka and Goshirakawa was short-lived.[6] By the ninth month Goshirakawa had in effect asked Yoritomo to destroy Yoshinaka, a request with which Yoritomo was happy to comply. After some political maneuvering of his own with Goshirakawa he dispatched to Kyoto two of his brothers, Noriyori and Yoshitsune, as generals. In the eleventh month Yoshinaka, incensed by this and other developments, burned down Goshirakawa's palace. On the third of the first month, 1184, Yoshinaka forced Goshirakawa to appoint him shogun.

Let us now return to the *Azuma Kagami*.

Twentieth day, first month. Gama no Kanja Noriyori and Kurō Yoshitsune, as the commander's emissaries, arrived in Kyoto, leading several tens of thousands of troops. Their purpose was to punish Yoshinaka. Today Noriyori entered Kyoto from the Seta [route]; Yoshi-

---

5. The first military exploit of Yoshihira, the oldest brother of Yoritomo and Yoshitsune, was the killing, in 1155, of his own uncle and Yoshinaka's father, Yoshikata. Subsequently Yoshihira hunted for Yoshinaka, but before he managed to find him, he was captured and killed following the Heiji Disturbance.

6. Some important factors quickly worked against Yoshinaka. His army, initially numbering several tens of thousands, was a hodge-podge assemblage of troops led by many disparate local clans and was never wholly under his control. Kyoto that year was ravaged by a famine, and a sudden intrusion of a host of rowdy, looting soldiers alienated the Kyoto townsfolk and aristocrats from Yoshinaka in short order. As Yoshinaka's estimation plummeted, his army dispersed. In his first attempt after occupying the Capital to carry out the mandate to destroy the Taira, he was miserably defeated. Yoshinaka, from rural, mountainous Kiso, was politically unsophisticated and was no match for Goshirakawa, who may be counted among the greatest political schemers in Japanese history.

tsune entered from the Uji route. Kiso [Yoshinaka] tried to fight them back on both routes with soldiers under the command of Shida Senjō Yoshihiro and Imai Shirō Kanehira, but they were all defeated. Noriyori and Yoshitsune, accompanied by Kawagoshi Tarō Shigeyori, [Kawagoshi] Kotarō Shigefusa, Sasaki Shirō Takatsuna, Hatakeyama Jirō Shigetada, Shibuya Shōji Shigekuni, and Kajiwara Genta Kagesue, hurried to Rokujō Palace to protect the emperor [Goshirakawa].[7] During this time, brave warriors under the command of Ichijō Jirō Tadayori ran in various directions and finally, near Awazu, Ōmi Province, had Ishida Jirō, a resident of Sagami Province, kill Yoshinaka.

Twenty-seventh day. Around two in the afternoon, express messengers from Governor of Tōtōmi Yoshisada, Noriyori, Yoshitsune, and Ichijō Jirō Tadayori arrived in Kamakura. They said that back on the twentieth a battle was completed in which his lordship's army killed Yoshinaka and his cohorts. Three of the messengers were summoned by his lordship and went to Ishitsubo, on the north side. While he was probing for much greater details, an express messenger from [Kajiwara] Kagetoki also arrived. He brought a list of the names of those vanquished and those taken prisoner. Various messengers came but it was not possible to make a record of their reports. His lordship is said to have observed movingly, more than once, that Kagetoki's considerateness was divine.

The entry for the twenty-seventh may need some explanations.

Kajiwara Heizō Kagetoki (d. 1200), who was on the side of Yoritomo's enemies during the battle of Mt. Ishibashi but deliberately overlooked him in his hiding place, joined him soon afterward, went on to become his "number-one aide" (*ichi no rōdō*), and wielded enormous power. During the war Kagetoki played a triple military role: field commander, superintendent of logistics and warriors, and inspector-general of officers. In the military command structure of the day his rank of *saburai daishō* (general of soldiers) was nominally far below that of someone like Yoshitsune, who bore the title of *sō-daishō*

---

7. In the absence, though not death, of Emperor Antoku, the new emperor, Gotoba (1178–1239), had been installed on the twenty-second of the eighth month of the previous year. The disagreement on the selection of a new emperor is said to have been the first incident that palpably estranged Yoshinaka and Goshirakawa: Yoshinaka pushed the late Prince Mochihito's son, and Goshirakawa, Antoku's younger brother. Goshirakawa won and remained the de facto imperial ruler.

(general of the army), but Kagetoki regarded himself as Yoritomo's *o-daikan* (special deputy) and would not easily defer to his direct superior in the field, Yoshitsune.

The passage above shows Kagetoki's awareness of his roles and Yoritomo's appreciation of it. Whereas other commanders merely reported on the victory and failed to provide many other details, Kagetoki sent a list of enemy casualties — and, though not mentioned, probably a report on his fellow commanders as well.

On the previous day Yoritomo had received from Goshirakawa an imperial command to destroy the Taira clan.

Twenty-ninth day, first month. The two generals of Kantō [Noriyori and Yoshitsune] left for the Western region with soldiers to subjugate the Taira clan. It is reported that all of them left Kyoto today.

First day, second month. Master Noriyori received his lordship's expression of ire. This is because during last winter,[8] while he was heading toward Kyoto to subjugate Kiso [Yoshinaka], at the ferry of Sunomata, Owari Province, he competed with his lordship's direct vassals (*gokenin*) to reach the other shore and as a result fell into a brawl with them. Hearing about this incident today, his lordship said, "It is extremely disquieting that anyone should mindlessly engage in personal squabbles before conquering the imperial enemy."[9]

Seventh day. It snowed. Around four in the morning, Master Kurō arrived at the hill in the rear of Ichinotani [called Bulbul's Passage] with the seventy-odd particularly brave warriors he had selected and set aside from the rest.

Separately, Kumagae no Jirō Naozane and Hirayama no Mushadokoro Sueshige, both residents of Musashi Province, secretly turned

---

8. By the lunar calendar, "winter" consisted of the tenth, eleventh, and twelfth months.

9. Like the episode concerning the presentation of horses to the carpenters, this story shows Yoritomo's disinclination to accord special treatment to his brothers. Indeed, for Yoritomo his brothers were often less important than the *gokenin* — those warriors with independent means who pledged personal allegiance to him. Yoritomo's ire was serious enough to merit another entry in the *Azuma Kagami;* on the sixth of the third month, the document reports, Yoritomo decided to "absolve Noriyori from his ire. It was because Noriyori had for days expressed his worries about the matter."

around, got out on the road in front of Ichinotani, and vied with each other in assaulting the fortress from the sea side, loudly calling out that they were spearheading the Minamoto forces. In response, Lieutenant of the Outer Palace Guards, Left Division, Hida no Saburō Kagetsuna, Etchū no Jirō Moritsugu, of the Middle Palace Guards, Lieutenant of the Middle Palace Guards Kazusa no Gorō Tadamitsu, and Akushitsu Kagekiyo, of the Middle Palace Guards, leading twenty to thirty horsemen, opened the wooden gate and fought them. Kumagae no Kojirō Naoie was wounded,[10] and Sueshige's soldier met a premature death.

Following this, Noriyori, along with men from Ashikaga, Chichibu, Miura, and Kamakura, hurriedly arrived. The warriors of the Minamoto and Taira were thrown into chaos, and their white banners and red banners mixing, they battled, making the mountains resound and the ground shake. Their momentum was such that even Fan K'uai, and Chang Liang wouldn't have been able to easily defeat them.

Furthermore, the castle and the boulders soared so high that horses found them impassable, and the valley was so deep that no human being had visited it for a long time. Master Kurō, accompanied by the warriors under the command of Miura no Jūrō Yoshitsura, attacked from Bulbul's Passage [this mountain is so rugged that nothing passes over it except wild boars, deer, rabbits, and foxes]; the Taira forces lost their composure and retreated in defeat, some running out of Fort Ichinotani whipping their horses, some in boats heading for the island of Shikoku plying poles.

In the process the Middle captain of the Inner Palace Guards, Third Rank [Taira no Shigehira], was captured on Akashi Bay by Kagetoki and Iekuni. The Governor of Echizen, Third Rank [Michimori], was killed near the Minato River by Gensan Toshitsuna. Including him, a total of seven—Satsuma Governor Tadanori[11], Wakasa Governor Tsunetoshi, Musashi Governor Tomoaki, Atsumori, of Fifth Rank, Narimori, former Etchū Governor Moritoshi—were seized and killed by the forces of Noriyori and Yoshitsune. Former Tajima Governor Tsunemasa, Noto Governor Noritsune, and Bitchū Governor Moromori were seized by Tōtōmi Governor Yoshisada.

---

10. Later that same day Naozane, Naoie's father, would find himself in a position to kill Taira no Atsumori, who was his son's age. The incident aggrieved him so deeply that he later would take Buddhist vows.

11. For Tadanori, see the Introduction, pp. xxix–xxx.

Yoshitune's assault on Ichinotani where the Taira forces had regrouped and built a castle-fortress is famous for its daring. Situated on the border of Settsu and Harima provinces (just west of present-day Kobe), and facing the Inland Sea in front and steeply rising hills in back, Ichinotani was ideal for defense. Noriyori, commanding 50,000 troops, attacked the Taira from the east along the coastal road; Yoshitsune, commanding 10,000, did so from the north, coming through a mountainous region.

Yoshitsune moved fast. He traversed in a single day a distance that normally would take two days: from Kyoto to the eastern edge of Mt. Mikasa where the three provinces of Tamba, Settsu, and Harima meet. On the fifth, after nightfall, he received a report that a Taira force of 3,000 troops was encamped about eight miles southwest. He quickly decided to attack, rather than rest for the night, and, torching everything in sight along the way, trounced the Taira force in no time. For the rest, we will turn to the *Heike Monogatari* (The Tale of the Heike).

At daybreak of the sixth, Kurō Onzōshi[12] divided his 10,000 horsemen into two groups and first sent forth Toi no Jirō Sanehira, with 7,000, toward the west side of Ichinotani. He himself wanted to ride down with 3,000 behind Ichinotani, from Bulbul's Passage, and took Tamba Route for a rear attack.

A number of soldiers said, "We hear this is a dangerous place. We don't mind getting killed fighting the enemy but don't want to get killed falling into a dangerous place. Dammit, isn't there a guide to these mountains?"

Hirayama no Mushadokoro, a resident of Musashi Province, stepped forward and said, "Sir, I, Sueshige, know how to guide you."

Kurō said, "You were brought up in the Eastern region and have seen these mountains in the Western region for the first time today, yet you say you can guide us. That doesn't strike me as terribly credible."

Hirayama said further, "I can't believe those are your words, sir. A poet knows about the blossoms of Yoshino and Hatsuse, a tough

---

12. *Onzōshi* means "honored son." When applied to the Minamoto, the term denoted a son in the direct line of family inheritance. In the rest of this account Yoshitsune will be simply called Kurō even when the term *onzōshi* is used.

warrior knows how to guide men into the rear of a castle the enemies have shut themselves in."[13]

That, too, sounded impertinent and rude.

Again, a young man who had just turned eighteen, by the name of Beppu no Kotarō, another resident of Musashi Province, stepped forward and said, "Sir, Monk Yoshishige, my late father, used to tell me, 'Whether because you were attacked by an enemy or while hunting in the mountains, if you're lost in mountain depths, toss the reins on an old horse and drive him ahead of you. You're bound to come out on a path.' "

Kurō said, "Well said! Come to think of it, there's a saying, 'Snow may cover the whole field, but an old horse knows how to find his way.' "[14]

So he put a gold-rimmed saddle and a bit polished white on an old whitish roan, tied the reins and tossed them over him, and, driving him ahead, went into the deep mountains he knew nothing about. Because it was the second month, the snow on the peaks had faded, mottled, looking like cherry blossoms in some places. In other places bush-warblers came up from the valleys to visit, wandering in the haze. As the men climbed up, white clouds soared, gleaming; as they climbed down, green mountains became rugged with steep cliffs. The snow on the pines had yet to fade, and the narrow mossy path barely existed. As the snow scattered in occasional gusts, they almost mistook it for plum flowers. As they whipped their horses along to the east and to the west, the sun sank beyond the mountain path, so everyone dismounted for encampment.

Musashibō Benkei[15] brought an old man to Kurō.

"Who's this?" Kurō asked.

"He's a hunter on these mountains."

"Well then, you've got to know this area well," he said to the man. "Tell us exactly what it's like."

"I'd be a darn fool if I didn't know this area, sir."

---

13. "A poet knows," etc., refers to the practice among the court poets of the day of routinely describing in their poems things that are required topics even though they may never have actually seen them. Yoshino and Hatsuse, both in present-day Nara, are famous for their cherry blossoms, an important poetic topic for the season of spring.

14. The original idea may come from a story about a Chinese general who left his country in spring on a military expedition. In winter, when he returned, he lost his way in the snow; thereupon, he released an old horse and, by following it, made it safely back to his fort.

15. A legendary monk-warrior who would remain steadfastly loyal to Yoshitsune to the very end.

"I'd like to ride down to the Taira castle-fortress in Ichinotani. What do you say about that?"

"That's absolutely impossible, sir," said the man. "Places like Ninety-Yard Precipice and Forty-Five-Yard Ledge are not passable, I think, for human beings. Much less so for the horses, I must say. Besides, within the castle they've dug pitfalls and have two-pronged spears implanted in them."

"Well, do deer go through them?"

"Yes, sir, deer do go through them," said the man. "When the world gets warm, the deer in Harima cross over to Tamba seeking to lie in deeper grasses; when the world gets cold, the deer in Tamba go over to Inamino, in Harima, seeking to graze where the snow is shallow."

"That sounds like a veritable riding-ground!" said Kurō. "If deer go through them, why can't horses? Take us there at once."

"I'm too old for that, sir," said the man.

"Don't you have a son?"

"Yes, sir, I do." The man then brought a young man by the name of Kumaō, who was eighteen years old, and gave him to Kurō. At once he was given a manhood rite, and because his father called himself Washio no Shōji Takehisa, he was to call himself Washio no Saburō Yoshihisa. Then Kurō had him ride ahead as guide. . . .

At daybreak of the seventh, Kurō, who had circled to the enemy's rear, rode up to Bulbul's Passage in back of Ichinotani and was about to ride down, when, surprised perhaps by his forces, two large stags and one doe scampered down to the Taira's castle-fortress in Ichinotani. Some warriors in the castle saw them and anxiously said among themselves, "Even the deer near a village are afraid of us and stay deep in the mountains. But these deer have rushed right into our midst. This is a sure sign that the Minamoto forces are riding down upon us from the top of the mountain!"

Takechino Mushadokoro Kiyonori, a resident of Iyo Province, stepped forward and said, "Who cares about that? These animals have come out from the enemy and there's no reason to let them by." He then shot the two stags dead and let the doe go by without shooting her. The former governor of Etchū[16] restrained him, saying, "What a thing to do, sir, shooting deer! Each one of those arrows could have

16. Taira no Moritoshi, one of the "generals of soldiers" deployed to defend the Bulbul's Passage side of Ichinotani. A powerful warrior, he would be killed by a Minamoto warrior in the ensuing battle.

defended us from ten enemies! You've committed a sin and wasted your arrows."[17]

Kurō for a while surveyed the castle-fortress far below and said, "Let's have horses run down to see what happens." Saddled horses were chased down. Some of them broke their legs and tumbled down; others ran down without any trouble. Three of the saddled horses gathered to the mountainside of Etchū Senji's shack[18] and stood there trembling.

Having watched this, Kurō said, "Ride down carefully and you won't injure your horses. Let's go down! Make me your model!"

First, with about thirty horsemen, himself at their head, he dashed down. A large crowd followed. It was such that the stirrups of those riding down behind hit the armor and helmets of those ahead. The slope was sand mixed with pebbles, and the men slithered down in a rush for about two hundred yards, then stopped at a table-like spot. Below that, though, was a huge moss-covered boulder dropping straight down for forty-five yards or so. The warriors were neither able to turn back nor seemed to think it possible to ride down farther. Bewildered and unable to move, they said among themselves, "This is the end of it!"

At that moment Sahara no Jūrō Yoshitsura came forward and said, "In Miura, just to chase a single bird, we race about in places like this mornings and evenings. This would be just a riding-ground in Miura!" With that he dashed down, and all the warriors followed suit.

As they went down, they encouraged their horses with muffled "Go, now, go!" It was so terrifying they kept their eyes closed as they went down. On the whole it didn't seem like a human feat but like a demon's or a deity's act.

Even before all of them reached the bottom, they raised a battle cry. It was three thousand horsemen shouting, but the echoes from the mountains made them sound like a hundred thousand.

Paddy Officer Murakami no Motokuni's men started the torching and burned down all the Taira's shacks and temporary huts. A fierce wind happened to be blowing, and as black smoke pressed down, the Taira warriors and soldiers panicked. Many rushed into the sea in front hoping to save themselves. There were a number of rescue

---

17. In Buddhism it's a sin to kill any sentient being.
18. The castle-fortress of Ichinotani, which was built in a brief period of time, is likely to have consisted largely of shacklike makeshift structures.

boats at the water's edge, but as the men vied to get on them and four to five hundred, even a thousand, armored men crowded into each, it simply didn't work. When the boats were pushed out only about three hundred yards from the shore, three large ones sank in a matter of a few moments.

After this it was decreed, "Let the nobles on board, but not the lesser ones," and the lesser ones who tried to board were slashed with swords and halberds. Knowing what to expect fully well, they nonetheless clutched and grabbed at the boats that rejected them. As a result, some had their arms cut off, others their elbows lopped off, and lay covered with blood at the water's edge of Ichinotani.

Noto Governor Noritsune,[19] who had not once lost in many battles, we don't know what his thoughts were this time, mounted a horse called Dusky Black and fled west. He then got on a boat on Akashi Bay in Harima and crossed over to Yashima, in Sanuki.

Because of Yoshitsune's rapid advance and daring, the battle at Ichinotani ended in a complete rout for the Taira: More than 1,000 soldiers were killed, among them nine generals, and those who were not killed or captured escaped across the Inland Sea to regroup in Yashima, on Shikoku Island.

Express messengers from Yoshitsune and Noriyori, sent to report on battle results, arrived in Kyoto the following day, the eighth, and in Kamakura on the fifteenth. Yoshitsune and Noriyori themselves arrived in Kyoto on the ninth, accompanied by only a few troops, with the rest of their armies to follow. They explained their hurry by saying that they wanted to know if the imperial court would allow them to march the full length of the main boulevard carrying the heads of the Taira generals they had killed. Retired Emperor Goshirakawa solicited opinions from his chief courtiers, and the Ministers of the Left, the Right, and the Center, as well as the Major Counselor, all advised that permission not be given. They argued that these Taira men had for a long time served the court in ranking positions and were even related to the imperial household. However, Noriyori and Yoshitsune argued that they were the enemies of their father and grandfather and that, furthermore, unless the march with the heads were allowed, there would be no incentive for the

---

19. At the outset of this series of battles, Taira no Noritsune had assured the Heike high command, to the latter's immense relief, that he would fight at the most dangerous spot.

Minamoto to pursue and destroy the remaining "enemies of the court." In the end Goshirakawa had to yield to the generals' insistence.

Thirteenth day, second month. The heads of the Taira men were brought together in Master Kurō's house in Rokujō Muromachi. They were the heads of Lord Michimori, Tadanori, Tsunemasa, Noritsune, Atsumori, Moromori, Tomoakira, Tsunetoshi, and Moritoshi. Then all these were carried to Hachijō Kawara. Imperial Police Lieutenant [Minamoto no] Nakayori and others accepted them, attached each to a halberd, attached also red tabs [each denoting a Taira man], and hung all of them from a tree facing the gallows. The crowds who came to watch them are said to have turned the place into a veritable market.

Fifteenth day. Around eight in the morning, the express messengers of Noriyori and Yoshitsune arrived in Kamakura from Settsu Province and presented his lordship with reports of the battles. The reports said, in sum: "Earlier, on the seventh, there were battles at Ichinotani. Many of the Taira clan lost their lives. The former Minister of the Center [Munemori] and others escaped by sea and headed toward Shikoku. The Middle captain of the Inner Palace Guards, Third Rank, was captured. Also, Lord Michimori, Tadanori, Tsunetoshi [these three were killed by Noriyori], Tsunemasa, Moromori, Noritsune [these three were killed by Tōtōmi Governor Yoshisada], Atsumori, Tomoakira, Narimori, Moritoshi [these four were killed by Yoshitsune], and a thousand others were beheaded. On the whole, each of the soldiers from Musashi, Sagami, and Shimotsuke did great work. Detailed reports will be orally given later."

Tenth day, fourth month. Kurō's messenger arrived from Kyoto. He said: "On the twenty-seventh of the previous month a session was held for official appointments[20] and the commander was appointed senior fourth rank. It was a reward for the destruction of Yoshinaka."

Twentieth day, sixth month. Earlier, on the fifth, an emergency appointment session was held. The list of appointments arrived today. The appointees suggested by the commander were accepted without exception. These were Acting Major Counselor Taira no Yorimori,

---

20. *Jimoku*. There were two regular sessions: the one for spring, which was mainly intended for appointing governors and other local officials, and the one for autumn, which was mainly for appointing court officials. There were also emergency sessions called *shōjimoku*.

Chamberlain Taira no Mitsumori, Governor of Kawachi Taira no Yasunari, Governor of Sanuki Tō no Yoshiyasu, Governor of Mikawa Minamoto no Noriyori, Governor of Suruga Minamoto no Hirotsuna, and Governor of Musashi Minamoto no Yoshinobu.

Twenty-first day. The commander gathered together Noriyori, Yoshinobu, and Hirotsuna, and toasted them. He then touched on their appointments by the court. Each one must have been overjoyed. In particular, Master Kurō had strongly expressed his wish for a recommendation for a government position, but the commander had somehow refused to accommodate it. Instead, he said, he had recommended Noriyori first, a special consideration which immensely pleased the latter.

Third day, seventh month. The commander told the Imperial Palace to dispatch Master Kurō to the Saikai for the destruction of the former Minister of the Center [Taira no Munemori] and other Taira men.[21]

Fifth day. Ōuchi no Kanja Koreyoshi's express messenger arrived. He said: "Earlier, on the seventh [of the sixth month], in Iga Province, Koreyoshi was assaulted by members of the Taira clan and a great many of the retainers he had counted on were killed." At this news various people turned up in a hurry and Kamakura was thrown into an uproar.

Second day, eighth month. It rained. Another express messenger from Ōuchi Kanja arrived. He said: "Earlier, on the nineteenth [of the seventh month], around six in the afternoon, Koreyoshi engaged in battle with the remaining men of the Taira clan. The rebels were defeated, but more than ninety men escaped. Among them were . . . former Governor of Dewa [Taira no] Nobukane's sons. . . . Koreyoshi had already vindicated himself. Could he expect a special reward?"

Third day. It rained. The commander summoned Ōuchi Kanja's messenger and gave him a letter detailing his response. In the main, it said: "It was most commendable that you attacked and defeated the rebels. Except that your asking if you did not deserve a special reward does not follow the logic of things. The reason is that one is appointed constable of a province (shugo), as you were, for the purpose of putting

---

21. Evidently nothing came of this suggestion. Considering the ceremony and pomp Yoritomo arranged for Noriyori when he sent him from Kamakura for the same purpose, as described in later entries, he may have made the suggestion without providing Yoshitsune with adequate troops. The Saikai, "the Western Sea," designates Kyūshū Island where the Taira clan had strong supporters.

down criminal elements. Nevertheless, you allowed yourself to be attacked by bandits and your retainers were killed. This happened because you had not prepared yourself well. It was your own fault. . . ."

The commander also dispatched a messenger to Kyoto. "The recent military actions in Iga Province must have been plotted by Governor of Dewa [Taira no] Nobukane's sons. These men nonetheless broke out of the encircling force, and their whereabouts are said to be unknown. We are certain that they are hiding in Kyoto. Find them out at once and kill them without hesitation." This message was to be delivered to Master Kurō. Adachi Shinzaburō departed as express messenger.

Sixth day. The commander summoned Governor of Mikawa [Noriyori], Ashikaga Kurōdo, and Lieutenant of the Middle Palace Guards Takeda. Also Tsunetane and other principal vassals came in response to his summons. These men were going to the Saikai to destroy the Taira clan, so they came for a farewell session. A banquet was held all day. As the time for them to leave came, each was presented with a horse. Among those given, the one for the Governor [Noriyori] was a horse his lordship had especially prized. On top of that Yoritomo accompanied the gift with a set of armor.

Eighth day. Clear. Governor of Mikawa Noriyori left for the Saikai as the commander's emissary for destroying the Taira clan. He marched out around noon. A flag carrier [the flag was rolled] and a bow carrier, side by side, went first. Next was the Governor of Mikawa [clad in a jacket dyed in shades of indigo, lightly armored, mounted on a chestnut]; next were a thousand-odd horsemen under his direct command, along with splendid horses, followed by Hōjō Koshirō, Ashikaga Kurōdo Yoshikane. . . .[22] The commander had a viewing stand made near the Inase River and watched the departing men.

Seventeenth day. Kurō's messenger arrived. He said that earlier, on the sixth, Kurō was appointed Lieutenant of the Headquarters of the Outer Palace Guards, Left Division, and commanded to serve on the Imperial Police as well. These appointments were not something he had asked for, but word was that the court was unable to ignore his various exploits and that some imperial honors were due; therefore, it was not possible for him to decline the honors firmly, Kurō said.

The news terribly angered the commander. Noriyori and Yoshinobu's receiving court appointments was something his lordship

---

22. The listing of Yoritomo's prized retainers that follows is omitted.

himself had thought of and recommended. Kurō's was something he had adamantly not permitted for some private reasons. Now it appears, his lordship suspected, that Kurō had acted on his own and asked for it. It seems that this was not the first time Kurō went against his wishes. Because of this, his lordship said, he would delay for a while naming him emissary for the destruction of the Taira clan.

The entry on this important incident may be a good occasion to explain Yoshitsune's changing titles. In the next (original) entry on him, which follows, and thereafter, Yoshitsune will often be referred to as *teii*, here translated "captain." *Teii* is a Chinese name (pronounced the Japanese way) for the second or third ranking officer (*suke* or *jō*) of the Imperial Police, so it may be assumed that for the chronicler Yoshitsune's presence on the police force had greater prestige.[23]

There are, at any rate, some discrepancies in Yoshitsune's court ranks and government posts. After his appointment to the lieutenancy of the Outer Palace Guards, Left Division, and a position in the Imperial Police, Yoshitsune also begins to be referred to as *taifu* and *hōgan*. *Taifu* is another name of "a gentleman of fifth rank," and *hōgan*, "judge," another name of the *jō* of the Imperial Police, a position to which someone of sixth rank was appointed. Regardless, to avoid confusion Yoshitsune will be called "captain" when he is referred to as *teii* or *hōgan*, even though his title in the Outer Palace Guards is *shōjō*, lieutenant.

It must also be borne in mind that loose military titles given to men on actual combat duty, such as *sō-daishō* and *saburai daishō*, were different from the titles given by the court to men holding specific positions.

Twenty-sixth day. The captain's [Yoshitsune's] express messenger arrived. Earlier, on the tenth, he had invited [Taira no] Nobukane's sons, Lieutenant of the Outer Palace Guards, Left Division, Kanehira, as well as Jirō Nobuhira and Saburō Kanetoki, to his house and killed

---

23. Yoshitsune himself seems to have preferred his title in the Outer Palace Guards in signing his name.

them and on the eleventh the court sent an envoy to Nobukane to relieve him of his post.[24]

Ninth day, ninth month. The commander sent a letter saying that the captain should place under his jurisdiction the lands in Kyoto belonging to Former Dewa Governor Nobukane and his family members.

Twelfth day. The messenger Mikawa Governor Noriyori had dispatched on the first arrived today and presented his lordship with a letter. It said that he arrived in Kyoto on the twenty-seventh of the previous month, that on the twenty-ninth he was given a government order to be the emissary for a punitive force, and that today [on the first of the ninth month] he left for the Saikai.

Fourteenth day. Kawagoshi Tarō Shigeyori's daughter left for Kyoto. She was to marry the captain. There was a previous promise and consent at the commander's suggestion. She departed accompanied by two of Shigeyori's sons, along with thirty-odd men.

Twelfth day, tenth month. The Governor of Mikawa, in Aki Province, gave rewards to men with achievements. This was done in accordance with the commander's order. Among them, Yamagata no Suke Tametsuna, a resident of the same province, received a special reward. It was because his military loyalty was particularly outstanding.

Twenty-fourth day. Governor of Inaba [Ōe no] Hiromoto [appointed on the eighteenth of the ninth month] said that earlier, on the eighteenth of the previous month, the captain was promoted to a higher rank while remaining in the same post. On the fifteenth of this month he was permitted to enter the court. On that occasion he rode a cart whose cover was decorated with an eight-leaf design and was accompanied by three men from the Palace Guards under his command and twenty attendant samurai [each mounted]. He danced in the garden, removed his sword and ceremonial scepter, and went into the palace proper.

Sixth day, first month [1185]. For some time the news was that the Eastern warriors who were in the Saikai for destroying the Taira clan had no means of engaging in battle because they had no boats and

---

24. The incidents involving Ōuchi no Koreyoshi and Taira no Nobukane are extracted from the *Azuma Kagami* to show Yoritomo's ambiguous attitude toward Yoshitsune. The extract is also made to show that even though the civil war between 1180 and 1185 was mainly between the Taira and Minamoto clans, allegiance of each member was not necessarily to his own clan, and that even after the main body of the Taira family was officially termed "the imperial enemy," not all the remaining members of the clan were so condemned.

they had run out of provisions. Accordingly, some time back his lordship had ordered construction of boats and the sending of rice to the provinces of the West. When he was about to send to the Saikai a message to this effect, an express messenger that Mikawa Governor Noriyori [who had left Kyoto on the second of the ninth month of the previous year] had dispatched on the fourteenth of the eleventh month of the previous year arrived today. His letter said that because of lack of provisions there was no strong agreement to fight among the soldiers, each thinking of his homeland, most wanting to get out and go home. Other than this the governor detailed matters in Kyūshū. He also asked for riding horses.

This letter dispelled some of his lordship's suspicions, but he still sent runners Sadatō, Nobukata, and Munemitsu. Of these, Sadatō and Nobukata were in Kyoto. So Munemitsu was told to pick them up in Kyoto. He carried with him detailed letters from his lordship. . . .[25]

He also sent a letter to his own vassals in Kyūshū [commanding them to follow the orders of the Governor of Mikawa and announcing that he] was going to send Captain Kurō to Shikoku. . . .

Twelfth day. The Governor of Mikawa moved from Suō Province to Akamagaseki[26] and wanted to cross the sea from there to attack the Taira clan, but having run out of food and with no boats, ended up staying there for several days against his wishes. The men from the East became extremely bored and many thought of their homelands. Even someone like Wada Kotarō Yoshimori[27] became intent on returning secretly to Kamakura. In the circumstances what else could we have expected of other men?

But there had been rumor for some time that Usuki Jirō Koretaka, a resident of Bungo Province, and his brother, Ogata Saburō Koresaka, wanted to be on the Minamoto side; so it was decided by

---

25. In his two letters—one largely written before the arrival of Noriyori's messenger, the other a reply to Noriyori's letter—Yoritomo, showing his acute awareness of the volatile, shifting allegiance among motley groups of soldiers, emphasized the importance of handling them with extreme care. He repeated his advice that Noriyori do his best not to "antagonize" the men of Kyūshū while "cajoling" the men from the East into "doing fine work." His strategy in attacking Yashima should be, he said, to use the men from the East as his core force while making Kyūshū men carry out the general assault.

26. An old name of Shimonoseki, a port town at the southwest tip of Honshū Island.

27. Yoshimori (1147–1213) was among the most dedicated and loyal retainers Yoritomo had. In the Western battles he was attached to Noriyori as his *saburai daishō* (general of soldiers).

agreement that boats would be summoned from these brothers to cross to Bungo Province, from there to break into the port of Hakata. Accordingly, the governor returned to Suō Province.

Twenty-sixth day. Koretaka and Koresaka, understanding the Mikawa Governor's wishes, offered a total of eighty-two naval boats. Also, Usanagi Kamishichi Tōtaka, a resident of Suō Province, offered provisions. As a result, the governor untied the moorings to cross over to Bungo Province.

First day, second month. The Governor of Mikawa reached Bungo Province. . . .

Fourteenth day. While the Governor of Mikawa was still in Suō Province, the commander had sent him a message: "Have Toi Jirō and Kajiwara Heizō talk to the men of the nine provinces [that make up Kyūshū] to make them join us. If as a result they appeared to yield to our side, enter Kyūshū. If not, entertain no thought of doing battle in that land. Cross to Shikoku at once and attack the Taira clan."

But now the governor, wanting to go to Kyūshū but without boats, was unable to advance. He happened to cross to Nagato Province, but with food running out, had to retreat back to Suō Province. The warriors were finally changing their minds, and among them there was no strong agreement to fight, or so the governor lamented. An express messenger bearing this news arrived in Izu Province today.

Accordingly, his lordship sent letters to the governor and some of his own vassals saying: "Should you return to Kyoto without carrying out the battles to the end, what would you have to make yourselves proud? We are sending you provisions: You must wait with patience. The Taira men are out of their homeland and are traveling, but they manage to maintain their military readiness. In contrast, you are my emissaries to destroy them. How can you not get special courage out of yourselves?"

Sixteenth day. The warriors of the Kantō left for Sanuki Province to destroy the Taira clan. Captain Yoshitsune led the van. Today, around six in the afternoon, he untied the moorings.

Since yesterday Minister of the Treasury [Takahashi] Yasutsune had been staying in the captain's inn with the pretext of looking at his armor. His intention was elsewhere, however, for he tried to restrain him by saying, "Sir, I don't know much about military matters, but, as far as I know, a general of the army has not once raced to be in the van. Shouldn't you first send out your second in command?"

The captain replied, "I have a special thought on that. I want to give up my life in the vanguard."[28] With this he went ahead and departed. His were crack troops.

The Taira clan had set up camps in two places. The former Minister of the Center [Munenori] had made a castle-fortress out of Yashima, in Sanuki Province, while the new Middle Counselor Tomonori had fortified the Barrier of Moji with government soldiers of the nine provinces, installing his headquarters on Hiko Island; thus they awaited the punitive forces. . . .

Eighteenth day. Yesterday the captain tried to cross the sea from Watanabe, but a storm suddenly arose, and many of the boats were damaged. So all the boats for the soldiers remained moored without a single exception. The captain saw this and said, "As a punitive force to destroy the Imperial enemy, we won't be able to avoid retribution if we tarry here even for a moment. Don't give a passing thought to the winds and waves!"

Around two in the morning he set out with the first group of five boats and around six arrived in Tsubaki Bay, in Awa Province [normally the route takes three days]. He landed, leading 150 horsemen, summoned Kondōshichi Chikaie, a resident of the province, to serve him as guide, and departed for Yashima. On his way, at Katsura Bay, he attacked Sakuraniwa no Suke Yoshitō [Sanni Nariyoshi's younger brother], and the latter bolted from his castle and disappeared.

The *Heike Monogatari* presents Yoshitsune's decision at Watanabe with far more color and drama.

In Watanabe the great and small lords who had assembled tried to assess the situation: "We have never trained ourselves in boat battles. What shall we do?"

Kajiwara [Kagetoki] said: "How about building 'reverse oars' in the boats for this battle?"

The captain: "What are 'reverse oars'?"

---

28. This utterance may suggest that by then Yoshitsune had sensed his relationship with Yoritomo had become untenable.

"When running a horse," Kajiwara said, "it's easy to turn him round to the left or to the right. But with a boat it's hard to turn it back quickly. So I suggest we build oars both at bow and stern, and add rudders to the sides, so we may go easily any which way."

"In battle," the captain declared, "even when you're determined not to retreat a single step, you often end up doing that when things get bad. What good is there in planning to run from the outset? This is a bad thing to hear when we're setting out. Whether reverse oars or upside down oars, gentlemen, you may build a hundred or a thousand of them on your boats. For me, the oars as they are will do just fine."

"A great general," Kajiwara insisted, "is someone who attacks where he should attack and retreats where he should retreat, so that he may preserve himself until he destroys his enemy. Someone who goes only one way is called a wild-boar warrior, and no one thinks him good."

"I don't give a damn whether it's a wild boar or a wild deer," the captain said. "In battle I feel good only if I attack flat out and win."

The warriors were afraid of Kajiwara and didn't laugh out loud, but, eyes batting and noses twitching, they giggled among themselves. The captain and Kajiwara, though on the same side, would fight with each other, they babbled among themselves.

Finally, when the sun set and night came, the captain declared, "Your boats have been repaired and they're as good as new. Congratulate yourselves with a bite to eat and a bottle to drink, gentlemen."

Making the pretense of doing that himself, he put arms in the boats, loaded them with rice, and lined up horses in them. He then said, "Hurry up and launch them!"

The sailors and helmsmen protested, "Sir, there sure is a tail wind, but it isn't normal. Offshore it must be blowing quite hard. We can't launch them, sir!"

The captain became furious.

"Whether you die in a corner of a field or a mountain or you lose your life drowned in the sea or a river," he said, "that's all fate determined by your previous life. Why should you worry that the wind may be strong out there on the sea?

"If I told you to go out into the head wind, I might be acting wrongly, but this is a tail wind. Simply because it's a bit stronger than usual, how can you refuse to go out on an important mission like this?"

He then ordered, "Shoot every one of them dead if they refuse to launch the boats!"

Satō Saburō Tsugunobu of Ōshū, of the Middle Palace Guards,[29] and Ise no Saburō Yoshimori stepped forward with arrow on bow and said, "What are you quibbling for? This is his order. Hurry up and launch them! If you don't launch the boats, we'll shoot each one of you dead!"

Some sailors and helmsmen heard this and said, "If we're going to be shot dead, fellows, we might as well rush to our death in the dread wind!"

So five out of the 200-odd boats raced out. All the other boats stayed behind either because their crews were afraid of the wind or scared of Kajiwara.

"You shouldn't remain because others don't come out," the captain said. "When things are normal, your enemy will be on the alert. You can beat your enemy by attacking him unexpectedly—as in these stormy winds and waves!"

The five boats were: one of the captain, one of Tashiro no Kanja, one of Gotō, of the Middle Palace Guards, and his son, one of the Kaneko brothers, and one of Gōnai Tadatoshi of Yodo, who was a boat magistrate.

The captain said, "Don't light the watch-fires on everyone's boat. Make mine the main boat and keep an eye on my watch-fires at bow and stern. If the enemy sees a lot of lights, he'll become suspicious and alert."

They raced through the night and covered in several hours the distance that normally took three days. They left Watanabe and Fukushima about two in the morning, on the sixteenth of the second month, and were blown to the land of Awa around six the next morning.

Nineteenth day. All through last night the captain crossed Nakayama on the border between Awa and Sanuki provinces, and today, around eight in the morning, he reached the bay facing the Imperial Palace at Yashima and burned the houses in Mure and Takamatsu. As a result, the former emperor[30] left the palace. The former Minister of

29. He and his brother, Tadanobu, were "given" to Yoshitsune by Fujiwara no Hidehira when Yoshitsune left Ōshū to join Yoritomo.
30. Antoku. Called "former" because the assumption was that he lost the imperial throne when the Taira took him out of Kyoto.

the Center [Munemori] led the members of his clan in getting out to the sea.

The captain [clad in a jacket made of brocade with red background and a suit of armor with its scarlet shaded darker toward the lower hem and mounting a black horse], accompanied by Tashiro no Kanja Nobutsuna, Kaneko no Jūrō Ietada, Kaneko no Yoichi Chikanori, and Ise no Saburō Yoshimori, galloped to the water's edge. They then exchanged arrows and stones with the Taira men plying poles on their boats. In the meantime, Lieutenant of the Middle Palace Guards Satō Saburō Tsugunobu, Lieutenant of the Middle Palace Guards Satō Shirō Tadanobu, Lieutenant of the Middle Palace Guards Gotō Sanemoto and his adopted son, new Lieutenant of the Middle Palace Guards Motokiyo, burned down the palace as well as the Minister of the Center's headquarters and houses. Black smoke soared into heaven, covering the bright sun.

At that juncture Lieutenant of the Middle Palace Guards Moritsugu, of Etchū, and Lieutenant of the Middle Palace Guards Gorō Tadamitsu, of Kazusa, [both Taira retainers] got off the boats and took up a position in front of the shrine to fight. In the ensuing battle the captain's retainer, Tsugunobu, was killed.[31] The captain was deeply grieved by this. He wrapped him in a robe and buried him in a Thousand-Pine wood. He also presented the monk who was to offer prayers for him with the splendid horse he had especially prized [named Taifukuro;[32] originally a horse in the retired emperor's stables; when he went on an imperial excursion as an attendant, the emperor presented it to him; he mounted it whenever he went into a battlefield]. This was his way of soothing his warriors. There was no one who did not speak of this act as marvelous.[33]

Twenty-first day. The Taira clan secluded itself in Shido Dōjō, in Sanuki Province. The captain, leading a troop of eighty horsemen, reached it. A Taira retainer, Lieutenant of the Outer Palace Guards, Left Division, Dennai, surrendered to him. Also Kawano no Shirō

31. The *Heike Monogatari* says Taira no Noritsune, a great archer, shot him. Noritsune was trying to shoot Yoshitsune down, but Tsugunobu and others made a protective formation in front of Yoshitsune. It may be recalled that Noritsune fled Ichinotani without putting up much of a fight.

32. Or "Fifth-Rank Black."

33. As the *Heike Monogatari* points out, the Taira commanders lost a crucial opportunity by failing to mount an aggressive attack—at least on the night of the nineteenth. Yoshitsune and his men were exhausted after a night in a stormy sea, battles and a forced march on the following day and night, followed by a series of battles the next day. Also, they were few in number.

Michinobu joined him with thirty naval boats. By then Master Yoshi-tsune had crossed over to Awa Province. . . .

Twenty-second day. Kajiwara Heizō Kagetoki and other warriors of the East reached the shore of Yashima in 140-odd boats.[34]

First day, third month. After nightfall an express messenger from Saigoku[35] arrived. Since people were busy speculating on the outcome of battle, a number of people gathered in a hurry to hear the news.

Second day. The express messenger last night turned out to be one from Shibuya Shōji Shigekuni. He said that earlier, in the first month, when the Governor of Mikawa crossed from Suō Province to Bungo Province, Shigekuni crossed the sea at the head of the troops and killed [Harada] Tanenao.

Eighth day. The captain's express messenger arrived from the Saigoku. He said that on the seventeenth of the previous month the captain, leading a troop of only 150 horsemen, untied the moorings at Watanabe, braving a stormy wind. Around six the next morning he arrived in Awa Province and fought some battles. The soldiers follow-ing the Taira clan either were killed or ran away. So on the nineteenth the captain headed for Yashima. This messenger left the scene without waiting for the outcome there. However, when he looked back from Harima Province there was black smoke soaring into heaven in the direction of Yashima. He had no doubt that the battle was already over and the palace and other buildings were burned down.

Ninth day. The Governor of Mikawa sent a letter to the commander from the Saikai in which he said: "Because there were a number of Taira strongholds there we approached Bungo Province in a state of readiness. But all the people had fled, so we had no means of acquiring provisions. As a result, several samurai, including Wada Tarō [Yoshimori] and his brother, Ōtawa Jirō, and Kudō Ichirō, wanted strongly to return home. It was by imposing my will that I restrained them and crossed the sea with them. I wish you would tell them something.

"Also I hear that Tanzō, Superintendant of the Kumano Shrines,[36] agreed, through the captain's suasion, to join the punitive forces and

---

34. The *Heike* says people jeered at Kajiwara and his men by comparing them to "flowers too late for a service, sweet flags on the sixth, or clubs brought long after a fight is over." Sweet flags here refer to those used for decoration on the fifth of the fifth month.

35. Shikoku Island, where Yoshitsune and his troops were.

36. An influential figure, because of his religious position, who initially sided with the Taira clan and was trounced in the first battle. His wife was Yoritomo's aunt.

some time back crossed to Sanuki Province and is now thinking of coming into the nine provinces. I understood that you put Yoshitsune in charge of Shikoku and me, Noriyori, in charge of Kyūshū. If you further select a man like that, it's not only that I'm bound to lose face, but also it is as if there were no other courageous man. I'm embarrassed to think what people think of this."

Eleventh day. The commander sent a reply to the Governor of Mikawa. He wrote that there was no truth in the rumor that Tanzō had crossed the sea. . . .

Twenty-first day. It poured. The captain wanted to head for Dannoura to attack the Taira clan but postponed it because of the rain.[37] In the meantime Gorō Masatoshi at the local government boat agency of Suō Province, being the boat magistrate of the province, presented him with fifty to sixty boats. In response Yoshitsune gave Masatoshi a letter. It said that he was now Lord Kamakura's direct vassal.

Twenty-second day. The captain untied the moorings of fifty to sixty naval boats and urged them on toward Dannoura. Since yesterday he had been gathering vessels and devising strategies. Miura no Suke Yoshizumi heard about this and came to meet him at the port of Ōshima, of the same province. The captain said to him, "You have already seen the Barrier of Moji. You should be our guide and lead us."

Following this order Yoshizumi went ahead and reached the shore of Okitsu, of Dannoura [a distance of about 3,000 yards from the Taira camps]. When they heard this, the Taira troops left Hiko Island plying their poles, passed Akamagaseki, and were now at Tanoura.

The *Heike Monogatari* describes another dangerous confrontation between Yoshitsune and Kajiwara no Kagetoki—this one just before the final battle of this civil war.

Kajiwara said, "Sir, allow me to be the first to go into battle today."
The captain: "If I weren't here."
"That isn't fair, sir. You realize you are the general of the army."

---

37. Yoshitsune's movements for about a month after he went to Awa Province following the Shido battle are unrecorded. He may have spent the month fighting various clans in Shikoku or persuading them to join the Minamoto. Dannoura is close to present-day Shimonoseki, at the southwestern tip of Honshū.

The captain declared, "The thought never occurred to me. Lord Kamakura is the general of the army. I've merely been asked to serve as his deputy and I'm no different from you."

Kajiwara, unable to get through his wish to be the first to go into battle, mumbled, "This man isn't born to be a leader of samurai."

The captain heard this. "You're the stupidest man in all Japan!" he said and put his hand on the hilt of his sword.

"I have no master other than Lord Kamakura!" Kajiwara spat out and also put his hand on the hilt of his sword. . . .

Although the two men were restrained by their aides, the *Heike* tells us, this confrontation, no less than the argument on "reverse oars," motivated Kagetoki to slander Yoshitsune later on. Slander Yoshitsune Kagetoki did, as we shall see, yet the confrontation, if it did take place, may be noted for something else also: Yoshitsune's acute sense that he was no more than a pawn on Yoritomo's chess board. In addition, at least in Kagetoki's eyes, he was becoming a dangerous pawn.

Yoshitsune was dangerous to Yoritomo because he, unlike Noriyori, was an exceptionally able military commander. Noriyori was ineffectual, didn't know what he was doing, and failed to win loyalty from his subordinates, of whom he perpetually complained. So, to Yoritomo he was safe. Yoshitsune, on the other hand, was effectiveness incarnate. A medieval practitioner of blitzkrieg, he knew delayed action could be fatal. He always put himself at the forefront of any military action, thereby winning fierce loyalty from his men, if not from fellow commanders. He might usurp Yoritomo as leader of the Minamoto clan.

Twenty-fourth day. On the sea off Dannoura at Akamagaseki, in Nagato Province, the Minamoto and Taira faced off. They rowed their boats and ships toward each other from three hundred yards apart. The Taira clan divided their five hundred vessels into three groups and, with Yamaga no Hyōdōji Hidetō and the Matsura Group as commanders in chief, they challenged and fought the Minamoto generals and commanders. Around noon the Taira were finally beaten into submission. . . .

Fourth day, fourth month. With the word that all the Taira had been annihilated, the captain's messenger hurriedly reached Kyoto. . . .

Eleventh day. Around two in the afternoon there was a pillar-raising ceremony for the South Holy Hall. The commander attended it. Meanwhile an express messenger from the Saikai had arrived to tell of the annihilation of the Taira clan. The captain had provided a scroll of registration[38] [Nakahara Nobuyasu is said to have written it]. . . .

Tō no Hōgan-dai [Fujiwara no Kunimichi] knelt before the commander and read the registration aloud. The Governor of Inaba [Ōe no Hiromoto], along with [Fujiwara no] Toshikane and Chikuzen Saburō [Koremune Takahisa], was standing by. The commander took the registration and unrolled it himself, and, as he held it in his hands facing toward Tsurugaoka,[39] he was unable to say a word. . . .

Twenty-first day. Kajiwara Heizō Kagetoki's express messenger arrived from the West. He had a relative of his present a letter. In the first part he described the battles and toward the end complained about the captain's disloyalty. . . .

> The Lord Captain, as your deputy, accompanied by your vassals, carried out the battles to the end. Nevertheless, he seems to think he alone should get all the credit even though, I submit, the victories were the result of the cooperation of many people. As I see it, many people strove to work together not because they thought of the captain, but because they held Your Lordship in awe. And yet, after the annihilation of the Taira clan his behavior has become even more excessive. All the soldiers are terrified of him, but he shows no inclination to be accommodating. Above all, I, Kagetoki, as Your Lordship's close aide and knowing Your Lordship's strict order, point out to him, whenever I see his misbehavior, that it may go against Your Lordship's wishes. But my words are turned against me, and I am even in danger of being penalized. Now that the battles are over and there is nothing to do, I see no reason to continue to serve him. I would like to be relieved of my duty as soon as possible and return home.

Twenty-sixth day. Today when the former Minister of the Center [Taira no Munemori] and other people who were captured alive entered Kyoto by the summons, the retired emperor secretly set out on his cart at Rokuō Bōjō to watch them. . . . All of them were taken to the captain's mansion at Rokujō Muromachi.

---

38. Of those important Taira people who were killed or captured alive.
39. Where the family shrine was located.

Twenty-ninth day. Runner Yoshieda left for the Saikai as the commander's messenger. The purpose was to deliver his letter to Tashiro no Kanja Nobutsuna. The letter said: I sent the captain as my emissary to the Saikai, having my vassals accompany him, but I hear that he acts as if he thinks he has authority on all matters. The warriors privately think they want to serve me, and resent him in various matters. Therefore, secretly circulate the word that henceforth those who want to be loyal to me may not obey him.

Fourth day, fifth month. Kajiwara Heizō Kagetoki's messenger returned to the West. Accordingly, the commander made him carry a letter in which he rebuked the captain. Do not obey his orders anymore. . . .

Seventh day. The captain's messenger [by the name of Kamei Rokurō] arrived from Kyoto. He presented the commander with the captain's letter vowing that he had no rebellious thoughts. The former Governor of Inaba [Ōe no] Hiromoto relayed it. The Governor of Mikawa [Noriyori] had sent a series of express messengers from the Saikai to give detailed reports. He had not acted freely in anything, so the commander had kindly thoughts for him. The captain tended to act on his own authority. Now that he had heard about the commander's displeasure, he did something like this for the first time. It was not something the commander could tolerate, and it merely provided fodder for furthering his fury.

Eleventh day. As a reward for capturing and presenting the former Minister of the Center [Munemori], the commander had been appointed Junior Second Rank on the twenty-seventh of the previous month. The letter of appointment arrived today. . . .

Fifteenth day. The captain's messenger [Hori Kagemitsu] arrived. He said that the captain was bringing with him the former minister of the center and his son. He had left Kyoto on the seventh and was expected to arrive at Sakawa Station tonight. He planned to enter Kamakura tomorrow. The lord of second rank [Yoritomo][40] had Lord Hōjō [Tokimasa] head for Sakawa Station as his messenger. The purpose was to welcome and receive the former minister of the center. He had Mushadokoro [Maki] Munechika and Kudō Kojirō Yukimitsu accompany him. His word to be conveyed was: The captain may absolutely not come into Kamakura; he must stay near there for a while until he is summoned. Koyama Shichirō Asatomo was to be the envoy for this.

---

40. Henceforth Yoritomo will be referred to as "the lord of second rank."

Twenty-fourth day. The captain had subjugated the imperial enemies as planned. In addition, he had brought with him the former minister of the center for the lord of second rank. He had not doubted that he would be rewarded for these deeds, but because there were recently rumors of his disloyalty, he suddenly became the subject of the lord of second rank's ire and was not allowed to enter Kamakura. He had already spent days idly at Koshigoe Station and grown so worried and depressed that he presented a plea[41] through the former Governor of Inaba [Ōe no] Hiromoto. Hiromoto showed it to the commander, but there was no clear word, except that in time there would be some instructions. . . .

Ninth day, sixth month. The captain, who had stayed near Sakawa for a while, returned to Kyoto today, taking the former Minister of the Center with him. The lord of second rank appointed Tachibana Umamitsu [Kiminaga], Asō Shōji [Munenobu], Usami Heiji [Sanemasa], and other stout men to go with the prisoner. The captain's thought for some time had been that if he came to Kantō he would be asked in detail about the process of subjugating the Taira clan. Also, he would be rewarded for his great exploits and his ambition fulfilled. That's what he had expected, but he was suddenly made to realize that this was not so. Worse, he was unable even to have an audience and had to return to Kyoto empty-handed. . . .

Thirteenth day. His lordship stripped the captain of all the twenty-four lands confiscated from the Taira clan and allotted to him. . . .

Twenty-ninth day, eighth month. Earlier, on the sixteenth, there was an emergency appointment session. The list of the appointments arrived today. Many members of the Minamoto clan received imperial consideration. These were [Yamana] Yoshinori, Governor of Izu; [Ōuchi] Koreyoshi, Governor of Sagami; [Ashikaga] Yoshikane, Governor of Kōzuke; [Kagami] Tōmitsu, Governor of Shinano; [Yasuda] Yoshisuke, Governor of Echigo; and Yoshitsune, Governor of Iyo.[42] As for Yoshitsune receiving a government position, the lord of second rank had previously steadfastly rejected any such move, but when it comes to the present governorship of Iyo, he had privately made the

---

41. The famous "Koshigoe Letter." A slightly abbreviated translation appears in *The Nobility of Failure*, pp. 85–86. The version cited in the *Heike Monogatari* is shorter.
42. Hereafter Yoshitsune will be often referred to as the Governor of Iyo.

request to Courtier Yasutsune earlier, in the fourth month. Since then disloyalty and other matters had been revealed, but he was no longer able to withdraw the request and so had left the whole matter to imperial judgment. . . .

Second day, ninth month. Lieutenant of the Outer Palace Guards, Left Division, Kajiwara Genta Kagesue and Yoshikatsubō Jōjin left for Kyoto as envoys. . . . Calling themselves his lordship's messengers, they were to visit Governor of Iyo Yoshitsune at his house and tell him to find out the whereabouts of the former Governor of Bizen [Minamoto no] Yukiie[43] and kill him. They were to see how the Governor of Iyo would react to this, Kagesue was told. Earlier, on the twentieth of the fifth month, the former Major Counselor [Taira no] Tokitada,[44] along with some others, were given a government notice of exile. But he was still in Kyoto, which infuriated his lordship; nevertheless the Governor of Iyo, as the said counselor's son-in-law, wanted to be considerate to him and allowed him to stay. Even worse, there was a rumor that he was intent on persuading the former Governor of Bizen Yukiie to join him in a revolt against Kantō. . . .

Twelfth day. Kagesue and Jōjin entered Kyoto. They spoke of the people to be exiled.

Sixth day, tenth month. Lieutenant of the Outer Palace Guards, Left Division, Kajiwara Genta Kagesue returned from Kyoto. In his lordship's presence he said: "I went to visit the Governor of Iyo at his house and said I was Your Lordship's messenger, but he refused to meet me on the ground that he was ill. The secret message I had was not something I could convey through another messenger, so I went back to my inn [at Rokujō Aburanokōji]. Two days later I went to visit again, and he met me, leaning on an armrest. He looked extraordinarily emaciated. He had several moxa marks.

"I brought up the subject of pursuing and destroying Yukiie. In response he said, 'I am not feigning this illness. I, Yoshitsune, would immediately bring to justice even a common criminal like a robber. Is there anything that needs to be said of Yukiie? He is

---

43. Yukiie was Yoritomo and Yoshitsune's uncle. He had initially raised an army with Yoshinaka. An unlucky soldier, he was defeated in a series of battles.

44. Tokitada (1130–89) is notorious for the observation quoted earlier: "Anyone who isn't a member of our clan has to be a nonhuman." He became influential because one of his sisters married Goshirakawa and another Kiyomori. He was one of the few ranking Taira members who were not beheaded but exiled.

not a member of another clan, but is, like me, a descendant of Rokuson'ō [Minamoto no Tsunemoto][45] who handles the bow and horse. You can't rank him with an ordinary man. I can't just send my retainers and simply make him surrender. I intend to treat my illness as soon as possible and, once cured, will devise ways. Tell this to his Lordship.' "

The lord of second rank declared, "Because he sympathizes with Yukiie he decided to pretend an illness. That's so obvious."

Upon hearing this, Kagetoki said, "The first day my son went he couldn't have a direct meeting with him, but two days later he had a meeting. When you think how he worked out the whole thing, if you don't eat for a whole day and don't sleep one whole night, you're bound to get tired. As for moxa marks, you can put any number of them on in an instant. And he had a couple of days to work on them! My guess is that he worked these things out in those two days. You shouldn't doubt for a single moment, sir, that the two of them share the same thought and are ready."

Ninth day. His lordship had an intense council for a few days on killing Iyo Governor Yoshitsune. Finally it was decided to dispatch Tosanobō Masatoshi. This mission was something that a great many people were in the mood to decline, but Masatoshi volunteered to sign a letter of acceptance and won his lordship's special word of gratitude. Just before his departure he came to his lordship, said that he had an old mother and infants in Shimotsuke Province, and asked for his lordship's compassion for them. The lord of second rank agreed on the spot and gave him Nakaizumi Village in Shimotsuke Province. Masatoshi was accompanied by eighty-three horsemen. These were Mikami Yaroku Iesue [Masatoshi's younger brother], Nishigori Saburō, Kadoma Tarō, Aisawa Jirō, and others. His travel time was determined to be nine days.

Thirteenth day. Earlier, on the eleventh, and today, Governor of Iyo, Fifth Rank, Lieutenant Yoshitsune secretly went to the Imperial Palace and pleaded his case, saying: "The former Governor of Bizen Yukiie has turned against Kantō and intends to revolt. This is because the order of the lord of second rank, of Kamakura, to kill him had reached his ear, and Yukiie had become resentful as he wondered why the lord of second rank wanted to kill his own innocent uncle—for

---

45. Tsunemoto (d. 961) was a grandson of Emperor Seiwa (850–880) who was given the family name of Minamoto to found the Minamoto clan.

what error or neglect? I, Yoshitsune, tried hard to restrain him, but in vain.

"In the meantime I, Yoshitsune, repulsed the heinous crimes of the Taira clan and brought the world back to peace and quiet. One would think these are great achievements. But the lord of second rank never thought of rewarding me but even stripped me of all the lands he had happened to allot to me. Worse, I now hear that he is plotting to kill me. In order to avoid this predicament I have already agreed to work with Yukiie. In the circumstances I must have a government order to pursue and destroy Yoritomo. Without imperial permission both of us intend to commit suicide."

The imperial reply was, "Try hard to placate Yukiie's resentment and fury."

Seventeenth day. Tosanobō Masatoshi, carrying the strict order from Kantō issued earlier and accompanied by Mizuotani Jūrō and sixty other horsemen, attacked the house of Governor of Iyo, Fifth Rank, Lieutenant Yoshitsune at Rokujō Muromachi. It happened that most of the governor's strong men were wandering near Nishikawa and only a few retainers were staying in his house. But accompanying Lieutenant of the Middle Palace Guards Satō Shirō Tadanobu and others, the governor himself opened the gate, dashed out, and fought. Yukiie heard about this, came and joined them from the rear, and fought for the governor. As a result, after a short while Masatoshi beat a retreat. The governor's retainers scattered in all directions to hunt him and his men. The governor hurried to the Imperial Palace to report that he was safe.

Eighteenth day. As regards Yoshitsune's request, a council was held yesterday in the Imperial Palace to determine whether or not to grant imperial permission. It happened that at the time there was no one to command the police force other than Yoshitsune. If he didn't receive imperial permission and resorted to violence, who did they have to order for their defense?

In order to avoid this predicament for the time being, it was decided that first an imperial command would be issued, then details would be explained to Kantō. If this were done, the lord of second rank was unlikely to be much offended.

Accordingly, the imperial command was issued. The presiding officer was the Minister of the Left [Fujiwara no Munetsune].

Eighteenth Day, Tenth Month, First Year of Bunji [1185]

Imperial Command:

Lord Minamoto no Yoritomo, Junior Second Rank, has single-handedly displayed his military prowess, but has already forgotten the imperial law. Therefore, we hereby order Former Governor of Bizen Minamoto no Yukiie and Lieutenant of the Palace Guards, Left Division, Minamoto no Yoshitsune to pursue and destroy his lordship.

Submitted by
Head of the Treasury
Major Controller of the Right
Assistant Director of the Office of the Empress's Household
Fujiwara no Mitsumasa

Twenty-third day. Yamanouchi Takiguchi Saburō Tsunetoshi's servant hurried from Ise Province and reported: "Saying that they were under the Iyo governor's order, people were recruiting soldiers. In the meantime, earlier, on the nineteenth, they surrounded the constable's office to kill him. Probably he couldn't get away. . . ."

Twenty-fourth day. After returning to his quarters,[46] his lordship summoned [Wada] Yoshimori and [Kajiwara] Kagetoki and ordered: "Go to Kyoto tomorrow. Gather the soldiers and register them; separately submit a list of those who ought to depart at dawn tomorrow." By midnight those vassals who gathered totaled 2,096, among them [Chiba] Tsunetane and other important ones, of which those who ought to go to Kyoto were fifty-eight, including [Koyama] Tomomasa and [Yūki] Tomomitsu.

Twenty-fifth day. At dawn today those brave warriors who agreed were named and made to depart for Kyoto. His lordship told them: "First, when you get to Owari and Mino, tell the residents of those provinces to fortify the ferries at Ajika, Sunomata, and other places. Next, as soon as you get into Kyoto, kill Yukiie and Yoshitsune. Show no mercy whatsoever. If they happen not to be in Kyoto, wait until I arrive. . . ."

Twenty-sixth day. Tosanobō Masatoshi and three of his party were hunted down and brought out of the depths of Mt. Kurama by the Iyo governor's retainers and beheaded today on Rokujō Kawara.

---

46. That is, after a grand and elaborate service held at the South Holy Hall, a description of which takes up most of the long entry on this day. For the South Holy Hall, see the entry on the eleventh, fourth month, 1185.

Twenty-ninth day. In order to suppress the revolt of the Governor of Iyo and the Governor of Bizen, the lord of second rank left for Kyoto today. . . .

Second day, eleventh month. The Governor of Iyo already planned to move to the West. In order to arrange vessels for that purpose, he first dispatched Captain of the Imperial Police [Fujiwara no] Tomozane. . . .

Third day. Former Governor of Bizen Yukiie [armor made of cherry-decorated leather] and Governor of Iyo Yoshitsune [jacket made of brocade against red background, armor made of pale-blue fabric] departed for the Saikai. First they sent a messenger to the Imperial Palace to say: "In order to avoid Kamakura's censure we are escaping to Kyūshū. We are aware that we should come to pay respects to Your Majesty, but we are not in proper attire, so we have already left."

Accompanying them were former Middle Captain [Taira no] Tokisane; Gentleman-in-Waiting [Ichijō] Yoshinari [Yoshitsune's half brother; Minister of the Treasury Ichijō Naganari's son]; Lieutenant of the Outer Palace Guards, Right Division, [Minamoto no] Izu Aritsuna; Hori Yatarō Kagemitsu, Lieutenant of the Middle Palace Guards Satō Shirō Tadanobu; Ise no Saburō Yoshimori; Kataoka Hachirō Hirotsune; Monk Benkei; and others. The entire force is said to have consisted of about two hundred horsemen.

Fifth day. The direct vassals dispatched from Kantō entered Kyoto. They first conveyed the lord of second rank's fury to the Minister of the Left [Fujiwara no Tsunemune].

Today, when the Governor of Iyo reached Kawajiri, members of the Minamoto clan of Settsu Province, Chamberlain Tada Yukitsuna and Toyoshima Kanja, blocked his way and shot some arrows and stones. The governor galloped into them, and they were unable to put up a fight. Nevertheless, many on the governor's force dropped away, and not many remained with him.

Sixth day. Yukiie and Yoshitsune boarded their vessels on the beach of Daimotsu, but a gale arose suddenly and fierce waves capsized their vessels, so they had to abandon their plan to cross the sea. Many of their group scattered and only four chose to stay with the Governor of Iyo: These were Lieutenant of the Middle Palace Guards Izu, Hori Yatarō, Musashibō Benkei, and the governor's mistress [called Shizuka]. They spent this night near Tennō Temple and then fled to some place.

Today an imperial command ordering capture and return of these two men was sent to various provinces.[47]

Seventh day. The lord of second rank stayed at an inn in Kisegawa so that he might gather together the warriors and hear what was going on in Kyoto. He was told that earlier, on the third, Yukiie and Yoshitsune had fled from Chūgoku toward the Saikai. The only thing was that the two men had been equipped with the Retired Emperor [Goshirakawa]'s command that the residents of Shikoku and Kyūshū obey their orders. . . . The lord of second rank was extremely depressed that the retired emperor had trampled upon his many achievements. Nonetheless he was greatly pleased when he heard the rumor that during the deliberations on whether or not to issue the said imperial command the Minister of the Right [Kujō Kanezane] had strongly supported him.

Today Yoshitsune was relieved of his present posts [said to be the Governorship of Iyo and the position in the Imperial Police].

Kujō Kanezane (1149–1207), a wily courtier who had already established communications with Yoritomo, heard, on the same day, that Yukiie and Yoshitsune had perished a few days earlier. He jotted down his thoughts on the matter in his diary *Gyokuyō:*

If the news were true, it would no longer be possible to recompense them for their services. This is to be regretted but it is a matter of great joy to the world. If they had positioned themselves in Kyūshū, the provinces along the routes to the island would have suffered and declined further because of the warriors sent to pursue and destroy them. In the provinces of the Kantō, too, because of the ensuing disturbances Yoritomo would not have been able to carry out his plans. As a result, both the high and the low in Kyoto would not have found any means of

47. The one ordering Yukiie and Yoshitsune to "pursue and destroy" Yoritomo. The imperial command sent to provinces appears to have been actually issued five days later, on the eleventh. According to the entry on that day, Goshirakawa became fearful of Yoritomo's ire and decided that Yukiie and Yoshitsune might be alive despite news that they had perished at Daimotsu.

survival.[48] Therefore, their deaths before achieving what they wanted to do can only be a great boon to the nation.

Yoshitsune has left great achievements; about this there is nothing to argue. In bravery, benevolence, and justice, he is bound to leave a great name to posterity. In this he can only be admired and praised. The only thing is that he decided to rebel against Yoritomo. This was a great traitorous crime. It must be because of this that Heaven meted out to him this punishing accident.

Eighth day. Because they [Yukiie and Yoshitsune] had already fled Kyoto, his lordship [Yoritomo] canceled his plan to go to Kyoto and left to return to Kamakura today.

Seventeenth day. There was rumor that the Governor of Iyo[49] was hiding in Mt. Yoshino, in Yamato Province, so the temple administrator, with the help of tough warrior monks, had been looking for him among the hills and woods for some days, but to no avail. However, around eight in the evening today, the governor's mistress, Shizuka, came down the Fujio Slope of this mountain and reached Giō Hall. She looked extraordinarily strange. Some warrior monks spotted her and took her to the temple administrator's office.

When questioned in detail, Shizuka said: "I am a mistress of Captain Kurō, Fifth Rank [the present Governor of Iyo]. From the beach of Daimotsu he came to this mountain and stayed here for five days, but hearing the rumor that the warrior monks had revolted against him, he disguised himself as an itinerant mountain monk and disappeared. At the time he gave me a great deal of such things as gold and silver and sent me off toward Kyoto with several servants. But these men soon stripped me of the valuables, and abandoned me in the deep snow of the mountain. That's why I wandered down here."

Eighteenth day. Following what Shizuka had said, warrior monks of Yoshino again went into the hills and valleys to hunt the

---

48. During that period Japan suffered from a series of great famines and other natural disasters. The situation was seriously aggravated by large groups of soldiers who, moving up and down the country, routinely indulged in looting, killing, and burning. The warriors' behavior was such that Yoritomo himself was forced to issue a series of stern injunctions—even to his top aides, such as Kajiwara no Kagetoki.

49. The chroniclers of the *Azuma Kagami* tend to be strict about the shifting titles, but here they have not taken note that Yoshitsune is no longer the Governor of Iyo or the captain in the Imperial Police.

Governor of Iyo. The temple administrator greatly pitied Shizuka and said that after taking good care of her for some time he would send her to Kamakura.

Twenty-second day. The Governor of Iyo braved the deep snow of Mt. Yoshino and secretly headed for Tafu Peak. He said it was to offer prayers to the soul of the Taishokkan.[50] He reached the Fujimuro quarter of the South Hall of the shrine, whose resident monk, a tough warrior monk calling himself Jūjibō, admired the governor.

Twenty-fifth day. Today Lord Hōjō [Tokimasa][51] entered Kyoto. Through the Governor-General of the Dazaifu and Middle Counselor [Yoshida Tsunefusa] he conveyed in detail to his majesty the lord of second rank's depression in regard to Yukiie and Yoshitsune's rebellion. Accordingly, today his majesty passed down his instructions, issuing an imperial command to hunt the two down without fail.[52]

Twenty-ninth day. Jūjibō, of Tafu Peak, spoke to the Governor of Iyo and said: "This temple isn't big, and there aren't many monks living here, either, so it will be difficult for you to hide yourselves here for a long time. I'd like to send you to a place near the Totsu River. It's so deep in the mountains that people and horses can't easily get to it."

The governor agreed, so the monk was overjoyed and sent the governor off along with eight tough warrior monks.

Fifteenth day, twelfth month. Lord Hōjō's express messenger arrived from Kyoto. He brought a detailed report on the goings-on in Kyoto. Lord Hōjō first confiscated the houses of the rebels. He made strategic arrangements so that those who were sympathetic to their evil acts, in particular those whose intentions had been revealed, would not be able to flee. . . . Next, the Iyo Governor's mistress was brought to him. Questioned, she said that when the Governor of Iyo left the capital, trying to go to the Saikai, he took her as far as the beach of Daimotsu. . . .

Eighteenth day, second month [1186]. There was rumor that the Governor of Iyo was living in hiding on Tafu Peak. This means, his lordship [Yoritomo] suspected, that the Governor's teachers, Tōkōbō

---

50. Fujiwara no Kamatari (614–669), who is enshrined in Danzan Shrine. The *taishokkan* was the highest court rank created after the Taika Reform and Kamatari was the first to receive it.
51. Tokimasa (1138–1215), father of Yoritomo's wife, Masako, became regent after Yoritomo's death and laid the foundation for the Hōjō's takeover of the Kamakura government.
52. This command was issued to Yoritomo.

Ajari, of Kurama, and Suō Tokugō [Shōkō], of Nara, are sympathetic to him. He ordered that they be brought to Kamakura.

First day, third month. Today, the Governor of Iyo's mistress, Shizuka, summoned, arrived in Kamakura from Kyoto. . . . Her mother, Iso no Zenji, accompanied her. . . .

Sixth day. Shizuka was summoned and questioned about the Governor of Iyo by Toshikane and [Taira no] Moritoki. She said that earlier she had spent some days on Mt. Yoshino. When told that her story could hardly be believed, she said, "It was not on the mountain but in a monastery there. But hearing that the warrior monks had revolted, the governor disguised himself as an itinerant mountain monk and left, saying he intended to enter the Great Peak.[53] The monk of the monastery accompanied him. In love with him, I went as far as the First Torii, but the same monk scolded me, saying 'Women aren't allowed to enter the Peak.' So I headed toward Kyoto. But the servants who accompanied me took my valuables and disappeared. So I wandered down to Giō Hall."

Further asked the name of the monk, she said she had forgotten. On the whole, what she had said in Kyoto and what she described now were different to a great extent. . . .

Fifteenth day. Former Governor of Iyo Yoshitsune, who had brazenly appeared in a number of places, offered prayers at the Grand Shrine [of Ise]. Saying it was for the fulfillment of his prayers, he donated a gold-decorated sword. It was the sword he had worn in various battles.

Eighth day, fourth month. The lord of second rank and his ladyship[54] paid their respects at Tsurugaoka Shrine. Next they summoned Shizuka to the colonnade. The purpose was to have her offer a dance to the shrine. Orders had been issued earlier, but she had not presented herself, using the pretext of illness.

"She is in unfortunate circumstances and in no position to make any excuse, but as the Governor of Iyo's mistress it would be extremely shameful to appear in a public place so soon, she says, and is very reluctant [to respond to your order]. Still," her ladyship said, urging, "she is a great dancer known to the whole land. We happen to

---

53. Ōmine, a mountain range in Yoshino regarded as sacred for spiritual training. To "enter the Great Peak" means to "start spiritual training."

54. Yoritomo's wife, Masako (1156–1225). As this episode shows, Masako was strong-willed. After Yoritomo's death, she ran the Kamakura government—first with her father, then by herself. She was called the "Nun Shogun."

have come to the shrine and she lives near here. We would regret it if we didn't see her perform."

Consequently, his lordship summoned Shizuka. His order was that her performance be to praise the benevolence of the Great Boddhisattva.

When she faced the stage, however, Shizuka continued to decline firmly, saying she had been terribly distressed in recent days and that, furthermore, she did not know how to dance. Nonetheless, when his lordship's order was repeated a few more times, she diffidently put her snow-white sleeves around her body and started the Song of the Yellow Bamboo. Lieutenant of the Outer Palace Guards, Left Division [Kudō] Suketsune played the drum. Even though he was born to a family that had produced outstanding warriors for several generations and he himself had lived in the dust arising from shield and halberd, he had done a chief's duties[55] and he himself sang and played music; that must be why he served in that role. Hatakeyama Jirō Shigetada did the rhythmic part.

Shizuka began by chanting a song:

> *Yoshino-yama mine no shirayuki fumiwakete*
>   *irinishi hito no ato zo koishiki*

> Treading on the white snow of the peak of Mt. Yoshino
>   he went away. How I miss him!

She then sang a song from the "farewell" category of music and again chanted a song:

> *Shizu ya shizu shizu no odamaki kurikaeshi*
>   *mukashi o ima ni nasu yoshi mo gana*

> Shizu oh shizu! Like the shizu spool, if only I could
>   repeat the past and bring it back![56]

---

55. *Ichirō jōjitsu. Ichirō* designated the chief of a group of people on a certain assignment, and *jōjitsu* "on duty."

56. A variation on the tanka in *Ise Monogatari*: "Like the *shizu* spool turned round and round, if only I could repeat the past and bring it back." *Shizu* is a type of ancient fabric which serves as a metaphor of the past.

Truly it was such a splendid spectacle in front of the shrine that dust on the beams surely must have trembled![57] Both the high and the low were deeply moved.

However, the lord of second rank said, "Anyone who shows his performing skill before the treasure hall of Hachiman Shrine must praise the glorious future of Kantō above all, but ignoring what I told her, she expressed her longing for the traitorous Yoshitsune and sang farewell songs. This is outrageous!"

His ladyship responded by saying, "While you were exiled and lived in Izu Province, you pledged your love to me. But my father, Lord Hōjō, fearful of the timing and the circumstances, secretly shut me up. Nevertheless, I responded to your call, wandered out into the darkness of night, and ignored the downpour to come to your place. Again, while you were out on the battlefield at Ishibashi, I, left alone on Mt. Izu, did not know whether you were dead or alive, almost fainting with anxiety day and night. If you speak of my distress then, it was exactly the way Shizuka must feel now. If she forgot the governor's love for many years and did not miss him or long for him, she would hardly be called a woman of fidelity. She simply used this opportunity to perform publicly and revealed her innermost feelings. This is most wonderful. You must bend over backwards to compliment her."

As a result of these words, his lordship contained his anger. In a while he had a robe [u no hana kasane][58] pushed outside the blind as a reward for her performance.[59]

Twentieth day. Today there was rumor that Yukiie and Yoshitsune were still in Kyoto, scheming with warrior monks of Mt. Hiei. His lordship [Yoritomo] was asked if he should issue some instructions. Accordingly, he sent a message to the Governor-General of the Dazaifu and Middle Counselor [Yoshida Tsunefusa], asking him to have some of those brave warriors[60] climb the mountain and find the warrior monks.

---

57. From a passage in a classical Chinese text, "moving the dust on the beams" is a metaphor for excellence in singing or any other musical performance.

58. U no hana kasane, "saxifrage or deutzia flower layers," is a robe with a "layered color combination, white over green." Kimono: Fashioning Culture, p. 219.

59. Clothes were the standard reward for performers. As a ranking court aristocrat, Yoritomo probably watched Shizuka's performance from a box seat with a see-through blind.

60. The ones left by Hōjō Tokimasa for policing Kyoto when he departed for Kamakura on the twenty-seventh of the third month.

Twenty-fifth day, fifth month. Express messengers from [Ichijō] Noriyasu, Military Aide Heiroku Tokisada, and Hitachibō Masaaki arrived. They brought the head of former Governor of Bizen Yukiie. . . .

Twenty-second day, sixth month. The express messenger from the Chief of the Imperial Stables of the Left [Ichijō Noriyasu] came from Kyoto. There was a report that the Governor of Iyo was living in hiding near Ninna Temple and Iwakura, so Secretary of the Criminal Bureau [Kajiwara] Tomokage, Lieutenant of the Middle Palace Guards [Gotō] Motokiyo, and other brave warriors were dispatched, but they found nothing. In the meantime there was rumor that some warrior monks on Mt. Hiei were taking care of him.

Tenth day, intercalary seventh month. An express messenger from the Chief of the Imperial Stables of the Left came. His letter said that the former Iyo governor's boy servant, Gorōmaru, had been arrested and questioned in detail; he said that the former governor had been hiding on the mountain until about the twentieth of the sixth month. If his confession were true, it would mean that Shunsō, Shōi, and Chūkyō, all warrior monks of Mt. Hiei, had been sympathetic to and supportive of him. Accordingly, the matter was brought to the attention of the head [of Enryaku Temple: Zengen] and the religious counselor to his majesty.[61] This was something of which his majesty, too, had been informed.

Also, Yoshitsune had the same name as his excellency, the Middle Captain of the Third Rank, so it was changed to Yoshiyuki.

"His excellency" here is Fujiwara no Yoshitsune (1169–1206), the second son of Kujō Kanezane. The two Yoshitsunes used different Chinese characters for their names, but one was an important aristocrat, the other a criminal: hence, the arbitrary change.

Who proposed the name change is a matter of speculation, but it may well have been Yoritomo. There is little doubt that he enjoyed ingratiating himself with Kanezane, a ranking aristocrat of the day. Four months earlier his recommendation had been accepted and Kanezane had become regent. Proposing to change his own brother's name because it sounded the same as that of a son of his admired friend would have been another nice gesture.

---

61. Jien (1155–1225). Later an archbishop, he brought together his brother, Kanezane, and Yoritomo. An accomplished poet, he wrote a history of Japan called *Gukanshō*.

As Yoritomo's irritation at the failure of anyone to capture his elusive brother grew, along with his suspicions of Kyoto people, a man by the name of Miyoshi Yoshinobu thought of pointing out—so the entry on the fifth of the eleventh month tells us—that Yoshitsune's new name, Yoshiyuki, could be interpreted to mean "going away without any mishap" and, therefore, "to be able to hide himself well." That was why, he said, Yoshitsune could not be captured. He brought the matter to Regent Kanezane, and Yoshitsune regained his original name—all in his absence.[62]

Twenty-sixth day, intercalary seventh month. A letter from the chief of the Imperial Stables of the Left came. In accordance with Gorōmaru's confession, the request was delivered to the head of the mountain [Zengen] that the monks sympathetic to the Governor of Iyo be lined up and handed over; thereupon, the head said that the fellow in question had already escaped. . . . Nevertheless, three were lined up and handed over as related to the fellow who had escaped, so these were given over to the Imperial Police. . . .

Twenty-second day, ninth month. Kasuya Tōta Arisue, in Kyoto, captured the Iyo governor's retainer, Hori Yatarō Kagemitsu [who had been hiding in Kyoto]. Also, at the Nakamikado Higashi no Tōin, he killed his retainer [Satō] Tadanobu. When Arisue raced to the place, Tadanobu, being naturally a tough soldier, fought back and could not be easily subdued. But the attack was made with a great number of people, so that in the end Tadanobu and his two servants killed themselves.

It is said that Tadanobu, who was with the Governor of Iyo for a number of years, had some time back parted with him near Uji, returned to Kyoto, visited a common married woman whom he used to meet secretly, and given her a letter. The woman showed the said letter to her husband at the time. The husband told this to Arisue, who, as a result, went to get the man.

Tadanobu used to be a close aide of General of the Eastern Pacification Headquarters [Fujiwara no] Hidehira. Back in the fourth year of Jishō [1180], when the Governor of Iyo left for Kantō, Hidehira

---

62. On the twenty-ninth of the eleventh month of the same year the court changed his name again—this time to Yoshiaki.

had selected him along with Tsugunobu from among his warriors known for their bravery and offered them to him.

Tenth day, second month [1187]. Former Governor of Iyo Yoshitsune managed to live in hiding in various places for some time and to escape time and again the punishing hands of his pursuers. Finally, after going through such provinces as Ise and Mino he reached Ōshū. This he did because he counted on the power and influence of Governor of Mutsu and Lay Priest [Fujiwara no] Hidehira. It is said that as he went, taking his wife, son, and daughter with him, all were either in the guise of itinerant mountain monk or child.

Fifth day, third month. Because various people's reports agreed that the Governor of Iyo was in Mutsu Province and that this was something Lay Priest Hidehira had arranged, his lordship had earlier told Kyoto to look into the matter closely. The commander of the Outer Palace Guards, Right Division [Noriyasu], said that, as a result, his majesty took some steps.

Eighth day. The Reverend Suō Shōkō, of Nara, had come in response to his lordship's summons. This is because he was the Iyo governor's teacher. For some days he had been in the custody of Koyama Shichirō Tomomitsu. Today the lord of second rank interviewed him and at once began questioning him. He said: "The Governor of Iyo is a criminal who wants to disturb our land. Accordingly, after he disappeared out of sight, his majesty has time and again commanded that he be hunted down in the mountains and valleys of all provinces and be killed. So everyone under heaven, high or low, has turned against him. Nonetheless, I have heard, Reverend, that you, alone, have not only offered prayers for him but also conspired to make arrangements for him. Would you explain to me what you mean by all this?"

Shōkō said in reply: "When the governor departed as Your Lordship's emissary to subjugate the Taira clan, I firmly agreed with him to pray that all his battles be completed without mishap. This I did with special concentration for some years. That was for the good of the country, was it not?

"When the governor had to hide himself because, he said, he was censured by Kantō, he came to Nara remembering our master-disciple relationship. At that time I gently advised him to be careful and remove himself from harm's way for the moment, so that he might have a chance to apologize to Your Lordship. I provided him with servant monks and sent him off to Iga Province. I have heard absolutely nothing from him since then.

"I did pray, yes, but not for rebellion; I did advise, but to placate his rebellious mind. Why should this be termed conspiracy?

"When you think of it, Your Excellency, the peace of Kantō is the result of the governor's military exploits, is it not? And yet you accepted slander, instantly forgot the services he had rendered, and took back the lands you had given him as a reward. Was it not natural for him, as a human being, to have rebellious thoughts?

"May I suggest, sir, that you reverse your attitude at once, decide to be reconciled with him, and call him back, so that the two of you may live like fish in the water? That is the correct way of ruling our nation. This I say not to defend myself, but because I seek some way of achieving national peace and quiet."

When he heard this, the lord of second rank understood the reverend's true intentions and asked him to become the resident monk of the Shōchōju-in[63] and concentrate on prayers for the prosperity of Kantō.

Fourth day, ninth month. Earlier, the lord of second rank had appealed to the court that Lay Priest Hidehira was protecting the former Governor of Iyo and contemplating rebellion. In response, the Office of the Retired Emperor had sent a letter of inquiry to Mutsu Province. At the same time, a runner had been sent from Kantō; he returned today. The word from Kyoto was that Hidehira had no designs to rebel. But the runner said that it appeared that he was already making preparations. Accordingly, the same runner was dispatched to Kyoto. He was to report what was happening in Ōshū.

Twenty-ninth day, tenth month. Today Lay Priest Hidehira died in his mansion in Hiraizumi, Mutsu Province. For some days he had been suffering from a serious disease. At the time of his death he left a will telling Yasuhira and his other sons to have the former Governor of Iyo succeed him as general and govern the province.[64]

Twenty-ninth day, second month [1188]. The commander of the Outer Palace Guards sent word that imperial messenger Shishō Kunimitsu and Officer of the Office of the Retired Emperor Kagehiro were going to be sent to Yasuhira, of Ōshū, concerning the former Governor of Iyo.

---

63. The temple earlier referred to as the South Holy Hall.
64. The will was ignored. Yasuhira, the second of Hidehira's three sons, succeeded him as head of the family and immediately put himself in intense conflict with his younger brother, Tadahira, who supported his father's wishes. In the end Yasuhira killed Tadahira before he himself was killed by Yoritomo.

Ninth day, fourth month. Officer Shishō Kunimitsu and Officer of the Office of the Retired Emperor Kagehiro left Kyoto on the twenty-second of the previous month. Their purpose was to order Yasuhira to arrest and hand over the Governor of Iyo. The two of them arrived in Kamakura today, carrying an imperial command and other documents from the Office of the Retired Emperor.

Twenty-second day, second month [1189]. His lordship dispatched to Kyoto a messenger [runner Tokizawa]. Since the Governor of Iyo had disappeared, the imperial handling of the matter had been lax and accommodating, so the man had been intent on criminal activities. His lordship said that the matter should be taken care of with urgency.

Twenty-fifth day. His lordship sent a messenger [runner Satonaga] to Ōshū. The purpose was to spy on Yasuhira's moves.

Twenty-second day, third month. Temple Administrator of Seishō-ji Hōkyō Shōkan came to Kyoto as a messenger. He presented his lordship's letter to the Governor-General of the Dazaifu and middle counselor. In it his lordship repeated his earlier request that Yasuhira's plea of innocence be accepted and that an Imperial command for pursuing and destroying him be issued immediately.

Twenty-second day, fourth month. The matter concerning the pursuit and destruction of the men of Ōshū was decided upon in the Imperial Palace earlier, on the ninth, with the assistant minister of the Treasury as presiding officer, even though the retired emperor was at Tennō Temple.

Thirtieth day, intercalary fourth month. Today, in Mutsu Province, Yasuhira attacked the Governor of Iyo. This he did in response to the imperial decision and the lord of second rank's order. The governor was in Secretary of Popular Affairs [Fujiwara no] Motonari's mansion at Koromogawa. Yasuhira, leading several hundred horsemen, raced to the place and fought. The governor's retainers tried to defend themselves, but all were killed. The governor went into the Buddhist Altar Hall, first killed his wife [twenty-two years old] and child [girl, four years old], and next committed suicide.

Thirteenth day, sixth month. Yasuhira's messenger, Nitta Kanja Takahira, brought the Iyo governor's head to the bay of Koshigoe and sent in a report. Accordingly, his lordship sent Wada Tarō Yoshimori and Kajiwara Heizō Kagetoki to the place for inspection. Each man wore a jacket and armor and was accompanied by twenty armored horsemen. The governor's head was placed in a tub lacquered black, immersed in excellent sake, and carried on the shoulders of two of Takahira's servants. Long ago, Lord Su even carried his own provisions himself; now Takahira had his men carry the governor's head. All those who watched this are said to have wiped their tears, soaking their sleeves.

KUSUNOKI MASASHIGE:
A GUERRILLA OF
UNFLINCHING LOYALTY

THE KAMAKURA BAKUFU (1185–1333), established by Minamoto no Yoritomo, never enjoyed the kind of systemic stability usually associated with the Tokugawa Bakufu (1603–1868). Yoritomo's practice of killing off potential political rivals[1] was entirely inherited by the Hōjō family that took over the military government as regents, and it could only have a splintering effect. Within the Hōjō family itself internecine struggles continued unchecked.

In the meantime, the imperial court, with institutional legitimacy as the true government, suffered from its own internal schisms, of which Kamakura was never loath to take advantage. However, even while the court remained deferential or acquiescent to Kamakura most of the time, there occasionally appeared men from among the aristocracy who became resentful enough of their secondary position to take action against Kamakura. Gotoba (1180–1239), who was installed as emperor in 1183 after his brother, Emperor Antoku, was taken out of Kyoto by the fleeing Taira clan, was one of them. In 1221 he, by then long "retired," raised an army against the Hōjō. He was easily defeated and exiled.

In 1331 Emperor Godaigo (1288–1339) took the same route. His military venture also ended in defeat; he was exiled, albeit briefly, and his imperial hegemony did not last long. But during the civil war touched off by his revolt a genius of guerrilla warfare emerged: Kusunoki Masashige (1294–1336). The following account of Masashige—the greatest nationalist hero until Japan's defeat in the Second World War—is taken from the *Taiheiki* (Chronicle of Great

---

1. In 1193, four years after killing Yoshitsune, Yoritomo had Noriyori murdered. He had started destroying powerful men in his own camp during the war against the Taira clan.

Peace), a historical narrative of Japan from 1318 to 1367.[2] A few abbreviated portions within the quoted narrative are bracketed.

Masashige's lineage given at the beginning of the account below has not been ascertained despite centuries of admiration for him and scholarly digging. Indeed, there are few facts recorded about Masashige before he came on the scene. One theory holds that he was able to wage the kind of guerrilla warfare he did because, beside being a free-moving warrior common at the time, he controlled an extensive commercial guild and had sufficient means of retaining the allegiance of a wide spectrum of people.

The account begins with Godaigo taking the unusual step of moving his court from Kyoto to a mountain temple to the south.

On the twenty-seventh of the eighth month in the first year of Genkō [1331], the emperor went to Kasagi Temple and established the Imperial Palace in its main hall. For the first few days, afraid of the power of the military government, not a single person came to visit. But after hearing that a Rokuhara force[3] was beaten in a battle at Higashi-Sakamoto, on Mt. Hiei, soldiers in provinces nearby, first among them the monks of this temple, began to gather in a hurry. Even so, not a single warrior of good repute came or a man with large holdings leading a hundred, two hundred, horsemen.

The emperor fretted that with such a puny force he would not even be able to protect the Imperial Palace. While so worried, he dozed and had a dream [revealing that something related to a camphor tree, *kusunoki*, might bring him luck]. When the day broke, he summoned a ranking monk of the temple's Jōju-bō and asked, "Is there a warrior by the name of Kusunoki near here?"

"I have yet to hear of a man nearby who bears that family name, Your Majesty," replied the monk. "However, to the west of Mt. Kongō, in Kawachi Province, there *is* a man called Kusunoki Tamon Masashige, of the Middle Palace Guards, and he has established his reputa-

---

2. The *Taiheiki*, which incorporates a number of legendary Chinese episodes, is studded with Chinese-style rhetorical flourishes. But dates and certain other factual data in the narrative are deemed surprisingly reliable. The book opens as Godaigo ascends the throne and ends as Hosokawa Yoriyuki assumes the regency for the third Ashikaga Shogun Yoshimitsu.

3. Rokuhara, east of Kyoto, had a *tandai*—Kamakura's outpost which was administrative, judicial, and, above all, military in nature. In one of the skirmishes a force supporting Emperor Godaigo defeated a Rokuhara unit.

tion in bow and arrow. He is a descendant of His Excellency Minister of the Left, of Ide, Tachibana no Moroe, a fourth grandson of Emperor Bitatsu, but it has been many years since he began living outside Kyoto. His mother, when young, went to pay her respects to Bisha-mon Temple on Mt. Shigi for a hundred consecutive days. As a result, she had an oracular dream and conceived him. That's why his boy-hood name was Tamon."

The emperor decided that this had to be the man revealed to him in his dream, and issued a command: "Summon him at once." Conse-quently, Kusunoki Masashige was quickly summoned, with Lord Fujifusa as imperial messenger.

When the imperial messenger carrying the command reached Kusunoki's fort and explained what happened in detail, Masashige thought that for a man of bow and arrow no honor could be greater than such a summons and, without further deliberation, came at once to Kasagi in secrecy. The emperor spoke through Lord Fujifusa:[4] "Concerning the punishment and subjugation of the Eastern barbar-ians,[5] His Majesty had a certain reason to turn to you, Masashige, and sent a messenger. He is deeply satisfied that you hurried to this place without wasting any time. Tell us your candid thoughts on the unifica-tion of our land: what schemes must be employed to win a swift victory and bring peace to the four seas."

Masashige respectfully replied: "Now that the Eastern barbar-ians' recent traitorous act has invited imperial censure, it should be easy to take advantage of their deteriorated and chaotic condition and punish them on His Majesty's behalf.

"In essence, for achieving the unification of our land we must have military power and strategic resourcefulness. If we fight them head-on in strength alone, it would be difficult to win even if we faced the provinces of Musashi and Sagami with all the soldiers of the sixty states combined. If we contest them with strategy, however, their might is likely to prove to be no more than a force that can shatter a sharp sword and break tough armor. It should be easy to defeat them, and there shouldn't be any need to fear them.

"Of course, since we are talking about war, please do not make up your mind by just looking at a victory or defeat in a single battle. As

---

4. An emperor normally spoke to his low-ranking subjects through an inter-mediary.

5. The Hōjō, because they operated out of the East.

long as you hear that Masashige—if only he—is still alive, please assume that luck will eventually be with the imperial force."

After making these reassuring remarks Masashige returned to Kawachi.

Kasagi Temple was on a craggy mountain so difficult to attack that the Rokuhara army had to spend almost a month doing little more than laying siege until, on the night of the twenty-eighth of the ninth month, a few men managed to scale a cliff and set fire to the temple. A few days later Emperor Godaigo was captured while straggling with a few of his men not far from Mt. Kasagi.

Long before then, in the middle of the ninth month, word had come to Rokuhara that Kusunoki Masashige had revolted, entrenching himself with 500 men on Mt. Akasaka. Meanwhile, notified of Godaigo's move Kamakura had begun sending large armies westward as early as the fifth of the ninth month.

The great host that came west from distant Eastern provinces were so sorely disappointed to learn that Kasagi Castle had fallen even before they entered Ōmi Province that none of them bothered to enter Kyoto. Instead, they headed for Akasaka Castle in which Kusunoki Masashige, of the Middle Palace Guards, had entrenched himself, some over the mountains of Iga and Ise, others crossing the roads of Uji and Daigo.

As they passed the riverbed of the Ishi River and looked up, they saw the castle was obviously a puny affair built in great haste: the moat wasn't carefully dug, the wooden fence was merely single-fold, and, within an enclosure one or two hundred yards square perhaps, twenty or thirty lookout towers were set up. Everyone who looked at it thought:

Well, what a pitiful enemy we've got here! I could grab the whole damned castle with one hand and throw it away, if that's what I wanted to. I wish by some kind of miracle Kusunoki could hold out for just one day, so I could get rewards for my booty and exploits!

So the attack force of 300,000 mounted soldiers jumped off and let go of their horses the moment they'd pressed close enough. They leapt into the moat, lined up under the towers, and began vying with one another to be the first to break in.

Now Masashige was someone who could "plot stratagems within his tents of encampment and ensure a victory a thousand miles away" as if born between the chests of Ch'en-p'ing and Chang-liang.[6] He had two hundred superb bowmen within the castle and had placed on a different mountain his own brother, Shichirō,[7] and Wada Gorō Masatō, accompanied by three hundred horsemen. The attackers never dreamed of any such thing. Furiously intent on breaking the castle in a single sweep, all at once a great many got to the bottom of the rising cliffs. Steady, rapid shooting began from atop the towers and through the openings. Within a short while those killed or wounded reached 1,000.

Thwarted, the men of the Eastern forces retreated somewhat from their initial attacking positions, saying among themselves, "No, sir, the way this castle is made, we can't possibly scale it in a day or two. Let's regroup, set up camp, and separately fight as called for." They took down the saddles off their horses, removed their armor, set up their tents, and rested in them.

Kusunoki Shichirō and Wada Gorō, who were looking down on all this from a distant mountain, decided that the time was right and divided their three hundred horsemen into two groups. Then, from the mountains to the east and the west, through the woods, carrying two banners with the chrysanthemum-on-the-water crest flapping through the pine wind, they advanced their horses quietly through swirls of mountain haze. The soldiers from the Eastern provinces saw them, and they were wondering whether they were the enemy or friendly forces, when the three hundred horsemen, from both sides, raised battle cries and, in wedge formations, galloped into the 300,000 soldiers massed like clouds. They raced to the east, west, south, north, brandishing their swords. A great many of the attackers were thrown into such consternation that they were unable to gather into formations.

At that juncture the three wooden gates of the castle suddenly opened at once and two hundred horsemen dashed out, shooting as fast as they could. The size of the attacking force was huge indeed, but they were so confounded that some jumped on their tethered horses and kicked and whipped them, while others tried to shoot from

---

6. "Plotting stratagems," etc., is a phrase in *Han Shu* (The History of the Former Han Dynasty). Ch'en-p'ing and Chang-liang are two strategists who served Kao-tsu, the founder of the Han Dynasty.

7. Masauji; later changed to Masasue.

unstrung bows. Several jumped onto a single suit of armor and squabbled over it, shouting, "It's mine!" Even while such things were happening, the attackers retreated to the riverbed of the Ishi River, scattering like baby spiders as they did so, some soldiers unaware that their master-commanders were killed, others that their own fathers were. The road of about three miles in between was so thickly strewn with abandoned horses and suits of armor that you couldn't step onto it without bumping into something. It appears that the people of the entire county of Tōjō enjoyed windfall profits.

The renowned Eastern soldiers had made an unexpected mistake and suffered a defeat in the initial battle. Perhaps because they decided as a result that Kusunoki's strategic resourcefulness couldn't be made light of, even though some advanced to Handa and Narabana[8] the main force did not seem eager to mount another attack soon. In the war council that was held, some argued that they should stay where they were for a while and, using guides from the region, cut down the trees on the mountains and burn down the houses to prevent a rear assault, and then attack the castle without any worry. But many among the soldiers from Honma and Shibuya[9] had had their fathers or sons killed, and these men were furious, saying, "What's the use of living on like this? We don't give a damn if anybody else comes with us. We'll just go attack them and die!" Prompted by these words, a great many raced forward.

The Akasaka Castle we've been talking about had rising layers of terraced paddies to the east, and it seemed somewhat difficult to attack it from that direction. But it was adjacent to flat land in the three other directions, and those sides were protected only, it seemed, by a single moat and a single-layer fence. That being the case, even if a demon or a god were inside, he couldn't possibly hold it for long, all the attacking soldiers thought, making light of the situation again. So the moment they reached where the castle was, they got into the moat, got to the other bank, and removed the obstacles, ready to climb up. But there was not a single sound from within the castle.

"This means," they decided, "that just like yesterday they're going to shoot at us and wound many, and when we start to run in confusion, they will release a force for a rear attack and throw us into chaotic battle."

---

8. Villages east of Akasaka.
9. Place-names in Sagami Province.

So the attackers divided themselves into a group of 100,000, which was directed toward the mountain at the rear, and a group consisting of the remaining 200,000, which surrounded the castle like rice, hemp, bamboos, or reeds. Even then, there was not a single arrow shot out of the castle nor was a single man seen. Emboldened by this, the attackers grabbed onto the fence to climb over it. Actually, though, the fence was two-layered, the outer layer to be cut off and dropped. Indeed, men within the castle simultaneously cut the ropes tying the outer fence on all four sides, so that the 1,000 attackers who had held onto the fence fell as if under a weight, and while they were pinned down, only their eyes moving, large logs and large rocks were thrown and hurled at them. As a result, in the battle this day seven hundred attackers were killed.

Punished as they were in battle for two consecutive days, not one among the many soldiers from the Eastern provinces was now willing to attack the castle. They set up camp in places near it, merely laying siege from a distance. They remained in that state for four or five days, but then they began to think: "It isn't manly to maintain such a passive offense. This is a castle on flat land with a circumference of less than four hundred yards, and only four or five hundred men are entrenched in it. If we, soldiers from the eight eastern provinces, are unable to attack it but end up merely laying siege, it will be the sort of disgrace for which people will make a laughingstock of us in years to come. This won't do.

"Come to think of it, before, we were so excited that we attacked without carrying shields or preparing proper attack weapons. That's why we created casualties uselessly. This time we'll change our approach."

So all the attacking soldiers were made to hold overhead shields to which hardened leather was nailed to make them hard to break. And even though it would have been easy to jump onto the fence because neither was the moat deep nor the bank high, in case the fence was again a hanging one they did not try to hold onto it thoughtlessly. Instead, standing in the moat they tried to pull it down with rakes. When it appeared that the fence was about to be torn down, however, men in the castle dipped up boiling water with three- to six-yard long ladles and poured it on the attackers. The boiling water got through the holes in their helmet-tops and the spaces in their shoulder-guards and burned them. Unable to bear it, the attackers dropped their rakes and shields and suddenly retreated, presenting a ludicrous spectacle. Even though no one really died on the spot, some had their arms and legs burned and could not stand, while others became ill with their whole bodies injured, and these numbered a couple of hundred.

The attackers had attacked with a new approach, and those in the castle had defended themselves with a new stratagem. The council decided that now there was nothing special that could be done but to wait until the enemy's food ran out. After this decision they altogether gave up any kind of battle; instead, they built a lookout tower in each camp and constructed obstacles around it as they laid siege. As a result, the warriors in the castle began to lose their mettle, with little to divert them.

Kusunoki had built this castle in great haste, with no time to prepare adequate provisions. In a mere twenty days after the battle had started and the castle was surrounded, there were only four or five days' worth of provisions left in the castle. So Masashige faced his men and said:

"We've won several battles and destroyed countless enemies. But their number is so great they didn't think anything of it. Meanwhile we're running out of food and there isn't any rescue force. Since I was the first among the soldiers of this country to rise with a decision to help His Majesty unify the land, I wouldn't hesitate to give up my life if the time was right and the act was just. Still, a courageous warrior is someone who takes precautions on an important occasion and chooses to plot things out.[10] For this reason I, Masashige, would like to let this castle be taken and make the enemy assume that I have committed suicide. Let me explain why.

"If they find out that I have committed suicide, the men from the Eastern provinces will be overjoyed and return to their lands. When they have, I'll come out and fight; if they come back here, I'll again withdraw into deep mountains. If I annoy the forces from the East in this fashion four or five times, they're bound to become exhausted. This is how by preserving myself I plan to destroy the enemy. Gentlemen, what do you think of this?"

His men gave him full assent, so at once they dug a large hole about ten feet deep in the castle, picked up twenty to thirty corpses from those killed and lying in the moat, threw them into the hole, piled up charcoal and firewood on top of them, and waited for a night

---

10. The Confucian *Analects* has a sentence: "Make sure to take precautions on an important occasion and choose to plot things out."

of powerful wind and rain. Masashige's fortune must have been what Heaven favored. A sudden wind began kicking up sand and the rain that also started fell like bamboos shot down from the sky. The night was pitch dark, and everyone closed up his tent.

It was exactly the kind of night they had been waiting for. Masashige left a man in the castle with the instruction: "When you have determined that we are four or five hundred yards away from here, set fire to the castle." Then the men removed their armor and left in fives and threes, mingling with the attackers, quietly passing by the officers' quarters and the pillows of the soldiers lying asleep.

When Masashige was passing in front of Captain of the Imperial Police Nagasaki Takasada's stable, an enemy soldier spotted him and asked, "Sir, why are you passing in front of our officer's quarters without announcing your name and so surreptitiously?"

"I'm one of the general's retainers, but I lost my way," Masashige said as he quickly walked away. The one who tried to stop him cried, "He's damned suspicious! I'm sure he's a horse thief. Shoot him dead!" And he himself ran up close and shot at him. The arrow struck Masashige's elbow and should have implanted itself deeply, but it did not; it bounced back, its direction reversed. Later, when Masashige checked the spot, he saw that the arrow had struck where he carried a talisman containing the Sutra of the Bodhisattva Avalokitesvara that he had believed in and read for many years. In effect, miraculous though it may seem, the poem in two phrases in praise of the bodhisattva[11] had blocked the tip of the arrow.

So escaping death to be brought by a deadly arrow, Masashige went on about 2,000 yards, then turned back to look. As had been agreed upon, the man left behind had already set fire to the officers' quarters in the castle. The men on the attacking forces were startled by the fire and raised battle cries: "Look, the castle's fallen! Don't let a single man get away!" They made a big commotion among themselves. When the fire quieted down and they went into the castle to check, they found a number of corpses burned in a large hole stacked with charcoal. When they saw this, there was not one among the many who did not praise Masashige, saying, "Poor fellow! He committed suicide. Though our enemy, he met his death with dignity as a man of bow and arrow."

---

11. "If you intently praise the Lord, the Bodhisattva Avalokitesvara will in the end hear your voice and absolve you of all sufferings."

On the fifth of the third month of the second year of Genkō [1332], Lieutenant of the Inner Palace Guards, Left Division, Tokimasu and Echigo Governor Nakatoki were appointed to the two Rokuhara offices and arrived from Kantō. For the last three or four years Suruga Governor Tokiwa Norisada had administered the two Rokuhara offices by himself, but he had firmly refused to continue, it was said.

Kusunoki Masashige, of the Middle Palace Guards, had let on in the previous year that he committed suicide and had his body burned at Akasaka Castle. The military government accepted this as fact, installed Yuasa Magoroku, the lay priest Jōbutsu, as constable in his place, and was satisfied in its belief that there would no longer be anything untoward in Kawachi Province. But, on the third of the fourth month, Kusunoki suddenly materialized leading 500 horsemen, broke into Yuasa's castle, and carried out a breathtaking assault.

Perhaps because Yuasa did not have adequate provisions on hand in the castle, he planned to have several hundred laborers carry provisions from Azegawa, his own land in Kii Province, and let them into the castle during the night. When Kusunoki got wind of this, he placed his soldiers at a strategic point, had them rob all the provisions and replace the contents of the rice bags with armor and weapons. These men then had horses and laborers carry those bags, with a couple of hundred of them accompanying them, pretending to be their guards. As they were about to get into the castle, Kusunoki put on a show of driving them away, starting a round of chasing and being chased among his own men.

Yuasa saw this and decided that the soldiers trying to bring in his provisions were fighting Kusunoki's force. He dashed out of the castle, and brought in all those enemy soldiers he shouldn't have. Kusunoki's men, having gotten into the castle as planned, quietly took out their armor and weapons from the rice bags and, after fully equipping themselves, raised a battle cry. In response, the men outside broke down the wooden gates or climbed in over the fence. Surrounded by the enemy both inside and outside the castle, Yuasa had no way of fighting and promptly surrendered.

Kusunoki added Yuasa's men to his own, making a force of seven hundred horsemen. With these he made the two provinces of Izumi and Kawachi follow his bidding, creating an even larger force. So on the seventeenth of the fifth month, he advanced close to Sumiyoshi and Tennō temples and took up a position south of the bridge at Watanabe.

While he was doing this, one express rider after another galloped from Izumi and Kawachi, reporting that Kusunoki was about to attack Kyoto. This threw the capital into considerable turmoil. The warriors raced to the east and to the west, and both the high and the low became miserably confounded. Even so, an amazing number of soldiers from in and out of the Kinai region gathered to the two Rokuhara outposts, and these waited for Kusunoki to come to attack Kyoto imminently. But there was no such sign. In the end they decided that contrary to what they had heard, Kusunoki's forces had to be small and that they themselves might as well go forward, attack, and crush him. The two Rokuhara commanders appointed Suda and Takahashi marshals and, joining together the soldiers of the forty-eight "watch-fire posts," those stationed in Kyoto, and men from the Kinai region, sent them off toward Tennō Temple. These totaled 5,000. They left Kyoto on the twentieth of the same month, took up positions in Amagasaki, Kanzaki, and Hashiramoto, and spent the night burning watch-fires, impatiently waiting for the day to break.

When Kusunoki learned of this, he divided his 2,000 horsemen into three groups, hid these main forces in Sumiyoshi and Tennō temples, and kept only about three hundred lined up south of the bridge at Watanabe with a couple of large watch-fires burning. His aim was, he said, to induce the enemy to cross the bridge, drive them into the deeper part of the water, and decide the outcome of the battle at once.

The day broke on the twenty-first of the fifth month. The 5,000 horsemen from Rokuhara, combining all the forces from various positions into a single unit, came to the bridge at Watanabe and surveyed the enemy forces facing them on the other side of the river. There were only a couple of hundred of them, and these *soldiers* were riding skinny horses, using straw ropes for reins. When Suda and Takahashi saw this, they said to themselves:

"This is just what we had expected. These bastards from Izumi and Kawachi are puny nothings. There isn't a single worthy man in the enemy force. We'll capture every one of them and hang their heads at the gallows at Rokujō Kawara.[12] That should gain us a lot of gratitude from the lords of Rokuhara!"

Even before they finished saying this, they dashed straight across the bridge, unaccompanied by a single man. Seeing this, the

---

12. A traditional execution ground on the Kamo River. See p. 123.

5,000 riders vied with one another in advancing their horses, some making them walk on the bridge, others making them wade through the shallows, before scrambling up the other shore. Kusunoki's men shot a couple of arrows from a distance, but without engaging in a single battle started to withdraw toward Tennō Temple. The Rokuhara forces, emboldened by what they took to be a winning momentum, chased after them, galloping breathlessly, chaotically, until they reached the farmhouses north of Tennō Temple.

Kusunoki, having decided that he had tired out the enemy forces, both men and horses, as much as he wanted, sent one group from the 2,000 men he had divided into three galloping out of the east side of Tennō Temple to face the enemy to the left; one group galloping out of the stone torii at the West Gate in a wedge-shaped formation; and one group galloping out of the pine trees of Sumiyoshi to make a crane-wing formation.

The Rokuhara forces were so much larger in comparison as to seem impossible to oppose, but they were so clumsy in their groupings that it now looked as if they had been surrounded by a much bigger force. Suda and Takahashi issued a command:

"The enemy has trapped us with a large force hidden in the rear. This ground is poor footing for the horses and we won't be able to fight. Lead the enemy out into the open, size up the condition of each force, and fight them again and again until we win!"

But the 5,000 soldiers, afraid their rear might be cut off, started to retreat toward the bridge at Watanabe. The Kusunoki forces took advantage of this and, raising battle cries, chased them from three directions. Near the bridge, when Suda and Takahashi saw the actual size of the Kusunoki forces, they galloped back and forth, back and forth, barking a command, "The enemy isn't large! Turn back and fight! You can't have a large river at your rear! Turn back, turn back!"

But now that a great many people were on the retreat, no one turned back, but everybody raced toward the bridge, ignoring its precarious condition. As a result, countless men and horses fell from the bridge and drowned. Even among those who tried to wade across the river, some who did not know where the water was deep or shallow died in the process. Some fell with their horses as they tried to ride down the bank and were shot on the spot. There were many who abandoned their horses and armor and tried to run, but not one tried to turn back and fight. So only a greatly reduced portion of the 5,000 horsemen scrambled back to Kyoto. The next day, who did it we don't

know, but a high notice board was put up at Rokujō Kawara with a
tanka verse written on it:

> *Watanabe no mizu ika bakari hayakereba*
> *Takahashi ochite Suda nagaruran*

> How rapid was the water at the crossing?
> The high bridge fell down and a corner field flowed away[13]

As was the habit among Kyoto children, this satiric piece was
turned into a song and sung or otherwise bounced back and forth with
laughter. As a result, Suda and Takahashi lost face, and they did not go
to their offices, feigning illness.

The two Rokuhara officers were disquieted to hear this and held a
council to mount another attack. They invited to the council Assistant
Minister of Civil Administration Utsunomiya who was in Kyoto, sent by
Kantō because the capital was too defenseless, and said to him:

"We know that, as has happened since ancient days, winning or
losing in battle sometimes depends on luck. Nevertheless, we lost in
the recent battle in the south because of our commanders' tactical
clumsiness, and also because of our soldiers' cowardice. So many in
the land ridicule us that there's no way of shutting their mouths.

"Now Kantō sent you here, sir, even after they sent Nakatoki, so
that you would pacify any criminal uprising. As things stand now, we
don't believe we can put up a meaningful fight no matter how many
times we gather together the defeated soldiers and send them off.
This, then, is a time of grave national crisis. Please, sir, sally forth and
eliminate the criminal."

Utsunomiya, showing no inclination whatsoever to decline, said:

"I do wonder about the advisability of sallying out with a small
force after a large one was defeated. However, ever since I left Kantō I
have been of a mind to think nothing of my own life in a time of crisis
like this. At this moment I'm in no position to tell whether I can win or
lose in battle. So I will simply go out to engage in battle, even by
myself. If I face any difficulty then, I may ask you for reinforcements."

With these words Utsunomiya left, looking grave and determined. Now that he was going to face a great enemy at the order of the

---

13. The original 5–7–5–7–7–syllable verse cleverly puns on three names: Watanabe
(crossing), Takahashi (high bridge), and Suda (corner field). Suda may also suggest
sudaku, "to gather in great numbers."

military government and had no intention of valuing his life, he did not even bother to return to the place where he was staying, but immediately after leaving Rokuhara he left the capital, around noon, of the nineteenth of the seventh month, and headed for Tennō Temple.

As far as Tō Temple, his force seemed to consist of only fourteen or fifteen riders, master and servants combined. But as his men, who were scattered throughout the capital, raced to join him, by the time he reached Yotsuzuka and Tsukurimichi he had 500 men. As they rode forward, they robbed horses from the people they met on the road, whether or not they were of families of influence and power, and drove off their laborers. As a result, travelers changed their routes and village people shut up their houses.

That night they took up a position in Hashiramoto and waited for the day to break. Not one of them thought they would return alive.

When Wada Magozaburō, a resident of Kawachi Province, heard about this, he came to Kusunoki and said:

"Sir, I understand Kyoto was incensed by its defeat in the battle the other day and has sent down Utsunomiya. Tonight he has arrived in Hashiramoto, but I hear his force is made up of no more than six or seven hundred horsemen. Even when we faced Suda and Takahashi's 5,000, we made them scamper away with a small force. Besides, we now have a winning momentum and our force is much greater, while our enemy, having lost his momentum, is small. No matter how masterful a soldier Utsunomiya may be, he shouldn't be able to do much. What would you say, sir, about attacking him tonight and making him run?"

Kusunoki pondered the matter for a while and said:

"Victory or defeat in battle doesn't necessarily depend on the size of the forces involved. The question is whether or not the officers and their men are united in their minds. This is why it's said, 'Make light of a great enemy; be fearful of a small force.'

"Now, when you think of it, Utsunomiya by himself has come forward to face me with a small force after a far larger force suffered defeat and retreated in the previous battle. This means there isn't a single man on his force who wants to return alive. On top of that, Utsunomiya is the best handler of bow and arrow in the Kantō. And the soldiers of the Ki and Kiyohara clans[14] think of their own lives so

---

14. The two clans served the Utsunomiya family.

lightly in a battlefield that they regard them as less worthy than dust. If seven hundred of these men fought with a single mind to decide the outcome, most of the soldiers on our side would be killed even if they had no mind to retreat.

"The fate of our land should not depend on this battle. We are bound to have to fight far into the future. If most of our soldiers are killed in initial battles, when we don't have many of them in the first place, who will come to help us in later battles? It's said, 'A good commander wins without fighting.' I'd like to follow this dictum for now and deliberately decamp and retreat tomorrow. That way we can make our enemy think he has earned an honor. Then, four or five days later, we'll light up watch-fires on the surrounding hills and give him a 'roast.' If we do that, it's just the Kantō warriors' habit—they're bound to get tired of the whole affair and everyone will begin to say, 'No, no, it's no good staying here for so long. We better go while we still have our honor.'

"The saying, 'Advancing or retreating depends on the occasion,' speaks of a situation like this. Look, it's almost daybreak. I'm certain that our enemy is very close to us now. Come along with me."

And so Kusunoki left Tennō Temple. Wada and Yuasa also withdrew, along with their men.

As the day began to break, Utsunomiya pushed forward to Tennō Temple with a force of seven hundred horsemen, set fire to the houses in Kōzu, and raised a battle cry. But no enemy came out because there were none of them there.

"They must be trapping us," Utsunomiya said, and gave an order: "The land around here has poor footing for horses and the roads are narrow. Don't allow the enemy to gallop into the midst of you and divide you or allow them to surround you from the rear!"

The Ki and Kiyohara men, their horses' feet aligned, galloped into the temple from the east and and west entrances. They repeated this maneuver a couple of times, but not a single enemy was there, only some embers left in the watch-fires burned out and abandoned in the gradually whitening night.

Utsunomiya felt he'd earned a victory even before fighting. He dismounted in front of the main hall, prostrated himself, and offered prayers to Prince Jōgū.[15] "This has not been brought about because of

---

15. Another name of Prince Shōtoku (574–622), who wrote Japan's first constitution. A devout Buddhist, he built Tennō and other temples.

my military strength, but because of the protection of the deities and buddhas"—as he intently thought this, he became blissful.

Soon he dispatched an express rider to Kyoto to report, "We have driven away the enemy at Tennō Temple in short order." There was no one among the many who heard the news—from the two officers of Rokuhara on down to the common soldiers of the hereditary and non-hereditary retainers—who did not praise him for his outstanding act.

Still, while feeling that he had made the enemy at Tennō Temple scamper away and thereby earned honor, Utsunomiya knew that with his small force he could not simply go ahead and march into the enemy camp; he also knew that he would not feel right if he went back without waging a real battle.

Even while he was trying to resolve this dilemma, four or five days passed. Then Wada and Kusunoki, who had rounded up four or five thousand warrior-bandits[16] in Izumi and Kawachi to join them, sent them, along with a couple of hundred soldiers, to the area surrounding Tennō Temple, and had them light up watch-fires. Utsunomiya's men were thrown into turmoil, exclaiming, "Look, the enemy has come out!"

As they watched in the gathering darkness, the fires visible in Akishino and Toyama villages and on the hills of Ikoma were more numerous than the stars on a clear night, and the watch-fires lit on the bay of Shigizu noted for its seaweed, as well as in Sumiyoshi and Namba villages, looked as if they would burn up the waves like the fishing fires burned on fishing boats. Throughout the hills and bays found in Yamato, Kawachi, and Kii provinces there was not a single spot where a watch-fire wasn't lighted. There were so many of them that the estimate of the enemy force ran to several tens of thousand.

This went on for three nights. And the watch-fires gradually came closer so that they seemed to begin to fill the entire universe—from the east and west to the south and north, from the northwest and southwest to the northeast and southeast, not to mention above and below—as if dark night was replaced by bright day.

Watching this, Utsunomiya was resolved to quickly settle the victory or defeat if the enemy came forward. He waited, with the saddle kept on his horse, the outer strap on his armor untied. But there

---

16. *Nobushi,* peasants and samurai who have become marauding bandits. In the age of great social upheaval the line between samurai and bandit must often have been thin. Masashige's father may have been classifiable as a "warrior-bandit" at one point.

was no battle, though the enemy kept up pressure. Utsunomiya's courage began to wear down, his spirit to fight to soften, and in the end a desire grew to just call it off and retreat.

At that point the men from the Ki and Kiyohara clans said, "In the end we wonder if it's a good idea to face a great enemy with our kind of small force. Let's say we earned some honor the other day when we drove our enemy off from this spot, and go back to Kyoto."

Everyone agreed to this proposal. And as Utsunomiya withdrew from Tennō Temple at midnight, on the twenty-seventh of the seventh month, and returned to Kyoto, early morning the very next day Kusunoki came back to replace him. Truly, if Kusunoki and Utsunomiya had fought to determine the outcome, it would have been a battle of two tigers or two dragons, ending in the death of both. Perhaps because the two of them thought this, Kusunoki withdrew once to plot stratagems 1,000 miles away, while Utsunomiya also withdrew once without losing his honor after a battle. There was not one man in the world who did not praise them as outstanding commanders of deep insight and far-reaching planning.

As time passed, people of considerable means, not only of nearby provinces but also of far-off lands, began to hear that Kusunoki Masashige, of the Middle Palace Guards, out at Tennō Temple, exercised enormous power but never gave trouble to ordinary people while remaining deferential and considerate to his officers and soldiers. As a result, a great many gathered to join him, in the end making his force so strong and large that it appeared difficult for Kyoto to send a punitive army against him with any ease.

There were no decisive battles throughout the year, but uprisings near Kyoto became so frequent that in the ninth month and the tenth month, 1332, Kamakura again dispatched large armies. In early 1333 these forces moved against three main targets: Akasaka Castle, now defended by the lay priest Hirano Shōgen, Yoshino Castle, defended by Prince Morinaga,[17] and Chihaya Castle, defended by Masashige.

---

17. Godaigo's son (1308–35) who abandoned the priesthood to work to defeat the Kamakura Bakufu. He succeeded in rounding up a good deal of support for the cause, briefly served as shogun, but was eventually arrested and killed. He is called Prince Otō.

Akasaka fell on the twenty-seventh of the second month, Yoshino on the first of the intercalary second month. What Hirano said to the enemy commander in surrendering—rather than fighting to the last man—tells a good deal about the unsteady state of personal allegiance of the fighting men. He said:

"Because Kusunoki subjugated the two provinces of Izumi and Kawachi and began to wield enormous power, I joined your enemy, against my own wishes, in order to get out of the predicament for the time being. I had meant to come to Kyoto to explain this in detail, but before I managed to do that, you came with a great force to press upon me."

The surrender was a mistake. Contrary to the enemy commander's promise of rewards and leniency, all two hundred two soldiers defending Akasaka Castle were bound up as criminals upon their surrender, sent to Kyoto, and beheaded at Rokujō Kawara.

Now the assault on Chihaya Castle began.

The attackers of Chihaya Castle numbered a million as the forces against Akasaka and those against Yoshino galloped to join the 800,000 that had headed there from the outset.[18] These packed the space for five to seven miles from the castle on all four sides, like the viewers of sumō wrestling leaving not an inch of ground unoccupied. The banners and flags flapping in the wind were more numerous than the pampas grass in an autumn field, while the swords reflecting the sun and glinting looked like the frost carpeting the withered grass at daybreak. Each time a great army moved, a mountain shifted its position; each time a battle cry rose, trembling, the axis of the earth shattered in an instant. Kusunoki, unafraid of such a force, putting up a defense in his castle with a small force of less than 1,000, with no one to count on or wait for, truly had an indomitable mind.

This castle had, to the east and the west, deep valleys cutting so steeply that there was no way of climbing them. To the south and the north, it lay contiguous to Mt. Kongō with peaks soaring high. Nevertheless, it was a small castle about two hundred yards high and with a circumference of two miles. So the attackers thought nothing of it,

18. The size of the Kamakura forces tends to be greatly exaggerated with Chinese-style hyperbole. It may be kept in mind, however, that any large military unit in those days was an assemblage of opportunistic groups whose numbers greatly fluctuated at a moment's notice.

making light of the situation. For the first couple of days they didn't even bother to set up their camps or prepare attack devices.

Indeed, many vied with one another climbing up to the wooden gates of the castle. The men in the castle were not at all perturbed by this but kept quiet. They simply threw down large rocks from the towers, shattering shields, and, as the men below moved about in aimless confusion, shot at them rapidly. Men tumbled down the slopes on all sides, falling on one another, wounded and dying. The number of these reached five to six thousand a day. Lieutenant of the Outer Palace Guards, Left Division, Nagasaki Shirō, being a marshal and required to make eyewitness records of casualties, had to keep twelve scribes plying their brushes without respite for three days and nights.[19] Consequently, an announcement was circulated: "Henceforth any soldier who engages in battle without a general's permission shall be punished." Thereupon the attacking forces suspended fighting for a while and concentrated on building their camps.

Now Kanazawa Umanosuke, the general at Akasaka, turned to Osaragi and Ōshū and made this statement:

"The other day we brought down Akasaka Castle, but that we managed to do not because of any exploits of our soldiers. We guessed the layout within the castle and stopped the water supplies, and that made our enemy surrender.

"When you look at the castle here, you can't believe that it has a stream of water coming into it, sitting as it does on such a small space on a hilltop. Also, there isn't any device for getting elevated water from a different mountain, either. The reason they still seem to have plentiful water is, I think, that every night they go down to get valley water running at the base of the mountain to the east. I suggest, then, that you order a couple of your able commanders to prevent them from getting the water."

"We agree entirely with you, sir," the two generals said. They then had Echizen Governor Nagoya set aside 3,000 men and, with him as general, take up a position near the water, with obstacles constructed along the paths that people from the castle were likely to take.

It happens that Kusunoki, a man endowed both with courage and resourceful thinking, had checked, when he began building this

---

19. One such record surviving from this battle concerns Kumagae Naotsune, a descendant of Kumagae Naozane (see p. 116). It details the wounds that he and his flag carrier sustained. Each wound was worth a reward.

castle, if there was a continuous supply of water. He had found that on top of the hill were five hidden water holes, which itinerant mountain monks passing it used secretly and which produced about 250 gallons of water a night. These holes never dried up even during the worst drought, and in ordinary circumstances the water from them should have been adequate to quench his men's thirst.

But during battle water was also needed to put out fires and people became thirsty far more frequently than usual. With this thought he decided that this water supply by itself would be inadequate. He had two or three hundred boat-shaped tubs carved out of large trees and filled them with water. In addition, he had the gutters of all the several hundred shacks linked up in such a way that all the rainwater could go to the tubs without a drop being wasted. At the same time, clay was laid at the bottom of each tub to prevent the water from going bad. With all this water it should be possible to hold out for fifty to sixty rainless days. And, anyway, if you waited that long, there was bound to be another rainfall.

Such was the profound thinking with which Kusunoki reasoned things out. Because of this people in the castle did not have to get water from the valley.

Meanwhile, the soldiers assigned to block the water would tense up every night, expecting men to come down at any moment. But that was at first. Later, they gradually became lax and, with the tension gone and deciding in the end that no one was coming down to get water, they began to neglect taking precautions.

Having observed this carefully, Kusunoki lined up a couple of hundred reliable bowmen and sent them down from the castle one night. With the day yet to break wholly under eastern clouds, these men pressed forward hidden in the mist, cut down the twenty-odd men standing watch near the water, following this up with a relentless attack with swords. Governor of Echizen Nagoya was unable to hold them back, and withdrew to his camp. Learning about this, several tens of thousand men among the attackers wanted to rush to fight. But the path was on the other side of the valley and trailed narrowly along the base of a hill. So not many soldiers managed to get there. While this was going on, Kusunoki's men picked up the abandoned flags and large-size tents and calmly went back to their castle.

The next day flags with a three-umbrella crest were raised and tents with the same crest spread above the main gate of the castle. Then soldiers inside called out and roared with laughter:

"Sir, these are all flags Lord Nagoya was kind enough to present us with, but they carry his lordship's family crest and are useless to others. May we perhaps suggest that some of his retainers come into our place to collect them?"

When worthy warriors saw this they all said, "Heavens, what a terrible embarrassment to Lord Nagoya!"

The members of the Nagoya family, greatly disquieted by this, barked an order: "All the men of our forces shall die, without exception, at the wooden gate of the castle!"

Accordingly, the 5,000 men of Nagoya's forces, with grim determination and utterly ignoring those who were shot and killed, rode again and again over dead bodies, tore away the first layer of obstacles, and many finally managed to reach the base of the other cliff of the moat. But the cliff was high and steep, and, for all the desperate drive they had, they were unable to climb it. They just glared up at the castle, trying to contain their anger, panting.

At that moment, about ten large trees laid at the top of the cliff were cut off and dropped, crushing and knocking down and killing four or five hundred attackers in swift succession. Even while the remaining soldiers were struggling chaotically to escape a similar fate, men on the towers in all directions shot directly down at them as they pleased, leaving few of the 5,000 untouched.

With that the battle of the day was over. But because these men, for all their furious bravery, did not accomplish anything great but allowed so many to perish, people never stopped saying, "Poor fellows! That's injury added to disgrace!"

Having seen these unusual battles, the attackers must have decided they should not take the enemy casually. Unlike the initial stage there was no longer anyone who would bravely volunteer to lead an attack.

Lieutenant of the Outer Palace Guards, Left Division, Nagasaki Shirō assessed the situation and issued an order: "Attacking this castle with sheer might alone will merely produce casualties and accomplish little. Simply lay siege until their food runs out."

As the fighting stopped entirely, the men soon had to fight unbearable boredom. So *renga* masters of the orthodox school[20] were summoned from Kyoto, and rounds totaling 10,000 verse links started.

---

20. *Hana no moto no renga-shi*. About *renga* (linked verse), see the Introduction, p. xxvii–xxix.

The opening verse on the first day was by Nagasaki Kurō Moromune, of the Outer Palace Guards, and went like this:

Sakigakete katsu iro mise yo yamazakura

Be first and show us your winning color, mountain cherry[21]

Lieutenant of the Outer Palace Guards, Right Division, Kudō Jirō responded with the second, which went:

arashi ya hana no kataki naruran

a storm is your enemy, I must say

Truly, both verses were skillful in the use of puns and they read elegantly indeed. But people realized later that by comparing the enemy to a storm when the first verse depicted the friendly forces as cherry blossoms, the second one ended up using expressions that ought to have been avoided.[22]

At any rate, because the entire army followed a general's order and stopped fighting, they must have found not many worthy ways of diverting themselves; while some spent whole days playing go and backgammon, others whiled away the nights indulging in contests such as "a hundred-tea tasting" and verse-matching. The soldiers in the castle became all the more annoyed by this, they themselves having no means of distraction.

When some time passed in that fashion, Masashige said, "Well now, friends, let's trick our attackers again and shake them out of their sleep."

He had twenty to thirty life-size dolls made with garbage, put suits of armor on them, and attached weapons to them. He then had these dolls placed at the base of the castle during the night, with foldable shields erected in front and, deployed behind them, 500 carefully selected soldiers.

---

21. In the original, *sakigake*, "to be first," means, in the military jargon of the day, "to ride out or run out ahead of everyone else to reach the enemy ground," an act traditionally regarded as highly commendable and honorable, although, as this account shows, it began to be discredited during this period. The word *katsu*, "to win," also has an obvious military association.

22. By following an utterly conventional (and safe) poetic notion that a storm is a foe of cherry blossoms in bloom, this one inadvertently manages to reverse the auspicious idea given in the opening verse.

As the night gradually turned light through the haze, the soldiers all at once raised a battle cry. When the attackers on all sides heard it, they raced to attack, shouting, "They're out of the castle! They're in their last desperate frenzy! They're finished!"

As arranged beforehand, Kusunoki's men at first pretended they were there to fight with arrows, thereby attracting more and more enemy soldiers. But they gradually climbed into the castle in small groups, leaving only the dolls behind the trees. The attackers, thinking that the dolls were real soldiers, gathered to kill them. Masashige, drawing them as close as planned, suddenly launched forty to fifty large rocks simultaneously. Three hundred of those gathered near were killed instantly, with the number of men gravely wounded reaching 500.

When examined after the battle, none of the soldiers who had seemed to be truly formidable men, never retreating a step, turned out not to be humans but dolls made of straw. The many men who had gathered to kill them but had been killed instead, struck with rocks or shot by arrows, could not add their deaths to their honor, while those who had been too afraid of them to go close merely ended up exposing their timidity, to their embarrassment. Either way, both groups became laughingstocks for all the people. . . .

On the fourth of the third month of the same year, an express messenger arrived from Kantō with an order, "You shall not suspend battle and spend your days uselessly." In response, the principal generals held a council and worked out a scheme: They would span a bridge over the deep moat steeply cut between this side and the enemy castle and send soldiers across it into the castle. For this purpose they summoned 500 carpenters from Kyoto and had them assemble lumber five or six, eight or nine inches thick and build a suspension bridge five yards wide and sixty yards long.

When the bridge was ready, two to three thousand thick ropes were tied to it, and it was pulled up erect with pulleys, then one end of it was dropped on the top of the cliff across the moat. It was so well built that one wondered if Lu Pan's "bridge to the clouds"[23] was perhaps something like it. In no time several thousand excited soldiers jumped on it and started to run up. Now the castle's fall appeared imminent.

But Kusunoki had made preparations for this. His men lit throw-torches, threw them onto the bridge in such a way as to make stacks of

---

23. Lu Pan, a master carpenter of Lu, is reputed to have made a ladder extendible to the clouds when his king was attacking Sung.

firewood on it, then directed at them torrents of oil with pumps. As a result, the fire started to burn the bridge girders, and the wind from the valley spread the flames. The soldiers who had first started to cross the bridge without much thought would have burned themselves in the raging fire if they advanced further, whereas they could not really turn back even if they tried to because those immediately behind them kept pushing them, not realizing what the difficulty was. Jump off the side they could not: It was too scary, the valley too deep with crags soaring in it. They were not in that writhing predicament for long, pushing and shoving, before the burning bridge broke in the middle and smashed into the valley. Several thousand soldiers fell in piles with it into a raging fire, and all without exception burned to death. The spectacle was such that one could wonder if the Eight Great Hells were perhaps something like this—where criminals are said to be skewered on sword mountains and in saber trees, scorched in raging fires and cooked in molten iron baths.

In the meantime, the warrior-bandits of Yoshino, Totsugawa, Uda, and Uchinokōri who had gathered in response to the command of Prince Ōtō [Godaigo's son Morinaga], 7,000 in all, hid themselves on this hill or in that valley and blocked the roads used by those attacking Chihaya. As a result, the soldiers gathered from various provinces soon ran out of provisions, and both men and horses became exhausted. Unable to wait any more for deliveries by land or water, they started to withdraw in groups of two or three hundred.

As they did, they were killed by the warrior-bandits who knew the region well and waylaid them at tactical spots in various places. The number of soldiers so killed day and night was anyone's guess. The few people who were waylaid but managed to save their lives abandoned their horses and armor or were stripped of their clothes. Some covering themselves with torn straw raincoats merely to hide their naked bodies, some wrapping grass leaves around their waists shamelessly, these turned into stragglers and streamed away in all directions every day. It was an unprecedented disgrace. . . .

While the assault on Chihaya Castle was continuing, in the intercalary second month Emperor Godaigo, who had been exiled to Oki Island in the previous year, escaped, and returned to Kyoto in the sixth month. Even before Godaigo's return, in the fourth month, Ashikaga Takauji (1305–58), one of Kamakura's important commanders, revolted, and on the twenty-second of the ninth month the Kamakura Bakufu came to an end, with Hōjō Takatoki committing suicide along with many others. Even though Masashige never won a decisive battle, his successful defense of Chihaya Castle is believed to have helped turn the tide against Kamakura.

Still, the fall of the Kamakura Bakufu merely set off another round of civil strife. Takauji, initially appointed General of the Ezo Pacification Headquarters by Godaigo, soon proved unwilling to follow his orders and, as Godaigo's reform measures soured, revolted once more—this time against the imperial court. By late 1335 Godaigo was issuing commands to "pursue and destroy" Takauji.

In the first month of 1336, Takauji returned to Kyoto from Kamakura where he had gone at Godaigo's command to "pursue and destroy" another rebel. But his army was routed by Masashige and others, and he escaped to Kyūshū. By the fourth month, however, he had regrouped more than sufficiently and, along with his brother, Tadayoshi, started to head back to Kyoto with large armies.

Courtier Yoshisada[24] sent an express rider to the Imperial Palace to report that because Lord Takauji and Courtier Tadayoshi were returning to Kyoto with large forces, he had withdrawn to Hyōgo to attempt to block them at a strategic point. Greatly alarmed by the news, the emperor summoned Captain of the Imperial Police Kusunoki Masashige[25] and told him, "Hurry to Hyōgo and join forces with Yoshisada to fight."

Masashige respectfully offered his opinion:

"Since Lord Takauji is returning to Kyoto leading forces of the nine provinces of Kyūshū, I am convinced that his forces are immense. Our forces are exhausted and small. If in such a state you confront and fight a large enemy force, which is also gaining momentum, you are bound to be defeated. For this reason, may I suggest that Lord Nitta be simply summoned back to Kyoto and His Majesty visit Mt. Hiei as he

24. Nitta Yoshisada (1301–38), who was appointed by Godaigo Lieutenant General of the Outer Palace Guards, Left Division, in 1333. By the time Takauji started his march back to Kyoto, Yoshisada had become Godaigo's top commander.

25. Godaigo appointed Masashige Captain of the Imperial Police and Lieutenant of the Outer Palace Guards, Left Division—the same appointments Yoshitsune received. In effect, the men holding these posts were the top imperial bodyguards.

did before?[26] I myself will return to Kawachi and try to block Kawajiri[27] with forces from the Kinai. If then we attack our enemy in Kyoto from both sides until his provisions run out, he will gradually become exhausted and weak while day by day we will gain forces racing to join us. At an appropriate moment Lord Nitta will press down the mountain, and I will come to attack from the enemy's rear. By so doing we may be able to destroy the imperial enemy in a single battle.

"I am certain that Lord Nitta himself thinks the same way. But he must feel that it would be a disgrace if he, as someone on the road, returned without waging a single battle and people thoughtlessly condemned him as ineffectual. I think that's why he has decided to stay in Hyōgo and fight.

"Many things may happen in battles, but what is essential is a final victory. Let us hope that His Majesty will think into the future and have his court come to the right conclusion."

The emperor responded by saying, "Truly, leave military matters to a soldier." But in the council held by ranking aristocrats Imperial Adviser Kiyotada repeated his view:

"There may be some grounds for what Masashige proposes. But even before Yoshisada, as special emissary commanded to subjugate Takauji, carries out his battles, His Majesty is being asked to abandon the imperial capital and visit Mt. Hiei for the second time within a year. This strikes us as making light of the throne; as well, such an action would undermine the position of the imperial army. Takauji may indeed return to Kyoto leading the forces from Kyūshū, but these forces are most unlikely to exceed those he led from the eight provinces of Kantō when he returned to Kyoto this year.

"In general, from the start of this war until the defeat of our enemy, our forces, though small, never failed to bring our great enemy into submission. This was possible not because our military strategies were superior; it was simply because our Emperor's destiny was what Heaven approved. This persuades us that it cannot be difficult to decide the outcome of this battle and annihilate the enemy outside the imperial capital. Masashige must go immediately, not sometime in the future."

---

26. To avoid Takauji's army when he returned to Kyoto in the first month of the year, Godaigo had gone up Mt. Hiei for "a visit." The Enryakuji, a large temple complex on that mountain, had its own sphere of influence and was able to provide such protection. As is clear from Masashige's subsequent argument, he is saying that Yoshisada ought to be part of the "visit."

27. The port town at the estuary of the Yodo River, an important transportation route between Kyoto and Osaka.

Masashige said, "Now that it has come to this, I see no use in voicing my disagreement." On the sixteenth of the fifth month he left the capital and headed for Hyōgo with 500 horsemen.

The *Baishō Ron* (On the Plums and Pines), a history compiled around 1349 from the viewpoint of the Ashikaga Shogunate, gives a somewhat different account of Masashige's argument:

> . . . . in spring earlier that year, when the news reached Kyoto that the shogun [Takauji] and his brother [Tadayoshi] headed from Hyōgo to Kyūshū, the emperor felt relieved and was sharing his joy with his ranking courtiers that there no longer was anything to worry about. It was then that Masashige submitted his opinion and said, "His Majesty should kill Yoshisada and summon Lord Takauji back in order to make peace between ruler and subject. I myself would serve as envoy."
>
> People said it was such a puzzling thing to propose and ridiculed Masashige in various ways. Thereupon, he submitted his view again and said, "The destruction of His Majesty's previous enemies can all be credited to Lord Takauji's loyalty. There is no doubt that Yoshisada brought down Kantō, but all the warriors under Heaven submit themselves to the general [Takauji]. The evidence of this is that his army, though defeated, was able to go to a distant place with even those in Kyoto gladly obeying and following him, abandoning His Majesty's victorious army. This should prove to His Majesty that Yoshisada has no personal appeal.
>
> "As I ponder the reality of the matter, I am certain that the two men will easily make the western provinces follow them and return to attack during the third month. When they do, there will be no way to defend ourselves and fight. His Majesty is thoughtful in a thousand ways, but when it comes to military matters, this humble Masashige cannot be wrong. It is my wish that His Majesty will reconsider the matter."
>
> As he made this statement, he shed tears. We think he was truly a brave warrior with profound insight.

Some historians think that Takauji's popularity among samurai and Yoshisada's ineffectiveness as military commander make it likely that Masashige made such a proposal. The *Baishō Ron* goes on to note that when the imperial court rejected his strategy, Masashige decided to be "the first to die" at the front.

So back to *Taiheiki*.

Masashige resolved that this would be his last battle. So with some thought, from his house in Sakurai he sent back to Kawachi his son, Masatsura, eleven years old that year, whom he had brought along. The instructions he left at the time were:

"It is said that a lion throws his cub down a stone wall several thousand yards high three days after its birth. If the cub has a lion's mind, he bounces back up halfway, without being told, and will not die. You are already eleven years old. If you retain a single word of mine in your ear, please do not go against what I now have to say. I think the coming battle will decide the fate of our land, and this will be the last time for me to see your face in this life.

"When people learn that Masashige has been killed in battle, assume that our land is bound to be run by General Takauji. But even if that happens, do not destroy our loyalty of many years and surrender to save your own life. As long as a single young man remains alive in our clan, hide yourself near Mt. Kongō and fight the enemy, if he comes, with the kind of determination you would need if targeted by Yang Yu,[28] comparing your righteousness with the loyalty of Chi Hsin.[29] That will be your first filial duty. . . ."

And so, as the day broke on the Twenty-fifth of the fifth month, around eight, in the rifts of haze in the offing, some boats came faintly into view. While people were wondering if they were boats returning from fishing or boats crossing the strait of Awaji, enjoying, as they were, the grand seascape, into a far wider sweep of the briny route there emerged tens of thousands of naval boats, rowing and churning starboard and port, with banners erected at bow and stern, a tail wind swelling their sails. Across the hazy, expanding surface of the sea, for a distance of about forty miles, they were continuous as they rowed, gunwale squeaking against gunwale, bow touching stern, suddenly turning the sea into solid land, their sails shutting the mountains out of view.

---

28. A legendary Chinese archer in the Spring and Autumn Period (B.C. 770-B.C. 403). He could hit a willow leaf from a hundred paces.

29. First Han Emperor Kao-tsu's subject known for his single-minded loyalty.

So innumerable were they that while looking at them in amazement people were wondering if even the number of soldiers who joined battle at the Red Cliff when Wu and Wei contested hegemony, or that of soldiers at the Yellow River when Great Yuan destroyed the Sung Court, could have exceeded the number of these, when from Ueno and Shikamatsu Hill, of Suma, as well as from Bulbul's Pass, several hundred banners with the crests of Futatsuhikiryō, Yotsumeyui, Sujikai, Hidaritomoe, and Yosekakari no Wachigai pressed forward like clouds, flapping in a continuous stream.

Both the naval boats in the sea and the soldiers on the land were far more innumerable than had been thought, far exceeding what had been rumored, and the men of the government army felt overwhelmed when they looked at their own forces. Still, both Courtier Yoshisada and Masashige were brave men endowed with the kind of mind that Kuang-wu had, who would make light of a large enemy while never making light of a small one. They showed no sign whatsoever of flinching, but began by leading their men to a small pine wood on Cape Wada and quietly deploying them.

One group, headed by Wakiya Uemon no Sagisuke as general and commanded by twenty-three of his relations, close and distant, had 5,000 horsemen, and these waited at Kyōgashima. One group, headed by Ōtachi Samanosuke Ujiakira as general and commanded by sixteen of his relations following him, had 3,000 horsemen, and these waited on the shore south of Tōrodō. One group, headed by Captain of the Imperial Police Kusunoki Masashige, who deliberately avoided mixing other forces with his, had 700 horsemen, and these waited at the station south of the Minato River to face the enemy coming on land. Middle Captain of the Outer Palace Guards, Left Division, Yoshisada, being commander in chief, was in charge of orders to be issued to his officers. He had curtains put up[30] on Cape Wada and waited with his 25,000 horsemen.

As the initial battles began and Yoshisada moved his forces in an attempt to prevent the enemy soldiers' landing, the distance between his forces and Masashige's became considerable.

---

30. To make an enclosure for temporary field headquarters.

Captain of the Imperial Police Kusunoki Masashige turned to his brother, Sword-bearer[31] Masasue, and said, "Our enemies have cut us off from front and rear, and we've been separated from our command post. We now have no way of getting out of this. Let's first smash into the enemies in front and drive them around, then fight the enemies behind us!"

"That's a good idea," Masasue agreed.

Then, with their 700 horsemen in front and back, they galloped into a great mass of enemies. The soldiers under Chief of the Imperial Stables of the Left Tadayoshi[32] saw the banners with the crest of chrysanthemum and water, thought these were worthy enemies, and tried to isolate and kill Masashige and Masasue. But each brother cleaved through them from east to west and drove them from north to south. Each one, when he saw a worthy enemy, would gallop side by side with him, wrestle him down, and take his head; when the enemy was unworthy, he would strike him with a swing of the sword and run him down. Masasue and Masashige met seven times and separated seven times. Each one's sole aim was to get close enough to Tadayoshi, wrestle him down and kill him.

Tadayoshi's 500,000 horsemen were pushed around so badly by Kusunoki's 700 that they started to turn back toward Ueno, of Suma. As they did, the horse Tadayoshi rode stepped on an arrowhead with his right foreleg and began limping. The Kusunoki force swiftly caught up and was about to strike at Tadayoshi, when Yakushiji Jūrō Jirō turned back and, as he met Tadayoshi on the bank of Lotus Pond, jumped off his horse and, brandishing a thirty-inch-blade halberd held at its metal handle, slashed at the neck and chest straps of the oncoming enemy horses, in no time felling seven or eight of them. In the meantime Tadayoshi switched horses with Jūrō Jirō and escaped into the distance.

When General Takauji saw Chief Tadayoshi being driven back by Kusunoki and withdrawing, he issued an order, "Send in reinforcements! Don't let Tadayoshi be killed!"

---

31. "Sword-bearer," *tatehaki*, is the title given to men assigned to guard the crown prince's quarters. There were thirty of them.

32. As noted before, Tadayoshi (1306–52) is Takauji's brother. His relationship with Takauji later soured and he was eventually killed by him.

At once 6,000 horsemen of Kira, Ishitō, Kō, and Uesugi galloped to the east side of the Minato River and encircled the Kusunoki force to cut off its rear. Masashige and Masasue turned back and attacked these forces, killing or wrestling the enemies down as they galloped in and out of them. In about six hours they had sixteen engagements. Their force was reduced gradually, until only seventy-three riders remained.

Even with this small force they could have broken out of the enemy and escaped, but since leaving Kyoto Kusunoki had had a mind to bid farewell to the world here, so he fought without retreating a step. But their spirit now drained, he and his men hurried into a house in a village north of the Minato River. When he removed his armor for disembowelment, he found eleven sword wounds on his body. Each of the remaining seventy-two men also had five to ten wounds. The thirteen members of the Kusunoki clan and their sixty retainers sat in two rows in the guest room with six pillars, chanted a Buddhist prayer ten times in unison before disemboweling themselves.

Masashige, sitting at the head of the group, turned to his brother, Masasue, and asked, "They say your thought at the last moment determines whether your next life is going to be good or bad. Tell me, brother, what is your wish in the Nine Realms?"[33]

Masasue laughed cheerfully and said, "I'd like to be reborn in the Human Realm seven times so that I may destroy the imperial enemy."

Masashige was pleased to hear this and said, "That's a truly sinful, evil thought, but I think exactly as you do. Well then, let us be reborn in the same way and realize our wish."

With this vow the two brothers stabbed each other and died side by side. The eleven other principal members of the clan, including Governor of Kawachi Usami Masayasu, Jingūji no Tarō Masamoro, of the Middle Palace Guards, and Wada Gorō Masataka, as well as the sixty retainers, disemboweled themselves all at once, each sitting in the place of his choice.

Kikuchi Shichirō Takeyoshi, who had come to observe the battles in Suma as the representative of his older brother, the Governor of Higo, happened upon Masashige's death. Perhaps he thought it would be a disgrace to see something like this and return. He also killed himself and fell into the fire.

---

33. The Nine Realms are those of hell, hungry demons, beasts, asura, humans, heaven, sravaka, pratyekabuddhas, and bodhisattvas.

KŌ NO MORONAO:
WHEN A WARRIOR FALLS
IN LOVE

THE *TAIHEIKI* (CHRONICLE OF GREAT PEACE), from which the foregoing account of the warrior-commander Kusunoki Masashige is drawn, incorporates a number of extended passages which digress from the main narrative line. The following tragicomic love story of Kō no Moronao (d. 1351)—a man who, failing in his attempt to seduce a married woman, resorted to brute force—makes up the second half of chapter 21.

The Kō family served the Ashikaga family as hereditary regents while the Ashikaga were local daimyo. Moronao continued in that position when Ashikaga Takauji (1305–58) became shogun in 1338. As shogunate regent, Moronao was in effect commander in chief of all the armed forces with allegiance to the Ashikaga and was therefore a powerful man.

Akashi no Kakuichi (d. 1371), who, along with Shin'ichi, performs a section from the *Heike Monogatari* (The Tale of the Heike) for Moronao at the outset, is thought to have given the final shape to the military tale, which, as one scholar has put it, is "an oratorio-like work made up of some 182 cantatas for solo bass voice and *biwa* (lute) accompaniment, each lasting for thirty to forty minutes."[1]

The incident occurred while Kō no Moronao, the Shogunate Regent and Governor of Musashi, was staying home for some time, feeling too indisposed to go to his office to work. His ranking vassals tried to amuse him every day by preparing sake and delicacies and

---

1. Barbara Ruch, "Akashi no Kakuichi," *Journal of the Association of Teachers of Japanese*, vol. 24, no. 1, p. 36.

inviting the ablest from the entertainment fields to demonstrate their skills in his presence.

Late one moonlit night, when everything had quieted down and the wind blowing over the bush clovers felt truly cold, two blind lute-playing musicians, Shin'ichi and Kakuichi, narrated the following story from the *Heike Monogatari*:

"Once during the reign of Konoe-in, a *nue*, a monstrous bird, flew to the roof of the Shishin Palace and cried night after night. At the imperial command Minamoto no Yorimasa[2] shot it down. The feat so pleased the retired emperor that on the spot he put his scarlet robe on Yorimasa's shoulder as a gift.

"Later, the retired emperor mused aloud:

" 'As the reward for such work, it won't be adequate just to raise his rank or give him a governorship that's unfilled. Come to think of it, Yorimasa appears to have developed an unbearable passion for Ayame ("Iris"), of the Fujitsubo quarter, and he's lately been despondent because of this. As a reward tonight, I'll give her to him. But I take it he's only heard about her and has never actually seen her. Let's assemble some ladies-in-waiting who look like her, and if he fails to pick the right one from among them, let's tell him, "Your love is as confused as a profusion of irises,"[3] and have a good laugh about it!' "

"So, out of the three thousand maids in his harem, he chose twelve beauties whom flowers would have envied and of whom the moon might have been jealous, had them dress exactly the same, and put them behind a gold-tinted gossamer curtain with no attempt to dim the lights.

"He then had Yorimasa summoned to the outer eaves of the Seiryō Palace and, through a gentlewoman of the wardrobe as his messenger, told him: 'As tonight's prize, I will give you an iris from the marshes of Asaka. Even if your hands become tired, pull the right one and make her your wife.'[4]

---

2. A warrior-poet (1104–80), who is described in the Introduction, pp. xxvii–xxviii. He was killed at the beginning of the war between the Minamoto and the Taira clans.

3. Alludes to the anonymous poem that opens the section on love in *Kokin Shū* (no. 469): "Cuckoos call, this is the fifth month with those irises, as profusely as those irises I'm in love!"

4. Alludes to a poem on summer by Fujiwara no Takayoshi in *Kin'yō Shū* (no. 138): "Irises tire your pulling hands with their long roots; how is it they grow in the marshes of Asaka?" Takayoshi plays on the fact that *asa* of Asaka means "shallow."

"Yorimasa, who was standing with his hands on the edge of the large floor of the Seiryō palace, became visibly confused as he looked from one woman to another, utterly incapable of hitting upon the right iris to pull. All the ladies were about sixteen years old, each with facial features so exquisite that no painter's brush would have been able to reproduce a semblance of them, all wearing necklaces of gold and green, radiating coquetry as peaches in their ripeness might.

"The gentlewoman of the wardrobe laughed to see this and said, 'When the waters increase, even the marshes of Asaka can confuse you!' Thereupon, Yorimasa responded with a poem:

> Samidare ni sawabe no makomo mizu koete
> izure ayame to hikizo wazurau

The fifth-month rains swamp the water-oats along the shore,
    making it hard to tell irises from one another and pull
        just one

"The retired emperor was filled with admiration for Yorimasa. He himself rose to his feet, took Lady Ayame by the sleeve, and gave her to Yorimasa, saying, 'Take her home as your wife.'

"So, Yorimasa not only added to his reputation as an archer by shooting down a *nue*; he also proved himself a distinguished poet by winning with a single poem Lady Ayame, whom he had adored for years and months."

As Shin'ichi and Kakuichi finished the narrative in tandem, with Moronao intently listening, his pillow pushed aside, those both inside the blind and out in the garden exclaimed, deeply moved. After the *Heike* narrators left, some of the young men and the hermits staying behind were heard saying among themselves, "It's nice that Yorimasa got a beauty as the reward for shooting down a *nue*, but he didn't get a plot of land or any substantial compensation. That's very, very bad."

Moronao strongly objected. "What you fellows have just said strikes me as utterly unacceptable. For a beauty like Ayame, I'd gladly give ten provinces or twenty or thirty plots of land." This put them to shame.

It happened that Jijū heard the exchange behind a sliding door. Formerly a lady-in-waiting for an upstart though ranking nobleman, she had seen some glorious days of imperial rule. But with the changing times her fortune had declined, and she was now a frequent guest at Moronao's house. Jijū opened the door behind Moronao and laughed and laughed.

"You all seem to have guessed wrong," she said. "As I see it, I don't think Lady Ayame of the past was such a beauty. About Yang Kuei-fei, it's said that 'she gave a smile, and all the beauties in the six palaces paled to naught.'[5] Even if they had lined up thousands and tens of thousands of ladies-in-waiting, would Yorimasa have failed to 'pull' her, if she had indeed been truly outstanding?

"You said, sir," Jijū turned to Moronao, "that you would give ten provinces for a lady-in-waiting like that. Well, if you ever saw someone like Nishi no Tai, of the Koki Palace, the daughter of Prince Hayata, who is maternally related to the former emperor, I bet you'd give Japan, China, and India."

She went on playfully to describe how beautiful Nishi no Tai was, citing Chinese legends and Japanese poems.[6] When she was finished, she started to withdraw and close the door. Moronao, overjoyed, held her by the sleeve, and asked, "Where is this princess? How old is she?"

"She's been the wife of a country gentleman for some time now," she said. "She's no longer as beautiful as she was when she was at the court, and she's past her prime — or so I had thought. But one day not long ago, on my way home from a shrine, I went to see her, and she turned out to be even more radiant than the cherry blossoms on a young tree when spring has arrived at long last. With the full moonlight pouring in, she had the blind facing south rolled up high and was plucking the lute. Some loose strands of hair had fallen over her face, but I could still see her exquisite eyebrows, eyes shaped like lotus leaves, and ineffable red lips — all of which, I dare say, would easily have bewildered the mind of the holiest of holies meditating in the depths of a rocky cavern. She was so dazzling!

"Alas, sad is the fate sometimes arranged by the marriage deity," she continued. "When you had expected her to be a retired emperor's consort or an empress, she didn't even become the wife of someone like the shogun who has now taken over the country. Instead, the former emperor gave her to En'ya Takasada, Captain of the Imperial Police, whose commanding voice is as effective as the cooing of a

---

5. A line from Po Chü-i's poem about the legendary beauty Yang Kuei-fei (719–756), "Song of Everlasting Regret." Emperor Hsuan Tsung (685–762) was ruined as a result of his infatuation with her.

6. Here the translation abbreviates the original account.

pigeon at the top of a tower and whose province is Izumo, where the beddings are too coarse for her imperial self.'"7

Moronao was immensely pleased. "The story you've told me is so fascinating I'd like to give you some presents," he said, and had placed in front of Jijū ten outer garments along with a pillow made of aloes wood. Jijū, flushed by the sizable gain she'd suddenly made, was hesitating to leave, when Moronao leaned over to her and said:

"Your incredible story has made me feel that my illness will go away soon, but at the same time I feel as if possessed by a new sickness. I humbly beg you: Would you be the go-between for this lady and me? If you do well, I'll give you a plot of land or any valuables in this house, as you wish."

This turn of events took Jijū by surprise. After all, it was not as if the lady in question were living alone. She wanted to say this, that it wasn't something that could be done. But she had sense enough to fear that, if she spoke up, she could lose her life or some other terrible thing could happen to her. So she said she'd try to talk to the lady, and went home.

Jijū was trying to figure out whether she should do this or that, when within a few days something unheard-of happened: Moronao, the Shogunate Regent, had a variety of sake and delicacies sent to her, along with a message, "You're taking time to get back to me," evidently to pressure her. Deciding that there was no way out of it, she went to see Takasada's wife, and in some embarrassment tried to persuade her.

"Just hearing me say something like this, lady, I know, will offend you terribly," Jijū began. "This is something one should forget after hearing about it, but it has happened the way it has, and I'd like to know what you can do about it.

"If you were good enough to console him as briefly as a dewdrop lasts, I'd think the future of your children would be guaranteed and, I dare say, even those of us who have no means of supporting ourselves would have somebody to depend upon. If you don't do it frequently, you needn't be afraid that people will notice as they are prone to notice the seine on Akogi Bay when it's dragged in.8 If it's as inconspicuous

---

7. Jijū is exaggerating somewhat. At the time of the story, in 1341, Takasada was one of the four commanders appointed to assemble military forces against the imperial forces threatening Kyoto.

8. Alludes to a poem: "If we meet as often as they drag in the seine on Akogi Isle, people will know eventually."

as dew fallen on a leaf of bamboo grass, who will begin to have suspicions?"

"What an extraordinary thing you're saying!" Takasada's wife lamented, and there seemed to be no way to approach her further on this matter.

Nevertheless, remembering the custom of suitors among the northern barbarians, who are said to place up to a thousand striped sticks in front of the houses of the women they covet, Jijū went to visit Takasada's wife every day and remonstrated.

"Once you put me in trouble," she said with resentment, "once you make me sink in an abyss in a river, there will be nothing you can do to help me, even if you pity me and regret what you've done. Suppose you pretend Lord Moronao is the late prince you used to serve and send him just one word in response?"

Such remonstrations merely discouraged Takasada's wife even more.

"No, please don't depress me any further, don't say any more of those things," she said, distressed. "If I become attracted to this pitiful person, there's always a chance that my poor reputation may rise as high as 'the fickle waves at Takashi Beach.' "[9]

So Jijū went back to Moronao and explained what had happened. Moronao's passion simply intensified. Hoping that if he conveyed his sentiments repeatedly Takasada's wife might relent, he decided to take a letter-writing route. He summoned an outstanding calligrapher, a hermit by the name of Kenkō[10] and had him write out his feelings in detail on a thin, "double-scarlet" sheet of paper so strongly incensed that if you touched it your hand might begin smoldering. He then waited impatiently for a reply. The messenger returned and reported: "Sir, the lady took your letter in her hand but didn't even open it and threw it away in the garden. I didn't want anybody to see it, so I've brought it back with me."

Moronao's feelings were greatly damaged by this.

"Well, well," he fumed. "Brush-handlers are so damnably useless. From today on, don't allow Monk Kenkō to come to my place!"

---

9. Alludes to a poem on love by Kii (dates unknown) in *Kin'yō Shū* (no. 501): "I wouldn't be splashed by the fickle waves of famed Takashi Bay, lest my sleeves become soaked." Translated: "I know you're fickle so I won't succumb to your sweet words, lest I be left alone weeping."

10. Yoshida Kenkō (1284–1350), author of the famous collection of essays, *Tsurezuregusa* (Essays in Idleness).

In the midst of all this, Yakushiji Jirōzaemon Kin'yoshi[11] happened by on some business. Moronao called him to his side and said with a bitter laugh, "Now we've got this woman who wouldn't even bother to read a letter I sent her, who's so outrageously indifferent to me. What would you suggest I do?"

"No human being can be like a rock or a tree," Kin'yoshi said. "Whatever this lady may be like, I can't imagine she won't bend when you long for her so. Why don't you send her a letter once again and see what happens?"

Thereupon he wrote a letter on Moronao's behalf, but there were no words in it except a single poem:

Kaesusae te ya furekento omouni zo
  waga fumi nagara uchi mo okarezu

You returned it, but thinking your hand touched it,
  I can't leave it alone, my own letter though it is

When the intermediary went back at once and delivered it, Takasada's wife, whatever may have struck her, looked at the poem, blushed, and stood there for a while with the letter in her sleeve. The intermediary thought her reaction wasn't bad and, tucking his sleeves backward, said, "Well, ma'am, how are you going to respond?"

Takasada's wife merely said, before withdrawing inside, "The nightgown, placed on top of the quilt."

The messenger hurriedly returned and explained how it had gone. Moronao looked pleased and thought about it. In a while he summoned Kin'yoshi.

"My intermediary says that in reply this woman said, 'The nightgown, placed on top of the quilt,' and left. Did she mean to say," Moronao asked, "that I ought to send her a silk gown? If that's the case, I can very easily have any kind of clothes made for her. Do you think that's what she meant?"

"No, sir," Kin'yoshi said. "She didn't mean anything like that. Among the poems on the ten commandments in the *Shin-Kokin*, there's one that goes:

---

11. Also known as Genka (1308?–81), a poet who was originally a member of Moronao's household.

Sanakidani omoki ga ue no sayo-koromo
waga tsuma naranu tsuma na kasane so

The nightgown, placed on top of the quilt, is too heavy:
  do not add to your spouse another's spouse[12]

I think she was alluding to it, saying that what you're asking her to do
is something she must avoid."

Moronao was greatly impressed by this.

"My goodness," he said, "you're an incomparable expert not in
the way of the bow and arrows alone, but in the way of poetry as well.
Let me give you a present."

He then personally took out a sword entirely painted in gold and
gave it to Kin'yoshi. Kenkō, by his bad luck, and Kin'yoshi, by his
good luck, at once switched their positions in the wheel of fortune.

After he heard about the reply, Moronao would summon Jijū
from time to time and say, sometimes threatening her with anger in
his eyes, sometimes remonstrating with his head hanging:

"I had long thought I'd give up my life in a grave moment for my
lord. But now I seem to be losing it for someone's wife who doesn't
give a damn, and I feel very sad about it. When my life is about to
expire, I'll make sure, lady, to take you with me, so that we may
together cross Mt. Death and the Sanzu River."

Jijū didn't know how to deal with such a man. But then it
occurred to her that Moronao might be disillusioned with Takasada's
wife if he saw her face after taking a bath and still with no makeup on.
So she said consolingly:

"Sir, be patient a while longer. As long as you feel, 'Not that I did
not see her, nor that I did,'[13] whatever I say will be of no avail. So I'm
going to arrange to have you see her, though from a distance."

Moronao smiled to himself to hear this and waited for the occasion as if it was just about to happen. Then, Jijū brought the news: A
girl who worked as a maid for Takasada's wife came to her, as instructed, and reported, "Tonight my master will be away and my
mistress will have a hot bath." And so, with Jijū as his guide, Moronao
sneaked into Takasada's mansion.

---

12. By Monk Jakunen (dates unknown); the subject is the Commandment against
Adultery. The poem appears as no. 1964 in *Shin-Kokin Shū*.

13. Alludes to a poem in Chapter 99 of *Ise Monogatari* (Tales of Ise): "Not that I did
not see you, nor that I did, but longing for you for no reason I brood all day."

As he crouched in a room with two columns and peered in through the space between the partitions, he saw a woman who seemed to have just come out of a hot bath. Beautifully flushed like a plum flower, she picked up by the hem a short-sleeved robe which was a translucent as ice and was lying softly on her body. Her long moist hair elegantly covered her body. There was a strong hint of the smoke from insense which apparently she had burned privately to perfume the undersides of her sleeves. Where in the world is she? wondered Moronao, confused. And as he thought of the dreamy flowers of the Goddess Shrine and the willows in the rain at Chao-chün Village,[14] he began to tremble violently as if possessed.

If enough time passed like this, the master of the house might return, Jijū feared, so she dragged Moronao out by the sleeve. But when they struggled out of the *hajitomi* door, Moronao fell flat on the porch and, no matter how she pulled him, he wouldn't get up. Jijū was afraid that he might even expire there. In the end she managed to get him home, but from that moment he just sank into the disease called love, and, whether asleep or awake, raved crazy things. Fearful of whatever might befall her, Jijū fled to a place in the countryside that no one could know of.

After that Moronao had no one to guide him. Not knowing what to do, he was aggreived, until he hit upon a plan: he spread the slanderous rumor in various ways that En'ya Takasada was plotting a conspiracy against the government and brought the matter to the attention of the shogun and the commander of the Outer Palace Guards, Left Division.[15] When Takasada heard about this, he saw that there was no way for him to save his life. He decided to flee to his own province for the time being, then raise an army by urging the members of his clan to join him, and discard his life in a battle against Moronao.

On the twenty-seventh of the third month [in 1341], at the crack of dawn, Takasada set out with thirty-odd young retainers who he knew had no thought of betraying him, each dressed in hunting garb and with a falcon on his arm, with the pretense of heading toward Rendaino and Nishiyama for gambling at falconing. At Terado, however, he and his men turned back toward Yamazaki and fled along the Harima Route. Meanwhile, he had his wife and children set out with

---

14. Alludes to a legendary Chinese goddess whose shrine had flowers of uncommon beauty, as well as to Wang Chao-chün, a legendary beauty in Emperor Yuan's court, who was sold to barbarians because she refused to bribe the imperial portrait painter.

15. Ashikaga Takauji and his brother, Tadayoshi.

twenty-odd retainers who were particularly close to him, pretending to make a round of visits to shrines and temples. In about an hour these people, too, turned away from their apparent destinations and fled along the Tamba Route.

In those days children readily turned against their parents, and younger brothers didn't think anything of losing their older brothers. Takasada's younger brother, Shirōzaemon, was no exception: he hurried to the Governor of Musashi and told him exactly what Takasada had done. When he heard the news, Moronao talked the matter over with his men for quite a while. But in the end, stung by his failure to get hold of Takasada's wife, he hurried to visit the shogun and said:

"Sir, about Takasada's conspiracy, I urged you to take care of it immediately, but you didn't listen to me. Now, at daybreak today, he ran away toward the west. If he gets to Izumo and Hōki and entrenches himself in a fort with members of his clan, it will become a grave matter to you, sir."

In consternation, the shogun at once started selecting men to go after Takasada. But those who happened to be there looked nervous and tense, each evidently wondering, Am I going to be asked to be one of them? Seeing this, the shogun decided that none of them was fit for chasing and killing Takasada. Instead, he summoned Yamana Tokiuji, Governor of Izu, Momonoi Tadatsune, Governor of Harima, and Ōhira,[16] Governor of Izumo, and told them, "I've learned that Takasada's now fleeing to the west. Go after him until you get him and kill him!" The three of them voiced no objection and solemnly accepted the order.

Tokiuji, who, unaware of what awaited him, had come in civilian attire, must have decided that if he went home to get into military gear and assemble a force, he would lose that much time and it would become that much harder to catch up with Takasada. He took armor from one of Moronao's young retainers, put it over his shoulders, tied the strings as he mounted a horse, and galloped out the gate. A total of seven men, a father, one of his sons, and retainers, soon reached the Harima Route and continued in hot pursuit. Not long afterward, a group of 250 warriors, including Tokiuji's first son, Captain of the Outer Palace Guards, Right Division, and his chief retainers, Kobayashi Minbunojō and Sakyōnosuke, barely armed and leaving in great haste, followed suit.

---

16. His personal name is missing.

Nor did Momonoi and Ōhira go home; each sent a servant home with the order to his men to follow with extra horses and arms, then rode out along the Tamba Route. Each time they came across someone on the road, they asked if he'd seen any suspicious group going west. The first responses were the same: "About twenty men guarding a lady in a palanquin hurried past. They must be several miles ahead of here now."

"Well, this means they haven't gotten too far. Let's wait for our forces running after us."

That night they stayed at an inn in Hōkabe.

Takasada's young retainers knew the pursuers would catch up with them any moment and tried to hurry. But hampered by the presence of a woman and children whom they had to look after in various ways, no sooner had they arrived in Kageyama, in Harima Province, than the forerunners among the pursuers caught up with them. Seeing that they could not get away, they at once carried the palanquin into a small house on the roadside. Then they faced the enemy. They removed their jackets so they could handle their bows better, and fiercely shot at the pursuers. Many of the soldiers of the pursuing group were not properly armed. As they rode forward to attack or ran forward with drawn swords, eleven of them were quickly shot and killed, and countless others were wounded. Nevertheless, the pursuers kept adding to their numbers, while those pursued began to run out of arrows.

So Takasada's men, deciding to stab their lady and her children to death first and then disembowel themselves, dashed into the house. What they saw there was so heart-rending that, tough warriors as they were, they could not hold back their tears. The lady, as beautiful as ever but distraught from continuous weeping, seemed ready to fade away and die. Yet, as she sat, holding her two children to her sides, she looked alarmed and agitated at what might happen to them.

In no time the pursuers came near the house, and one of the men was heard giving a command: "Remember why we're doing this. Even if we kill Captain En'ya, unless we capture his lady alive, we won't fulfill the Lord Regent's wishes. Keep that in mind!"

On the spot Hachiman Rokurō decided to smuggle out En'ya's second son, then three years old, who was clinging to his mother. He gathered him up in his arms, went to a nearby roadside prayer hall, and handed the boy to an itinerant monk who happened to be there, saying, "Would you, sir, make this little boy your disciple and take him to Izumo? Would you see to it that he will grow up and become the proprietor of a plot of land?" Rokurō then gave the monk two *kosode* kimono[17] as a gift.

"No problem, sir," said the monk as he received the boy and the gift without hesitation.

Rokurō was pleased how easily he had accomplished his mission. He hurried back to the house and said to the other men, "As long as I have any arrows left, I'll defend all of you. Go inside and stab the lady and the child to death, set fire to the house, and disembowel yourselves."

Then a member of the En'ya clan by the name of Munemura, who was Governor of Yamagi, dashed into the house. Holding up the drawn sword he was carrying, he put its tip below the lady's chest, which was more virginal than the snow and more exquisite than the flowers, and pushed the sword in. Scarlet blood spurted out and with a faint cry the lady fell forward in her silky robe. Her son, who was five, alarmed by the sword, burst out weeping. Crying "Mommy!" he clung to his mother who was no more. The Governor of Yamagi fortified himself, held the boy in his arm, and, placing the hilt of the sword against a fence, skewered himself and the boy together all the way through to the sword-guard and died.

The remaining twenty-two men were all relieved to see this. They untied their topknots to let their hair loose,[18] bared the upper parts of their bodies, and, whenever an enemy approached, dashed forward to fight with swords. They knew there was no way they could save their lives. They also knew that to continue killing in the circumstances would merely be adding to their sinfulness. But they hoped that by holding up the enemy a while longer the captain might go that much farther. So they went on fighting for about four hours, from time to time dashing forward with a shout, "I am En'ya! I am Takasada! Kill me, and show my head to Moronao!"

Finally, when they ran out of their last arrows and there was not a single man who was not wounded, they set fire to the entrance of the house, ran into it as the fire grew fierce, and, each disemboweling himself in his own way, were all burned to death.

---

17. *Kosode* means "short sleeve." As Liza Dalby puts it in *Kimono: Fashioning Culture,* the "kosode (small sleeve) garment took its name in contradistinction to gowns with great, billowing, fingertip-covering sleeves."

18. To show readiness to die.

When the house burned down, Momonoi's and Ōhira's men brushed aside a pile of ashes to check. Underneath was En'ya's wife; she was like a pheasant which is reputed to burn to death protecting her chicks from field fires: her baby, slashed with the tip of a sword while in her womb, was half out of her belly, covered with blood and ashes. Also, among the many who had died by disembowelment and were lying upon one another was one who, with a small boy in his arms, was pierced with a single sword. Momonoi and Ōhira decided that the man could be no other than Captain En'ya, but that his head was too damaged by fire to be worth taking back. They then returned to Kyoto.

Meanwhile, Yamana Tokiuji and his young retainers, who rode along the San'yō Road, were passing in front of Takara Temple, in Yamasaki, when someone called out from far behind, "Halt! I have a letter from the Lord Regent! I have a message for you!"

As they reigned in their horses and turned to look, a man, about three hundred yards away, shouted, "I've ridden too hard and my horse is too out of breath to come as far as where you are! Turn back, please!"

Tokiuji himself dismounted and gave a command to several of his men, "Find out what the whole thing is about, and hurry back."

Five men rode back and, as they came near the messenger, jumped off their horses: "Tell us what's happened, sir!"

The man gave a big grin and said, "To tell you the truth, I'm no messenger from the Lord Regent. I work for Lord Takasada, but I didn't know he'd decided to become a refugee, and so couldn't accompany him. I'd like to give up my life right here for my master and then talk about how I did it in Hell."

No sooner had he said this than he drew his sword and slashed at the men. Their fight lasted for quite a while. When he had wounded three men and himself received two cuts, the man must have seen that his end had come. He quickly disemboweled himself and died.

"We were tricked by this bastard and we lost time. The refugees have gone that much farther." So grumbling, Tokiuji and his men spurred their horses on even harder than before.

They traveled the distance of about forty-five miles from Kyoto to the Minato River in four hours. There, at the Minato River, Tokiuji said, "Our horses are too tired for us to get near our enemy before the end of day. Let's let our horses rest tonight before continuing the chase."

But Tokiuji's son, captain of the Outer Palace Guards, Right Division, who was fourteen that year, selected some impatient young men, called them together, and said, "Our fleeing enemy is afraid of us, so they'll keep running during the night, too. We can't wait for the break of day for nothing just because our horses are tired. If we do anything like that, we'll never be able to catch up with our enemy and kill him. Those of you who are good riders will agree with me. We won't tell this to my father, the Governor. Let's catch up with the enemy tonight and kill him on the road!"

With this he pulled up his horse and mounted it; so did one warrior after another, soon a total of twelve, Kobayashi Minbunojō the most senior among them. And these men galloped into the night to resume their chase.

During the night they traveled the distance of about forty miles. By the time they reached the Kaku River the night had whitened into daybreak. The men looked at the other shore through the rifts of "mist over the river" through which, says a poem, "the sleeves of distant people can be seen."[19] Indeed, about thirty men, who did not appear to be ordinary travelers, were hurrying their horses, hoof sounds chaotic. Determining at once that these were En'ya and his men, the captain of the Outer Palace Guards, Right Division, spurred his horse down to the river's edge and called out:

"Sirs! You're hurrying your horses. Am I wrong to see that you are Lord Takasada and his men? Now that you have made the shogun your enemy and you have us as your pursuers, how far do you think you can flee? Hold your ground, fight for your lives like soldiers, so that you may leave your names for as long as this river!"

En'ya Rokurō, the captain's younger brother, turned to his men and said, "I'm ready to fight and die here. You men go on ahead, defending yourselves with arrow wherever you have to, so the Captain may flee. Never allow yourselves to be destroyed all in a single fight!"

Rokurō then worked out with his men a fighting plan which included the part after his own death, and a group of seven men, led by himself, turned back. The captain of the Outer Palace Guards, Right Division, and his twelve warriors splashed into the river as a single group. As they crossed it, their horses flanking one another, Rokurō and his six men, all on horseback, lined up on the other shore and shot at them. The captain received three arrows, one that pierced

---

19. Alludes to a poem on autumn by Major Counselor Minamoto no Tsunenobu's Mother (dates unknown) in *Go-Shūi Shū* (no. 324): "Is it daybreak? Through the rifts of mist over the river the sleeves of distant people can be seen."

one of the side flaps of his helmet and two that pierced the sleeve of his left arm, before he galloped up the shore. At once En'ya Rokurō drew his sword, and all the men struck at one another as they galloped past each other time and again.

Kobayashi Sakyōnosuke was struck off his horse by Rokurō and was about to be beheaded, when the captain ran up, blocked Rokurō, and cut him down. The remaining six were all killed, too, each in a different way. Their heads were hung on the roadside, before the captain and his men resumed their chase without taking time to rest.

During that time, En'ya Takasada and his men had gone on ahead about three more miles. But by then his retainers' horses were too tired to move any farther and were abandoned along the road, the men following barefoot. It may be that Takasada then decided it was inadvisable to stay on the main road. At Gochaku Station they took a different road and headed for Mt. Oshio. When the captain's group came up close behind them, three of Takasada's men turned back and, with a grove of pine trees as their shield, shot at the pursuers as fast as they could put arrows to their bows. In no time they shot down six men riding at the front. When their arrows were exhausted, they drew their swords and fought until they were killed. This nonetheless enabled Takasada to escape. The chasers' horses were also all too tired. The captain decided that it was no longer possible to catch up with Takasada on the road, and calmly turned back with his men.

On the last day of the third month, Takasada arrived in Izumo Province. On the first of the fourth month, Yamana Tokiuji, Governor of Izu and the commander of the punitive force, along with his son, the captain, reached Yasugi, in the same province, with more than 300 men on horseback. Immediately Tokiuji circulated a notice throughout the province: "Takasada's revolt has been exposed. We have come here to punish him. Anyone who kills him and brings his head to us, be he one with no official rank or one with no samurai status, shall receive a reward."

Hearing this, not only those unrelated to Takasada but also his relatives and blood relations had their greed stirred up and forgot all the favors they had received from him. As a result, soldiers of his own as well as other provinces blocked the roads or waited in ambush, or else went hither and thither to find and kill him.

With no place for him to hide for a single day, Takasada decided to climb a hill in Sasau and fight, and was hurrying there, when a young servant of his who had escaped along the Tamba Route ran up to him and said, "Sir, for whom do you think you are saving your life? Why are you trying to build a fort? The men accompanying your ladyship were caught by the enemy at a place in Harima called Kageyama, and they stabbed your ladyship and your sons to death. Then, without a single exception they disemboweled themselves and died. To come to you and tell you this, I've kept my negligible self alive."

Having barely finished saying this, the man slashed his belly and fell in front of Takasada's horse. Infuriated, Takasada said, "I couldn't live away from my beloved wife and children even for a brief while, but now they're gone. What's the meaning of going on to live? This is all so painful. I will be reborn seven times as Moronao's enemy, so he'll know what all this means to us."

So saying, he disemboweled himself, fell headlong from his horse, and died. At the time, only one retainer, Kimura Genzō, was by his side, as Takasada had sent out the thirty-odd young retainers he had with him to check out places that could be turned into forts. Genzō jumped from his horse, cut the head off the Lord Captain, wrapped it in his jacket, and buried it deep in the mud of a paddy some distance from there. He then disemboweled himself, took his intestines out, covered Takasada's neck with them, leaned on the dead body, and, holding it, died.

Later, Tokiuji's soldiers followed Genzō's muddy footprints to the paddy, recovered Takasada's head, and sent it to Moronao.

Of those who saw or heard about this incident, there was not a single person who did not say, "Captain En'ya was a loyal man who did not commit a single crime. But once slandered, he was forced to cut his life short. It's like Shih Chi-lun, of Chin, who was destroyed because of Lu-chu, who scattered to death like a flower in Chin-ku."[20]

Moronao thereafter piled up evil acts and was in time destroyed. In our opinion, there is truth in the saying, "To those who benefit others Heaven necessarily brings happiness; to those who harm others Heaven necessarily brings calamity."[21]

---

20. Shih Chi-lun was executed because he refused to give up his favorite concubine Lu-chu. See Burton Watson's *Meng Ch'iu: Famous Episodes from Chinese History and Legend*, pp. 154–155.

21. Rephrasing of an observation by Meng Tzu (Mencius): "To those who love others and those who benefit others Heaven necessarily brings happiness; to those who slander others and those who harm others Heaven necessarily brings calamity."

TAKEDA SHINGEN AND
UESUGI KENSHIN:
TWO WARLORDS

URING JAPAN'S "AGE OF WARRING STATES" several outstanding warlords emerged. Among them, Takeda Shingen Harunobu (1521–73), of Kai, and Uesugi Kenshin Terutora (1530–78), of Echigo, are often cited together. They were neighbors who confronted each other five times at a place called Kawanakajima,[2] and their characters contrasted distinctly. Shingen was a careful administrator who prompted a retainer to compile his words and deeds in many volumes, Kenshin a soldier pure and simple whose spirit of fair play was admired even by his enemies, Shingen among them.

Indeed, if, by happy coincidence, the best-known words on governance during this prolonged period of civil war come from Shingen, so does the best commendation of Kenshin. Shingen's wisdom on how to run a country is summarized in the following homiletic verse:

> *Hito wa shiro hito wa ishigaki hito wa hori*
> *nasake wa mikata ada wa teki nari*

> The people are the castle, the stone wall, and the moat;
> compassion makes a friend, vengeance a foe

It is a famous historical anecdote that the Confucian scholar Ogyū Sorai (1666–1728), visiting the place where Shingen's residence used to be, was surprised by its small size:

---

1. The "Island-in-the-River," a triangular flatland formed where the Chikuma and Sai rivers merge.

Ah! Lord Kizan [Shingen], with his heroic military prowess, moved troops from the five provinces of Kai, Shinano, Suruga, Hida, and Kō-zuke, and his impregnable way overwhelmed the lords of the Eastern provinces; in the end not one appeared who was able to oppose him. But, compared with his great achievements, his residence was so small, so simple!

Sorai may have been indulging in Chinese-style hyperbole, for it was Shingen himself who made a highly credible assessment of his worthy opponent, Kenshin. When he knew he was soon to die, he gathered his top commanders and gave instructions. One had to do with his heir, Shirō Katsuyori (1546–82):

As for Katsuyori's fighting, he must first make a truce with Terutora. Kenshin is such an honorable soldier that he won't do anything petty to young Shirō. Especially, if he speaks to him and says, "May I count on you," nothing should go wrong. I, Shingen, being childish, was never able to say to Terutora, "I count on you," and in the end I wasn't able to strike a truce with him. Katsuyori must go to Kenshin and say, "I count on you." With Kenshin you can do that without embarrassment.[2]

For an account of these men we will turn to the *Nihon Gaishi* (An Unofficial History of Japan), written in Chinese by the historian and poet Rai San'yō (1780–1832), and, for the most famous battle between them, to the *Kōyō Gunkan* (A Military History of the Great Men of Kai), generally attributed to Obata Kanbē Kagenori (1573–1663). Both books have been faulted for historical inaccuracies, but both have also been praised for achieving their goals. For if San'yō succeeds in giving effective portraits of many of Japan's distinguished military commanders, Kagenori succeeds in giving a vivid sense of how warlords tried to manage both war and peace.

In the following narrative, Shingen's name changes from Katsuchiyo to Harunobu to Shingen. Kenshin, too, undergoes similar changes. Also, at first his family name is Nagao; he did not acquire the name of Uesugi until 1561 when Uesugi Norimasa (1523–79) transferred to him his title of *Kantō kanrei*, (Governor-General of the Kantō).

---

2. Similar sentiments were expressed by Hōjō Ujiyasu (1515–71). Comparing some of his contemporary warlords, Ujiyasu said: "Kenshin is the only man who, once he agrees to do something for you, carries out his obligations no matter what happens to himself. That's why I'd like to have his undershirt so that I might cut it into pieces and give each piece to each of my young commanders as an amulet. If I were to die tomorrow, Kenshin would be the only one I would consider asking to look after my family."

SHINGEN'S UNHAPPY RELATIONSHIP WITH HIS FATHER

[Takeda] Nobutora fought and defeated [Governor of Kazusa] Kushima, the strong man of Suruga. On that day a son was born, so he was named Katsuchiyo;[3] later he was called Harunobu. He was always composed and wily. Nobutora favored a younger son, Nobushige, and wanted to get rid of Harunobu. Harunobu deliberately acted dumb and incompetent to hide his true self. When put in positions to have to compare himself with Nobushige in talent and skill, he would make sure to come out the inferior. Or he would fall from a horse to be helped up. Nobutora's commanders were contemptuous of Harunobu. Harunobu in the end secretly conspired with Imagawa Yoshimoto,[4] the lord-governor of Suruga. Yoshimoto was his sister's husband. In the fifth year of Tenbun [1536], Yoshimoto made a request to the imperial court, adopted Harunobu as his son, had him take the manhood rite, had him appointed Master of the Banquets and Governor of Shinano.

In the eleventh month Nobutora took his soldiers to Shinano and attacked Unnokuchi Castle. The lord-president of the castle, Hiraga Genshin, fought back well. Nobutora assaulted him with 8,000 soldiers and was still unable to bring him down the following month. Then there was a great snowfall. Nobutora's commanders held a council and said, "It's already late in the twelfth month. Let us withdraw. Our enemy will not tail us."

Nobutora followed the advice. Harunobu asked to take up the rear. Nobutora laughed and said, "You want to take up the rear because you know the enemy won't tail us. Nobushige would never do such a thing." Harunobu insisted and took up the rear with 300 soldiers. When he was several miles behind the main force, he stopped his men to bivouac and warned them: "Don't remove your armor. Don't take off the saddles. Feed your horses and then have some food. We'll leave around four in the morning. Just follow me where I go."

---

3. The name means something like "victory forever." It was a rather common name in those days.

4. Yoshimoto (1519–60), a warlord of considerable influence, would later be killed by Oda Nobunaga (1534–82) in the Okehazama Battle (see the next chapter). Nobunaga, who started the unification process, is depicted as a devious and cowardly man in this account.

His soldiers secretly derided him for this, saying, "The wind and the snow are so terrible. What's the use of these precautions?"

When four in the morning came, Harunobu promptly decamped, turned back to head for Uninokuchi, raced through the snow with the 300 riders, and reached the castle at daybreak.

Genshin had already dispersed his soldiers, staying in the castle only with a hundred. Harunobu divided his soldiers into three groups and himself led one group into the castle, leaving two groups outside with their banners up to work in unison with his men inside. The soldiers within the castle could not assess the size of the enemy and surrendered without fighting. Harunobu beheaded Genshin, returned with the head, and gave it to Nobutora. Nobutora's men were greatly surprised. Yet Nobutora would not give him any word of praise, saying, "It was cowardly of you to abandon the castle." His commanders privately admired Harunobu but would not dare praise his achievement. Harunobu himself continued to act dumb.

Nobutora was violent by nature and inconsistent in reward and punishment. The people of his province suffered because of this. Harunobu secretly conspired with the elder retainers Obu Hyōbu and Itagaki Nobutaka to strengthen his ties with Imagawa Yoshimoto. Yoshimoto, who was worried about Nobutora's strong resistance, wanted to manipulate the latter's province by helping Harunobu. Nobutora was not aware of this.

In the fifth month of the seventh year [1538] Nobutora wanted to drive Harunobu to Suruga. He put him in Obu's care and went to Suruga himself to consult Yoshimoto about this. Yoshimoto detained Nobutora and would not allow him to go back. As a result, Harunobu became independent in Kai. None among the commanders was unwilling to give in completely and take his orders.

However, hearing about the upset, the neighboring provinces wanted to take advantage of the situation. Also, many of the peasants of Shinano moved out to side with Murakami Yoshikiyo. In the sixth month the lord-president of Suwa Castle, Suwa Yorishige, and the lord-president of Fukashi Castle, Ogasawara Nagatoki, combining their forces into an army of 10,000 soldiers, came to attack. Harunobu, leaving Commander of Mounted Soldiers Hara, Governor of Kaga, to stay to defend, himself struck out to Nirasaki with 6,000 men to fend off the attackers. He assembled farmers and tradesmen of Kaga and Fuchū, 5,000 in all, and made each one carry a paper banner and march forward with drums and battle cries. The enemy withdrew and ran.

SHINGEN EXPANDS
HIS TERRITORY

Harunobu became arrogant and arbitrary, indulged in banquets and
other pleasures, and delighted in composing verses in Chinese, while
neglecting government. There were none among his retainers who dared
warn him. Itagaki Nobukata feigned illness and, secretly inviting to his
home a monk who was good at composing verses in Chinese, studied
verse composition for a couple of months. He then came out of his house
and sat in on a banquet where he offered to compose verses. Harunobu
would not believe it. Nobukata insisted and was granted his request.
On the spot he composed verses on the five topics given. Harunobu was
immensely pleased and asked, "How did you manage to be like this?"

Nobukata seized the chance to warn: "Sir, your father was so
unreasonable that you finally drove him away. Now you are acting just
the way he did. How do you know that someone might not do to you
what you did to him?"

Harunobu was struck by the truth of this and started again to
concentrate on government.

In the third month of the eleventh year [1542] Yoshikiyo, Nagatoki, and Yorishige, along with Kiso Yoshitaka, came to attack with
soldiers assembled in Shinano. Harunobu's commanders became
afraid. Harunobu said, "There are four of them working together, but
they may not necesssarily agree among themselves. We should engage them in battle and defeat them."

For deception Harunobu widened his moat and heightened his
earth wall. The four men regarded this as an expression of timidity[5]
and unhesitatingly advanced into Harunobu's territory. Harunobu
marched out during the night and, taking advantage of misty rain,
pressed forward and struck, handing the enemy a resounding defeat.
The four men regrouped and came to Hirasawa. Harunobu struck and
defeated them again. From then on they came to attack every year, but
Harunobu won each time.

Harunobu recruited Yamamoto Kansuke. A man from Mikawa,
Kansuke was a wall-eyed cripple. He had once studied military strategy with Ogata so-and-so and having that knowledge sought employment with Imagawa Yoshimoto. Yoshimoto's old retainers all treated

---

5. That is, they thought Harunobu was taking a defensive posture in preparation
for a siege.

Kansuke with contempt and Yoshimoto himself saw nothing special in him. Kansuke remained on the parasitic fringe for several years. When Itagaki Nobukata heard of his reputation, he recommended him to Harunobu. Harunobu summoned and saw him, talked with him, and was immensely pleased. On the spot he gave him holdings worth 200 *kan*[6] and gave him the name Haruyuki.

In the eleventh month Harunobu took nine castles in Shinano, using Haruyuki's stratagems. In the thirteenth year [1544] he trapped and killed Suwa Yorishige using Nobukata's stratagems and took Yorishige's daughter as a concubine. The next year she gave birth to Katsuyori; he was called Shirō. Harunobu already had his first son, Yoshinobu. So he made him his heir and made Katsuyori inherit Yorishige's house. In the fifth month of the fourteenth year [1545] he fought and defeated Ogasawara Nagatoki and Ina.

In the third month of the fifteenth year [1546] he attacked Toishi Castle. Murakami Yoshikiyo, commanding 6,000 soldiers, came to the rescue. Harunobu's spearheads, such as Amari Bizen and Yokota Bitchū, were all killed, and his force was about to be crushed. Haruyuki spoke up, "Sir, don't try to stop the enemy's spearhead head-on. Make it veer to the right and we'll win." Harunobu said, "Even my soldiers don't always obey my command. How could I possibly move the enemy as I wish?"

Haruyuki requested to borrow soldiers from those in the rear and struck out to the left. Yoshikiyo's army veered to the right. Harunobu's army recovered its spirit, pressed forward, and defeated the enemy. Because of this achievement Haruyuki's holdings were increased to 800 *kan*. Haruyuki went to Suruga for a visit. All those who used to deride him now extolled him. Yoshimoto regretted this.

Hearing that the Kai soldiers were exhausted at Toishi, Uesugi's commanders came over Usui Pass with 20,000 soldiers. Harunobu sent Nobukata for defense. He then took on the task himself. In the ninth month he attacked and defeated the Uesugi army. Sanada Yukitaka and his son Masayuki all did good work. Also, using Yukitaka's stratagems, Harunobu trapped and killed 500 crack troops under Murakami Yoshikiyo.

In the eighth month of the sixteenth year [1547], Harunobu took Shiga Castle. Yoshikiyo sent his army to Uedahara. Itagaki Nobukata, commanding the van, was not prepared; he had just won a battle. Yoshikiyo took advantage of his neglect, attacked him with his entire

---

6. An equivalent of 1,000 koku or 5,000 bushels of rice.

force, and killed him. Harunobu went out with reinforcements. Yoshikiyo, leading commandos, dashed into his camp, and even engaged in a sword fight with him; but he fell from his horse and in the end suffered a terrible defeat.

In the eighth month of the eighteenth year [1549], Harunobu invaded Kōzuke. Also he fought with Ogasawara Nagatoki in Suwa Field and made him run. In the third month of the nineteenth year he invaded Kōzuke again. Nagatoki withdrew when he heard that Harunobu had come out again.

At this time Imagawa Yoshimoto established a marital connection with Hōjō Ujiyasu, the lord-governor of Sagami.[7] He then came on behalf of Ujiyasu and made a request: "Sir, Ujiyasu is about to fight Uesugi and take Kōzuke. It is his wish that you refrain from making a move ahead of him." Harunobu agreed and allied himself with Ujiyasu and Yoshimoto.

In the same year Harunobu had his head shaven and called himself Shingen. Shingen held up a mirror and, looking at himself in it, said, "My face resembles Acala's."[8] At once he summoned a painter and had his portrait made and, after having a sword and a rope added to it, declared, "Even if our four neighbors launch an assault into our land after my death, they won't dare do anything outrageous if they see this image of mine."

Shingen continued to attack Murakami Yoshikiyo. He also attacked Takashina, Suda, and Shimazu. In the twenty-second year [1553] he invaded the four counties surrounding Kawanakajima. Yoshikiyo and others were unable to hold him back. They consulted one another and decided that Uesugi Kenshin was the only one who could oppose Shingen. Accordingly, they all went to join him.

KENSHIN'S CONFLICT
WITH HIS BROTHER

[Nagao] Tamekage had four sons. The first was called Harukage; the next, Kageyasu; the next, Kagefusa; and the last one, Kagetora. Kagetora was called Torachiyo[9] in his childhood; he was born of

---

7. See note 2 of this section.

8. An angry manifestation of the Vairocana, the central Sun. In Japan he is usually depicted as a demonlike figure seated on a rock and enveloped in giant flames, with teeth bared, eyes furious; in that posture, he grips a sword in his right and a rope in his left.

9. The name means something like "tiger forever."

Tamekage's second wife. When mentioned first in history, he is eight years old, sharp and imperturbable. Tamekage did not love him. He drove him to Tochio, wanting to make a monk of him. Kagetora did not take to learning matters related to monkhood. When Tamekage died, many of his commanders gave their allegiance to Kagetora.

However, there was a Minister Teruta Hitachi, who had been favored by Tamekage. Taking advantage of Harukage's mediocrity, he conspired with his two sons, Kuroda Hidetada and Kanatsu so-and-so, as well as Nagao Toshikage, the lord-president of Sanjō Castle, to put Harukage forward as heir and kill Kageyasu and the rest. Kagefusa ran out. They chased and killed him inside the outer gate. Kagetora, then thirteen years old, also ran. A gate keeper hid him under a bamboo floor. When night came and he opened the floor, he found Kagetora fast asleep. He woke him and secretly let him out. Kagetora went to Kasugasan Temple. The monk of the temple, holding his hand, escaped to Tochio, where he hid him in the house of his wet-nurse's husband, Honjō Yoshihide. Yoshihide, along with Usami Sadayuki, protected him with greatest care. Sadayuki was a hereditary commander of the Uesugi clan. He loved to read books and was versed in astronomy and military strategy. Once he decided to help Kagetora, he established a deep relationship with him.

When Kagetora heard that the rebel would not leave him alone but would keep hunting him down, he left the place to avoid him. Like his fourteen followers, he dressed like an itinerant monk, wearing leggings and straw sandals as he departed. Climbing Mt. Yone, he looked over the city below and said, "One of these days when I raise an army to recover my land, I will make sure to set up camp here." Finally he reached Sendanno.[10] He wept, offered prayers, and said, "I, your son, will make sure to annihilate your enemy and soothe your angry soul." In the end he made a round of the provinces of the Hokuriku and Tōsan, closely observing and mapping the shapes and locations of mountains, rivers, castles, and lakes before returning.

Someone informed the rebel of Kagetora's whereabouts. The rebel sent a troop to capture him. Kagetora, working with Yoshihide and Sadayuki, raised an army. He took Tochio Castle, made it his headquarters, and waited to receive his orders from Uesugi Sadazane.[11]

---

10. Where his father, Tamekage, was trapped and killed by Enami Kazuyori.
11. The daimyo of Echigo Province and, therefore, Kagetora's overlord.

In the spring of the thirteenth year [1544] Toshikage and Hidetada came to attack, commanding soldiers. Kagetora not only defended himself but trounced them: He killed Toshikage and made Hidetada run. In the fourteenth year he sent Jin'yo Masatsuna to Kyoto to request an imperial command to destroy the rebel. In the fifteenth year the rebel frequently came to attack. Kagetora won each time he fought.

In the sixteenth year [1547] Harukage sent a clansman, Masakage, to attack with a great force. Sadayuki wanted to go out and fight. Kagetora climbed up the castle, surveyed the enemy, and said, "The enemy has come from a distance but has no logistical support. He won't stay here for long. If we wait until he begins to withdraw, and attack, we can win."

Past midnight Masakage began to withdraw as expected. Kagetora, with 3,000 horsemen, opened the gate and galloped out, fought the enemy at Shimohama and made him run. When the enemy reached Mt. Yone, Kagetora restrained and halted his soldiers; when the enemy was about to go over the pass, Kagetora urged his men to resume pursuit, and again defeated the enemy.

Sadayuki turned to his commanders and asked, "Gentlemen, do you know why our lord restrained and halted his soldiers when he did?"

"No, we don't know, sir."

Sadayuki said, "If you press against your enemy when he's climbing a steep place, he'll turn back and attack. If you allow him to go over a pass and then attack from a higher position, he won't be able to hold himself up. Our lord is young, but as we've seen, he can assess an opportunity and change himself at will. He's far ahead of whatever I might be able to plot."

Masakage surrendered, and Harukage, cornered, committed suicide.

In the eighteenth year [1549] the people of his land begged Kagetora to return. Teruta and others, entrenched in Sanjō, still would not surrender. In the nineteenth year Kagetora attacked Sanjō, brought the castle down, and killed Teruta. The rebels, with the remaining soldiers, held out at two castles in Niiyama and Kurotaki. Kagetora wanted to mount a final assault, but Uesugi Sadazane happened to die, and he could not. In the twentieth year he sent one of his commanders, Takanashi Sadayori, who attacked and brought down Niiyama Castle, and killed Kuroda Hidetada. Usami Sadayuki brought down Kurotaki Castle and killed Kanatsu. Echigo was completely pacified.

In the twenty-first year [1552] the commanders and soldiers together expressed their wish to have Kagetora as their master. Kagetora said:

"I was pressed by people both high and low into fighting my brother with an army. I had not expected him to take his own life. In the circumstances, if I were to become lord-governor of Echigo, the whole world is bound to say that I've robbed this land. Now this place is more or less pacified. You may choose a different master. I will leave, become a monk, and make clear what my true intentions were."

He shaved his head and called himself Kenshin. When he was ready to leave for Mt. Kōya, all the commanders signed a petition begging him to stay and govern the land. Kenshin said:

"You install a master because you intend to follow his orders. If you don't intend to follow orders, you needn't have a master. If you agree not to go against the orders I issue from now on, I will agree to stay."

On the spot he made a pledge to his commanders. The next day he issued an order, rounded up the sixteen ministers known for manipulating his orders, and put them to death at Rinsen Temple. His commanders were left in trepidation.[12]

In the fifth month Kenshin was appointed Junior Assistant President of the Board of Censors and promoted to Junior Fifth Rank, Lower Grade. He said, "It is not right for an imperial subject to receive government positions and rank without making proper acknowledgments." In the second month of the twenty-second year [1553] he obtained permissions to pass through the provinces on the way and, leading 2,000 soldiers, entered Kyoto through the Hokuriku Route. He first went to the Imperial Palace to pay his respects, then had an audience with Shogun Yoshiteru.[13] He returned in the fifth month.

---

12. The killing of sixteen "ministers" is probably a Chinese-style exaggeration. There survives Kenshin's lengthy letter to his religious teacher, dated the twenty-eighth of the sixth month 1556, in which he expresses his wish to become a hermit-pilgrim. But as soon as the news got out, Echigo faced another civil war. As a result, Kenshin changed his mind and made his main retainers and powerful local clan leaders sign a letter pledging their allegiance and, as was the custom of the day, provide him with their closest relatives as hostages.

13. Yoshiteru (1536–65), the thirteenth Ashikaga shogun. The Ashikaga shogunate was by then in the final stage of decline, and Yoshiteru would be killed by Matsunaga Hisahide (1510–77), one of the more colorful usurpers of the day.

KENSHIN BATTLES WITH
SHINGEN AT KAWANAKAJIMA

Murakami Yoshikiyo, Takanashi Masayori, Suda Chikamitsu, Shimazu Norihisa, and others came from Shina to surrender, begged an audience with Kenshin, and said, "Sir, we've been the targets of Takeda Shingen's invasion, and we can't find a place to settle down. We have heard Your Lordship's great reputation. We would be most grateful if you could give us a hand and rescue us."

Kenshin said, "Gentlemen, you are by no means the sort of people to stand below someone else. You have nonetheless come to entrust yourselves to me. I must say you know me. Still, I have now put an end to the civil strife in my land. Of course, I have Kaga and Etchū as my father's enemies. I always want to destroy those provinces, with the final aim of raising my banners in Kyoto. This simple wish is all I have. But I won't be a true man if I meet someone who knows me and do not do what I can for him."

He then asked Yoshikiyo, "Tell me, sir, how does Shingen use his soldiers?"

"The way he moves his army, sir," Yoshikiyo said, "he indulges neither in keeping it on the march for long nor allowing it to stay in one place for long. Every battle of his is aimed at a final victory."

"He aims for a final victory," Kenshin said, "because his true desire is to cultivate the land. I am not the same. I meet an enemy and I fight him. In essence, I try not to get my spear blunted."

He issued an order throughout his land to gather soldiers in Odahama on the twelfth day of the tenth month. Commanding 8,000 mounted soldiers, he entered Shinano and set fire to some of the castles belonging to the Takeda clan. Advancing farther, on the first of the eleventh month he bivouacked at Kawanakajima.

Hearing this, Shingen requested reinforcements from Imagawa and, commanding 20,000 foot soldiers, went to Amenomiya Ferry. He then dispatched Yamamoto Haruyuki and three other men to spy on the enemy. They came back and reported, "The Echigo army is quite alert, sir. You should have cordons of soldiers and make the enemy buckle under without fighting."

Shingen followed the advice. The two armies encamped with water between them. Kenshin challenged Shingen to fight. Shingen would not come out. They faced each other for twenty-seven days. Kenshin sent a messenger and had him say:

"I have heard, sir, that the way you use your army, you never allow it to stay in one camp for long. If that is the case, why do you try not to settle the outcome with me? I have no resentment or vengeful thoughts against you. I am doing this only for Yoshikiyo and others.

"Dare I ask, Why did you rob them of their lands? If you do not want to fight with me, return their lands to them. If you do not want to return their lands to them, fight with me."

Shingen responded by saying, "It is admirably righteous of you to protect Yoshikiyo. Nevertheless, as long as I remain alive, you, sir, will not have your way. If you want to fight, you start it."

Kenshin said, "Agreed."

At once he held a council and promised to begin battle the next morning. That night he issued a command, made a circular formation with seven units combined, and at early dawn advanced across the bridge. Shingen, putting together fourteen units, tried to fight them off. From six in the morning to two in the afternoon they contested the bridge, giving chase and being chased, the outcome of the battle unresolved. Kenshin divided his army, had a group cross the river upstream and come out behind the Kai army. The Kai army saw this and retreated. Yokota Gensuke and Itagaki Saburō, as well as seven commanders from Suruga, were killed. Similarly, many of the Echigo soldiers were killed or wounded. Kenshin assembled his soldiers and went back.

THE FOURTH BATTLE AT KAWANAKAJIMA [14] ACCORDING TO THE *KŌYŌ GUNKAN*

On the sixteenth day of the eighth month of the fourth year of Eiroku [1561], an express messenger from Kawanakajima, Shinano, arrived and reported: Terutora has come out and is encamped on Mt. Saijō, facing Kaizu Castle, and he is saying that he will make sure to bring the castle down. His army consists of about 13,000 men.

Lord Shingen left Kōfu on the eighteenth day of the same month and on the twenty-fourth arrived in Kawanakajima. He made camp

---

14. Historians think that the greatest confrontation between Shingen and Kenshin took place in 1555, not, as the *Kōyō Gunkan* says, in 1561. San'yō's accounts of the five confrontations between the two warlords also differ from the generally accepted history in dates and details of the battles. For example, what San'yō describes as the second battle, occurring in the eighth month, 1554, incorporates some of the incidents that are usually thought to have happened in the fourth one, which took place in 1561.

this side of Kenshin's on Mt. Saijō, occupying the Amenomiya Ferry. Kenshin's men expressed worry, saying that their retreat route to Echigo was cut off and that they were as if "bagged." But Terutora showed no concern whatsoever.

Lord Shingen stayed where he was for five days and on the sixth day, the twenty-ninth, crossed Hirose Ferry and entered Kaizu Castle. But Kenshin ignored his administrator's opinion and remained on Mt. Saijō as he had done for some time. Obu Hyōbu urged Lord Shingen to engage in a decisive battle. When Lord Shingen summoned Minor Controller of the Popular Affairs Ministry Baba and asked his counsel, Baba, too, advised a big battle.

Lord Shingen said, "Among my able commanders, Governor of Yamagi Obata died of illness this past June, while Governor of Mino Hara sustained thirteen wounds at Warikadake Castle this summer and hasn't recovered from them, so I couldn't bring him, either." He then summoned Yamamoto Kansuke and ordered him to consult Baba to work out the preparations for the battle the next day.

Kansuke said, "Of your 20,000 men, sir, 12,000 should be sent to Kenshin's camp on Mt. Saijō to begin battle around six tomorrow morning. The Echigo forces, whether they win or lose, are bound to cross the river and withdraw. When they do, the group led by your aides-de-camp and the men of their two reserves will attack them from rear and front to finish them off."

Accordingly, it was decided that ten commanders—Censor Kō-saka; Junior Secretary of the War Ministry Obu; Baba; Governor of Bitchū Oyamada; Lieutenant of the Outer Palace Guards, Left Division, Amari; Sanada Ittokusai; Aiki; Governor of Shimozuke Ashida; Oyamada Yasaburō; and Governor of Owari Obata—would go over to Mt. Saijō to begin battle at six in the morning.

It was also decided that twelve commanders—the aides-de-camp group led by Obu Saburō, of the Middle Palace Guards, who was to be in the middle, the Tenkyū[15] and Anayama to the left, and Secretary of Palace Repairs Naitō and Governor of Bungo Morozumi to the right, with Hara, of the Hayato Office, and Shōyōken to the left and Tarō Yoshinobu,[16] then twenty-four years old, and Mochizuki to the right,

---

15. Tenkyū means "the Bureau of Horses" or its chief and here refers to Nobushige, Shingen's brother. It may be recalled that when they were young, their father, Nobutora, favored Nobushige over Shingen. The two seem to have gotten along with each other after Shingen kicked out Nobutora.
16. Shingen's son.

flanking them, and Assistant Director of the Palace Kitchen Bureau Atobe, Imafuku Zenkurō, and Junior Secretary of the Ministry of Ceremonial Asari bringing up the rear—all told, a force of 8,000—would set out around four in the morning, cross the Hirose Ferry, and deploy themselves so that they might begin fighting the enemy as he withdrew.

When Kenshin, on Mt. Saijō, detected signs of food preparations made by the spearheading aides-de-camp, he assembled all of his commanders and said:

"Fifteen years ago, in the year of the Sheep, when Shingen was twenty-seven, and I, Kenshin, eighteen, we began to fight. Since then we have engaged in battle a number of times. But each time Shingen was careful not to make errors in his deployment and in the end gave the impression that he dominated the battlefield, with me as loser.[17]

"Now I see that he is preparing for battle tomorrow. And what I see as clearly as if reflected in a mirror is this: his strategy is to divide his men into two groups, one of them to come over to this camp to begin battle, with the other to finish off my aides-de-camp as they cross the river to withdraw.

"Let me outwit him in this instance. We will soon cross the river and spend the night there. As the sun rises we will attack Shingen's forces to start a battle and throw them off before his spearheads hurry to get to us. We'll see to it that Shingen's aides-de-camp and mine will have a fight. Shingen himself and I myself will grapple with each other so that we may stab each other to death or, if that isn't possible, strike a truce. Either way tomorrow's will be a once-in-a-lifetime battle!"

Terutora equipped himself with armor and around ten on the night of the ninth day of the ninth month decamped from Mt. Saijō, crossed the Amenomiya Ferry, and moved to the other side. As he did so, not a single sound was heard even though there were as many as 13,000 men. This was because on a battlefield, by combat regulations, each Echigo man was made to prepare three-men's worth of food at each breakfast time, so did not need to prepare food for the evening; as a result, there was no sign of fires being made.[18]

---

17. The *Kōyō Gunkan* is written to extol Shingen, hence this imposition of self-deprecation on Kenshin. In fact Kenshin is thought to have often had the upper hand on Shingen.

18. The success of this spectacular redeployment of a large army, which was accompanied by a considerable number of horses besides, would be difficult to account for only by lack of fires for making meals. Kenshin, for example, may have left some troops on Mt. Saijō to maintain bonfires to give the impression that his army was still encamped there.

On the tenth day of the ninth month, at daybreak, Lord Shingen crossed the Hirose Ferry, deployed his 8,000 men, and was waiting for the first report of his spearheads, when, as the sun rose and the mist completely dissipated, he saw Terutora's 13,000 men positioned right before him and very close indeed. Kenshin was his powerful enemy and, even with an equal number of troops, it would have been a dangerous battle for him. But he had only 8,000, Kenshin 13,000. Even if we win, the Takeda men thought—and with reason—a great many of us will be killed.

Lord Shingen summoned a Shinano warrior by the name of Urano, a man accomplished in bow and arrow, and sent him out as a scout. Urano returned from the scouting, sat respectfully in front of him, and said, "Sir, Terutora has already left."

Lord Shingen, being a discerning general, said, "Do you suppose someone like Kenshin crosses a river during the night and then, as the day breaks, leaves without doing anything? Tell me, how did he leave?"

Urano said, "Sir, he would circle along our formation and come up to our front. As he repeated this move a number of times, he gradually went off toward the Sai River."

On hearing this, Lord Shingen said, "I can't believe you say such a thing, Urano. That's a formation called 'wheeling,'[19] and it's employed when you want your aides-de-camp to clash with your enemy aides-de-camp. This means Kenshin wants to make this his final battle with me."

Lord Shingen at once began redeploying his men.

Kenshin placed a powerful commander by the name of Amakazu, Governor of Ōmi, along with a unit of 1,000 foot soldiers, far behind the front, and appointed a commander by the name of Naoe, with 2,000 soldiers, magistrate of provisions, Kenshin himself leading a force of 10,000. Then, with a commander by the name of Kakizaki as spearhead, Kenshin heading the second group, they charged headlong, banners tilting, starting the battle in a single sweep.

Almost at once, one unit of Kenshin's aides-de-camp turned around to the right of Shingen's camp, drove off Lord Yoshinobu's fifty mounted aides-de-camp, along with about 400 troops, and cut into Lord Shingen's aides-de-camp. 3,600 or 3,700 soldiers, friends and

19. A wheel-shaped formation from one part of which small units of mounted soldiers gallop out continually to combat the enemy.

foes combined, were thrown into a melee, stabbing and getting stabbed, slashing and getting slashed, some grabbing each other's armored shoulders, grappling and falling down; one would take his enemy's head and rise to his feet, when someone, shouting, "That's my master's head," would skewer him with his spear, and a third, seeing that, would cut that man down. The Kai forces were so taken up by what was happening right in front of them they didn't even know where Lord Shingen was. The same was true of the Echigo forces.

At that moment a warrior wearing a pale-green sleeveless jacket, his head wrapped in a white kerchief, riding a light cream-colored horse, a three-foot drawn sword in hand, galloped straight up to Lord Shingen, who was sitting in his chair, struck at him three times, barely missing him each time. Lord Shingen stopped the blows with his battle-fan. When later examined, the fan had eight sword cuts. His chief attendant and the head of his twenty-man bodyguard, twenty men in all, each a brave warrior, ferociously fought back, even while surrounding him lest friends or foes spot him, cutting down anyone who came close. Ōsumi Governor Hara, the chief attendant, took up Lord Shingen's spear, which had blue shells inlaid in its handle, and stabbed at the warrior in the pale-green sleeveless damask jacket on the light cream-colored horse. He missed. He stabbed at the top of the warrior's armor but hit the forward part of his horse's rump. The horse reared straight up, then bolted. When later inquired about, the warrior turned out to be no other than Terutora.

Among Lord Shingen's aides-de-camp, Obu Saburō, of the Middle Palace Guards, along with his men, repelled Echigo's first spearhead, Kakizaki and his men, and pursued them for about 300 yards. Anayama and his men, too, pursued Kenshin's retainer, Shibata, for about 400 yards. All that while Lord Shingen had only his chief attendant, twenty-man bodyguard, and seventeen or eighteen pages, Tsuchiya Heihachi and Naoda Kihei among them, but would not withdraw a single step, standing at the spot where he rose from his chair.

But all of the nine other units on the Kai force, Lord Tarō Yoshinobu's included, were defeated, and they retreated toward the Hirose Ferry on the Chikuma River. Among them, the Tenkyū and Governor of Bungo Morozumi were killed; among the aides-de-camp and commanders of foot soldiers, Yamamoto Kansuke, the Lay Monk Dōki and Hajika Gengorō were killed. Lord Shingen received two light wounds on his arm, and Lord Tarō Yoshinobu received two wounds.

Most of the people had decided that in this battle Lord Shingen had lost, when the ten spearheading commanders who had gone to Mt. Saijō and realized that they'd been duped by Kenshin, and who, hearing the gunshots and battle cries, had vied with one another in crossing the Chikuma River, began attacking the Echigo forces from their rear and charged and charged as the latter retreated.

Kenshin, indomitable though he was, was accompanied only by a warrior by the name of Wada Kihē. He had to let go his honored horse, Hōjō Tsukige, and, riding his administrator's reserve horse, retreated to Mt. Takanashi.

Lord Shingen's warrior by the name of Yamadera took back the Tenkyū's head from the man who had taken it, and, in so doing, killed him, bringing back *his* head along with the Tenkyū's. As for Morozumi, a warrior under his command, Ishiguro Gorō, of the Middle Palace Guards, and a masterless warrior from Mikawa by the name of Naruse, took his head back and came back with the heads of some Echigo men.

In this battle, the round that started at around six in the morning ended mostly as a victory for Terutora, of Echigo, and the round that started at around ten ended as a victory for Lord Shingen, of Kai. The number of Echigo men killed, including ordinary soldiers, reached 3,117. With the lists of their heads Lord Shingen raised a victory cry around four in the afternoon. On that occasion Minor Controller of the Popular Affairs Ministry Baba held his lordship's sword, and Moroga, a warrior in the vanguard of Shinano, held his bow and arrow.

EVENTS FOLLOWING THE KAWANAKAJIMA CONFRONTATIONS

In the eighth month of the seventh year of Eiroku [1564], Kenshin himself inspected the border with Shinano Province. Shingen also took up a position facing him. The commanders of both houses tried to persuade their masters, saying, "Sir, simply because of four counties, you have had military confrontations with your powerful enemy for twelve years now and lost a great many of your officers and soldiers as a result. This has only benefited the provinces surrounding us. Please do not do it again."

Kenshin and Shingen agreed, and each promised to select a wrestler, have the two fight, and allow the winner's side to take Kawanakajima. Uesugi's wrestler won. Thereupon Shingen took only Kaizu Castle, and everything else belonged to Kenshin. Kenshin restored Murakami Yoshikiyo and Takanashi Masayori and had them regain their villages. . . .

Earlier, Imagawa Yoshimoto had fought [Oda] Nobunaga, and had been defeated and killed.[20] His son Ujizane was dumb and feeble and left the administration to his favorite subject, Miura Yoshishige. The people of his land would not obey him. Our lord Tokugawa [Ieyasu][21] once belonged to Imagawa. He now belonged to Oda. His army grew every day. At the time [Shingen's father] Nobutora was still alive, living a wanderer's life in Shinano. He sent a man to Shingen to say, "Suruga is in chaos. Tokugawa is about to possess it. You should go ahead and take it." Shingen did not reply.

Shingen's province did not have any coastline. He obtained salt from the Tōkai. Ujizane conspired with Hōjō Ujiyasu and secretly closed the supply routes for salt. Kai suffered greatly. When Kenshin heard this he sent a letter to Shingen and said, "I hear, sir, that Ujiyasu and Ujizane torment you by means of salt. This is cowardly and unjust. I fight you, but I fight with bow and arrow, not with rice and salt. I beg you, sir, that henceforth you obtain salt from my land. The quantity may be large or small, depending on your need."

He then ordered merchants to supply Shingen with salt at an equitable price. . . .

In the first year of Genki [1570] a clan under Sano Masatsuna took over Iimori Castle to fight Masatsuna. Hōjō Ujimasa[22] aided the attack with 40,000 soldiers. Masatsuna informed Kenshin of the emergency. In the first month Kenshin left and marched day and night. When he heard that Ujimasa planned to divide his troops, one group to fend him off, the other to launch a sudden assault on the castle to bring it down, he said to his commanders, "Even if I fight and defeat Ujimasa, it will be of no use if I fail to rescue the castle from falling into

---

20. The fifth month, 1560. See note 4 of this section.

21. Tokugawa Ieyasu (1542–1616) founded the Tokugawa Shogunate. For those under the shogunate, San'yō among them, reverence for Ieyasu as the "founding father" was required as a matter of course: hence "our." A son of a small local clan in Mikawa, Ieyasu was forced to spend most of his first twenty years a hostage.

22. Ujiyasu's oldest son (1538–90). He committed suicide when an overwhelming army commanded by Toyotomi Hideyoshi surrounded his Odawara Castle.

the enemy's hand. I will go into the castle by myself and defend it firmly. Put forward Yoshiharu as your commander and advance."

Kenshin then led eighty riders and passed right in front of Ujimasa's army and entered the castle. He was wearing a black cotton robe, but no armor. He held a cross-billed spear as he rode past. The enemy soldiers pointed at him and said, "That's Kenshin." In great consternation they did not dare block him or attack him. His commanders then arrived. Ujimasa's army was crushed and fled. Kenshin scotched Iimori Castle, made a round of Shimotsuke and Kōzuke, and entered Umayabashi. . . .

In the second month of the second year [1571], Shingen led his soldiers to the east[23] and, arriving in Tōtōmi, attacked Takatenjin Castle. In the fourth month he entered Mikawa and brought down eight castles. Tokugawa [Ieyasu] came out to the rescue. But seeing the stern, inviolable lineup of Kai's army, he did not dare go into battle. Nobunaga, hearing that Yoshiaki[24] was inviting Kenshin and Shingen to join him, became mortally afraid. He intensified his flattery of Shingen, sending him a letter of apology in which he said, "Ieyasu has come very close to your land. It must have been some error on his part. I will point it out to him. I would be grateful if you would not reprimand him." Shingen replied and said, "Sir, I do not know what you are talking about."

Tokugawa sent two messengers to establish a favorable link with Kenshin, proposing, with a firm pledge of alliance, to attack Shingen from two sides. Murakami Yoshikiyo's son, Kunikiyo, who was in Echigo, strongly supported this move. In the fourth month of the third year [1572], Kenshin, commanding 10,000 soldiers, came out to Shinano and set fire in Naganuma, thereby showing his support from a distance. When Katsuyori, who was in Ina, received the news of this danger, he took 800 soldiers to defend the place. Kenshin said, "He wants to fend me off with such a small number of soldiers. He certainly is worthy of being Shingen's son. I will add to his reputation

---

23. The ultimate goal of any warlord worth his salt was to "put up his flag and drum in Kyoto," as San'yō makes Shingen say in the preceding, untranslated section. Shingen finally began to make that move.

24. Yoshiaki (1537–97), the fifteenth Ashikaga shogun. The year 1568, when Nobunaga entered Kyoto supporting Yoshiaki's legitimacy as shogun, is traditionally regarded as the end of Japan's "age of warring states." Yoshiaki regarded Nobunaga as a mere supporter. Nobunaga regarded Yoshiaki as his puppet. As a result their relationship became strained almost at once, with Yoshiaki constantly seeking other warlords' aid in trying to subdue Nobunaga.

as a man of bravery." He pulled back his soldiers, then entered Etchū and subjugated the Shiina and Jinbō clans.

In the tenth month Shingen, taking advantage of Kenshin's immobility because of snow,[25] again went to Tōtōmi and brought down Futamata Castle. Nobunaga secretly sent soldiers to help Tokugawa. In the twelfth month Shingen advanced and took up a position in Mikata Field, thereby threatening Hamamatsu Castle. As a challenge he set fire to the town surrounding the castle. The soldiers in the castle would not come out. Shingen feigned withdrawing. The solders in the castle rushed out. Noto Governor Uehara said to Oyamada Masayuki, "Tokugawa's formation is simple. I see Oda's banners moving. We should defeat them."

Masayuki forwarded the message to Shingen. Shingen moved his troops back. Masayuki, along with Katsuyori, Yamagata Masakage, and Baba Nobumasa, was the spearhead. First, Masayuki and Masakage made a joint retreat. Katsuyori and Nobufusa followed this with a thrust into the enemy core. Meanwhile Shingen dispatched Tango Governor Yonekura to launch an attack from the flank, and resoundingly defeated Tokugawa.

Some commanders begged Shingen to attack Hamamatsu. Kōsaka Masanobu said, "No, that won't do. If we attack but can't bring it down in twenty days, Nobunaga is bound to come to help with a great force. If we then end up facing him for several months and if Kenshin comes out to Shinano, we'll be forced to go back to the rescue. If that happens, Nobunaga will say, 'I even repelled Shingen.' That will harm our lord's great reputation."

Shingen retreated to encamp in Osakabe. During this battle he captured Oda's commander, Hirade Hirohide, and sent his head to Nobunaga with a letter of censure announcing he was severing their relationship. Even then Nobunaga did not stop making various excuses.

In the first month of the first year of Tenshō [1573], Shingen brought down Noda Castle. He became ill and went back. Nobunaga begged Shogun Yoshiaki to persuade Shingen to stop moving his army. Shingen declined, listing Nobunaga's five crimes. In the second month he had Akiyama Haruchika lure Iwamura Castle into surrender. The wife of the commanding officer of the castle was Nobunaga's

---

25. Echigo (present-day Niigata), Kenshin's province, faces the Japan Sea and is famous for great snowfalls.

aunt. Haruchika took her away and made her his wife. Many soldiers from Kyoto and its vicinity came to say congratulations.

Shingen recovered from his illness and set off again. He said, "With this expedition I am determined to enter Kyoto." Accompanied by 30,000 soldiers he came to Mino. Nobunaga went out with 10,000 soldiers to defend himself. Yamagata Masakage, with 800 riders, ran up against him. Nobunaga fled without fighting and redoubled his efforts to beg for a truce. Shingen would not listen. He turned and entered Mikawa and encamped in Hiraya.

SHINGEN'S DEATH

In the fourth month Shingen's illness recurred. He determined that he would not recover, summoned his commanders, and gave them instructions on things to be done after his death. He ordered Katsuyori to serve as his deputy until Nobukatsu grew up.[26] He warned him, saying, "You must restrain yourself lest you indulge in moving your soldiers and destroy our country. If I die, there will be only one man under Heaven: Kenshin. You must request his support and entrust this country to him. Once he agrees to be entrusted, he will never join with his neighbors to invade you." These words finished, Shingen became unconscious. After a while he awoke briefly, called Yamagata Masakage, and said, "Tomorrow, raise your flag at Seta."[27] He then died. He was fifty-three years old.

His commanders hid his death in accordance with his orders. Because his brother Nobutsuna looked like him, they put Nobutsuna in a palanquin and went back. The word was, "Because of illness Shingen has returned to his country."[28] On the night of his death he had met all the messengers from various lands. Also, he had signed in advance several hundred blank sheets of paper to be used to respond to written inquiries. As a result of all this no one invaded the land.

Shingen constantly read a range of books. He took Sun Tzu's words and had them written on his flag: "Immovable as a mountain,

---

26. Nobukatsu was Katsuyori's son. It may be recalled that it had been decided earlier that Katsuyori would inherit the Suwa family.

27. Seta, which is on the left bank of the Seta River, in present-day Ōtsu City, Shiga, was traditionally regarded as the eastern entrance to Kyoto.

28. The Kōyō Gunkan says it was another brother, Nobukane, who pretended to be Shingen. Kurosawa Akira based his movie, Kagemusha, on this story.

destructive as fire, quiet as a forest, swift as a wind."[29] Baba Nobufusa once asked, "Sir, the wind may be swift, but doesn't it cease as soon as it rises?" Shingen said, "In moving an army I'd like to be as swift as I can. Should I have to cease, my second in command would continue." Nobufusa said, "You would then be counting on the second round for victory." In that way the master and his subjects investigated military matters. Everything was done in that fashion.

In the end all of his neighbors heard about Shingen's death. Hōjō Ujimasa rushed a messenger to tell Kenshin of the news. Kenshin happened to be having his meal. He put down his chopsticks and lamented, "I have lost my good rival. We won't have a hero like that again!" For a long time after he privately wept for him.

Kai's four long-standing commanders, Baba Nobufusa, Yamagata Masakage, Naitō Masatoyo, and Kōsaka Masanobu, took turns trying to persuade Katsuyori to request a truce with Kenshin. Katsuyori would not listen. He was by nature self-confident and used his own counsel. He increasingly favored Nagasaka Chōkan and Atobe Katsusuke, who were close to him even while Shingen was alive. He wanted to send out soldiers to Mino. The four commanders each said this would not do. Chōkan and Katsusuke recommended the move and let him send out soldiers. It happened that Mikawa's army surrounded Nagashino, and the move was stopped at once.

In the fifth month Katsuyori dispatched Nobufusa to rescue Nagashino. The Mikawa army placed some soldiers in ambush, burned firewood, and, pretending that it had set fire to its own camp and escaped, offered itself as bait. The Kai men wanted to give chase. Nobufusa said, "The smoke is white. They didn't burn down their camp." He sent out some riders to check it out. As expected, they found soldiers waiting to waylay them. At once they retreated and encamped in Kurose. They brought down a castle and went back. In the meantime Masakage headed to Hamamatsu but did not gain any advantage and went back.

In the second month of the second year [1574], Katsuyori went out to Mino and brought down various forts. In the fifth month he attacked and brought down Takatenjin. Back home he gave a banquet for his men. Masanobu and Masatoyo said to each other, "This banquet

---

29. Reference to section 3, chapter 7, "On Battles," of the *Sun Tzu:* "An army survives by deception, moves for advantage, and changes by dispersal and concentration of forces. It is as swift as a wind, quiet as a forest, destructive as fire, immovable as a mountain, unfathomable as darkness, vigorous as thunder." San'yō somehow reverses the order of the listing.

portends the fall of the Takeda clan." Masanobu tried to persuade Katsuyori, saying, "Sir, you are becoming used to victories and aren't trying to restrain yourself. To stir up resentments in your neighbors isn't good for long-term planning. You should give back the lands to the two houses and work out a truce so that you may eventually take over the Eastern region and assemble a sufficient force."

The two favorites blocked the move. As they recommended, Katsuyori went out to Tōtōmi. He crossed the Tenryū River but did not encounter any enemy and turned back. On his way back, in Ina, he found Nobutora. The man was already eighty. Katsuyori wanted to carry him home. But seeing that Nobutora was as violent as ever, he gave up the notion.

Observing that Shingen's neighbors and the Kai soldiers no longer frequently contended with one another, Nobunaga sensed that Shingen must have died, and for a while tried to confirm it.

After Shingen's death Nobunaga concentrated his attention on Kenshin. He deprecated himself and exalted Kenshin, trying to be as subservient as he had been to Shingen. He made his sister marry Jinbō Nagasumi. Nagasumi was Uesugi Yoshiharu's older brother and was on Kenshin's side. So Nobunaga openly linked himself with Kenshin, while secretly working out schemes against him. With similarly secret planning he invited some of the commanders under the Uesugi clan to pledge allegiance to him. Kenshin wrote to censure his treacherous act. Nobunaga wrote back to make excuses. Kenshin would not listen.

Hatakeyama Yoshitaka's commanders, Yusa Danjō and others, poisoned Yoshitaka and surrendered to Nobunaga with Nanao Castle as a trophy. In the seventh month Kenshin, commanding 30,000 soldiers, went to subjugate the west. He attacked Nagasumi at Kibune Castle and brought him down, entered Kaga and conquered Kanazawa; he then moved his soldiers to attack Nanao, and, with Yoshiharu as commander, took Noto with effort. Yusa and others begged Nobunaga for help. Nobunaga, attacking Nagashima at the time, was unable to come. In the ninth month the castle fell, and Kenshin killed Yusa and others. He then had his soldiers rest; the second day was the night of a thirteenth-day moon, which was bright and clear. He distributed sake to his army and assembled his commanders. As the drinking reached its peak, Kenshin made a poem:

Frost fills the camp, the autumn air fresh.
Several lines of geese pass, the moon at midnight.

Echigo mountains, now Noto scenery taken.
No matter: People back home think of this expedition.

He selected officers and soldiers who were good at singing verse and had them sing this.

When he finished the administrative matters of the country, he went back. Nobunaga came to the rescue with a great army, but when he learned that the castle had already fallen, he left. Still, he sent a messenger to Kenshin to convey his apologies.

BATTLE OF NAGASHINO

This year Nobunaga invited Mikawa's commander, Okudaira Nobumasa, to surrender and had him defend Nagashino against Kai. In the fourth month of the third year [1575], Mikawa's accounting officer, Ōga so-and-so, secretly sent a letter to Kai, pledging to revolt if Kai attacked. Katsuyori took up a position at Nire Castle. When he heard that Ōga's scheme had been exposed and Ōga killed, he went back.

In the fifth month Katsuyori left Masanobu with 10,000 soldiers to defend against Echigo; he himself led 15,000 and surrounded Nagashino, encamping in Dōko Temple. He had his uncle, Nobuzane, defend the fort at Tobinosu. Tokugawa requested Nobunaga for reinforcements. Nobunaga would not come out. Messengers were sent three times, but he would not agree. A messenger said, "If you don't help us, we will give Tōtōmi to Takeda, become his vanguard, and take Owari. Also, Shingen is dead. Sir, why are you so afraid?"

Thereupon Nobunaga came to help, with himself as commander. His soldiers numbered about 70,000. Even then, worried about clashes with Kai's mounted soldiers, he built three layers of fences and lined up 10,000 guns for defense.[30]

Katsuyori wanted to fight. Nobufusa, Masakage, and Masatoyo all counseled against it, saying, "The enemy forces are new, and their spirits are high. It is best to avoid them for a while. Or else, attack the castle at once. We may suffer casualties but we should bring it down before going back."

---

30. Actually, 3,000 harquebuses. The harquebuses of the day had a range of less than a hundred yards and took time to reload. To make up for these weaknesses, Nobunaga for the first time divided the gun unit into three and had the three groups shoot by turns. The fences were built to block the onslaught of Takeda's famous mounted soldiers.

The two favorites said, "Today is the day for a battle to conquer the two enemies. Don't listen to those old and cowardly people."

Nobufusa said, "In today's battle we the old and cowardly will all die. You gentlemen will simply run away."

In the end Katsuyori made Muroga Yukitoshi and Oyamada Masayuki stay and surround the castle, and he himself advanced and crossed the river. The next morning the enemy assaulted Tobinosu from the flank. Nobuzane was defeated and killed. Our camp looked back at this and became restless.

The enemy men issued a challenge to battle. Masakage was the spearhead of the left wing. He dashed ahead, broke through a fence, was hit by a bullet, and died. Nobufusa was the spearhead of the right wing. Along with Sanada Noriyuki and Tsuchiya Naomura, he broke through a fence. Noriyuki and Naomura were also hit by bullets and died. Muroga Yukitoshi came and begged, "Sir, shouldn't we lift the siege?" Katsuyori said, "You may." Before he said this, most of his forces had perished.

Nobufusa rushed a man to Katsuyori to say, "Sir, leave this place at once. I beg you. I will stay here and die." He stayed on with eighty horsemen to fight and lost all of them. He climbed a hill and, seeing that Katsuyori was now far away, shouted loudly to the enemy, "I am Baba, Governor of Mino. Kill me if you can and win a big reward!" Enemies gave him multiple stabs, and he died.

The two favorites got away first. Masanobu must have known of the defeat of the Takeda forces beforehand: With 8,000 soldiers he came to the border to meet Katsuyori and take him home. He reminded him of the earlier warnings and asked him to marry a Hōjō woman, so as to fend off the two enemies. Katsuyori followed this advice. . . .

KENSHIN'S DEATH

This year Katsuyori sent a messenger to request a truce with Kenshin so that he might retaliate against Oda. Kenshin agreed and offered to take Katsuyori's son as hostage. Katsuyori did not approve. About that time Tokugawa attacked Futamata Castle. The commanding officer of the castle, Yoda Yukinari, defended it firmly and did not surrender. Accordingly, Tokugawa attacked and brought down Suwanohara, in the end attacking Oyama. Katsuyori said, "Does he think I'm too disabled to come out again?" He assembled 20,000 soldiers and went to the rescue. The enemy lifted the siege and left.

In the twelfth month Yukinari died. Tokugawa came out to attack again. Yukinari's son, Nobushige, put up a defense. Katsuyori ordered him to abandon the castle and withdraw. Iwamura fell again. Nobunaga killed his aunt by his own hand.[31]

In this month Katsuyori received Hōjō's daughter and married her. After returning from the ceremony, Masanobu said, "Tonight I can sleep well for the first time."

In the spring of the fourth year [1576], Katsuyori took his soldiers to Tōtōmi and faced Tokugawa in Yokosuka. Katsuyori wanted to fight. Masanobu counseled against it and said, "You lost many of the old commanders in the Nagashino battle. I am the only one left. Do you mean to kill me, too?" Katsuyori withdrew and, after building a fort in Sagara, went back.

Echigo's commanders tried to persuade Kenshin by saying, "Sir, the Kai army was defeated again. You should take advantage of this."

Kenshin said, "I fought Shingen fifteen or sixteen times but was unable to take his country. Now he's dead. If I act in contempt of his poor son, take advantage of his defeat, and get his country, how can I face the world with clear conscience?"

In the third month Kenshin entered Etchū, took Hasunuma, captured and killed Shiina Yasutane, and had a commander of his enter Hida and conquer the Ema clan. . . .

Nobunaga secretly invited Chō Shigetsura, a resident of Noto, and Matsutō Hikotsugu, a resident of Kaga, to persuade the Ikkō bandits[32] to move north. In the fifth year [1577] Shigetsura assembled soldiers and made Anamizu Castle his base. In response the castles of Komatsu, Ataka, and Mt. Daidō revolted. At this juncture Tsutsui Junkei and Matsunaga Hisahide,[33] who were based in Yamato, sent letters of allegiance to Kenshin in the distance, begging him to come west. At the same time they sent a pledge to Mōri to the far west, in their attempt to attack Nobunaga from the east and the west.

In the ninth month Kenshin himself as commander attacked and brought down Anamizu, killed Shigetsura, and attacked Komatsu

---

31. See pp. 223–224.

32. Adherents of the Ikkō sect, which initially found converts mainly among the peasants in Kaga, Noto, Etchū, and Echizen. They were often rebellious and at times took over whole provinces.

33. See note 13 of this section.

and Ataka. Nobunaga sent to the rescue five of his commanders, Shibata Katsuie and Maeda Toshiie among them, commanding 48,000 soldiers. He himself secretly came to help. Kenshin attacked and brought down the three castles. He advanced to the Yusurugi Bridge and, encamping twenty-five miles from Oda's army, sent a messenger to obtain a pledge to begin battle the following morning. Nobunaga again escaped by night. Kenshin laughed out loud and said, "Nobunaga is quite good at running. If he had stayed around, I could have kicked all of his men into the water."

Kenshin advanced and attacked Kanazawa and brought it down. Entering Echizen, he attacked Oda's forts as he went, drove off the defending soldiers, and moved on, setting fire to everything. The smoke and dust filled the sky. Nobunaga retreated to Kitanoshō, then retreated and entered Nagahama.

As the cold set in and the snow began to fall, and hearing that Hisahide and others had already been defeated and killed, Kenshin wanted to take his army home. He sent a letter to Nobunaga and said, "Shingen is already dead. That you, sir, leave Shirō[34] to Ieyasu, while yourself staying in Azuchi, must mean that you are making preparations against me. You've had easy fights with your enemies in the Kyoto region. You have yet to observe a northerner's skills. With your permission, sir, I'd like to come west to meet you with soldiers from the eight provinces[35] next spring, on the fifteenth day of the third month. Try, sir, not to regard me, Kenshin, the way you do the leather-sandaled city folk." He said this last because at the time the people in Kyoto loved to wear leather sandals. He had a messenger take this letter, along with 2,000 bolts of Echigo fabric as a gift.

Nobunaga met the messenger and said, "Please go back and report this to Lord Echigo for me. I, Nobunaga, have no reason to contest his lordship. Should he come to visit, I would take off my swords and, carrying nothing but a fan on my hip, ride out alone to receive him and guide him into Kyoto. His lordship is a man of justice. I know he would never rob me of the lands I struggle to manage."

The messenger returned and conveyed these words. Kenshin laughed and said, "Nobunaga is a treacherous soldier. He is trying to put me off guard with sweet words. I hear that in the Nagashino battle he tormented Shirō, of Kai, with fences and guns. The next year he is

---

34. Takeda Katsuyori.
35. Echigo, Etchū, Kaga, Noto, Hida, Shinano, Kōzuke, and Sado.

bound to try something similar with me. I have no intention whatsoever to be trapped by his schemes."

In the tenth month Kenshin returned to Echigo and sent out written appeals every other day to raise armies from the eight provinces under his control, with the target date of the fifth day of the third month. As for the soldiers in Kaga and to its west, he planned to pick them up as he moved along.

The news made the Kyoto region quake. Nobunaga sent a messenger to inform Katsuyori of this, begging him to forget what had happened between them in the past and to restore their old relations. He said, "If Kenshin comes west, Ieyasu and I will block him on the Northern Route. I hope, sir, that you will then immediately move to Echigo. If we win, you may keep the land you take." Katsuyori did not reply.

In the third month of the sixth year [1578], soldiers of the Hokuriku provinces gathered like clouds in response to Kenshin's appeals. Kenshin himself reviewed them, made pledges, and was about to set out. Two days before setting out, an illness struck, and he died two days later. He was forty-nine. He died five years after Shingen did.

ODA NOBUNAGA:
THE WARLORD AND POETRY

THE LIFE OF ODA NOBUNAGA (1534–82), who started the process of unifying war-torn Japan but was assassinated before achieving his goal, is linked to verse in a fascinating way: No versifier himself, he made his debut as a warlord singing a song about the transience of life; and his assassin, who in effect helped fulfill that prophecy, took that step after participating in a verse-composing session.

One of the most inspiring battles in Japan's "age of warring states" is the one at Okehazama. In it, Nobunaga, leading less than 2,000 men, attacked Imagawa Yoshimoto (1519–60), leading 25,000, and won. In the fifth month of 1560, Yoshimoto, the most powerful warlord along the Pacific Coast ("The Number One Bowman of the Eastern Sea"), headed west for Kyoto with an army combining the forces of the three provinces of Suruga, Tōtōmi, and Mikawa. Nobunaga, situated in Owari, was in his way but was not regarded as capable of putting up a credible fight. Indeed, by the morning of the nineteenth of the fifth month, only a day after arriving in Owari, Yoshimoto brought down two of the five forts built against him: Marune Fort, commanded by Sakuma Daigaku Morishige, and Washizu Fort, commanded by Oda Genba, with both commanders killed.

How Nobunaga faced an invader with overwhelming forces and mounted a successful counterattack is memorably told by Ōta Gyūichi (1527–1610?) in his *Shinchō-kō Ki* (Biography of Lord Nobunaga), which he is said to have written on the basis of notes he took while still "running about on active duty" as a bowman under Nobunaga.

On the eighteenth, when he received news of Yoshimoto's arrival in his territory, Nobunaga was in his main fort, Kiyosu Castle.

Oda Nobunaga

His conversations that night contained nothing remotely related to military matters, as they consisted of social gossip. When he found it was very late, he gave his men leave to go home. His house administrators derided him among themselves as they left, saying, "Well, the adage, 'When luck runs out, the mirror of one's wisdom clouds up, too,' is meant for this kind of behavior."

As expected, toward daybreak, messages from Sakuma Daigaku and Oda Genba arrived, one following the other, reporting that the enemy had already begun attacking Mt. Washizu and Mt. Marune.

On hearing this, Nobunaga danced the Atsumori dance, singing:

A man lives for fifty years.
When compared with the Lowest Heaven,[1]
it's like a dream, an illusion.
Is there anyone who, given life once,
never fades away?

This done, he commanded, "Blow the conch shell! Give me my equipment!" He then put on his armor, ate his breakfast standing, put on his helmet, and sallied forth. Accompanying him at that moment were his pages, Nagato Governor Iwamuro, Hasegawa Hashisuke, Sawaki Tōhachi, Hida Governor Yamaguchi, and Gatō Yasaburō.

The six of them, master and retainers together, galloped straight over the seven miles to Atsuta, where, in front of Gendayū Shrine, he looked east and saw smoke rising from Washizu and Marune, both forts evidently fallen. At the time there were six men on horseback and about 200 foot soldiers. If he pushed forward from the beach side, that would have been the shortest way, but the tides were up and would not have allowed horses to pass. So he and his men galloped through the hillside road from Atsuta, first arriving at the fort at Tange, then at the fort at Zenshō Temple where Sakuma [Uemon] had set up camp. There he counted his men and reviewed the situation. The reports said:

---

1. *Geten.* It refers to *Shiō-ten,* one of the Six Realms of Desire, and *Shiō-ten* is called *Geten* because it is located at the lowest stratum. In this "heaven" one day and night is the equivalent of fifty years of a human life.

His enemy Imagawa Yoshimoto, leading an army of 45,000 men,[2] was resting his men and horses on Mt. Okehazama. At noon on the nineteenth, he lined up his men to face northwest and said, "I couldn't be more pleased that you men attacked and brought down Washizu and Marune." He then had three rounds of nō chanting performed. This time Ieyasu[3] was the first to attack; leading men in red coats, he carried provisions into Ōtaka Castle, struggled at Washizu and Marune, and, because of all the difficulties he had had, was now resting his men and horses at Ōtaka, where he set up camp.

Seeing Nobunaga going to Zenshō Temple, the two commanders Sasa Hayato no Shō and Chiaki Shirō headed toward Yoshimoto with a light brigade of 300 men, but they were swamped in a sudden onslaught, both men, along with fifty riders, killed in battle. Yoshimoto saw this as a sign that even Heaven's demon or devils or gods would not be able to bear the brunt of his might. Feeling delighted about this, he had nō chanting performed in leisurely fashion as he laid out his camp.

These reports heard, Nobunaga decided to move to Nakajima. His house administrators loudly protested, holding on to the bit of his horse, saying, "Sir, the road there is flanked by deep paddies. Once you step into them, you won't be able to move. Besides, you'll be forced to march in a single file. That will make the puny size of our forces perfectly visible to the enemy. This is out of the question, sir!" But Nobunaga wrung himself free and moved to Nakajima. At the time his men are said to have numbered less than 2,000.

At Nakajima he again tried to move his men forward. This time, his administrators held on to him and succeeded in stopping him. Thereupon, he harangued his men:

"All of you, listen to me carefully. The enemy soldier came here, eating food in the evening and marching throughout the night. He had to carry his provisions into Ōtaka, worked hard at Washizu and Marune, and is exhausted with all the difficulties he's had. We, on the other hand, are a fresh army. Besides, you all know the saying, don't you, 'Don't be afraid of a large enemy because your forces are small. Luck resides in Heaven.'

---

2. Yoshimoto spread the rumor that he was leading an army of 40,000 men. The biographer further inflated the figure.

3. Tokugawa Ieyasu (1543–1616), who unified Japan and established his own shogunate. At the time he was going by the name of Matsudaira Motoyasu and, though he had his own castle, was Yoshimoto's virtual hostage. Sometime after Yoshimoto's death, he became Nobunaga's important ally. Hence this special reference to the enemy commander.

"If the enemy attacks, retreat. If he retreats, give chase. The idea is to wrestle him down and destroy him in the chase. Don't capture anybody. Just leave him alone. If we win in this battle, those of you taking part will bring honor to your houses, your reputation assured in generations to come. So do your best!"

While he was making this harangue, the following men—

Maeda Matazaemon, Mōri Kawachi, Mōri Jūrō, Kinoshita Utanosuke, Nakagawa Kin'emon, Sakuma Yatarō, Mori Kosuke, Ajiki Yatarō, and Uozumi Hayato

returned, each carrying the head or heads of the enemies he killed. After repeating his words to these men, Nobunaga took his forces to the hillside. Suddenly a downpour as fierce as catapulted ice stones struck the enemy in the face, Nobunaga's troops from the rear. The rain was so powerful that the camphor tree growing near the pines on Kutsukake Pass that would have required two or three men with arms spread to surround it tipped east and fell. The fierceness of it was such that people wondered if the Great Deity of Atsuta had started his own war.

The moment the sky cleared, Nobunaga lifted his spear and shouted loudly, "Attack now! Attack!" The enemy, seeing an assault coming forward like black smoke, suddenly fell back like a wave rolling back. Bows, spears, guns, banners, and battle-markers were thrown into confusion, as the enemy fell back and retreated, abandoning even Yoshimoto's lacquered palanquin.

Nobunaga barked a command, "That's his camp. Attack!"

It was around two in the afternoon that he directed his attack east. At first about 300 riders made a complete circle around Yoshimoto as they retreated, but as they fought the assaulting forces two, three times, four, five times, their number gradually decreased, and in the end only about fifty riders were left.

Nobunaga himself dismounted and rushed forward with young warriors, felling enemies forward and backward, as young men in their fury attacked chaotically, blade clashing against blade, sword-guard splitting swordguard, sparks flying, fire spewing. In all this, enemy and friendly warriors never confused themselves with each other, distinguishing themselves by color. Many of Nobunaga's horse-tenders [cavalrymen] and pages were wounded or killed.

Hashimoto Koheita attacked Yoshimoto, but, his knee slashed, fell down. Mōri Shinsuke cut Yoshimoto down and took his head. . . .

The place known as Okehazama is a valley, an extremely difficult terrain where deep paddies prevent mobility and high and low places are combined intricately. Those who fled into deep paddies could only crawl about, unable to get away. With these Nobunaga's young soldiers caught up, each taking two or three heads, bringing them to him. Nobunaga announced that he would conduct formal inspection of the heads at Kiyosu but he was more than satisfied to see Yoshimoto's head. He returned to his camp along the road he had taken earlier.

The "conversations" mentioned at the outset are *o-hanashi*, sometimes called *o-togi*. The conversations a master or a lord had with his ranking aides, though often idle or merely entertaining, formed a vital source of information or provided an occasion for assessment or analysis. This particular night Nobunaga's aides who gathered around him must have expected him to discuss how to respond to Yoshimoto's invasion, asking each one for his opinion. Instead, he whiled away most of the evening or most of the night, *not* talking about the pressing issues. That is why his house administrators were put off.

The verse Nobunaga sang as he danced is from a Kōwaka dance called *Atsumori*. This dance-narrative is an extended version of a brief, affecting episode in the *Heike Monogatari* where Kumagae no Jirō Naozane (1141–1208) is forced to kill Taira no Atsumori (1169–84), a teenage enemy commander his own son's age.[4] The verse is part of Naozane's thoughts as he realizes the transience of this world and decides to take Buddhist vows.

Such explanations aside, imagine a modern-day general dancing a dance expressing the transience of life, accompanied by his own singing, before leading his men into battle!

Nobunaga is known to have often sung this particular verse from *Atsumori*. But his love of songs was obvious. For example, he is said to have encouraged his soldiers to follow him and sing a song three times before springing out of their positions for assault on a battlefield. Still, as noted, he himself evidently did not compose much verse. There is, however, one episode where he appears as a versifier.

The episode, which forms a part of *Shinchō Ki* (Biography of Nobunaga) by Oze Hoan (1564–1640),[5] describes the time when Nobunaga entered Kyoto

---

4. See note 10, p. 117.
5. A revised version of Ōta Gyūichi's *Shinchō-kō Ki*. In defense of his rewriting Hoan said that Gyūichi's account was "simplistic" and "choppy," and that it had "oversights"

as the first official military backer of the fifteenth and last Ashikaga shogun, Yoshiaki (1537–97). Some decades before then the Ashikaga shogunate had come to exist in name only. Yoshiaki's own brother, the thirteenth shogun Yoshiteru (1536–65), was attacked and killed by his aides, and he himself became a refugee. (How Yoshiteru refused to flee from an on-coming army and, by implanting a number of drawn swords in the floor of the middle of his room, fought, wielding one sword after another, until he was overwhelmed and killed, is part of samurai lore.)

The shogunate had come to exist in name only, but it had one vital reason for existence. Ever since Japan became the so-called warrior's domain in the mid-twelfth century, anyone willing to engage in struggles for hegemony, provincial or national, faced a dilemma: if you say you can do anything you please to grab the position you want, you're also allowing that anyone can usurp your position. To deal with this dilemma, most warlords issued stern injunctions against violating the master-subject relationships, while strongly affirming the ultimate one – that between emperor and his top aide in charge of military affairs, the shogun.

So Yoshiaki, even while leading a precarious life as refugee, could still make shogunate claims as he sought from warlords military support to enable him to become shogun. In the second month of 1568 some of those who had assassinated Yoshiteru installed Yoshihide (1540–68), Yoshiaki's nephew, as fourteenth shogun. But Yoshihide was obviously a puppet and lineally not legitimate. In the end, in the seventh month of the same year, one of Yoshiaki's chief vassals, Hosokawa Fujitaka (better known by his later name, Yūsai: 1534–1610), persuaded Nobunaga, the rising star then, to back Yoshiaki.

Here's the episode in question from *Shinchō Ki*.

When Lord Nobunaga reached Kōjō-in, of Mii Temple, whispers spread here and there and people throughout Kyoto, both noble and base, high and low, who had often heard that he had defeated all his enemies, no matter how strong, and pacified a number of provinces, wondered how much more terrifying than a demon or a god he must be; and, now that he was about to enter Kyoto, they became fearful of all sorts of calamities that might befall them.

---

and "omissions," which made him "worried that those whose achievements have been overlooked might be aggrieved." Arai Hakuseki, whose account appears on pp. 273–286, reports his mother's remark that her forbears are mentioned in *Shinchō Ki*.

Indeed, their fears seemed to far exceed those of children who scare themselves by talking about demons who cross the oceans from a foreign country, strike and kill them with pebbles,[6] and devour them as their only food. Some people fled to such neighboring provinces as Tanba and Wakasa, whether they had relatives or not there, while others boarded riverboats on Yodo to go to distant islands. Still others, especially those with names to protect, sent away their wives and children as well as furniture and other valuables to acquaintances they thought trustworthy, while themselves staying home so they might congratulate Lord Nobunaga on his entry into Kyoto. However, even these people continued to worry, as those who knew one another got together and wondered what might befall them, some trying to convince themselves by thinking aloud, "Well, who knows, something good may happen to us because we're staying here." Finally, on the twenty-eighth of the ninth month, Lord Nobunaga arrived at Tōfuku Temple, and all the assessments made earlier proved useless.

At once the renga masters, Shōha and Shōshitsu Shinzen, and among doctors, Nakarai Roan and Suichiku-in Dōzō, and those who'd established their reputations, each in his own field, plus the so-called elders, of Upper and Lower Kyoto, who would take part in any council at a moment's notice, all came to thank Lord Nobunaga with various presents. Among them Shōha went straight to him, with two tip-spreading fans on a tray. Everyone held his breath, thinking, What in the world is he doing? when Shōha, kneeling in front of the lord, and even before adjusting his formal attire, said:

Nihon te ni iru kyō no yorokobi

two held in your hands, the joy today

Lord Nobunaga followed it with:

mai asobu chiyo yorozuyo no ōgi nite

these are the fans with which to dance and play for thousands of generations!

---

6. Pebbles were vital weapons for boys when they fought among themselves. In addition, pebble-throwing was often an integral and of course dangerous part of a rambunctious festival. So the image of a demon killing children with pebbles was, at the time, far less incongruous than it may appear today.

When they heard this story, the old and the young throughout Kyoto were so impressed they couldn't say anything more. "This gentleman is such a ferocious warrior that we had expected him to behave the way Kiso did when he entered Kyoto in the ancient Juei era,[7] but he's turned out to be such an elegant person, hasn't he? Now we can expect nice things from him perhaps," people said, encouraged in their hearts, and breathed a collective sigh of relief.

Here, what I have translated as "tip-spreading fan" is *sue-hirogari no ōgi*. This translation, no less than the original expression, is redundant in a way: When you open a fan, its outer end spreads out. But *sue* of *suehiro* also means "the future," and *suehiro* or *suehirogari* is a celebratory name of the fan. By presenting Nobunaga with *suehirogari no ōgi* the renga master Shōha (also known as Jōha; the family name, Satomura: 1524–1602) was congratulating the warlord for entering Kyoto as shogunate military supporter. Evidently everyone saw that by making this move, Nobunaga, in effect, placed himself in the position of "issuing orders to the world under heaven," as the expression of the day went.

However, Shōha's real trick lay in bringing *two* fans or *ōgi nihon*, for *nihon* also means "Japan." In other words, by saying "two of these propitious things held in your hands, today you must be overjoyed," Shōha also meant "Japan held in your hands, today you truly deserve our congratulations!" In response to this invitation to take part in the composition of a renga, Nobunaga tactfully ignored the blatantly flattering pun and said that the fans—in a traditional Japanese dance an indispensable prop—were only proper for a celebratory dance. The phrase, *mai asobu*, "dance and play," conjures the images of the crane and the tortoise, two creatures inherited from China as symbols of longevity, and the phrase, *chiyo yorozuyo*, "a thousand, ten thousand generations," is a congratulatory set phrase.

Shōha may have been a remote relative of one of Nobunaga's commanders, Akechi Mitsuhide (1524?–82), who killed his lord fourteen years later, in 1582. By that year Nobunaga had gained control of one third of the country, by one estimate. Even though not all the warlords may have had the ambition to "issue orders to the world under heaven," he still had a number of powerful contenders to subdue.

---

7. Kiso Yoshinaka (1154–84), the first Minamoto commander to enter Kyoto after the Minamoto rebelled against the Taira in 1180. See pp. 113–114 and note 6.

In the third month of the year, Nobunaga destroyed Takeda Katsuyori (1546–82), a menace to the northeast, and turned his attention to the west. He ordered his ablest commander, Toyotomi Hideyoshi (1536–98), to start a massive campaign to subjugate the western warlords who had not yet pledged allegiance. Hideyoshi brought down one fort after another, until he reached Takamatsu Castle, in Bitchū Province. It was a difficult castle to scale, so he surrounded it with water to starve them out. But then Mōri Terumoto (1153–1625) came to the rescue with an army estimated to be six times as large as Hideyoshi's. Hideyoshi sent a request to Nobunaga for reinforcements. Nobunaga, apparently deciding to use this opportunity to subjugate not only the warlords of Chūgoku, but also those of Shikoku and Kyūshū, first ordered Mitsuhide and five other commanders to repair to their home provinces and raise armies. He himself planned to lead an army.

For Mitsuhide's subsequent action, we turn to *Shinchō Ki*. In both Sakamoto and Kameyama he had a fort, and the one in Kameyama was his residential castle.

On the twenty-sixth of the fifth month of the tenth year of Tenshō [1582], Koretō, Governor of Hyūga [Akechi Mitsuhide], before leading an army to Chūgoku, went from Sakamoto to Kameyama Castle, in Tamba. The next day he climbed Mt. Atago and while staying at the shrine that night he is said to have drawn a sacred lot[8] two or three times. On the twenty-eighth of the same month he held a renga session at the Nishi no Bō. It began:

Toki wa ima ame ga shita shiru satsuki kana   Mitsuhide

Now is the time to rule the world: It's the fifth month!

minakami masaru niwa no natsuyama   Nishi no Bō

the water upstream increases at the summer hill in the garden

hana otsuru ike no nagare wo seki-tomete   Shōha

the brook from the flower-scattering pond having been dammed

---

8. *Mikuji*, a small, folded piece of paper in which your fortune is predicted.

This hundred-unit sequence finished, he returned to Kameyama. He must have drawn the sacred lot with something in mind as well; for from the make-up of the opening verse it was later guessed that this renga was planned as a prayer for [the successful execution of] a secret scheme. . . .

On the first of the sixth month, Koretō, Governor of Hyūga Mitsuhide, in Kameyama Castle, summoned Akechi Samanosuke, Akechi Jiemon no Jō, Fujita Dengo, Saitō Kuranosuke, and Mizo'o Katsubē no Jō, and said to them secretly: "Gentlemen, I'd like you to give me your lives. If you agree, we may continue our discussion. If not, behead me this instant."

He said this so bluntly the five men were startled and their good spirits vanished. With their breathing quickening, they merely looked at one another. At last Samanosuke spoke up: "Sir, we have held you up as our master until today. Why, then, shouldn't we see you through this grave crisis? No matter what you may have in mind, I, Sama-no-suke, will follow you." At these encouraging words, the remaining four also gave consent.

When he heard this, Mitsuhide said, "Gentlemen, I'm pleased that you've agreed to work with me. To put the matter simply, I have several reasons to kill Lord Nobunaga. And I think the time is pressing. I've been driven into a corner from which there is no escape. This is why I've decided to revolt. . . ."

That day, around seven in the evening, he left Kameyama, with those five men as spearheading generals. After passing Mt. Ōe, they pressed forward at utmost speed, so that by the daybreak of the second the forerunning groups arrived outside Kyoto. As soon as they did, they surrounded Honnō Temple, where Lord Nobunaga was staying and, after raising a great battle cry, shot arrows and guns into the temple. . . .

A number of reasons have been advanced to explain why Mitsuhide, who had served Nobunaga since as early as 1567, decided to revolt at that particular juncture. The most persuasive reason, according to the historian Kuwata Tadachika, is Mitsuhide's accumulated resentment against his lord who often treated him, a commander of distinction, like a mere foot soldier, publicly insulting him on some important occasions. Considering Nobunaga's tyrannical nature, recorded by his contemporary foreign observers such as the Jesuit priest Luis Frois (1532–97), some of the insults Nobunaga is said to have accorded Mitsuhide ring true.

At any rate, Nobunaga had left his main fort, Azuchi Castle–the most extravagant military structure ever built in Japan till then–on the twenty-ninth of the fifth month, and arrived in Kyoto the following day. The purpose of his stay in Honnō Temple was to hold a tea ceremony to display the great Chinese tea utensils he had collected since his first official arrival in Kyoto, in 1568. This partly explains why he took only about thirty pages along with him, but not a sizable group of armed soldiers. In contrast, his son Nobutada, who had preceded him to Kyoto, had taken 2,000 cavalrymen.

On the first of the sixth month he had the tea meeting as planned, with Torii Sōshitsu, a wealthy merchant from Hakata, Chikuzen, as guest of honor. Along with a group of aristocrats as "companion guests," Nobutada also took part. Following the tea ceremony, Nobunaga played go with the master Hon'inbō Sansa until late into the night. After Nobutada took his leave, he went to bed. For the rest of what happened the following morning, we go back to *Shinchō-kō Ki*.

. . . . both Nobunaga and his pages at first thought that some lowly people were making the racket, but in time that proved not to be the case. There were battle cries, and gunshots flew into Nobunaga's quarters. He asked, "Is this a revolt? Whose plot is this?" When Mori Ran[maru] said, "These appear to be Akechi's men, sir," he said, "There's nothing we can do," and, without a moment's hesitation, withdrew into his quarters, with the men on duty there joining him.

Yashiro Katsusuke, Ban Tarōzaemon, Ban Shōrin, and Murata Kichigo ran out of the stables brandishing swords and were killed. Other than these, a total of twenty-four *chūgen*[9] were killed in fighting at the stables, among them Tōkurō, Tōhachi, Iwa, Shinroku, Hikoichi, Yaroku, Kuma, Kogomawaka, Torawaka, and his son Ko-Torawaka.

Those who were killed in the inner quarters were–

The three brothers of Mori Ran[maru], Mori Riki[maru], Mori

---

9. Men whose status is between servant and samurai.

Bō[maru], Ogawa Aihei, Takahashi Toramatsu, Kanamori Ginyū, Sugaya Kakuzō, Ueozumi Katsushichi, Takeda Kitarō, Ōtsuka Mataichirō, Karino Matakurō, Susukida Yogorō, Imagawa Magojirō, Ochiai Kohachirō, Itō Hikosaku, Kukuri Kame, Oida Kame, Yamada Yotarō, Iikawa Miyamatsu, Sofue Mago[maru], Kashiwabaranabe Brothers, Hariami, Hirao Kyūsuke, Ōtsuka Magozō, Yuasa Jinsuke, Ogura Shōju [maru]. These pages were killed while attacking repeatedly. Yuasa Jinsuke and Ogura Shōju[maru]—these two heard the news at an inn in the town, mingled among the enemy, ran into Honnō Temple, and were killed. At the entrance of the kitchen, Takahashi Torazō put up a good defense for a while, doing incomparable work.

Nobunaga at first took up a bow and shot two or three times, but his time must have come: his bowstring snapped. Afterward he fought with a spear but was wounded at the elbow and withdrew. Then to the women who had been around him until then, he said, "There's no need for you women to stay with me. Hurry out!" and chased them out. By then the fire set to the temple was coming close to him. He must have decided he shouldn't show his body; he went into the innermost part, closed the door from inside, and pitilessly disemboweled himself.

It happens that Luis Frois, whose church, as he explained in his letter, was "situated only a street away from the place where Nobunaga was staying," has left us a somewhat different account of Nobunaga's last moments:

> . . . some Christians came just as I was vesting to say an early Mass, and told me to wait because there was a commotion in front of the palace and that it seemed to be something serious as fighting had broken out there. We at once began to hear musket shots and see flames. After this another report came, and we learned that it had not been a brawl but that Akechi had turned traitor and enemy of Nobunaga and had him surrounded. When Akechi's men reached the palace gates, they at once entered as nobody was there to resist them because there had been no suspicion of their treachery. Nobunaga had just washed his hands and face and was drying himself with a towel when they found him and forthwith shot him in the side with an arrow.

Pulling the arrow out, he came out carrying a *naginata*, a weapon with a long blade made after the fashion of a scythe. He fought for some time, but after receiving a shot in the arm he retreated into his chamber and shut the doors.

Some say that he cut his belly, while others believe he set fire to the palace and perished in flames. . . .[10]

Not long after Nobunaga's assassination, some people began linking Mitsuhide's opening verse to his action several days later, as Hoan did in his account. *Toki*, which means "time," also was the name of the clan from which Akechi branched out, so one can be more explicit in interpretation and read a straightforward announcement in the verse: "Now's the time for a Toki to rule the world: It's the fifth month!"

Legend has it that the renga master Shōha was taken to task by Hideyoshi, who hurried back from the west and attacked and defeated Mitsuhide. Shōha wriggled out of the predicament, it is said, by saying that someone had changed a single character in the transcript of the renga session, from *ame ga shita naru* to *ame ga shita shiru*, thereby changing the meaning of the verse from "we're in the rain" to "to rule the world." It is also said that because he immediately sensed what Mitsuhide meant in his opening verse, he tried to counsel against this with his link, by using the word *seki-tomu*, which means "dam," "block."

Some have discounted the linkage, so to speak, arguing that a commander as cautious as Mitsuhide would not have revealed his rebellious intent in such a public forum. Still, to us of later generations, it is fascinating that Nobunaga, who made his debut as a warlord with a snatch of verse on his lips, should be linked to another verse in his death.

On the fifteenth of the following month Hosokawa Fujitaka, who had refused to respond to Mitsuhide's invitation to join him, held a renga session with Shōha and others to commemorate Nobunaga's death. The three opening verses of the hundred-unit sequence are recorded in *Sōken-in Dono Tsuizen Ki* (Record in Memorial to Lord Sōken-in), which Hideyoshi's scribe and ranking aide, Ōmura Yūko, wrote, following the grand funeral Hideyoshi gave Nobunaga. Sōken-in was a temple Nobunaga built next to Azuchi Castle;[11] it was also his posthumous Buddhist name.

---

10. Michael Cooper, *They Came to Japan: An Anthology of European Reports on Japan, 1543–1640*, p. 103.

11. To have himself worshipped, according to Frois. See *They Came to Japan*, pp. 101–102.

Kurozome no yūbe ya nagori sode no tsuyu　　　　　　Fujitaka

Black-dyed, evening lingers with dew on my sleeve

Tama-matsuru no no tsuki no akikaze　　　　　　Ryōgo-in

over the field for the requiem, the moon, the autumn wind

wake-kaeru kage no matsumushi ne ni nakite　　　　　　Shōha

as I return, bell-crickets in the shadow cry out

PART THREE

The Way of the Warrior

HŌJŌ SŌUN:
''LORD SŌUN'S TWENTY-ONE ARTICLES''

AMONG THE MANY *kahō*, "house laws," and *kakun*, "house lessons," left by warlords and other samurai, the group of twenty-one articles attributed to Hōjō Sōun (1432?–1519), known as *Sōun-ji Dono Nijūichi Kajō* (Lord Sōun's Twenty-one Articles), is especially admired for the simplicity and practicality of what the articles say.

Sōun ("Swift Cloud"), who originally called himself Ise Shinkurō Nagauji, was an undistinguished wandering samurai well into his forties. In 1491, when he was nearly sixty years old, he took advantage of the rift between two branches of the Uesugi clan and established himself as lord of Izu Province, part of present-day Shizuoka Prefecture. From then on his influence and domain in the Kantō region increased and in the end he founded the Hōjō clan that lasted for five generations. His success as a warlord derived from his generosity to the peasants, for whom he reduced taxes, and to his retainers, among whom he distributed most of what he gained.

Because a samurai of unremarkable military lineage seized control of a province, the year 1491 is often marked as the beginning of Japan's "age of warring states."

The following "lessons" are thought addressed to samurai retainers, rather than to the heirs of the Hōjō house.

Item: Above all, have faith in the Buddha and in Shinto deities.

Item: Rise, yes, very early in the morning. If you rise late, even your servants will become lax and unusable. You will be failing to do your duties, both official and private. If this begins to happen, you are bound to be given up by your master, so be extremely careful.

Item: In the evening, go to bed no later than two hours after sunset.[1] Night robbers are most likely to sneak in during the four hours around midnight. If you indulge in useless, long chattering in the evening and go to bed near midnight or even later, you'll end up having valuables stolen and ruining yourself. Your reputation outside your household will also suffer. Don't burn up wood and oil for no purpose in the evening.

Get up a few hours before sunup, wash yourself with cold water, and offer prayers. Put yourself in order and give instructions for the day to your wife, children, and retainers. Report to work before sunup. An old saying has it, "Go to bed an hour before midnight and get up a few hours before sunup," but this depends on the person. Still, getting up a few hours before sunup is beneficial to you. If you sleep until after sunup or even close to noon, you won't be able to report to work and carry out your duties, nor will you be able to do your own errands. This is no good. Your daily schedules will not be met.

Item: Before you wash your hands and face, go around and check the toilet, the stable, the garden, even how things look outside the gate. Then tell an appropriate person to clean the places that have to be cleaned first, and quickly wash your hands and face. Water may be available in abundance, but don't simply dump the water you've used for gargling.[2] Though you're in your own house, if you cough loudly, you'll allow yourself to appear inconsiderate to others, and that's unseemly; so cough, if you must, inconspicuously. As they say, "Bend under heaven, step softly on the ground."[3]

Item: Offering prayers is for your own sake. Simply keep your mind straight and pliant, honest and law-abiding. Be respectful to those who are above you, and be compassionate to those who are below you. Accept things as they are: what you have as what you have, what you don't as what you don't. Doing so seems to accord with the wishes of the Buddha and Shinto deities. Even if you don't pray, by keeping this in mind you will enjoy various deities' protec-

---

1. Or *itsutsu*, which designates about two hours between one hour and three hours after sunset.

2. It isn't clear what other use the water could be put to.

3. The original proverb describes someone with a guilty conscience. Here it is used to mean the importance of being humble.

tion. Even if you pray, though, if your mind is crooked, you'll be abandoned by Heaven's Way. So be careful.

Item: Don't think your swords and clothes should be as good as those of other people. Be content as long as they don't look awful. Once you start acquiring what you don't have and become even poorer, you'll become a laughingstock.

Item: Not to mention when you report to work, but even when you decide to stay in your house because of some illness or some errands to tend to, take care of your hairdo early.[4] It is out of the question and careless of you to appear among people in an unkempt state. If you start becoming lax about yourself, even your servants will begin to imitate you. It's unseemly to run around [trying to fix your hair hurriedly] simply because a colleague happens to come to visit.

Item: When you report to work, never go directly to see your master. Go to the waiting room and observe your colleagues and others. Present yourself to your master only when summoned. Otherwise, you may be shocked.[5]

Item: When your master calls your name, respond with a quick "Yes, sir!" even if you are sitting some distance from him, swiftly go forward, and, when you're near him, crawl toward him. Listen humbly to what he has to say. Then quickly leave, do what you're told to do, and report back to him what you've found, exactly as it is. Don't try to show off your talent. Also, depending on the matter, seek the advice of some thoughtful people on the reply before conveying it to your master. Try not to credit yourself for everything.

Item: In your master's presence, don't linger near those gossiping. Stay away from them. Needless to say, you should never gossip about yourself or laugh conspicuously. If you do that, not only your superiors but also your colleagues will give up on you.

Item: There's the saying, "Do everything with others, and you'll have no trouble."[6] Rely on others in everything.

Item: Whenever you have a little bit of time for yourself, read a book. Always carry something with characters written on it with you and look at it when no one's looking. Unless you accustom yourself to

---

4. Because of the topknot and the practice of shaving the pate, a man in those days had to do more than just brush his hair.
5. By what is not clear from the context.
6. The meaning of the original saying cited is not clear.

them, asleep or awake, you'll forget them. The same is true of writing.[7]

Item: When you have to walk past the elders lined up in the corridor for the master's audience, you must bend at the hips and lower your hands. It's absolutely out of the question not to show deference or humility but to stomp past. All samurai must behave humbly, deferentially.

Item: Never say a single word of falsehood or even half of it to anyone, high or low. Even when joking, tell the truth. If you continue to say false things, it will become your habit and people will begin to torment you. In the end they'll give up on you. You must be prepared to think it a disgrace for your lifetime if someone accuses you.

Item: Anyone without any knowledge of tanka composition must be said to be untalented and shallow. Study it.

Be careful about what you say, at any time. People can tell what you're thinking from a single word.

Item: Whenever you have time off from your service to your master, work at horse-riding. Learn the basics from an expert, and learn the handling of the reins and other things on your own.

Item: Seek good friends in writing and learning. Avoid bad friends in go, chess, pipes, and flutes. Not knowing these things is not a disgrace for you, nor is there evil in learning them. It's simply that you'd rather not waste your time on them.

Whether someone's good or bad entirely depends on his friends.

Whenever three people take a road, there's always one who's worthy as a teacher. Choose that one person and follow him. By looking at the one who isn't good, you correct your ways.[8]

Item: When you have time off from your service and go home, you should go from the stable to the rear of your house and repair the four walls and the fences and block the holes dogs make in fences. A careless maid might take the thatch from the eaves for kindling and, having taken care of the need of the moment, give no thought to what may happen later. Keep in mind that such things happen to everything.

Item: At sundown, close the gate tight and open it only when someone must come in or go out. Otherwise, something bad is bound to happen in the future.

---

7. Amusing but realistic advice in view of the enormous number of Chinese characters that have to be memorized in order to be able to read and write. The problem was much more acute in Sōun's days when no formal educational system existed.

8. The last two sentences are from Book VII of *The Analects*.

Item: In the evening, check yourself the sources of fire in the kitchen and your wife's room, firmly tell her to be careful, and make a habit of taking preventive measures against a fire from your neighbors. Do this every night. Noble or lowly, wives tend to have no thought about these things and to be lax, leaving valuables and clothes scattered about.

Even if you have servants, don't think only of telling them to do everything. Do things yourself first so that you may know what they're like. Only then think of having others do them.

Item: Always work at reading, writing, martial skills, archery, and horse-riding. There is no need to detail this. Hold literary skills in your left hand, martial skills in your right. This is the law from ancient times. Never neglect it.

MIYAMOTO MUSASHI:
GORIN NO SHO
(BOOK OF FIVE ELEMENTS)

IYAMOTO MUSASHI (1584?–1645) is famous for perfecting the art of using simultaneously both the long and short swords that every samurai traditionally carried. Musashi himself called the technique *niten'ichi*, "two heavens as one," or *nitō'ichi*, "two swords as one." It is said that he was able to pursue this unusual way of sword-use in part because he was tall and strongly built.

Gorin no Sho, "Book of Five Elements," which Musashi wrote toward the end of his life, from 1640 to 1642, is a tract on *heihō*, an all-encompassing term for the art of fighting. In the following translation of excerpts from it, the term may be rendered variously to express notions ranging from military strategy to actual combat to swordsmanship.

The word *gorin* in the title of the book refers to the five elements that make up the phenomenal world in Buddhist belief: earth, water, fire, wind, and air (or emptiness, the void). The use of these elements to name the five "volumes" of the book is judged to be largely for convenience, and their philosophical connections are thought to be tenuous. But I have included Musashi's own explanations given in "The Five Volumes that Make up this Book."

Musashi's reputation as a swordsman seems to have been considerable even before his death, but few facts are known about him, not even the exact year and place he was born. Most of his actions depicted in later narratives and dramas are based on legend and fiction. Take the opening remarks of *Gorin no Sho*:

Miyamoto Musashi

Ever since I was young, long ago, I've been mindful of the art of fighting; I had a duel for the first time at age thirteen. I beat my opponent then, a swordsman called Arima Kihē, of the Shintō School. At age sixteen I beat a powerful swordsman called Akiyama, from the Province of Tajima. At age twenty-one I went to the capital and met prominent swordsmen, engaged them in several fights, but never failed to gain a victory. After that I went to various parts of the land, encountered swordsmen of different schools, and all in all had sixty-odd fights, but I never once lost my advantage. All this happened while I was from age thirteen to age twenty-eight or -nine.

This innocuous paragraph already contains a biographical point subject to debate. The original word for "the capital" is *tenka*, which also means "Number One under Heaven" or the best in the world. Since the heads of the Yoshioka family had served the Ashikaga shogunate as instructors of swordsmanship and could therefore be described as "the best," the original sentence may be interpreted to mean Musashi's fights with two Yoshioka brothers as described in *Niten Ki* (Record of Niten), the biography of Musashi written by his adopted son, Iori:

> In the spring of the ninth year of Keichō [1604], when [Musashi] was twenty-one years old, he went to the capital, and fought Seijūrō, the first son of Yoshioka Shōzaemon and the Number-One-Swordsman-under-Heaven, in Rendaino, outside Kyoto, to determine who was superior. Seijūrō had a real sword, but Musashi struck him with a wooden sword. Seijūrō fell down, unconscious. His disciples helped him up on a board, carried him home, and treated him with some medicine; he revived. After this he gave up swordsmanship and had himself tonsured.

Iori goes on to say that Seijūrō's younger brother Denshichirō challenged Musashi and was instantly killed, so that Seijūrō's disciples, with his son Matashichirō as their leader, challenged him. But Musashi managed to kill Matashichirō, too, along with several other swordsmen, and got away.

However, the record of the Yoshioka family gives an entirely different account: It was Seijūrō who defeated Musashi by injuring his brow, and when challenged by Seijūrō's disciples, Musashi simply disappeared.

In any event, Musashi has been admired both for his no-nonsense approach to the art of fighting and killing *and* as a seeker of the Way.

FROM THE *EARTH* VOLUME

When I was past thirty and looked back upon what I'd done, it occurred to me that I had won not because I had reached the ultimate in swordsmanship. Was it because I was born with a skill in this art or did not stray from heaven's logic? Or was it because swordsmen of other schools weren't quite up to it? With a resolve to gain some deeper principles from then on, I trained mornings and evenings and eventually crossed the path of swordsmanship when I was about fifty years old. Ever since that time I've had no more path to explore further and have simply spent months and years. In accordance with the logic of swordsmanship, I have followed various arts and skills as they have taken me, so that I've had no master in anything.[1] Even as I prepare this book, I do not intend to borrow ancients words from Buddhism or Confucianism, nor to allude to ancient things in military accounts and military laws. I simply wish to reveal my view of my own school, its true essence, by making Heaven's Way and the Bodhisattva Avalokitesvara my models, and take up my brush and set out to write it down at three-thirty on the night of the tenth day of the tenth month.

Fighting is the law for any samurai house. Above all someone in a commander's position must practice it, and even a soldier must know it. . . .

First, as is often said, "A samurai must have both literary and martial skills":[2] to be versed in the two is his duty. Even if he is awkward, a samurai must train in martial arts to a degree appropriate to his status. On the whole, if you are to assess the samurai's mind, you may think it's simply attentiveness to the manner of dying. When it comes to the manner of dying, of course, there is no difference between the samurai, priests, women, and even peasants; everyone must know his obligations, think of what would be disgraceful, and be prepared to die when the moment comes. The samurai pursues martial arts, however, in order to excel in everything, be it winning a duel or winning a combat with several men, be it for your master or

---

1. Musashi pursued the arts of serving tea, writing renga, painting, and sculpture. Some of his slash-like monochromatic paintings are highly admired.

2. For a famous commentary of Musashi's contemporary, the Confucian scholar Nakae Tōju, on the accomplished samurai's duty to be versed in *bunbu ryōdō*, "literary (civilian) and martial (military) skills," see the Introduction, p. xxiii.

for yourself, with the resolve to establish your reputation and distinguish yourself. The samurai does these things through the virtue of martial arts.

Some people may think that even if you learn martial arts, they will be useless in actual battles. That may be so, but the true spirit of martial arts requires that you train in ways to be useful at any moment and teach men so that they may be useful in everything.

. . . [Anyone who pursues the way of the warrior] should not limit himself to swordsmanship. If you acquire expertise only in swordsmanship, you will find it hard to know even what swordsmanship is all about. Of course, you will never see the way of the warrior.

"THE FIVE VOLUMES THAT MAKE UP THIS BOOK"

. . . In the *Earth* volume, I give an overall picture of the art of fighting and my view of my own approach. It is difficult to know the true Way through swordsmanship alone. From large places one knows small places, from the shallows one goes to the depths. Because a straight road is made by leveling the earth and hardening it with gravel, I call the first volume *Earth*.

Second, the *Water* volume. We make water our model and turn our mind into water. Water adjusts itself to a square or round vessel with ease, turns itself into a single droplet or into a vast ocean.[3] It has the color of aquamarine depths. With that clarity I will write out my approach in this volume. Once you definitely understand the principle of swordsmanship, the ability to defeat a single person at will means the ability to defeat all the people of the world. . . . A commander's strategy, which requires him to make something large out of something small, is comparable to the making of a giant Buddhist statue from a foot-high scale model. . . .

---

3. A reference to *Lao Tzu* (sec. 8): "Supreme good is like water. Water benefits everything, yet doesn't compete. Because it doesn't compete, it doesn't suffer from any accusation. It settles where ordinary people don't want to be. So it's close to the Way." The noncompetitive nature of water is evident in the ease with which it fits into a container of any shape. Water also is content to settle down at the lowest place; hence the statement: "It settles where ordinary people don't want to be." (This is the first half of the paragraph. Following one interpretation one sentence is moved here from the end of the second half.)

Third, the *Fire* volume. In this volume I will write about fights. Fire can be large or small and can acquire an extraordinary ferocity. . . . In combats, a one-to-one combat is the same as a clash between armies of thousands of men. . . . [But] large things are easy to see, small things hard to see. That is to say, an affair involving a great number of people can't be turned around instantly [so what's happening can be readily observed], whereas in an affair involving just one man his mind changes so quickly it's hard to learn the changes in detail. . . . The changes occur so fast you must train yourself to get used to them every day until you begin to regard them as normal and your mind stops changing. . . .

Fourth, the *Wind* [also, School, Style] volume. I call this the *Wind* volume because here I do not write about my own approach but the art of fighting in general, along with the various schools that make it up. . . . Without knowing the others well, you can hardly know what you are.[4]

In any field, no matter what you do, there's always a false Way. Even if you work at what you do every day, if your mind is not on the right track, you are not following the true Way when seen from a correct perspective, even though you yourself may think you're taking a good path. Unless you follow the true Way, what may be slightly off course at the beginning will later turn into a great divergence. . . .

Fifth, the *Air* [also, the Void] volume. I call this the *Air* volume because once you mention the air, what can you call its innermost part or its entrance? In the art of fighting, once you comprehend its nature, you let it go; it has its own freedom, you acquire an exceptional skill on your own, and when the time is right, you know the rhythm, you strike, you hit. All this is the Way of the Air. I write about entering the true Way naturally in the *Air* volume.

''TWO SWORDS AS ONE''

I started to talk about using two swords because samurai, commanding officers and regular soldiers alike, wear two swords right on their hips. In the old days they were called *tachi* [big or long sword]

---

4. A reference to *Sun Tzu* (vol. 3, sec. 6): "If you know both your enemy and yourself, you won't be in danger even if you fight him a hundred times; if you don't know your enemy but do know yourself, you will sometimes win, sometimes lose; if you know neither your enemy nor yourself, you will be in danger in every battle."

and *katana* [sword]; now they are called *katana* [sword] and *wakizashi* [side-arm]. That any samurai carries these two weapons I don't need to explain in detail. In Japan samurai have worn them on their hips, whether or not they know how to use them, as a matter of duty. I've decided to call my approach *nitō'ichi* [two swords as one] in order to make the advantage of using the two known. . . .

In this "Two Swords as One" approach, the beginner must train by holding the *tachi* and *katana* in each of his hands. In giving up your life, you would want to make use of all the available tools of war. It can't be your true wish not to use all of them but to be killed with one of them remaining on your hip.

Nevertheless, even if you hold a sword in each of your hands, it is exceedingly difficult to use both the left and the right hand at will. This is why I teach students to get used to using a sword with one hand.

I wouldn't say the same thing about large weapons such as the spear and halberd, but the swords, both long and short, are tools you carry in one hand. To hold a sword with both hands is awkward:[5] It's awkward when you're on horseback, awkward when you're running. It's awkward in the swamps, muddy rice paddies, stony ground, on steep slopes, and in crowded places. In your left hand you hold a bow, a spear, or whatever other tool it may be, so you must use your sword with the remaining hand. Holding a sword with both hands is not the true way. If or when you find it hard to strike the enemy dead with one hand, you may dispatch him with both hands. There's nothing complicated about it.

For anyone willing to learn to brandish a sword with one hand, I talk about two swords and make him learn to wield the long sword with either hand. For anyone, the first time he takes it up, the long sword is heavy and hard to brandish. But everything is hard the first time you take it up: The bow is hard to draw, the halberd hard to wield. In each case, though, you get used to the tool: In time you gain the strength to draw the bow, and as you become accustomed to wielding the long sword, you will learn the knack and find it easy to wield. . . .

You wield the long sword in a spacious place, the short sword in a confined place; this is the first thing you learn. In my approach you

---

5. Practically all the schools of swordsmanship in Musashi's days taught holding a single sword with both hands. Musashi rejects this as impractical in actual combat.

win with the long sword and win with the short sword. For this reason I don't specify the length of the sword but regard the essence of my approach as the resolve to win with either blade. . . .

In the way of the warrior those able to wield a sword have traditionally been described as *heihōsha* [martial-arts experts]. In martial arts, if you are good at shooting an arrow, you're called an archer; if you have mastered the gun, you're called a gunman; if you can use the spear well, you're called a spearsman; if you learn to use the halberd, you're called a halberdsman. Following this practice, someone who has learned the way of the sword should be called either a long-swordsman or a short-swordsman. The bow, the gun, the spear, and the halberd are all tools of the warrior, and each should be a way of mastering martial arts.

Nevertheless, the sword alone is associated with the mastery of martial arts. There is a reason for this. With the virtue of the sword you govern the world, you govern yourself. This is why the mastering of martial arts originates in the sword. . . .[6]

"RHYTHM IN MARTIAL ARTS"

In everything there is rhythm; however, the rhythm in martial arts, in particular, is something you can't master without hard training.

Among the rhythms readily noticeable in our daily life are well-tuned, exquisite rhythms in Nō dancing and in accomplished musicians' pipes and strings. You move on to martial arts, and there is also rhythm and timing in shooting the bow, shooting the gun, and even riding a horse. . . .

In martial arts there are a variety of rhythms. First, you must learn to attune yourself to your opponent, then learn to disconcert him. To learn, in rhythms large and small, slow and fast, how to be aggressive, to pause, or to go against your opponent's rhythm is crucial in martial arts. In a martial combat, you must learn the rhythm of each opponent; and, with a rhythm he can't imagine, you win by creating a sophisticated rhythm out of the rhythm of the Void. . . .

In "Two-Swords-as-One," you work mornings and evenings, evenings and mornings, and gradually come to have a mind broad

---

6. This observation is based on Japan's ancient sword worship.

enough to comprehend the strategies for both large-scale battle and one-on-one combat. . . .

Anyone who sincerely desires to learn these strategies has ways of disciplining himself:

1. Think of things that aren't evil.
2. Train yourself in the way [of swordsmanship].
3. Try your hand in various arts.
4. Know how things are done in various professions.[7]
5. Be able to measure the gains and losses of everything.
6. Learn to be able to pass judgment on various professional matters.
7. Perceive and understand what you can't see.
8. Pay attention to the smallest details.
9. Do nothing useless.

FROM THE *WATER* VOLUME

''MENTAL BEARING''

In martial arts, let the bearing of your mind be no different from its normal state. In normal times, and in times of martial arts, try to be no different: Keep your mind broad and straight; do not stretch it taut; do not allow it to grow in the least lax; do not make it lean to one side but hold it at the center; keep it quietly fluid, doing your best to maintain it in a fluid state even while it *is* fluid.

When you are quiet, your mind shouldn't be quiet; when you're moving fast, your mind shouldn't at all be moving fast. Your mind shouldn't follow your body, nor should your body follow your mind. Your mind must be cautious while your body is not. Your mind should lack nothing while having no excess. Superficially you may have your mind appear weak, but you must keep it strong inwardly, lest people can tell what you really are.

If you have a small body, you must know whatever there is to know about having a large body; if you have a large body, you must

---

7. In some untranslated passages of this book, Musashi demonstrates his detailed knowledge of carpentry in comparing the command structure and the duties of each soldier to that of the carpenters' guild and the work of its members. However, comparing the samurai to carpenters appears to have been common in those days.

know whatever there is to know about having a small body. Large or small, it is crucial that you keep your mind straight and try not to play favoritism to whatever you are.

Do not allow your mind to become muddied. Keep it broad and maintain your judging ability in a broad place. It is most important that you continue intently to polish your judging ability and your mind. Hone your judging ability; acquire the ability to tell the right and wrong under heaven and know the good and bad of things. Try all the arts to experience what is sought in each field. Then, after you have learned not to be easily deceived by anyone, you can say you have acquired judgment in martial arts. . . .

"PHYSICAL BEARING"

In holding your body, your face shouldn't be downcast or up-turned, tilted or twisted. Do not allow your eyes to be distracted easily. Do not knit your brow, but keep the space between your eyebrows wrinkled, lest your eyes roll. Taking care not to blink, narrow your eyes a little. With your face relaxed, keep your nose straight, your lower jaw a little forward.

As for your head, keep the muscles in back straight, your nape tight. Treat your body from shoulders down as one. Hold both shoulders down, your spine erect. Do not stick your buttocks out. Put strength into your legs from knees to toes. Thrust your belly out lest you bend at the hips. There is something called "wedge-tightening": you put the weight of your belly on the scabbard of your short sword lest your belt slacken.

On the whole, in martial arts it is most important that you regard your normal bearing as the same as your bearing at a time of fighting and your bearing at a time of fighting as the same as your normal bearing. . . .

"EYEING THINGS"

You eye things in a sweeping, broad fashion.

As for the two manners of seeing things, *kan* (observing) and *ken* (seeing), the eye for *kan* is strong, the eye for *ken* weak; seeing distant things as if they are close at hand and seeing close things as if they are distant is special to the art of fighting. Knowing your opponent's sword and yet not in the least seeing it is important in the art of fighting. . . .

This way of seeing things applies both to a large-scale battle and a one-on-one combat. It is crucial that you observe what's happening on both sides of yourself without rolling your eyes. . . .

''THE PATH OF THE SWORD''

By knowing "the path of the sword" well, you can freely wield the sword you always carry, even with two fingers. If you try to wield it unnaturally fast, its path becomes blocked and you can't wield it. You must wield it as naturally as you can. When you try to wield it as if it's a fan or a knife, the sword goes out of its path and you can't wield it. This is called "knife-whittling" [i.e., useless], and that way you can't cut a man apart.

After you strike your sword down, you lift it along the path that comes naturally to it, and after you wield it sidewise, you return it along the crosswise path that comes naturally to it. You stretch your elbows in a most comfortable way and wield your sword powerfully. This is what's called the path of the sword. . . .

''ON 'POSITIONING AND NONPOSITIONING' ''

"Positioning and nonpositioning" means not intending to position your sword. Nevertheless, because there are five ways of positioning it,[8] you also can't help positioning it. No matter which direction you may hold your sword in accordance with the enemy's move, the place, and the situation,[9] the idea is to hold it in a way which will enable you to cut your enemy most easily.

You may start out holding your sword in an upper position, but if you lower it a little as the occasion requires, you are taking a middle position, while if you lift it a little to gain advantage, you are taking an

---

8. In the preceding paragraphs, which are untranslated, Musashi has described five basic ways of positioning the sword or swords at the outset of a sword fight—middle, upper, lower, left, and right—adding, characteristically: "Though the positions are differentiated into five types, all are meant to cut a person."

9. See "Knowing the Situation," later in these excerpts.

upper position. Likewise, a lower position will become a middle position if you raise the sword a little. The sword you position to either side of you will also move into a middle or lower position if you edge it to the middle, depending on where you are. This is why I say you are and are not positioning your sword.

In any event, once you take up a sword, you must be prepared to cut your enemy down regardless of how you do it. . . .

"STRIKING WITH 'NO-THOUGHT, NO-FEATURE' "[10]

When you and your enemy are about to strike each other, your body and your mind turn into a single striking movement and your hands strike out of the void naturally, swiftly, powerfully. This is called "no-thought, no-feature," and is of crucial importance. . . .

"FACING MANY ENEMIES"

"Facing many enemies" is when you must fight a great number of enemies all by yourself.

You draw both the long and short swords, spread them wide to the left and right, both lowered. If your enemies attack you from all sides, aim to chase them in one direction. Of the attackers, you must judge who's coming first, who next, and quickly step forward to deal with the first one. You must maintain a perspective on the overall situation. As the enemies strike, simultaneously wield in different directions both the sword in your right hand and the sword in your left hand, cutting the enemy in front with the sword striking forward, cutting the enemy moving on your side with the sword being withdrawn. It's no good to wield the swords in different directions and then wait. You must quickly bring them back to their original positions. As a new enemy steps forward, you vigorously attack him, crush him backward, and, as you do so, move to deal with the next one that comes forward, and destroy him. Do your best to force enemies to

---

10. *Munen musō* in Japanese, "no-thought, no-feature" is the ultimate state a Buddhist can attain where the consciousness of the ordinary mind has no place. *Musō* is a translation of the Sanskrit word *animitta*.

form a single file like fish, you as their pursuer, and as you see them get entangled in their formation, strike powerfully.

If you frontally attack your enemies as they form a crowd, you can hardly make progress. Also, if you start wondering which of your enemies will step forward first, that will put you in a waiting stance, and you can hardly make progress. Respond to your enemies' rhythm, know their weakness you can take advantage of, and win.

If you practice with your friends often until you learn the knack of forcing the whole group into one file, you can deal with one enemy or ten or twenty enemies without any worry. . . .

. . . Even a road of a thousand miles you can traverse only by moving forward one step at a time. You must take it to be the duty of a samurai to give unhurried thought to this art and practice it, trying to defeat today what you were yesterday, defeat someone inferior tomorrow, and defeat someone superior the day after . . . never allowing your mind to be sidetracked. No matter what kind of enemy you may defeat, though, if you do so in a way contrary to what's laid down in this approach, you will not be following the true path. If you grasp this principle, you will see how you can defeat fifty to sixty men single-handedly. When that happens, you will be enlightened in the strategy for large-scale battles as well as one-on-one combats with the wisdom gained through swordsmanship. I call practicing for a thousand days *tan*, "training," practicing for ten thousand days *ren*, "discipline." . . .[11]

THE *FIRE* VOLUME

''ON CHOOSING YOUR POSITION''

In selecting a position for yourself, we speak of "carrying the sun on your back," that is, facing your enemy with the sun behind you. If the place doesn't allow you to have the sun behind you, try to have it to your right. In a room, you likewise try to have a light either behind you or to your right.

You want to have the space behind you not too small, the space to your left ample, and the space to your right somewhat small.[12] During the night, too, if it's a place where you can see your enemy, you must

---

11. Musashi here divides into two the word *tanren*, which means "discipline, drill."
12. Evidently Musashi thought that in using two swords it was important to keep your right sword free to avoid being attacked from that flank.

remember to position your swords by "carrying a fire on your back" or having any light to your right.

We also speak of "looking down on your enemy"; this means you try to place yourself higher, if only a little. In a room, one such place is the side of the room with the alcove.

Once a fight begins and you start chasing your enemy, try to chase him to your left and corner him in a spot where he has little maneuverability behind him—or, in any case, into an unmaneuverable spot.

Concerning such an unmaneuverable spot, we speak of "not showing the place to the enemy," which means not allowing him time to look around, but continuing to close in on him without relaxing a moment. In a room, too, as you chase him toward a threshold, a lintel, a door or sliding door, a latticed balcony, or toward a pillar, the notion of "not showing the place to the enemy" applies. No matter where you chase him, it must be toward a place with poor footing or with some obstacle on either side or both. You must concentrate on taking advantage of the place, on "gaining victory through the place." . . .

"KNOWING THE SITUATION"

In strategy for a large-scale battle, sizing up the situation means knowing the rising or declining state of your enemy's mood, knowing the number of his soldiers, and making an accurate judgment on how he is from the way things are, so that you may take the initiative and fight with the conviction that you will win with the strategy you have set, including the number of soldiers you have decided to deploy.

Similarly, in one-on-one combat it is crucial to be knowledgeable about the school of swordsmanship to which your enemy belongs, to make an accurate judgment of his personality, and to spot his strong and weak points, so that you may take the initiative and use tactics he doesn't expect by knowing the high and low of his shifting moods and by cleaving into the rhythmic break.

If you have a strong intellect, you never fail to size up any situation. When you attain freedom in the art of fighting, there should be many ways of winning through a good assessment of your enemy's mind. Ponder ways of doing so.

''BECOMING YOUR ENEMY''

"Becoming your enemy" means putting yourself in your enemy's shoes.

When you think of it, if someone who's stolen something runs into a house and shuts himself up, we tend to think of him as a formidable enemy to deal with. But if you put yourself in his position, you'll see that he must be feeling cornered and desperate, having turned the whole world into his enemy. Having shut himself up, he's a pheasant, whereas you, the one who breaks in to get him, are a hawk. . . .

In large-scale battles, too, you tend to think your enemy is strong and take cautious steps to avoid calamity. But if you have a good number of soldiers on your side, know how strategies work, and have a fair grasp of ways of defeating your enemy, there's nothing to worry about.

In a one-on-one combat, too, you must "become your enemy." Most likely he's thinking that you know the art of fighting well, have a fabulous grasp of swordsmanship, and are, in short, an expert in the field, so that meeting someone like you he's bound to lose. . . .

''MOVING THE SHADOW''

"Moving the shadow" is something you do when you can't tell what your enemy is thinking.

In a large-scale battle, when you can't judge the moves your enemy is planning to make, you pretend to launch a strong attack to see his hand. Once you see his hand, you have a great advantage, and it will become easy for you to win.

In a one-on-one combat, too, when you have an enemy with a sword behind you or on either side, if you make a sudden show of striking, he is bound to reveal his intentions in his sword. Once his intentions are revealed and known to you, that's an advantage, and you respond to it and move to defeat him. . . .

''BEING INFECTIOUS''

"Infection" occurs in everything. Sleepiness is infectious, and so is yawning. . . .

In a large-scale battle, when your enemy looks restless, hurrying to achieve his goal, you pretend to be paying no attention to it and move slowly; the enemy, infected, will think that's the way to do it, and become lax. Seizing that moment of infection, you empty your mind and launch a swift, powerful attack, and win.

In a one-on-one combat, too, you make both your body and mind slow down, and the moment your enemy becomes lax, you seize the initiative, make a powerful, swift attack, and win. . . .

"FRIGHTENING THE ENEMY"

One becomes frightened by everything. We are speaking of our tendency to be frightened by something unexpected.

In a large-scale battle, by frightening the enemy, we are not only speaking of something visible. It is possible to frighten him with your voice, by making something small seem large, or by making a sudden move at his flank. He can be frightened by anything. And the moment he's frightened, you take advantage of it and win.

In a one-to-one combat, too, you can frighten your enemy with your body, frighten him with your sword, frighten him with your voice, or frighten him with a sudden move he doesn't even have in mind, and responding to that moment of fear, you move on to win. . . .

"THE OFFICER KNOWS HIS SOLDIER"

"The officer knows his soldier" means this: When the matter finally comes to battle, you face it with firm conviction that as far as what you're going to do is concerned, you have constantly studied the art of fighting and have gained a perfect knowledge of it, so that your enemy is no more than your soldier whom you can dispose of as you like and move about as you wish. . . .

FROM THE *WIND* VOLUME

. . . When you seek out and look at other schools of swordsmanship, one school touts the technique of using a longer sword and concentrates on the power of the blow you deliver. Another school upholds a short sword and pursues the art of fighting with it. Yet another school devises a great many ways of using the sword and tries to teach the art of fighting through the positionings of the sword, calling some *omote*, and some *oku*.[13] I have revealed in this volume how all these are not the true Way. . . .

"THE MANY WAYS OF USING THE SWORD"

Some people devise a great many ways of using the sword and teach them. They do this, I suppose, because they must make something to sell out of the art of fighting and for that they must impress beginners by saying they have devised many ways of using the sword. This is to be repudiated in the art of fighting. The reason is this: if you think that there are many ways of cutting a person, you'll end up distracted.

In fact, there isn't much variation in the manner of cutting a person. For those who know the use of the sword or for those who don't, for women or for children, there aren't many ways of striking a person to kill. Other than cutting the person down, there's only stabbing and slashing sideways. Because the purpose is above all to cut the person, there can't possibly be many ways of doing so.

Nonetheless, depending on the place or in accordance with the circumstance, you may find yourself, for example, in a spot so tight above or at your flank that you must hold your sword in such a way it won't be obstructed. For this reason, we think there ought to be five fundamental ways of holding the sword. If you add to these and say you can also cut a person by twisting your arms, bending your body, jumping, or moving backward, you aren't being truthful to the true Way. You can't cut a person by twisting your arms, bending your body, jumping, or moving backward. Such things are utterly useless.

In my approach you hold both your own body and mind straight and win by distorting and bending your enemy and twisting his mind. . . .

---

13. *Omote* literally means "front": hence the beginner's state, the techniques for the beginner. *Oku* literally means "innermost": hence the state of ultimate accomplishment, the techniques for someone accomplished.

"ON *OKU* AND *OMOTE*"

In the art of fighting, how can we call some aspects *omote*, others *oku*? In some other arts, people talk about *gokui*, "the ultimate state or wisdom," and *hiden*, "secret transmissions," and there may be entrances that lead to the ultimate understanding of the art. But when it comes to exchanges of blows with your enemy, you can't say you're fighting with *omote* or that you are cutting him down with *oku*.

In my approach, the way I teach, I first let those who have just started learn what they can learn fast in accordance with their skills; only later, as I judge that their minds are unwinding, I teach them things that were beyond their comprehension—gradually, those deeper principles of fighting. Still, on the whole I make them learn only those things related to actual fighting, and I must say there isn't anything like "entrances that lead to the ultimate understanding of the art."

When you think of it, suppose you go to the depths of the mountains: When you decide to go a step deeper, you often end up coming out of the mountains.[14] In any field, there are times when some aspects of *oku* can be effective, and times when "entrance" aspects can be good.

In any event, as regards the principles of fighting, what shall I hide, what shall I reveal? For this reason, in teaching my approach I dislike things like *seishi* and *batsubun*.[15] I'd rather weigh the intellect of each person who studies with me and teach him the straight Way by making him get rid of various bad habits that come with the attempt to learn the art of fighting, so that he may attain the law of the samurai, the true Way, and acquire an undisturbed mind by himself. . . .

THE *AIR* VOLUME

The essence of the art of fighting I call "Two-Swords-as-One" I write out in the *Air* volume. By *air*, I mean the place where nothing

---

14. Musashi may be alluding to a homiletic tanka apparently current at the time, which may be translated: "Alack, I again find myself close to a village, having tried to go too far into the hills."

15. *Seishi* is a written pledge to train as a student; *batsubun* a letter of censure. The ability to issue *seishi* and *batsubun* meant an ability to recruit students and earn income. Some of the elaborate arrangements for pledge and censure often led to the stultification of what was taught.

exists, things that are unknown. Of course, the air is the void. By knowing what is, you know what isn't; that is the void.

Ordinarily, the vulgar view holds that the place where things are not understood is the void. But that is not the true Void, for there everyone remains lost. In the art of fighting, too, if a samurai who pursues his duties doesn't know what the *law* for him is, he hasn't attained the state of void. Someone like that will continue to be distracted in various ways and may describe something irrelevant as void, which of course is not the true Void.

If he firmly masters swordsmanship while also training hard in other martial arts; if he is not at all in the dark about what he is expected to do as a samurai and practices it, undistracted, every day and every hour; and if he polishes the two mental components of *shin*, "the mind," and *i*, "the will," and hones the two eyes of *kan*, "observing," and *ken*, "seeing," thereby reaching the place where nothing is clouded, distracting clouds having all cleared up, then the samurai will know what the true Void is.

While he does not know the true Way, he may think that not the Buddhist law or worldly laws but his own is the sure Way and *the* good thing. But when seen in the light of the Straight Way of the Heart or in accordance with the Great Square of the World, what he believes in often proves to be contrary to the true Way, distorted as it is by his tendencies to favor his own thoughts and viewpoints.

A samurai must know this and try to base his deeds on the straight Way and make the true Heart his path. When he widely disseminates the art of fighting and grasps that which is correct, enlightened, and all-encompassing, he can begin to regard the Void as the Way, the Way as the Void.

ARAI HAKUSEKI:
"MY FATHER"

rai Hakuseki (1657–1725), who, by dint of his learning, attained the position of chief counselor for the sixth shogun Tokugawa Ienobu (1662–1712; shogun, 1709–12), had a wide range of interests: history, geography, international affairs, religion, linguistics, and classics. Among his books, the autobiographical *Oritaku Shiba no Ki* (Breaking and Burning Firewood) is known for the lively portrait of his father, Masanari (1601–82), a samurai whose youth was spent in the years, as Hakuseki puts it, "not far removed from the days of warring states." What follows is the description of Masanari in the opening sections of the book.

People in the old days would talk when they had something to say, and would not say unnecessary things. Even when they said something they had to, they would say it not in many words but in its essence. My late father and mother were like that, too.

When my father was seventy-five years old, he contracted typhus. When he seemed close to death, a doctor came and recommended *dokujintō*.[1] My father used to say, "It may be all right for young people. But when you're old, it's bad to forget your life is limited and try to prolong it miserably with medicine. You must always keep this in mind."

Remembering these words of his, someone wondered how he would confront this situation. But with the sudden disease and heavy breathing making even the onlookers feel the pain, the medicine, along with ginger juice, was given him. With that he began to breathe better, and in the end was cured of that illness.

---

1. Hot medicinal drink made by boiling down carrots, sometimes mixed with ginger.

Later, my mother asked him, "While ill, why did you always lie with your back turned to us? Also, why did you not say a word to us?"

"Well," he replied, "even when I had an extreme headache, I had never shown my suffering to others. So I thought it wouldn't do if I behaved differently. Also, I had seen many people in their fevers say the wrong things, so I thought the best thing would be not to say anything. That's why I behaved the way I did."

From incidents like this, you can guess his conduct in normal times. Because he was like that, to my regret, I found it hard even to ask him what I did want to ask, and in time he passed away. As a result, many things remained unasked.

My father said, "They say that for some reason my father lost the land he governed and retired in the same land. His eyes were big, he had an ample beard, and he looked intimidating, but as I recall, when he died he still had no gray hair.

"Every time he ate a meal, he would take chopsticks out of a chopstick case, which was lacquered black, with a picture of irises. When he was done eating, he would put them back in the case and place the case by his side.

"I once asked the old maid who had brought me up about this. 'In a battle long ago,' she said, 'he brought the head of an enemy of good standing to the camp of his general. "You must be tired from fighting. This is for you," the general said and, pushing forward the portable meal table he was eating from, gave it to him along with the chopsticks. It was an honor at the time. That's why even now he keeps them close by.'

"I asked about this when I was just a little boy, and it isn't clear to me when and where the battle took place, who 'the general' was. The only thing he said to me that I remember even now was when I was playing with a friend my age. He heard me say, 'You say such insulting things,' and said, 'For a man to be insulted is a disgrace. What you just said you may have said playfully, but it's like allowing yourself to be insulted. You shouldn't do that.' "

When my father was young, the times were not far removed from the days of warring states,[2] and people loved to act righteously

---

2. A year before Masanari was born, the Sakigawara Battle was fought in which Tokugawa Ieyasu (1542–1616) gained control of Japan. In 1614 and 1615, when Masanari was in his mid-teens, two battles were fought through which Ieyasu completed his hegemony by destroying the remaining supporters of his former lord, Toyotomi Hideyoshi (1536–98).

and valued being principled in ways, I hear, that are different from today in many respects.

My father spent a number of years running about east and west, without settling down in one place. When he was thirty-one, shortly after he began service with Assistant Minister of Popular Affairs Minamoto no Toshinao,[3] he was put in charge of three foot soldiers who were alleged to have committed robbery by night and were arrested and shut up in the lookout tower atop the main gate. Told of this, he said, "Sir, as long as you are putting me in charge of these men, I request that you not take their long and short swords away from them."

His request granted, he was given the swords. He had someone carry them, climbed up to the lookout tower, and handed them back to the three men.

"Gentlemen," he said, "if you want to escape, cut off my head first. It's not possible for me alone to fight the three of you. This means my own swords are utterly useless."

As he said this, he tied up his own swords with a three-foot-long towel and threw them down. He then stayed with them, sleeping and eating with them. About ten days later, it was determined that the talk about the three men's robbery was unfounded. They were nonetheless deemed unfit for service and were eased out of the Kohō's house.[4] When the time for them to leave came, the three men said to my father:

"How unspeakably worthless did our master find us, that he should put us in the hands of one man? We must make him realize our worth, we thought, but if we killed you when you weren't even carrying your swords, he would conclude that we were worthless after all, and that pained us. So we decided, If we were put to death, that would be that. But should we survive, we will find some way of easing our pain by avenging ourselves.

"As it turned out, because of your compassion we were *not* deprived of our swords, and now we can mingle among samurai once again. We tell ourselves never to forget your compassion, and we feel our pain dissipate."

This is what he told me.

---

3. Tsuchiya Toshinao (1607–75), a daimyo with a small fiefdom in Kazusa Province. "Assistant Minister," etc., was his ceremonial court rank.

4. *Kohō* is a Chinese name of the Ministry of Popular Affairs. Hereafter Toshinao will be referred to by this title.

Not long afterward, he was selected to do important work and ended up staying to serve with the Kohō house.

As I remember him after I was old enough to notice things, my father had set daily routines and never changed them a bit. Around four in the morning he would get up without fail, wash his body with water, and do his hair by himself.

On cold nights my mother would say, "You should use hot water." But he would restrain her, saying, "We shouldn't even dream of troubling our servants."

When he passed seventy, my mother would say, "I've grown so old myself I can't bear the cold of the night." She would bury the burning charcoal in the ashes of the fireplace, putting her feet in the fireplace as she lay close to it. She would also put near the fire a kettle with water in it and give my father hot water when he got up.

Both were devoted to Buddhism. After doing his hair every morning my father never neglected to change his clothes and offer prayers to the Buddha. On the days commemorating the deaths of their parents they themselves cooked rice and offered it to the departed souls. They never asked their servants to do the work.

If the day had not yet broken after all this was done, my father would sit to wait for the morning and, after daybreak, would leave for work. His quarters were to the south, and the gate from which he left to work was to the north. In the morning he would take the path on the east side and in the evening the path on the west side. He wore *setta*, sandals with leather soles, and as he passed, he made sure to make loud footsteps, so that everyone heard him approach; infants would stop crying.

In the eighth month every year the Kohō went to Mōta County, in Kazusa Province, which he governed, and came back in the middle of the twelfth month.[5] After his return, he would never fail to summon my father and, in private, question him on what had happened during his absence.[6] Every year, my father would only say, "There's nothing particular to report, sir."

Years passed in a similar fashion, until finally the Kohō said, "Our house may certainly be small, but it isn't as though only a few

---

5. Under the Tokugawa system daimyo and vassals with the rank of *hatamoto*, "aide-de-camp," were required to spend every other year or half of each year in Edo. See the Introduction, p. xxii.

6. Masanari had the position of *metsuke*, "inspector," under Toshinao and was responsible for keeping watch on the behavior of Toshinao's vassals.

men were left during my absence. It isn't possible, is it, that in all these years nothing has happened? Still, year after year, you tell me, 'There's nothing particular to report.' I don't see how this can be.' "

"Sir, important matters are reported to you at once," my father replied. "As for minor matters, I discuss them with the people in charge of affairs during your absence and settle them. As a result, there is as yet nothing particular for me to report to you."

After this, too, the Kohō would summon my father without fail upon his return from Kazusa Province. He would tell him things he saw while there and, after many hours had passed, allow him to take his leave.

"He never asked what happened in his absence again," my father said.

In the fall of the second year of Shōhō [1645], when the Kohō was assigned his turn in guarding Suruga Castle,[7] my father had some business to tend to at the Kohō's place in Kazusa Province and went there, so did not join the group accompanying him. When the next spring came around, he was told by messenger to make his appearance in a hurry. At once he went from Kazusa Province to Suruga.

"In those days the residential quarters for the men on duty at the castle were still only surrounded with fences made of bamboo tied together," my father said. "As a result, every night many of the young samurai climbed over the fences to go out and play, and the elders accompanying the lord would say, 'There's no way of stopping them.' That's why the Kohō had summoned me.

"In these circumstances, I thought, our reputation will suffer even if just one man is accused of doing anything criminal. I had an idea.

"Soon I toured the area around the residential quarters and placed guards at appropriate places. I had four or five guard houses built and placed two foot soldiers in each for protection. Every night, after sunset until daybreak, I myself made an inspection tour, commending those who were not neglecting their guard duty while warning those who were. I did this until our shift was over, without sleeping a single night. As a result, the matter ended without anyone going out to play in the night."

---

7. Suruga Castle was Tokugawa Ieyasu's original stronghold.

In the fourth year of Shōhō [1647], the Kohō was assigned fire-watch duty on Mt. Nikkō[8] and was required to stay there for a hundred consecutive days. In the following year he was also assigned guard duty[9] at Ōsaka Castle. At that time, too, he took my father along. After he left here, until he got there, stopping at various places on the way, my father did not lie down to sleep for a single night. On the road he would doze on horseback and, after arriving there, while at work during the day, he would only take a catnap sitting up when he had the time to do so. Because he did not lie down to sleep night or day, after a long while he ended up suffering from something close to night blindness. One day on his way back from Ōsaka, the evening fell as he neared Mishima Station, but he was unable to see the lamps lit at each house, as he recalled, laughing.

"Sir, why did you do what you did at the time?" I asked him later.

"Well, there was a reason for that, son," my father said. "There was this so-and-so, a young hereditary samurai, who committed a grave crime. He thought that if it came to light he wouldn't be able to escape punishment, so before bolting, he killed a young one with a sword in order to make it look as though the crime were to repay some grudge. The Kohō hated him for this act and searched for him but couldn't find him.

"So he thought that if he arrested the man's aged mother, the man might come out. He arrested and held her, but the man didn't come out. As months and days passed, the mother died in jail. Then someone secretly told me that the fugitive was stalking the Kohō in the guise of an itinerant priest.[10]

"If what I've heard is true, I thought, he's likely to seek a chance while the Kohō is traveling like this. That's why I inconspicuously deployed guard soldiers every night and did the inspection myself, just as I had done in Suruga. Everybody thought that I was merely doing the things I'd done before."

After he resigned his post, my father told me a story in relation to something that had just happened:

---

8. The Tōshō-gū on Mt. Nikkō was built to enshrine Tokugawa Ieyasu. The Tokugawa government required daimyo to take turns serving on the fire-watch duty at the shrine.

9. The Tokugawa government required daimyo to take turns "guarding" the four gates of Ōsaka Castle, the western outpost of the government.

10. Or komusō. The komusō were members of a Zen sect; they did not practice the tonsure, wore a tube-shaped hat that entirely hid their heads, and, as they visited from house to house to beg for money, played the shakuhachi. They wore a sword.

"A fellow by the name of Ashizawa lost his father when he was young, but the Kohō gave him his father's fief and kept him in close attendance. When the man was about twenty, the Kohō summoned me, so I went. He was sitting on something, with a sword laid on his lap. I thought he looked different from normal. He said, 'Come closer.' I made the move to take my short sword from my waist to go near him, when he said, 'Get close to me the way you are.' When I went up close to him, he declared, 'I am about to summon Ashizawa and kill him myself for punishment. Stay where you are.'

"I was there without making a reply. After a while, he said, 'You didn't say anything in response. Is it because you have thoughts of your own?'

" 'Yes, I do, sir,' I said. 'Ashizawa often says, "I lost my father when an infant, but I have managed to grow up like this because of my master's vast kindness. For me to repay his favor, I can't be like an ordinary man."

" 'Ashizawa is born to be bold, but he's still young and does many stupid things. What monstrous thing has he done now? Still, someone who isn't like him when young perhaps can't do anything useful when he grows old. As I was thinking these things, I failed to respond at once. I apologize, sir.'

"The Kohō did not say another word and I, too, had nothing more to say. After a while, he said, 'Mosquitoes have collected on your face. Shoo them away.' I moved my face, and six or seven mosquitoes, which, bloated with blood, had grown to look like silverberries, fluttered down to the ground. I took out a tissue from my breast, wrapped them in it, put it in my sleeve, and waited. After another while, he said, 'You may go home to rest.' So I left.

"The man in question always liked to drink and would at times become wild when drunk. So I spoke to a man by the name of Seki, who was his good friend, and the two of us forced him to give up drinking, not neglecting to warn him against it all the time. As a result, after years and months, he was even given his father's position.

"Now, the Kohō is dead, but I hope Ashizawa will not trash what we initially told him but carry out his duties to the end."

He said this when the gentleman in question, after a long interval, got drunk again and behaved terribly.

In the Kohō house was a man by the name of Katō. He looked a little over sixty when I was about twenty. His grandfather is said to have been a general of soldiers[11] in Satomi, in Awa, and defended a castle in a place called Sanuki, in Kazusa Province. In his house were two treasured swords called the Snake Sword and the Monkey Leader. I saw the Snake Sword myself. The blade was on the slender side and it was about three feet long.

The Monkey Leader was so called, it was said, because it was a sword he'd begged from a monkey leader. I was supposed to have seen it. When he was sixteen, Katō killed his own young retainer with it. He slashed at the man when the latter was preparing marinated fish, and as he did so, he also cut a celadon bowl in two, crosswise. That was what everyone said.

After my father resigned his post, I happened to mention this sword to him.

"We have no one else with us now, so I'll tell you this," he said. "You shouldn't accept everything people say at face value. The sword that cut the bowl was the one I gave you when you were small.

"At the time Katō lived in a row house and was my next-door neighbor. He lived on the second floor. Once the master and servant quarreled loudly and I was concerned about it, when I heard Katō run down the stairs. Here we go, I thought, grabbed my sword, and rushed to the place. Katō had already given his man a slash, but his arms weren't strong enough perhaps, the wound hadn't had much effect. The servant man was about to attack him with a cutting knife, so no sooner had I drawn my sword than I struck him, and I struck him aslant, from shoulder down, together with the bowl that was in front of him. After a pause, I said to Katō, 'Give him the finishing stroke,' wiped the blood off my sword, put it back in its sheath, and hurried home. Later, people gathered and the whole thing eventually turned into an honor for the Monkey Leader.

"My sword originally belonged to a man by the name of Gotō, who was from Kōzuke Province. His older brother once made a sideways swipe with this sword and sliced his enemy's head horizontally into two. Gotō said he used to play with the skull as an infant. After I heard that, I begged him for the sword, and did so for a number of years, until he let me have it. You must take exceptional care to keep it close to you, so that you may hand it down."

This is the sword now placed in a slender decorated sheath, the one called The Lion.

---

11. Or *saburai daishō*. See p. 115.

For that matter, my excellent short sword, which Kiyokuni made, used to be owned by a grandson of someone who was said to be Governor of Tamba Okabe, who was with the house of Takeda, of Kai.[12] He was a cousin of the Kohō's father, Tadanao, and lived in Echizen Province. Tadanao, when young, asked him to join him, wanting to make him a direct vassal, but Tadanao passed away not long afterward, and this gentleman ended up spending his whole life in the Kohō house.

When this gentleman was thirteen, sometime in the fall, he went out into the field, alone with a servant-boy who was sixteen, to catch shrikes. Suddenly a wounded wild boar emerged. The servant, abandoning his master, climbed up a nearby pine tree. The master, who was thirteen, waited with his back against the pine tree. The boar ran straight toward him and was about to ram into him. He drew his short sword and stabbed the beast, but the beast grabbed the sword frontally with his mouth, up to its sword guard, and tried to run him down. His back against a large tree, the boy could not easily be pushed down. As the boar pushed and pushed, he bent back the sword guard, which was made of silver, by about an inch, and split his own head from the snout halfway to the brain; with the sword swallowed up to its sword guard he dropped dead.

Being a grandson of a man of great reputation, this gentleman had had many such experiences since he was an innocent boy. My father asked for and got the sword and bequeathed it to me.

On another occasion my father said to me, "You should never say to someone, face to face, that what you carry is a sharp blade. When I was young, someone heard someone else say that his sword cut exceptionally well, so the man said, 'By Heaven, you act rudely as if no one else is around you. Do you suppose anyone would carry a sword that doesn't cut? Come on, man, see for yourself whether my sword cuts or doesn't cut!' and he drew his sword. It was only because the men who happened to be with them restrained him that nothing came of it in the end. People in the old days were like that."

By the time I began to notice things, my father had few strands of dark hair left. His face was squarish, his forehead rose high, his eyes were large, and he had an ample beard; he was short but

---

12. See the chapter "Takeda Shingen and Uesugi Kenshin."

large-boned, and he looked strong. He was by nature too disinclined to show joy or anger. Even when he laughed, I don't remember him doing so loudly. Much less so when he scolded someone; I never heard him raise his voice. When he said something, it was sparingly; he never carried himself lightly. I never saw him act surprised, make a fuss, or look bewildered. For example, when he had moxa treatment, he would say, "It's useless to have a few, small moxa pieces," and he had large moxa pieces, and not a few of them, placed in five to seven spots, and had them burn at the same time, showing no pain whatsoever.

In quiet moments he would always clean his quarters, hang an old painting on the wall, and, with a couple of flowers of spring or fall thrown in a vase, spend the whole day facing them, sitting with his eyes closed. Or at times he would do some drawing, but he did not like to use colors.

Except when he was ill, my father would not ask other people to do things for him; he always did everything for himself. At morning and evening meals, he did not have more than two bowls of rice.

"When you hold your bowl in your hand," he would say, "from its weight you can tell whether there's more or less rice in it. Depending on the weight of the rice, eat more or less of other things, and try not to take an amount exceeding what's needed to fill your stomach.

"Even if it's something that's agreeable to your palate, don't eat too much of one thing. You may be hurt by it. If you aren't selective but eat a little bit of everything, things perhaps control one another, and you seldom are hurt by the food, I think."

Normally he would eat whatever you offered him, never saying, "I'd like to eat this or that." As the exception, he would say, "Please serve whatever becomes available and fresh at the start of each season," and he would enjoy it together with his family. As for sake, a mere drop through his throat would make him terribly drunk, so he would simply hold a cup in his hand to share the conviviality of the occasion. He liked to drink tea.

As for the clothes he wore, when at home he would wear things washed clean, never wearing soiled ones even when he went to sleep. When he went out he made sure to wear new and fresh things. Even then he never used articles that weren't proper to his state.

"In the old days," he would say, "people always took great care not to look bad even if they were to die suddenly."

This was even true of things like fans.[13] "You might drop your fan in a crowd or forget it somewhere," he would say. "Even from something like a fan you can guess what its owner is like."

His fan, accordingly, was of the so-called old style: About a foot long, its ribs were unlacquered, its paper had gold and silver dust blown on the ground, and for the picture on it, he would make certain to select one painted by a craftsman of good repute. When it comes to weapons, such as the long and short swords, I don't have to say a word.

After he passed seventy, my father developed pain in his left elbow. On account of this he offered to resign from his post, but the Kohō would have none of it. From then on he went to work wearing only a *sayamaki* sword[14] that was two inches wide and about a foot long, making a servant carry his long sword until he reached his office. When I think of it now, it must have presented a strange spectacle, but people didn't object to it, and of course the Kohō didn't seem to want to say anything. Come to think of it, my father must have thought, If something happens, it won't do if you carry a sword but can't use it. On the other hand, I have pain and can't possibly use a sword. Well then, if it's something useless, I might as well not carry it myself.

Until his death my father always kept this *sayamaki* close at hand and, following the word he left when he died, I sent it to the person he adopted as a child and brought up, who now lives in Michinoku. As for its decorations, the iron part had waves carved on it; the sheath was lacquered black except for the part called "thousand coils," which had gold foil underneath. After taking the tonsure, he kept it in a bag made of "toad-skin" leather.

Many years after my father's death, Ryōya, a former resident monk of Kōtoku Temple, told me a story.

"I didn't have a chance to see your father when he was young," he said. "When he was past eighty I had occasion to see him in action right in front of my eyes.

"A deranged drunk broke in here and, brandishing his sword, chased people away. There was no one who would go out and face

---

13. A fan was an indispensable part of a well-dressed person's paraphernalia.

14. A short sword without a sword-guard. It had a long string attached to its sheath, which was used to fasten the sword to the belt. The name *sayamaki*, "sheath-coiled," comes from the way the sheath was carved in such a way as to make it look as if a vine were coiling around it.

him, except your father: Leaning on his cane, he came out of his room. I wondered if he knew what was going on, and was worried about the danger, but there was nothing I could do. I was merely watching through the crack in the gate.

"Your father walked straight up to the man. When the man raised his sword, he grabbed that arm. The next moment he took the man's sword as he kicked him down, and threw it into a nearby ditch. Then he went back to his room.

"The man couldn't even stand up, lying there in drunken stupor. Only then did our young monks come out from here and there, kept watch on him, and when he sobered up sent him away."

When I was seventeen or eighteen, I happened to drop in front of my father what was called an "arresting cord,"[15] which was used to tie up a man and was made of slender blue strings braided together, with a hook attached at its end, and which I then had in my breast.

"What is this?" my father said and picked it up. After a while he said, "When I still held my former post, I used to carry one like this in my flint bag. That's because when there was someone who'd committed a crime, I would have my subordinates arrest him. I carried one in case they happened not to have one with them.

"After I was freed from my post, it became useless, so I used it to tie a cat, as you know. I don't have to tell you that you must learn all the warrior's skills. But there are skills that you must practice according to your station, and there are skills that you must not. This is not the kind of implement you should carry with you. You are not so young as not to realize something as simple as this."

Another time he told me a story.

"When I was young, there was a man by the name of so-and-so of Echizen.[16] He, too, disappeared and his whereabouts remained unknown.[17] Years later, I left Michinoku and, on my way toward the

---

15. Or *torihimo*. The Japanese, being Japanese, developed some intricate and, shall we say, artistic ways of tying up a criminal with this cord.

16. Hakuseki's own inserted note says: "Called Kurobē. It was an unusual way of calling oneself. 'Except,' my father said, 'in those days some people called themselves by the name of the province of their birth. It may be that he was someone born in Echizen.'"

17. Hakuseki has just cited a story, told by his father, of a samurai who committed a petty transgression, then committed a series of murders to hide the embarrassment, and disappeared.

San'yō Road, reached the Oak Tree Slope.[18] There I passed by a man carrying firewood on his back. When I had gone ahead by twenty to thirty yards, someone behind me called my name, so I turned to look. The man carrying firewood on his back had taken down the firewood and was walking toward me, removing the kerchief that wrapped his head. Puzzled, I walked back.

" 'It happened such a long time ago, sir, that you may have forgotten me,' he said. 'I am so-and-so. I wondered why in the world you are passing through a place like this all by yourself. All this feels like a fabulous mystery.'

"I looked, and, sure enough: Even though he didn't resemble the person I used to see long ago when he was in his youthful prime, there were suggestions of the man I could not possibly forget. It all felt like a dream.

" 'Sir, how on earth have you become like this?' I exclaimed, and told him a little about myself.

" 'Well then,' he said, 'you now have some moments of leisure. I'd like to hear about what has happened since we parted and about the people who used to be such good friends of mine. You must come to my place and stay with me tonight. Where I live isn't far from here.' So I went along.

" 'I have an aged father,' he said, 'but I ran out of means of supporting him. There was someone I knew in a place near here, called Higai, so I decided to come here to seek help from him. That's why I ended up doing something like this to make a living. This is something I would have been too ashamed to volunteer to tell, but you reminded me of so much of the past that I couldn't contain it but revealed myself.

" 'My father is extremely old-fashioned,' he continued. 'He may get unduly confused if someone he doesn't know suddenly comes upon him. I think I should tell him what happened. Please wait here for a while.'

"He made me stay outside a ramshackle house and went in. A while later he came out to welcome me, so I went in. There was an old man, about eighty, making a fire, who said, 'We're having you, a visitor, stay with us, sir, but I'm afraid we have no decent food to offer. Still, I hear that you were my son's good friend, and I shouldn't really be ashamed of what we have to offer. Please share with us what helps father and son fend off starvation, and spend the night here.'

---

18. One of the steep roads on Mt. Hakone.

"And so he entertained me by sharing boiled wheat mixed with vegetables. When night fell, he went in the one room that was there to lie down to sleep, saying, 'If this old man stays here, the two of you may not be able to relax.'

"The two of us, now left face to face, broke and burned firewood and continued to reminisce about what had happened long ago and more recently. When it was very late, our man went in where his father was lying and brought back two bamboo tubes that looked like carrying poles. He opened the parts that were their lids and took out a sword, about three feet long, and a short sword, about two feet long. Then he took out two sword guards from his breast and, turning his back against the light of the fire, unsheathed and inspected the two swords, then placed them in front of me. Both looked icy, their hilts decorated with gold; the sheaths were enfolded in *kairagi* leather.[19]

" 'Even when I was serving our lord,' he said, 'I was so incompetent that I wasn't able to earn enough stipend to support my father. Then I became the only one to serve him. That is why I withdrew from society and took up work like this. In the circumstances I shouldn't have regretted parting with any of the things I used to carry with me.

" 'Still, as long as I have any energy left, I thought I should keep at least a single set of swords with me. This is why I have so far steadfastly refused to let these go. As you can see, it may not be for long that my father remains in this world. If I'm lucky enough to carry out my filial duty, we may have another chance to meet.'

"As he said this, he shed tears.

"When the day broke, he prepared some meal and offered it to his father, and gave it to me, too. He accompanied me three miles before parting. After that, there was no way of hearing about him. I don't know what happened to him; there was also no one who saw him again."

---

19. *Kairagi* is the tough leatherlike skin of a tropical ray, which was sometimes used to decorate and protect the sword hilt and sheath.

YAMAMOTO TSUNETOMO:
HAGAKURE
(HIDDEN IN LEAVES)

Y AMAMOTO TSUNETOMO (1659–1721) was a retainer of the Nabeshima fiefdom, in Hizen, present-day Saga and part of Nagasaki, on the island of Kyūshū. Tsunetomo, who had served Mitsushige, the second lord of the Hizen fief, from his boyhood, asked for permission to take Buddhist vows when Mitsushige became gravely ill in the fifth month, 1700. He explained that he decided to do so because disembowelment to follow one's master had already been proscribed — as indeed it had been, four decades earlier. Permission was granted, and Mitsushige died a few weeks later. When Tashiro Tsuramoto (1678–1748), a young admirer of Tsunetomo, began to visit to record his observations, Tsunetomo had lived as a hermit for ten years.

Tsunetomo's observations, along with samurai anecdotes, Tsuramoto gathered together in eleven volumes under the title *Hagakure* (Hidden in Leaves). Tsunetomo's self-consciousness of Hizen's remoteness from the cultural and social centers of Kyoto and Edo accounts for his caustic use of the words "urbane" and "urban."

What follows are excerpts from the first volume.

The way of the warrior, I've found, is to die. In a situation with a choice, you can only choose at once to die. There's nothing complicated about it. With calmness you just go right ahead. Talk such as, "You're missing the mark" or "It's a dog's death," may be good for a sophisticated warrior's way, urbane style. But, for us, in a situation with a choice it isn't necessary to hit the mark. We all want to live.

There's always a better reason for what you want. If you miss the mark and live, you'll be a coward. That's the tricky line. If you miss the mark and die, you may be crazy but it won't be shameful. That's the solid way of the warrior. If you relive your death every morning and evening and remain in a constant state of death, you will achieve freedom in the warrior's way and complete your duty without making a mistake during your life.

Because you try to do everything with whatever little bit of wisdom you have, you remain concerned about yourself, go against heaven, and do evil things. To a third party watching you, what you do is unseemly, feeble, narrow, and unworkable. When what you have seems far from true wisdom, you had better consult those who are wise. Because it is not their business, they will be unselfish, and what they understand with their straight wisdom will meet the Way; to a third party watching you, it will look firmly rooted and solid, like a giant tree with many roots. One man's wisdom is like a log stuck into the ground.

The retainers who are determined to take their lord's side, leave everything, good or bad, to him, and remain completely dedicated to him, are not easily distracted by other things. A lord who has two or three such men is on secure ground.

In my long experience, when things were going well, there were many who made themselves conspicuous by serving their lord with wisdom, considerateness, or arts. But as soon as the lord retired or died, so many of them turned their backs and began culling favor with their new, rising lord. Just remembering such people disgusts me. Those of senior rank and junior rank, as well as those accomplished in the arts, provided service as though vying to be the first among equals. But when the time came for them to sacrifice their lives for their lord, they suddenly became weak-kneed and did few elegant things. This is why someone who is of no special use can prove himself worthy of a thousand men at a time of emergency; this someone is the one who gave his life to his lord years ago and has since lived completely in harmony with him.

When the late lord Mitsushige died, there was such an example: I was the only one determined to accompany him in his death, though some later imitated me. Many ranking officials who used to brag and make themselves prominent turned their backs once the lord closed his eyes. "In the bond between lord and retainer devotion is what counts" is a saying I had thought was worn out, but there and then it came back alive before my eyes. If you make up your mind here and now, you can make a superior retainer of yourself.

In the Nabeshima fief, proscription against disembowelment to follow one's lord had become part of the clan regulations in 1661 when a member of the Nabeshima clan, Yamagi Naohiro, died and it became known that thirty-six of his top retainers were contemplating suicide. When told of this, Mitsushige, the lord of the fiefdom then twenty-nine, had the following message delivered to the thirty-six men. His argument lucidly captures the samurai ethos of the time:

> Our lord [i.e., Mitsushige] hears that you men, mindful of your master's favors, have agreed among yourselves to disembowel yourselves in order to follow him. He appreciates this as divine.
>
> However, if Yamagi had told you to disembowel yourselves after his death, our lord is not aware of it. He would like to know if you are. If you are not, doing so would be useless. If you appreciate Yamagi's great favors, remember his son Ōsuke is young; protecting and serving him so that he may successfully inherit the Yamagi house will truly be repaying Yamagi's favors and at the same be loyal to Ōsuke. So you ought to give up the thought of disembowelment.
>
> Should you, however, force the issue and disembowel yourselves, your descendants would not be allowed the right of inheritance. Of course, some of you may be so deeply appreciative of your master's favor that you might disembowel yourselves regardless of the discontinuation of your descendants and reputable houses. In the circumstances, even if just one of you disemboweled himself, Ōsuke would not be allowed to inherit the Yamagi house and the house itself would be discontinued. That would make you disloyal. Consider this well.

The thirty-six men tearfully agreed to forego their plans. Informed of their decision, Mitsushige was immensely pleased and made the proscription against this type of disembowelment legally binding. Two years later, in 1663, in issuing amendments to "The Regulations for the Military Houses," the Tokugawa Shogunate followed suit by appending an "oral command" from the shogun Ietsuna:

Since old times we have warned that disemboweling oneself to follow one's lord is disloyal and useless. But because no one has made this explicit, in recent years too many men have disemboweled themselves after their lords' death. Henceforth, masters must firmly and continuously tell those who entertain such thoughts not to commit this act after they die. If even then someone commits it in the future, the deceased master will be held responsible. Also, his son who succeeds him will be deemed inadequate for failing to stop that act.

Later, the prohibition was incorporated as an article.

To advise someone to correct a bad habit is a matter of great importance, compassion, and service. What you have to take pains over is the way you give the advice. It is easy to see good and bad in someone; it is also easy to point the bad things out. Most people think it kind to say things that people don't want to hear and that are in fact difficult to say, and when someone doesn't accept what they tell him, they say they've tried, and give up. This is useless. It's the same as embarrassing someone or saying bad things about him to his face. It's no different from saying something just so *you* may feel better.

To advise someone about a bad habit, you must first determine whether or not he is going to accept your opinion. You must become his close friend so that he may take your words as trustworthy. You must then devise ways of bringing up the subject, as in relation to something he likes to do, or think of an appropriate moment to do so. When you are writing a letter or taking leave, you may bring up something bad about yourself. Or, to make him realize what you're getting at without your saying so, you may first praise him for good things or otherwise be extremely careful to make him feel better. In this manner he will take to what you have to say as readily as he takes to water when thirsty. Correcting someone's bad habit in this fashion is what we mean by giving good advice. It is an exceptionally difficult thing to do.

Most bad habits can't be corrected because they've been with the person for years. I myself have had some experience in this. Nevertheless, if colleagues try hard to correct their friends' bad habits, they can serve their master with one mind. It will also be an expression of great compassion. But how can you expect to correct someone's bad habit if you do no more than put him to shame?

Not long after I seconded Sawabe Heizaemon at his disembowelment, Administrator Nakano Kazumo sent me a letter of praise from Edo where he was stationed. It was full of extravagant words, such as "You have solidified the reputation of your clan." At the time I thought it was too much for him to say such things to a mere second. But as I later gave more thought to it, I saw that he had done it as a man of knowledge and experience. You must praise a young man when he has carried out a samurai assignment correctly, however trivial it may be, so that he may work with even greater determination and courage. I received a prompt letter of praise from Nakano Shōkan the Elder as well. I kept both letters. Yamamoto Gorōzaemon, my nephew, presented me with a saddle and a set of stirrups.

In 1682 when he was twenty-three, Tsunetomo was asked by his cousin Heizaemon to serve as his second or beheader the night before he was to disembowel himself. Heizaemon and several of his friends had engaged in illegal gambling, and he and two others had been condemned to death. After some hesitation Tsunetomo agreed to his cousin's request and wrote a formal letter of consent.

As is explained in the entry quoting the letter: "Since the days of old it has been said that the ultimate misfortune for a samurai is to be asked to serve as a second. This is because even when you execute the job well, it won't add to your reputation, whereas if by any chance you botch it, it will be regarded as the mistake of your life."

The second selected for one of the two other men did indeed botch his job. He drew his sword too far from the condemned man and, failing to behead him with a single stroke, had to "slash him up."

Monk so-and-so is among the most accomplished men in recent times. His generosity is immeasurable. That's why his large temple is managed well.

"I was put in charge of a large temple even though I'm a sickly man not worth speaking about," he said. "I thought I'd make errors if I decided to do the whole work myself and do it well. So I do what little I can, and when I'm not feeling well, I have my deputies run various things, hoping only that nothing disastrous will happen."

His predecessor's predecessor was too strict, and people grew tired of him. His predecessor delegated too much and was in some ways careless. Since the present monk took office, people have been satisfied.

When you think of it, he manages things well because he has a firm grasp of things, large and small. Also, from time to time he leaves things to his deputies and lets them take charge without interference. But, if asked, he gives instructions in a manner that shows there's nothing he's in the dark about.

Some time ago, the resident monk of a Zen temple summoned a fellow prone to mouth clever things and flaunt his enlightenment, and said, "You're getting in the way of the Law. I'll kill you!" He then beat him up. I'm told the man became a cripple.

Both monks have many good qualities. The latter is also known to take advantage of his illness.

Naki na zo to hito ni wa iite arinubeshi
kokoro no towaba ikaga kotaen

I can keep telling people the rumor's unfounded;
how shall I reply if my heart asks?[1]

Nothing is more valuable than the second half of this poem. I think we should repeat it like a prayer.

People tend to say things but not to do much else. Clever people today are only interested in decorating their exteriors to look wise and hide what they really are. They are inferior to those who are pure. Pure people are honest. If you look into your own heart, as in the second half of the poem quoted above, you have no place to hide yourself. Your heart is a good investigator. We'd like to maintain

---

1. An anonymous tanka on love in the *Gosen Shū* (no. 726) with the heading: "A man, who continued to secretly visit a woman living with her parents, said, 'Well, no one will know about this for a while.' [So the woman responded with a poem]." By the Edo Period the poem had come to be taken as a homiletic piece meaning something like, "A gentleman looks upon himself and corrects his ways."

ourselves in such a way as not to be embarrassed when we meet this investigator.

A certain swordsman said when he became very old:

"During your lifetime training there are stages.

"At a low level you train very hard but can't master the art. You know you're no good, and people agree. As long as you stay at that stage you can't serve your master.

"At a midlevel you may still not be able to serve your master, but you notice things that are wrong with you and also see things that are wrong with others.

"At a high level you are a master of the art. You can boast about it, delight when people praise you, and lament how others haven't reached your level. At that level you can serve your master.

"At a level somewhat higher you pretend to be unconcerned. People know you're good. This is where most people stop.

"There is, however, a level a step above, let's say, a superior stage, in the way of swordsmanship. When you go deep into the way, you realize there are no limits in the end. There is no point where you can say this is it, and you see starkly how inadequate you are. So you spend the rest of your life without even thinking of becoming accomplished or without thinking of boasting, let alone looking down upon others.

"Yagyū Munenori is said to have observed, 'I have yet to learn how to win a fight with others, but I have learned to win a fight with myself.'

"You try to be better today than yesterday, better tomorrow than today, and so on, day after day, for the rest of your life. There is no end to it."

Yagyū Munenori (1571–1646), an outstanding swordsman who taught swordsmanship to the first three of the Tokugawa shoguns, Ieyasu, Hidetada, and Iemitsu, has left a famous treatise on his Shinkage school, *Heihō Kaden Sho*.[2] Among his other distinguished students was Nabeshima Motoshige (1602–54), a son of Katsushige, the second lord of the Nabeshima fief under the Tokugawa

---

2. A complete translation of the tract is included in Hiroaki Sato, *The Sword and the Mind*.

Shogunate. He thought so highly of Motoshige that he dedicated to him a beautifully bound edition of his treatise. As a result, the Shinkage school of swordsmanship was accepted as standard by the members and retainers of the Nabeshima clan.

Murakawa Sōden, Tsunetomo's uncle and an accomplished swordsman of the Shinkage school, has left the following anecdote about Munenori:

"Yagyū Munenori's ultimate statement on swordsmanship is, 'The truly accomplished swordsmen have no use for swordsmanship.' As evidence, he told a story.

"Once a certain shogunate aide-de-camp came to him and asked to study swordsmanship with him. Upon seeing the man, Munenori said, 'Sir, what are you telling me? I see that you are already accomplished in some school of swordsmanship. I'd like to accept you as you are; without studying with me you may call yourself my student.'

" 'But, sir, I have absolutely no training in swordsmanship of any kind!'

" 'Well then, you must have come here to make fun of me,' Munenori said. 'You are not saying, are you, that an instructor to the shoguns can't tell the real thing when he sees it?'

"But the aide-de-camp vowed that he was telling the truth. So Munenori asked, 'If that is the case, you must have had some kind of enlightening thought that has made you what you are today.'

" 'Sir,' the man said. 'One day when I was a child, it occurred to me that what a samurai is all about is that he thinks nothing of his life. I became gravely worried about this realization, but after several years it dawned on me that that's the way it is. Since then I've thought nothing of dying. Other than this, I haven't had anything like an enlightening thought.'

"Munenori was greatly moved. 'So I've seen the real thing after all. To me, in that one thing lies the ultimate of swordsmanship. So far I have had hundreds of students, but I haven't revealed the ultimate to a single one of them. You don't need to take up a wooden sword. You are accomplished in your own way.'

"On the spot Munemori handed the man a certificate of mastery."

In *Bushidō Kōsha Sho* (Those Accomplished in the Way of the Warrior) is written: "For an accomplished man there is a way of establishing his reputation in soldiering that does not entail actual training." Herein lies a seed of misunderstanding for later learners. There should be "also" added after "there is." Again, Shida Kichinosuke said, "When you are forced to choose to live or die, you better live." Shida is a man of bravery, and said this as a joke. Nevertheless, young men misunderstand this and think that he said something dishonorable for a samurai. Alongside this you should put something else he said: "When you don't know whether you should eat or shouldn't, you better not eat; when you don't know whether you should die or live, you better die."

In the relevant paragraph of *Bushidō Kōsha Sho*, published in 1617, its author, Ogasawara Sakuun Katsuzō, says: "The advantage of being an accomplished man is that as such he has a way of establishing his reputation in soldiering that does not entail actual training. It is the advantage of using words to make your small experience in soldiering sound impressive. It lies in learning, and learning lies in your ambition. Learning in soldiering does not necessarily mean reading books. You must try to listen to the stories of experienced people, while at the same time not interrupting your training in soldiering."

Shida Kichinosuke was a relatively low-ranking samurai, but because of his brilliance his advice was greatly valued by those in the highest echelons. He was also admired for his bravery. However, it appears he spent most of his time indulging in strange behavior, pretending to be greedy and stupid, saying incredible things. Once when he was traveling as an eye-medicine merchant, he was attacked by a group of bandits. He cut three of them down, injured two others, and chased away the rest. He kept the incident to himself, but the story eventually came out. When someone said to him, "Sir, you are a great swordsman," he is said to have responded, "Absolutely not. I'm a coward. I thought I'd be killed if I just stood around, but I cherished my life, so I cut them down before they cut me down."

When a group met to discuss the promotion of a certain man, it was pointed out that some time back he had drunk an excessive amount of sake; the group, therefore, unanimously agreed not to promote him. But the man in question spoke out and said, "If you give up on somebody because he once made a mistake, you won't be able to find people who can serve our master usefully. Someone who once made a mistake regrets it, becomes careful, and so can serve his master usefully. You should promote me."

Someone asked, "Do you guarantee your statement?"

"Yes, sir, I do."

Everybody asked, "What is your guaranty?"

"The fact that I made a mistake," he said. "Somebody who hasn't made a single mistake is dangerous."

So he was promoted.

So-and-so ended up disgracing himself because he did not revenge himself in a quarrel. The way you revenge yourself is to walk into your enemy's place, prepared to be killed. When you're killed, it won't be shameful. Because you think you must successfully carry out your revenge, it becomes too late. Once you start saying things like, "They've got too many on their side," you let time pass, and in the end you agree among yourselves not to do it. Even if there are thousands of them on the other side, you must go, determined to cut down as many of them as you can, as they come. That's an accomplishment. That's what you have to do.

Similarly, it was a mistake that Lord Asano's masterless samurai didn't disembowel themselves at Sengaku Temple after their night assault.[3] It was also in error for them to postpone again and again the attempt to kill their enemy, Lord Kira, after letting him kill their master. It would have been a matter of grave regret indeed if Kira had died in the meantime, of illness, for example. Those urban people are brainy and clever, and are skilled in doing things in a way that draws praise. They don't do things in an unthinking fashion as people in the Nagasaki Quarrel did.

Again, the Soga brothers' vendetta was unnecessarily postponed, with Sukenari missing an excellent opportunity when he was invited into the enemy's camp. That was unfortunate. What [Soga] Gorō said was right.

---

3. See the next chapter.

The "Nagasaki Quarrel" is an incident that took place in Nagasaki on the twentieth of the twelfth month, 1700, two years before the successful assault on the Kira mansion by the forty-seven samurai. On the basis of a record kept at the time, the incident may be summarized as follows:

When two Nabeshima samurai, Fukabori San'emon and Shibahara Buemon, walked past a servant of Takagi Hikoemon by the name of Sōnai on a snow-covered muddy road, a splash from either San'emon or Buemon soiled Sōnai's kimono. Flaunting the fact that he worked for Hikoemon, a ranking official, Sōnai extravagantly cursed the samurai. San'emon and Buemon became furious and kicked Sōnai down into the mud and beat him up. Sōnai ran away, vowing to return with his men to retaliate.

That night Sōnai did return with a dozen men. San'emon and Buemon, having anticipated this, tried to fight back with swords. But evidently better qualified in intentions than in fighting skill, the two men were overwhelmed in no time and severely beaten before Sōnai and his men left.

When San'emon's son, Kaemon, learned what had happened to his father, he ran toward Hikoemon's house for revenge. Buemon's servants and other relatives joined him, and the next morning a total of twelve men broke into Hikoemon's house and, without suffering any casualty on their side, killed most of the men inside, including Hikoemon. When the fight was over, San'emon and Buemon disemboweled themselves, saying their wishes were fulfilled.

On the twenty-first of the third month of the following year, the Edo government's verdicts on those involved in the incident reached the Nabeshima fiefdom: death by disembowelment for the remaining ten men, and exile for the nine who came to Hikoemon's house to help—though after the fight was over.

The "Soga brothers' vendetta" refers to the killing, in 1193, of Kudō Suketsune by Soga Jūrō Sukenari (1172–93) and his brother Gorō Tokimune (1174–93) to avenge their father.

In 1193, beginning on the fifteenth of the fifth month, Minamoto no Yoritomo (1147–99) sponsored large-scale hunting on the outskirts of Mt. Fuji. Suketsune and the Soga brothers took part along with a great number of other samurai. According to *Soga Monogatari*, the narrative of the vendetta Tsunetomo here refers to, on the night of the first day, while spying on Suketsune, Jūrō is spotted by the latter's son and is invited into his camp where a banquet is being given. Jūrō is summoned to Suketsune's seat and hears him deny any wrongdoing in relation to his father, explaining that all that's said is nothing but slander. He then even dances at his enemy's request. However, deciding to carry out the revenge with his brother, he deliberately lets go the chance to kill Suketsune.

Told of this afterward, Gorō says, "The timing was so good you should have killed him, even though, come to think of it, I'd certainly like to kill him with you, too." Later on, he also says, "That was like going to a treasure mountain and coming back empty-handed. But I'm glad you restrained yourself."

So Tsunetomo's commentary on Gorō's reaction is only half right.

Jūrō and Gorō successfully carried out their vendetta thirteen days later. But in the mayhem following Suketsune's slaying, Jūrō was killed. Gorō managed to escape but was soon arrested and beheaded.

I shouldn't be criticizing such things, but I say them because we are looking into the way of the warrior. Unless you think about such things before something happens, you won't be able to act properly when you face a real situation, but will mostly end up shaming yourself. You listen to people and read books so that you may have a resolve in anticipation of a real event.

The way of the warrior is something you must contemplate in every detail, day and night, on the assumption that you may not be able to live through the day. You may win or lose, depending on the circumstances. But you can't shame yourself. You must die. If you have shamed yourself, you must revenge yourself on the spot. No wisdom is required for this. An accomplished warrior doesn't think whether he's going to win or lose, but dashes into the place of death with single-minded determination. In so doing he rids himself of all "illusions."

Tsunetomo's assertion that a samurai must act with unthinking, single-minded determination in order to avoid disgracing himself or to shed the disgrace already suffered may strike some as bizarre. But Tsunetomo's contemporary, the noted Confucian thinker and military strategist Yamaga

Sokō (1622–85), for example, believed in much the same thing; among the dicta he has left is, "The moment you're touched by a sense of pity, you must rise against your enemy no matter how few soldiers you may have on your side."

Sokō's observation may be traced to the Chinese philosopher Mencius, who said, "The feeling of pity is the beginning of virtuousness"—i.e., the moment you spontaneously respond to your sense of pity, you've already begun to ascend toward the ultimate virtue. Apparently Sokō interpreted the word "pity"—*sokuin,* in Japanese—in a broad sense, using it to mean something like "a triggered emotion." Some say Sokō's school of thinking was behind the actions of later military men such as General Nogi Maresuke (1849–1912) and Admiral Yamamoto Isoroku (1884–1943).

Until about fifty or sixty years ago, a samurai used to wash himself with cold water every morning, scent the shaven top of his head and his hair with incense, clip the nails of his hands and toes, rub them with a piece of pumice, then polish them with sorrel, to make himself presentable in every way. Above all, he took care not to let his weapons rust; he kept them dusted and polished to have them always ready.

The fact that a samurai used to make himself presentable may suggest he was trying to be a dandy; perhaps, but he never tried to be fashionable. He was ready to be killed in battle at any moment of the day. But if he was killed when not presentable, that would reveal that he hadn't been ready, and he would be dismissed by his enemy and despised as unsightly. That's why a samurai, young or old, tried to keep himself presentable. You may think I'm exaggerating or that I'm repeating myself, but that's what a samurai's job is all about. There's nothing special or hard about it. If you always maintain yourself in readiness to be killed in battle, if you completely hold yourself in a state of death as you serve your master and act in military situations, you will never shame yourself.

There is a way of bringing up a warrior's son. From infancy, encourage him to be brave. No matter what happens, do not scare him or cheat him. Cowardice acquired in childhood will remain as a flaw for life. As a parent, try not to be careless and show a boy that he can be scared of thunder or that he doesn't have to go into dark places. Telling scary stories to make him stop crying is a terrible thing. Also, if you scold an infant boy too severely, you'll make him diffident.

Make sure that he will not develop bad habits. Once he develops a bad habit, just telling him to get rid of it won't work. Make him learn gradually the proper manners and speech. See to it that he will not develop greedy tendencies. In other ways you may be normal; if the boy is normal, he will grow up all right.

People are right in saying that if parents don't get along with each other, their son grows up to be unfilial. Even birds and beasts learn, from their birth, by looking at their parents and listening to them.

Also, if the mother is unthinking, she may end up ruining the relationship between father and son. Because she tends to love her son blindly, she may side with him when the father criticizes him, in effect the mother and son united against the father, and the son may end up not getting along with the father. This is a terrible thing. You may even think that she is doing that hoping her son will take care of her in her old age.

Confucius said, "When you make a mistake, don't hesitate to correct it." If you correct your mistake immediately, the effect of the mistake will be vastly reduced. Trying to cover it up is unseemly, and you will suffer from it.

For example, if you realize you have said something you shouldn't have said, you should admit it at once. If you do that, what you have said won't remain and you don't have to be worried about it. If someone criticizes you even then, you should say, "I have said what I have by mistake, so I have admitted it. If you feel that's not enough, there's nothing more I can do about it. I didn't say what I did with you in mind, so I'd be grateful if you could pretend I didn't say what I did. We all can't avoid saying this or that about other people, can we?"

In any event, you should never tell a secret or talk about other people. Also, if you are with a group of people, you should be careful about each word you utter.

When it comes to handwriting, nothing seems better than that which is mannerly and meticulous. But, in reality, such handwriting is often stiff and base. There should be something that goes beyond the standard rules. This applies to every other thing.

The *metsuke*[4] can do harm unless he knows what his function is. The position of *metsuke* was created to aid in governing the country. Because the lord by himself can't see and hear everything in detail, the *metsuke* is expected to report to the lord clearly and accurately how the lord is conducting himself, the good or evil acts of the administrators, the justice or injustice of the government's verdict, what people are saying, and the joys and sufferings of his lowly subjects, so that the lord may justly govern. His position is so called because its true purpose is to provide the lord with an eye.

For all this, many in the position of *metsuke* are prone to concentrate on evil acts of lowly people they see and hear about. Since evil acts never cease, this brings unnecessary harm. Among the lowly those who are honest are rare. But their evil acts seldom harm the country.

Also, prosecutors must conduct their investigations with the inclination to favor what the criminals say, so that they may not be punished. Doing so will in the end help the lord.

The way of the warrior lies in frantic death—walking into the place of death without flinching. At times the slaying of one man may be carried out by fifty to sixty men. Lord Naoshige has commented: You can't achieve anything great in sanity. A warrior can only become insane and die a frantic death. In the way of the warrior the moment you begin to *think*, it's too late. The way of the warrior has no use for loyalty or filial devotion; it is simply frantic death. Within the frantic death itself are both loyalty and filial devotion contained.

Ittei[5], said "You make yourself unnecessarily unworthy if you look at what a truly accomplished man does and think that you can't be that good. A truly accomplished man is a human being; so are you. The moment you decide you can't be inferior and you take up something, you've already grasped the essence of the matter at hand. Deciding at age fifteen to be accomplished in scholarship was what

---

4. Inspector; literally, "eye-attached."
5. Ittei, or Ishida Yasubō Nobuyuki (1629–93), was a Confucian scholar and a counselor to Nabeshima Mitsushige. When he was thirty-three, his feudal bondage to Mitsushige was severed because of an incident, and he was put under a form of house arrest. Pardoned seven years later, he lived the rest of his life in retirement, writing a number of books. He greatly influenced Tsunetomo.

that great man was all about.[6] He wasn't the great man that he was because he made the decision and then worked hard to become a great man."

Ittei also said: "The moment you decide to become enlightened, you are."

A samurai must be careful about everything and try not to show any weakness. Untrained in how to say things, he is prone to say things like, "I'm a coward," "At such a time I'd run away," "That's scary," and "It hurts." Such are the things you should never say, be it as a joke or to be playful or while in sleep or in delirium. Anyone with insight may see what you are really like. You should always keep this in mind.

In the *Yoshitsune Gunka* (Yoshitsune's Military Verse),[7] is one that says, "A commander must often speak to his men." Not only when doing so is appropriate but also in normal circumstances, a commander should say even to ordinary soldiers things like, "You've done a fine job again," "I'd be grateful if you worked particularly hard this time," and "You're such a great fellow!" If the commander says things like these, his men won't mind giving up their lives for him. Such words play a crucial role.

My father Yamamoto Shin'emon Yoshitada used to say: "The ultimate asset for a samurai is the people he has. You may think you yourself can serve your lord adequately, but you can't do a warrior's work by yourself. When it comes to money, you can borrow it from somebody else. People don't suddenly materialize before you. You must take care to maintain able people with considerateness. When you have people working for you, you mustn't think of filling your mouth with food first, but give it to them first. Then they will stay with you."

As a result, those who knew my father used to gossip among themselves, "No one of Shin'emon's status and rank has as many people as he does" or "Shin'emon has more people than I do." Many

---

6. Alludes to the famous pronouncement of Confucius: "At age fifteen I decided to be accomplished in scholarship; at thirty I established myself; at forty I stopped being confused; at fifty I knew the principle of heaven; at sixty I followed my ear; at seventy I followed my heart's desire but never overstepped the bounds of propriety."

7. A collection of homiletic verses for warriors attributed to Minamoto no Yoshitsune (1159-1189). For Yoshitsune, see the chapter on him.

of the men he trained in his employment went on to serve directly under Lord Katsushige as spear-bearers. When he was ordered to head a military unit, he received the lord's word: "When it comes to the members of his unit, Shin'emon may replace them with the ones he likes." In addition, a special stipend was issued, so Shin'emon could fill the entire unit with his retainers.

At any regular moon-viewing session, Lord Katsushige used to send out Shin'emon's men to get ritual saltwater at Terai, saying, "Have the members of Shin'emon's unit do the work. They don't mind going into deep places to get the water."

When your lord depends on you like this, you can only serve him with dedication and care.

In *Kusunoki Masashige Hyōgo Ki* is the statement, "Surrendering is something a samurai never does, be it for deceiving the enemy or for the emperor." That's the way a loyal subject should be.

Kusunoki Masashige Hyōgo Ki (Record of Kusunoki Masashige in Hyōgo) is a book of sayings attributed to Kusunoki Masashige (1294–1336),[8] which, as legend has it, Masashige himself gave to Onchi Wada, in Hyōgo, before riding into a hopeless battle. The original passage Tsunetomo refers to reads:

> When you are surrounded by your enemy on all sides and you are the only one left, if you decide to surrender with the thought of carrying out a plot against the enemy later, you are no longer a courageous man. Once you think of your survival by a plot against the enemy, you will never carry that plot out because when the time comes you will think of some other thing that's beneficial to your life. Tension exists only while you're carrying out your action, regarding your enemy and your death as one and the same.

---

8. See the chapter on him.

THE FORTY-SEVEN SAMURAI:
AN EYEWITNESS ACCOUNT,
WITH ARGUMENTS

O N THE NIGHT OF the fourteenth of the twelfth month—or, to be more exact, before daybreak on the fifteenth—of the fifteenth year of Genroku, 1702, a band of forty-seven men broke into the Edo mansion of Kira Kōzukenosuke Yoshinaka[1] and killed Kira and many of the men staying with him. They immediately reported their action to the proper authorities, providing a list of the participants as well as an explanation: They had assaulted and killed Kira to avenge their lord, Asano Taku-minokami Naganori.[2]

Early in the previous year, during the annual reception of imperial messengers in Edo Castle, Asano, a daimyo on the reception committee, had attacked and wounded Kira, the lord of a *kōke*, "high house," the highest-ranking hereditary specialist in protocol appointed to guide Asano and others on reception etiquette. The government did not deliberate for long before coming to a decision: condemning Asano to death by disembowelment on the same day, while praising Kira for his restraint. The government also put Asano's brother, Daigaku, then a shogunate aide-de-camp, under house arrest and confiscated Asano's castle in Akō, Harima Province. The men who broke into the Kira mansion, led by Asano's house administrator, Ōishi Kuranosuke Yoshio, were some of those who had become "masterless" as a result.

---

1. As elsewhere noted, samurai in higher positions were often accorded a court rank as well as a court title. Kira Yoshinaka, who was born in 1641, carried the title of *kōzukenosuke*, "Lieutenant Governor of Kōzuke," as well as the rank of "Minor Captain of the Inner Palace Guards, Left Division," and junior forth rank.

2. Asano, who was born in 1667, received the court title of *takuminokami*, "Chief of the Bureau of Carpentry," in 1680, when he was thirteen years old, along with the rank of junior fifth rank. Following tradition, both *kōzukenosuke* and *takuminokami* will be often used in lieu of actual names in the rest of this section.

Nearly fifty days after the vendetta, on the fourth day of the second month, the men received the government's verdict on their action: death by disembowelment. The sentence was carried out at once, and the men—who had been broken up into four units and placed in the custody of four daimyo houses on the day they killed Kira—were all dead before the end of the day.

There prevailed in that period an adjudicative principle known as *kenka ryōseibai*: In a quarrel the two parties involved are equally to blame. Partly because of this, the government's handling of Asano and Kira was felt to be unjust—the impression strengthened by Kira's notoriety as an arrogant and coercive bribe-taker who used his special knowledge and position without any sense of embarrassment. Only a few years earlier another daimyo in Asano's position had seriously contemplated killing the man.

Nevertheless, Japan then was a society that had accustomed itself to prolonged domestic peace and the capricious, often heavy-handed rule of the fifth Tokugawa shogun Tsunayoshi (1646–1709), who, among other things, issued an edict forbidding the maltreatment or killing of all living things, from mosquito larvae to cats, dogs, and horses. (Human beings were evidently not counted among living things: Those who violated the edict were often put to death.) As a result, the vengeance carried out by a highly disciplined group of men, in seeming defiance of the government, shocked and won widespread admiration. Naturally, the government's decision on the avengers, when it came, provoked profound indignation among the general populace. It also generated spirited debate among scholars, who were mostly Confucian.

The vendetta itself was given its first dramatization a mere twelve days after the avengers disemboweled themselves. It has since continued to spawn plays, legends, treatises, fictions, and, of course, movies.

It should be noted that the number of people who surrendered themselves to the authorities after the killing of Kira was forty-six. There has been a good deal of speculation on what happened to the forty-seventh, Terasaka Kichiemon. Some say he panicked and ran away just before the men broke into Kira's house; others that he received special instructions from the leader, Ōishi, and left the group after the vendetta was completed. Here I follow the prevailing practice of assuming that the group consisted of forty-seven men.

What follows are the first part of an eye-witness account of what happened on the day Asano Naganori wounded Kira Yoshinaka, and some of the subsequent arguments made on the revenge.

Okado Denpachirō (1659–1723), who in 1697 was appointed an *o-met-suke*, which in this instance may be given as "deputy inspector-general," was on duty when the incident occurred. As a result, he, along with one of his colleagues also on duty, was assigned to question Asano. In addition, together with another deputy inspector-general, he was appointed a *fukushi*, "assistant marshal," to see to it that Asano's disembowelment was properly carried out.

The position of *o-metsuke* was a powerful one, its chief responsibility being to "spy" on shogunate aides-de-camp and other direct vassals for the shogun. It might be thought that in his line of duty an *o-metsuke*'s superior was an *ō-metsuke*, "inspector-general," whose main responsibility it was to "spy" on daimyo. But the Tokugawa Shogunate was a government of deliberate redundancies and divided responsibilities, where an *o-metsuke* reported, and was accountable, not to his titular superior, an *ō-metsuke*, but only to a *wakadoshiyori*, "deputy administrator," while an *ō-metsuke* reported to a *rōchū*, "administrator." The position of *rōchū* was first in government rank, and that of *wakadoshiyori* second, except when the emergency position of *tairō*, "grand administrator," was created. These separate chains of command in part explain Denpachirō's intransigence to Inspector-General Shōda Yasutoshi (1650–1705).

The Tokugawa Shogunate was also a government of collective decision making. The top administrative position, in normal times, of *rōchū* had four or five simultaneous appointees, who served in pairs every other month; so did the position of *wakadoshiyori* as well as that of *ō-metsuke*. When it comes to *o-metsuke*, there were as many as twenty-four appointees at any time, as Okado himself notes.

In his original account Denpachirō speaks mostly of himself in the third person, often making a slip and referring to himself in the first person. In the translation the account is given uniformly in the first person for better narrative flow.

MEMORANDUM OF OKADO DENPACHIRŌ

On the fourteenth of the third month of the fourteenth year of Genroku [1701], the two deputy inspectors-general on duty were Ōkubo Gonzaemon and I, Okado Denpachirō. However, all the twenty-four deputy inspectors-general were on hand, with Kuru Jūzaemon and Kondō Heihachirō on overnight duty. About an hour before noon there was a great commotion in the palace, and a message was promptly delivered to the room for the deputy inspectors-general: "Just now, in the Pine Hallway, there was a quarrel, even injury. I don't know who his opponent was, but Lord Kira Kōzukenosuke of the High House was wounded with a sword!"

At once all of us deputy inspectors-general hurried to the Pine Hallway, where we found Kōzukenosuke in the arms of Shinagawa Koreuji, Governor of Buzen, on the wooden verandah near the Cherry Room, shouting in a delirious, high-pitched voice, tongue trembling, "Bring doctors, please!" He had run from a corner of the Pine Hallway toward the Cherry Room, and the tatami had blood spilled all along the way.

On one side was Asano Takuminokami, face flushed and swordless, held down by Kajikawa Yosobē, saying in a subdued tone: "Sir, I'm not deranged. I understand why you are holding me down like this, but please let me go. I failed to kill him, and I'm ready to be punished. I would not try to injure him again. Unloosen your arms. Allow me to put on my headgear, allow me to straighten my crested robe, so I may await an order in accordance with the Regulations for the Military Houses."

But Yosobē would not relax his hold. So Takuminokami tried to reason with him: "I am at the least the lord president of a castle with holdings of 50,000 koku. Certainly I behaved in a manner inappropriate for this place, and I profoundly regret it. Nevertheless, I am wearing a formal robe. If you continue to hold me down in this unseemly fashion, my robe will become crumpled. I have absolutely no grievance against the shogun, have no intention of acting against him. I do regret I failed in my attempt to kill, but that's what happened and there's nothing more I can do about it."

Still, Yosobē continued to pin him down to the tatami, twisting him, so the four of us, Gonzaemon, Jūzaemon, Heihachirō, and I, received him in our custody, straightened his headgear and crested robe, placed him in a corner of the Cycad Room sectioned off with screens, and took turns watching over him. This immensely pleased him.

Kōzukenosuke was similarly sectioned off with screens, in the northern corner of the Cycad Room, with four deputy inspectors-general accompanying him. He asked, "Is there enough distance between Takuminokami and me? Won't he come over here again?" The inspectors said, "Don't worry, sir. We're here with you."

In no time, in places like the dismounting areas of the Main Gate and Sakurada Gate there was a great commotion among those who didn't know the names of the people involved in the quarrel and were worried about their masters, some coming in as far as the Main Entrance and Inner Entrance—or so reported Assistant Inspectors Mizuno Mokuzemon, Machida Ibē, and others, who asked, "We've stopped them at various gates, but they don't believe what we say. What shall we do?"

At once I gave instructions to the Office of the Architect, which prepared pine boards for public announcements with "*Asano Takuminokami wounded Kira Kōzukenosuke with a sword. Both men are under investigation in the palace. No unruly behavior shall be tolerated among retainers*" written on both sides in large brush strokes, and had them erected at all the dismounting areas. The commotion ceased immediately, except among the retainers of Asano and Kira who remained in a state of agitation—so we stated to the administrators and deputy administrators who had gathered in one room.

Administrators Tsuchiya Masanao, Governor of Sagami, and Ogasawara Nagashige, Governor of Sado, and Deputy Administrators Katō Akihide, Governor of Etchū, and Inoue Masamine, Governor of Yamato, who had gathered in one room, decided among themselves and ordered Kondō Heihachirō and me to investigate what Takuminokami had to say, while ordering Kuru Jūzaemon and Ōkubo Gonzaemon to investigate what Kōzukenosuke had to say. The short sword with which Takuminokami had struck Kōzukenosuke had already been taken and put back in its sheath, and in the section for the doctors in the Cypress Room Takuminokami, whose headgear and crested robe had been returned to him, was wearing a hemp kamishimo,[3] with six assistant inspectors sitting to his left and right.

---

3. The *kamishimo*, "upper-lower," was "a two-item set worn over kosode. The lower part consisted of a hakama tied at the waist. The upper section, *kataginu*, was a vestlike affair with whalebone stays stretching the material at the shoulder into stiff wings of fabric. Anything that has ever been said about the use of shoulder pads to project an

I said to him:

"Sir, concerning what you did today and what you have to say about it, the two of us have been ordered to investigate, and we do intend to examine your words in accordance with the regulations. Do you understand, sir?" I continued, "You became oblivious of where you were and went so far as to wound Kōzukenosuke with a sword. Tell us what you have to say about that."

Takuminokami would not make excuses for himself in any way, but said:

"Gentlemen, I have absolutely no grievance against the Shogun. I only had a personal grudge, and because of an accumulated anger I momentarily forgot myself, decided to kill Kōzukenosuke, and wounded him. No matter what punishment may be given me, I'll have no complaint. Nevertheless, I truly regret my failure to kill the man. How is he?"

When we replied, "The wounds are shallow, but he's an old man. Besides, they're on his face, so we aren't sure he'll ever recover," Takuminokami's face showed joy. After this, he would merely repeat, "I have nothing more to say, I'm afraid, gentlemen. I simply wait for the decision in accordance with the law." So Takuminokami was again taken to the Cycad Room and made to stay there.

As for Kōzukenosuke, similarly, in the section for the doctors in the Cypress Room his official robe was returned to him, and he was made to wear a hemp *kamishimo*. However, for some reason the *noshime* robe[4] hadn't been readied, and someone else's had to be borrowed for him. And in the same spot the two officers in charge told him:

"Sir, Asano Takuminokami, who seemed to have a grudge against you, went so far as to wound you with a sword. We've been ordered to conduct a detailed investigation of the matter, and would like to examine your words in accordance with the regulations. What kind of grudge had you provoked against yourself, so that Takuminokami, becoming oblivious of where he was, went so far as to wound you with a sword? You are certainly aware of the reason for it, and we trust you will tell us exactly what it is."

---

image of authority in the West must apply in triplicate to the kataginu," according to Liza Dalby, the author of *Kimono*. The *kamishimo* made of hemp was the samurai's formal wear in normal circumstances.

4. The samurai's formal wear to be worn under the *kamishimo* or any other formal outer garment. It was made of silk and had simple stripe patterns around the waist and sleeves.

Kōzukenosuke replied, "I am absolutely not aware of anything that might have generated a grudge against me. I'm convinced Takuminokami became deranged. Besides, I'm an old man. Why should anyone entertain a grudge against me? I am absolutely not aware of anything whatsoever. Other than that, I have nothing to say."

After this the four of us, Kuru Jūzaemon, Kondō Heihachirō, Ōkubo Gonzaemon, and I, consulted Inspectors-General Sengoku Hisayoshi, Governor of Tamba, and Andō Shigetsune, Governor of Chikugo, and reported the matter to the deputy administrators, who in turn reported it to Administrator Ogasawara. Then the four of us directly provided Administrator Ogasawara, with Administrator Tsuchiya also present, with detailed explanations of what Takuminokami and Kōzukenosuke had said. The matter was further reported to Lord Matsudaira Yoshiyasu, Governor of Mino.[5] We then received word that we would have further instructions in time and that we ought to stay in our room for a while. During this time two inspectors-general took turns guarding Takuminokami and Kōzukenosuke. Also, in response to Kōzukenosuke's request that his wounds be tended to, two palace doctors, Amano Ryōjun and Kurisaki Dōyū, examined his condition with his colleague Shinagawa Koreuji, Governor of Buzen, present. They determined that the wounds were shallow, and tended to them accordingly.

In time Chief of Service Nagakura Chin'ami conveyed the word:

"Deputy inspectors-general who investigated Takuminokami and Kōzukenosuke, and others, all come forward.

"Deputy Administrators Lord Katō Akihide, Governor of Etchū, and Lord Inagaki Shigetomi, Governor of Tsushima, had a meeting and made a decision.

"Concerning Asano Takuminokami, awhile ago he, becoming oblivious of where he was, and because of a long-standing private grudge, wounded Kira Kōzukenosuke with a sword. This was intolerable. He is ordered to be placed in the custody of Tamura Ukyōnodayū and to disembowel himself.

"Concerning Kōzukenosuke, he was aware of where he was and would not fight back. This was highly commendable. Shogunate Doctor Yoshida Ian is ordered to provide him with medicine, and

---

5. Yanagisawa Yoshiyasu (1658–1714), who was rapidly promoted by Shogun Tsunayoshi from an obscure, low position to the status of daimyo, then appointed *rōchū*. Because of shogunate favoritism, Yoshiyasu was more equal than the other men of the same rank.

Palace Doctor Kurisaki Dōyū to tend to his external wounds, so that he may have a good rest and recuperation. He may leave as he pleases, accompanied by his colleague from the High House."

All of us deputy inspectors-general heard these words gravely. We forwarded our protest:

"As for placing Takuminokami in Tamura Ukyōnodayū's custody, we will at once relay the message. At the same time, however, as for making these decisions public, we'd like to request that some time be given before we respond properly."

Meanwhile word was sent to Tamura Ukyōnodayū that he make necessary preparations in accordance with set rules.

Then, through Nagakura Chin'ami we—Denpachirō, Jūzaemon, Heihachirō, and Gonzaemon—sought a meeting with the deputy administrators, and I made the following statement:

"A while ago when we investigated what Takuminokami had to say, as I reported exactly, he said he had no grievance against the Shogun. He merely had a profound grudge against Kōzukenosuke, so that he forgot himself and, despite the gravity of the place, struck at him with a sword. He agreed that this was a serious, intolerable act. And his straightforward response was that no matter what punishment was given him, he would have nothing to complain about.

"Nonetheless, he is at the least a lord president of a castle with holdings of 50,000 koku and, in addition, from a house whose main branch is a daimyo with large holdings. When these things are considered, ordering disembowelment at once, today, as has been done, is too casual a measure. We fear that we occupy negligible posts, but as long as we are thought fit to serve in the position of deputy inspector-general, it would be a disservice on our part if we failed to point out our superiors' oversight when there is one, and we are afraid that Takuminokami's being ordered to disembowel himself on the same day is such an oversight. It is because of this that we dare point this out in disregard of the wrath this might bring down upon ourselves.

"Furthermore, Kōzukenosuke may indeed have shown restraint, but if Takuminokami, a daimyo of 50,000 koku, in fact had the kind of grievance against him that made him abandon his house, forget where he was, and strike at him with a sword—even supposing that he had become deranged, it would be difficult to say that Kōzukenosuke had done nothing blameworthy.

"In the circumstances, if you take at face value the result of the investigation conducted in some haste by only the two of us, the main branch of the Asano family, especially in view of the fact that it is of nonhereditary vassalage, might at some later date decide, should something untoward happen, that the shogunate handling of the matter was too casual.

"For this reason, concerning Takuminokami's disembowelment, we must request that inspectors-general, along with us, conduct a reinvestigation, and that a decision be made after an appropriate number of days have passed, whatever the penalty then may be. Until that time, Kōzukenosuke should be ordered to watch out for his own behavior, while a reinvestigation of him is also conducted. If he proves all right and it also turns out that he had done nothing deserving grievance and that only Takuminokami's derangement made him strike at him with a sword, treatment in his favor should be accorded him. Giving him favorable treatment today for his action today, we're afraid, is too casual. This we must dare point out."

Deputy Administrators Inagaki and Katō said, "You make perfect sense. We see that you are determined to fulfill your role of deputy inspector-general. We will relay your words to the administrators."

While we waited, the two deputy administrators returned and said, "The protest you made is entirely understandable. However, this is a case Lord Matsudaira had already heard and made a decision on, so they say you must accept what you were told earlier."

I, Denpachirō, alone protested further.

"Sir," I said. "If it is solely Lord Matsudaira's decision, I must ask that our statement be conveyed further up to the shogun. This is such a one-sided punishment that any daimyo of non-hereditary vassalage would be embarrassed to hear of it. Please do convey our statement to the Shogun at least once. Of course, if the matter has already been conveyed to him and the decision contains his thoughts as well, I must be pleased to accept it. But if Lord Matsudaira alone heard the case, I must request strongly that our protest be conveyed to the Shogun."

So Deputy Administrators Inagaki and Katō once again conveyed my protest to Lord Matsudaira. This angered Lord Matsudaira, who said, "I indeed haven't told the Shogun of this, but I, the administrator, have heard the case and made the decision. I find it hard to believe that the protest is brought to me yet again. Denpachirō deserves a penalty equivalent to house arrest. Have him stay in his room."[6]

---

6. Some historians say that the decision to condemn Asano to death was probably made by Shogun Tsunayoshi himself.

This message was brought by Deputy Administrator Inoue. The two deputy administrators who were involved earlier, perhaps feeling sorry for me, did not return.

While I stayed in a room as under house arrest, a place for disembowelment was set up at Tamura Ukyōnodayū's house. Kira Kōzukenosuke left the palace accompanied by Ōtomo Yoshitaka, Governor of Ōmi, and all the imperial messengers also left. Because of the confusion following the incident of the day, by the time the reception ceremonies were completed, it was already evening.

In the meantime, the deputy administrators sought a meeting with Administrator Akimoto Takatomo, Governor of Tajima, who agreed to allow me to leave. His words, as conveyed to me, were:

"Concerning the incident earlier today in which Asano Takuminokami injured Kira Kōzukenosuke with a sword and a decision was handed to each as a result, you made your protest twice, and that was correct. You made the protest out of respect to the Shogun, and that, we think, is commendable. However, in bringing your protest *twice* to the administrator you made a misjudgment.

"Nonetheless, the fact that you took your responsibilities seriously enough to make the protest is, as we said, commendable, so that you need not place yourself under house arrest. You may leave at once, and carry out your various assignments."

So I had a discussion with my colleagues, and we decided that Gonzaemon and I would go as assistant marshals for the disembowelment of Takuminokami.

I asked my colleagues, "What about the protocol and other matters involving Takuminokami's disembowelment? I was under a form of house arrest for some time, and I don't know in what kind of place it's going to be done."

I learned that Inspector-General Shōda Yasutoshi, Governor of Shimofusa, had been ordered to go as marshal. Accordingly, I met the Governor of Shimofusa and said:

"From some time back until a few minutes ago I was under a form of house arrest, and I wasn't informed of anything. Now I've learned that you will serve as marshal, and I've been asked to serve as an assistant marshal. I assume, sir, that you haven't made an oversight, but may I ask if you have already checked Tamura Ukyōnodayū's preparations and other matters?"

The governor replied, "I've been having those matters checked for some time, and you needn't worry."

So I said, "I see that you've settled everything."

Immediately preparations were made to go to Tamura Ukyō-nodayū's, and the attendants were reselected. By the time all of us left Edo Castle in one group, it was already nearly five o'clock on the evening of the fourteenth of the third month. Each of us two deputy inspectors-general had a foot soldier as attendant and was accompanied by four constables from the City Magistrate's office. I wore a *fukusa kosode*[7] and a hemp *kamishimo*. Inspector-General Shōda led the way, followed by me, Denpachirō, then by Gonzaemon. As we proceeded toward Ukyōnodayū's mansion, we saw his advance men already near the Sakurada Gate, who seemed to run ahead to announce our approach. Indeed, as we arrived, Ukyōnodayū's three house administrators and three officers welcomed us at the gate, and one from each group accompanied the inspector-general to guide him in. Similar treatment was accorded to us deputies, as we were taken to the main guest room. Tamura himself was at the main entrance to welcome us.

The governor said to Ukyōnodayū, "We brought the message that we were ordered to put Takuminokami in your custody and have him disembowel himself. Please make yourself ready, sir." He then proposed to see Takuminokami.

At this point Gonzaemon and I said, "Sir, we'd like to inspect the place for his disembowelment."

The governor said, "I took a look at a drawing of it a while ago, so that's done. Neither of you need to inspect it."

I insisted: "A while ago, sir, I was under a form of house arrest and while I stayed in my room you said you took care of everything. As a result I didn't even have a chance to look at the drawing you mention. Also, while we were still in the palace, I asked you how things were, and you told me that you had looked after everything. You further indicated that at a later time you would tell us how things were. We left the matter at that.

"Nevertheless, the position of assistant marshal is an important one, and you are not alone in this assignment. If we haven't even see the drawing, and if, after the sentence has been carried out, it were found that there was an oversight of any kind, it wouldn't be good for

---

7. The samurai's formal crested wear made of silk, which, like the *noshime*, was worn under a *kamishimo*, etc.

us. You may have seen a drawing, but we must inspect the place. Then we can see to it that Takuminokami carries out the sentence. I insist that we inspect the place."

The governor said, "As long as I've been appointed marshal, an assistant marshal doesn't have to give me orders. However, you are a deputy inspector-general, and I can't give you orders, so make the inspection as you please. Later, after all is finished, we will make our statements as we please, reporting the matter separately. If any of us commits an oversight, he will explain it himself. Do as you please."

So the two of us, Gonzaemon and Denpachirō, inspected the place, and found things that looked like large outdoor benches laid out in the yard of the inner guest room, with white-hemmed tatami laid over them, a curtain hung around them, and sliding screens with oiled paper set up against them. The arrangement was too stern in every respect.

We summoned Ukyōnodayū and demanded:

"We'd like to know whether this place was set up after providing the Governor of Shimofusa with a drawing and obtaining his approval or following his own order. Even if you set it up following the order of an inspector-general, Takuminokami is a lord president of a castle. Above all, the decision to punish him was made in accordance with the Way of the Samurai. In the circumstances, it is intolerable to have him disembowel himself in a yard. No matter how formal and respectful you may make it, a yard is a yard. Even if you treat the man himself in crude fashion, this has to be done in a room. We don't understand this. We must report this."

Ukyōnodayū became visibly angry at our words.

"I brought the matter up with the inspectors-general," he said, "and I had them look at a drawing and received their approval. Since that was done, I find it hard to understand what you are telling me now. I myself heard your argument with the Governor of Shimofusa awhile ago. In the circumstances, each of you should go ahead and make a separate statement."

"Indeed we will," I said. "Even though Takuminokami acted improperly, he is a gentleman of fifth rank. Furthermore, he is the lord president of a castle with holdings of more than 50,000 koku. If he, as such and as Chief of the Bureau of Carpentry, is ordered to disembowel himself, he must be treated as a lord president of a castle and a gentleman.

"On the other hand, if further investigation were made, and if, after some days, depending on the penalty, he were deprived of his court title and his court rank and became once again Matashichirō[8] and then were punished, the situation would be different. Indeed, that would be the way it should be. But punishment has been ordered while he remains in his capacity as Chief of the Bureau of Carpentry. This means, I understand, that daimyo treatment must be accorded to him.

"I thought it hard to predict what might be found out about the two men involved, and petitioned that Takuminokami's disembowelment be delayed for several days. But the petition was turned down and I was ordered to put myself under a form of house arrest."

Now Ukyōnodayū understood my reasoning very well and in some embarrassment expressed the view that the matter should have been handled in a better way. In the end, though, he said, "Now there's nothing we can do."

By the time these arguments took place, it was getting very late in the day.

We then turned to the governor and lodged a serious protest: "Sir, we have thoroughly inspected the place and found it highly at variance with what we had expected. Because of this possibility, a while ago we discussed the matter with you and expressed our hope that there would be no oversight in anything. We specifically asked how you had had the preparations made, and your reply was that there was no oversight. Accordingly, we left the matter to you. You seemed to indicate that you didn't want us to interfere, and we left things as they were. Now, look what has happened, sir. We certainly will have to make our statements separately later."

The governor became exceptionally angry at this.

"Do whatever you please," he said. "All this is a matter that should concern me, the marshal. Go ahead and report whatever each of you may think."

A serious dispute was about to ensue, when Ukyōnodayū appeared and announced:

"Sir, just now someone who calls himself Kataoka Gengoemon[9], Asano Takuminokami's retainer, has shown up and said,

---

8. Asano Naganori's name as a young man.
9. Kataoka Gengo'emon Takafusa (1666–1702). Before coming to Ukyōnodayū's mansion, he had written a report on the incident and dispatched it to Akō. He would also write the second report, following Asano's disembowelment.

'I've learned that my lord has been ordered to disembowel himself at your house. Because this will mean an eternal farewell between master and subject, may I ask you to allow me to have a glimpse of my lord?'

"I tried to turn him back a couple of times, but he asked me to convey his wishes to you at least once. He looked so upset in making this request that I thought he might do something untoward if I turned him down. So here I am, sir."

The governor wouldn't respond to this directly, merely saying, "I don't think this is important enough to be brought to the attention of the marshal." He wouldn't say that the request should be granted or that it should not.

So I said to Ukyōnodayū:

"There should be no problem about that. There is a way of doing it, however. When Takuminokami comes out to the place of disembowelment and the sentence is read out to him, make the retainer you mentioned shed his sword, bring him with several guards, and let him have a glimpse of his lord from some distance. You shouldn't make the guarding of the man appear too heavy-handed, for, even if he wanted to rescue his lord and jumped up, the many retainers of yours who are there would restrain him at once. Allowing a glimpse is an act of compassion in the circumstances, and I would approve of it."

Then I turned to the governor and asked, "What do you think, sir?" His reply was, "As you please." So what I said was accepted.

By the time these exchanges were over, it was close to six o'clock. Soon Ukyōnodayū told Takuminokami:

"Sir, it has been awhile since Inspector-General Shōda Yasutoshi, Governor of Shimofusa, and Deputy Inspectors-General Okado Denpachirō and Ōkubo Gonzaemon arrived as marshals and announced their mission. Now you may proceed to the place set up for the purpose. We have prepared appropriate clothing for you."

He then took, we were told, the prepared clothing out of a long trunk and laid it on its lid.

While this was going on, we three marshals sat in the main guest room. Because of the earlier arguments the inspector-general remained silent with us deputy inspectors-general except when there was some business to tend to. In a while Ukyōnodayū came and said:

"I conveyed the decision made earlier solely by you, Deputy Inspector-General Okado Denpachirō, sir, to Takuminokami's retainer Kataoka Gengo'emon. He said he was immensely grateful, and asked me to convey his sentiments to you. We made him shed his swords in a room next to the inner guest room, and have him guarded with many of my retainers."

I said, "Please keep him under strict surveillance, and be very careful."

At this the Governor of Shimofusa put on a sardonic smile. Obviously, the marshal was at odds with his assistants in every matter. The two of us, Denpachirō and Gonzaemon, had been arguing with the governor for some time. In particular, I had been making my own thoughts public since that morning to such an extent that I had even been ordered to place myself under a form of house arrest. As a result I expected to be relieved of my position the next day. Indeed, because I, his assistant, protested on every matter, the governor seemed bemused.

Ukyōnodayū added, "When Takuminokami prepares to disembowel himself I will bring out his retainer Kataoka Gengo'emon. I will allow Gengo'emon to view his lord until the latter reaches his place."

Before all of us proceeded to the place of disembowelment, the governor said to Takuminokami in the main guest room:

"Sir, today, in the palace, you became oblivious to where you were, and because of your personal grudge, you went so far as to injure Kira Kōzukenosuke with a sword. It was decided this was an intolerable act, and you have been ordered to disembowel yourself."

"Indeed, sir," Takuminokami responded. "I am grateful nonetheless that in accordance with the martial custom I have the honor of having been ordered to disembowel myself. In addition, sir, even though this is an assignment given to each of you, it is exceptionally considerate of you to have come as far as this place as marshals."

As he accepted the sentence, he looked no different from his normal self.

"I have a little inquiry to make, sir, if I may," he added. "I do not mean to delay the time of disembowelment, but how is Kōzukenosuke?"

The governor replied, "It was ordered that his wounds be tended to, and he left the palace."

"Well, deputy inspectors-general," Takuminokami said, "you must have dealt with him. As I recollect, when I struck at him I wounded him in two places. What do you say the effect of those blows was?"

The two of us, Denpachirō and Gonzaemon, responded in unison: "As you say, sir, you wounded him in two places. They were shallow wounds, it is true, but he is an old man; worse, you wounded him in places that tend to be fatal. He may try to recover from them the best he can, but your blows were so hard and painful we aren't sure that he will."

When he heard this, Takuminokami almost shed tears as he gave a broad smile.

He then said to Ukyōnodayū, "Now, lead me to the place, sir." He said these words in a most normal fashion, we thought.

When we reached the place of disembowelment, it was past six o'clock. Each of us took his seat.

As he seated himself, Takuminokami said, "I have a request to make of the marshals. I take it that you have kept my long sword in your custody. I'd like my second to use that sword and, afterward, keep it as my gift."

The governor, who heard the request, asked, "Assistant marshals and deputy inspectors-general, what do you think of this?"

"We should do as requested," we said. Takuminokami's long sword was indeed in our custody, and we at once arranged to have it brought to us. Takuminokami then requested an inkstone box and paper. We gave them to him. While his sword was being brought, Takuminokami pulled the inkstone box toward him, slowly rubbed the ink stick against the stone, took up the brush, and wrote:

Kaze sasou hana yori mo nao ware wa mata
haru no nagori o ikani toka sen

The wind seems to lure away the cherry blossoms as well,
    but I—how shall I deal with what remains of spring?[10]

While we were having his sword handed to his second, Assistant Inspector Isoda Takedayū, Takuminokami waited. Assistant Inspector Mizuno Mokuzaemon received the poem above and brought it to Ukyōnodayū, and while the latter was formally accepting it, Isoda, the second, came out and reported that in accordance with the ancient custom he had done his seconding duty and witnessed the completion of Takuminokami's disembowelment.

---

10. This poem recalls the one by Fujiwara no Kintsune (1171–1244) that is included in the *Hyakunin Isshu* (One Hundred Poems by One Hundred Poets): *Hana sasou arashi no niwa no yuki narade furiyuku mono wa waga mi narikeri* (Cherry blossoms lured by a storm, all this snow—but, no, what is falling is nothing but myself).

It was understood that Ukyōnodayū would handle Takuminokami's corpse and other matters, so leaving the rest to him, everyone left.

Okado Denpachirō's fears came true: the main branch of the Asano family, with holdings of 370,000 koku, remonstrated with the government over its handling of Takuminokami, and Inspector-General Shōda Yasutoshi, Governor of Shimofusa, was demoted, according to the government records, in the eighth month of the same year. (Denpachirō reports the demotion was ordered only five days after the incident.)

Denpachirō was also demoted, but in the next year, and the reasons are not clear. He himself thought that the action was taken not only because he was importunate in his protestations, but also because when Shōda and some others were demoted he had wondered aloud why *he* was not being subjected to a similar treatment, and this probably offended some in higher positions.

Kajikawa Yosobē (1647–1723), who seized and held down Takuminokami after the latter's attempt to kill Kōzukenosuke, was praised by the government and his holdings were increased by 500 koku. But popular sentiment was against him on the grounds that he'd prevented Takuminokami from carrying out his wishes.[11]

Around two on the afternoon of the day that Takuminokami attempted to kill Kōzukenosuke, Hayami Tōzaemon and Kayano Sampei, from among Takuminokami's retainers stationed in Edo, were dispatched to take the news to Akō; around nine in the evening, two others, Hara Sōzaemon and Ōishi Sezaemon, followed, to tell of Takuminokami's death by disembowelment. By taking one express palanquin after another, without rest, these men covered the distance of 620 kilometers (380 miles) in four and a half days.

The news threw the Asano clan into turmoil and heated debate. The condemnation of a lord president to death by disembowelment meant the government's confiscation of his holdings and disenfranchisement of his retainers. The immediate question, which had to be resolved before the government's emissaries came, was how to respond to this measure honorably. House Administrators Ōishi Kuranosuke and Ōno Kurobē, along with about 300 retainers of the Asano family, deliberated on the question day and night.

---

11. Perhaps because of this Yosobē wrote his own account of the incident to explain his action in *Kajikawa-shi Hikki* (Mr. Kajikawa's Writing).

Three main arguments emerged. Some people spoke for a peaceful surrender of the castle, the symbol of daimyo rule, and an equally peaceful dispersal of retainers. Some advocated putting up a fight against the government forces and, as they were sure to lose, for all to kill themselves as the castle was taken. A third group argued for surrendering the castle and then disemboweling themselves to follow their lord in death. Some, especially among those stationed in Edo, even insisted on attacking Kira Kōzukenosuke at once and killing him.

Disenfranchisement in most instances gave a samurai few prospects: He could either hope for a slim, uncertain chance of reemployment with another clan, seek to establish himself in one of the few jobs thought worthy of samurai, such as teaching, or expect at some point to abandon his samurai status to make a living as a commoner. On the other hand, the question of how to acquit oneself honorably in the face of disgrace for himself or his lord gave a samurai only one choice: to eradicate the disgrace, which often entailed death or, at the least, hardships of all kinds. (He could also decide to live with the disgrace, of course, but that was no honor at all.) The prospect of taking such an action was evidently unpalatable to many Asano men: dispersal began even before the final decision was made, and, a few days before the shogunate emissaries arrived to "receive" the castle, Ōno Korobē, who held the rank of *jōdai garō*, "acting lord president," disappeared with a good deal of the money he had been entrusted with and other valuables.

In the end the course of action that emerged out of the third group's argument was supported by Ōishi Kuranosuke and won the allegiance of sixty-one retainers, including Kuranosuke himself and his twelve-year-old first son, Chikara: to surrender the castle peacefully—ostensibly to seek to reestablish the Asano family, but with the understanding that they would kill Kira Kōzukenosuke. Even though some attempts were in fact made to reestablish the Asano family, killing Kōzukenosuke was, it appears, the focus from the outset. As Kuranosuke put it in one of his letters to a monk friend, "It would do no good to have [Takuminokami's brother] Daigaku pardoned [from his house-arrest status]. . . . As long as Kōzukenosuke is allowed to serve the Shogun, if he were put to work side by side with Daigaku, Daigaku would have nothing to show, no matter how admirably he might behave."

So began a chain of secret plotting, feints, hardship, anguish, and sacrifice. And one year and eight months later, the killing was accomplished.

ARGUMENTS

Hayashi Nobuatsu (1644–1732), in On Revenge.

> Nobuatsu, also known as Hōkō, was an outstanding Confucian scholar who served as the first *daigaku no kami,* the superintendent of all scholarly activities under the Tokugawa Shogunate.
>
> (The poem appended at the end and the commentary preceding it is the original editor's addition.)

For their deceased lord Ōishi [Kuranosuke] and forty-five other samurai-retainers of a daimyo in the Western region banded together to achieve a single aim and, on the fourteenth of the twelfth month of the fifteenth year of Genroku, carried out their revenge and were taken prisoner. The shogun ordered some officials to investigate the matter in detail and consider it closely; he then determined the nature of the crime, issued an order, and had the members of the band kill themselves.

Someone said: "The Three Relationships and the Five Bonds[12] are the basis of courtesy and the principle of enlightenment, and their application does not change depending on the age, ancient or modern, or upon the place, distant or close. Further, our ancestral kings established laws and clarified regulations, spread them throughout the world, and transmitted them to us their heirs.

"In particular, the relationships between master and subject and between father and son are the essence of the Three Relationships, the basis of the Five Bonds, and the ultimate of Heaven's Way and human ethics, and there is no place between heaven and earth where one can escape from them.[13] Because of this those who compiled the *Rites* said, 'One doesn't live under the same heaven with the enemy of one's master or father.[14] That is, the urge emanates from a firm, irrepressible feeling; there's nothing personal or private about it.

---

12. The Three Relationships are those between master and subject, father and son, and husband and wife. For the Five Bonds, see the "five ethical principles," Introduction, note 6, p. xxiii.

13. "In the World of Men," Chuang Tzu quotes Confucius as saying: "That a son should love his parents is fate—you cannot erase this from his heart. That a subject should serve his ruler is duty—there is no place he can go and be without his ruler, no place he can escape to between heaven and earth." (*The Complete Works of Chuang Tzu,* translated by Burton Watson, pp. 59–60).

14. *The Book of Rites.* The original refers only to one's father. Denial of coexistence is one way of saying you mustn't rest until you kill the one who killed your father.

"In the circumstances, if you are not to allow revenge, you will in effect go against the law of our ancestral kings and wound the hearts of loyal subjects and filial sons. When it comes to killing avengers, it is worse than trampling upon the law and annulling the meaning of punishment. With such an action, how can you propose to improve human ethics?"

I replied: "The righteousness of revenge can be clearly seen in *The Book of Rites* and *Rites of Chou*, as well as in *Spring and Autumn Annals*; also, various Confucian scholars of T'ang and Sung debated it. An especially detailed discussion is given by Mr. Ch'iu in his supplement to the *Lectures on Great Learning*. Allow me to debate the matter from my own understanding of what is meant in various books and commentaries.

"If you debate it from the standpoint of the forty-six men, carrying out revenge with a resolve not to allow the enemy to live under the same heaven was something that they had to do by 'sleeping on a coarse straw mattress with a sword for a pillow.' To value one's life and live with a disgrace is not a warrior's way.

"If you debate it on the basis of law, anyone who breaks the law must be put to death. Even if the forty-six men were carrying out the will of their deceased lord, they could not have escaped the fact that they were breaking the law of the land. Their act was willful and defied the authorities. To arrest and put them to death for the general populace and their descendants to see was, therefore, a way of clarifying the nation's legal foundations.

"True, the two standpoints are not in the same category, but they can exist as parallel without contradicting each other. Above are a humane ruler and wise counselors, and they clarify the law and issue orders; below are loyal subjects and righteous men, and they express their indignation and carry out their resolve. If because of the law the forty-six men had to submit themselves to death, as they did, why on earth should they have any regrets?

"Ancient men said, 'When a peaceful rule lasts long, the people's minds become lax.' It is of course fortunate that we should now have a world comparable to that of Yao and Shun, and that the people should be prospering and enjoying themselves as never before. As a result, however, warriors throughout the land had begun to indulge in munificence and grow negligent, to gather in large numbers and idly chatter their time away, and to learn to be content to be gentle and mild.

"At such a time that incident occurred. It woke the men and excited them, made them realize that they must ever be ready to carry out a righteous action, that the ruler can have confidence in his subjects, and that subjects can be loyal to their ruler.

"Ah, the death of Wang Chu helped recover Ch'i,[15] Yen Chen-ch'ing helped revive the T'ang Dynasty in ite mid-period.[16] Those who speak loudly of these men now know what they're talking about because of this incident. Those forty-six men were also outstanding men of the kind that appear once in a lifetime to enlighten the world. They should be discussed in the same breath with Yü Jang[17] and T'ien Heng."[18]

Mr. Hayashi also wrote a poem [with the heading: "Last year, on the fifteenth of the twelfth month, Ōishi Kuranosuke and forty-five former subjects of Asano Takuminokami, with single-mindedness, avenged their lord and revived righteousness. This year, on the forth of the second month, the government made a decision and by its order put them to death."]

In breaking into the gate they bested Ching K'o.[19]
The wind is cold over the I-shui, a brave man's heart.

---

15. During a Yen attack on the State of Ch'i, the Yen general Yueh Yi surrounded at a distance the city where Wang Chu lived, and sent for him with the promise of making him a general, along with the threat that, if he declined, his city would be razed. Wang Chu, though a commoner, had a great reputation for wisdom. He declined, saying, "A loyal subject never serves two rulers, a chaste wife never changes her husband. . . . I'd rather be boiled to death than lose my righteousness." He then hanged himself. Hearing this, many of the nobility who had fled Ch'i returned and revived the state. See "The Biography of T'ien Tan," Chap. 82, of the Shih Chi of Ssu-ma Ch'ien.

16. Yen Chen-ch'ing (709–786), a ranking courtier, became the first to raise an army against An Lu-shan when the latter took advantage of his favored position with Emperor Hsüan Tsung and established himself as emperor. Later, when another man revolted, Yen went to see him as imperial emissary, but he was arrested and, after three years' imprisonment, murdered. In addition to his loyal acts, Yen is famous for his masterly calligraphy.

17. Yü Jang, in trying to avenge a lord who treated him well, changed his voice and appearance by swallowing charcoal and painting lacquer on his body, in order to approach his enemy. Failing in his second attempt, he stabbed himself to death. See "The Biographies of Assassins," Chap. 86, Ssu-ma Ch'ien's Shih Chi.

18. T'ien Heng committed sucide, rather than respond to a summons from Emperor Kao, once his rival. Following a magnificent funeral Kao gave T'ien Heng, the two men accompanying him also committed sucide, even though the emperor had honored them with the rank of colonel. When informed of T'ien Heng's death, his 500 followers living in remote islands all killed themselves. See "The Biography of T'ien Tan," Burton Watson's translation from the Shih Chi, vol. I, pp. 245–251. In Hayashi's poem cited, "a shallot song" is a threnody for nobility.

19. Ching K'o a scholarly swordsman, was entrusted with the task of assassinating the man who later became the first emperor of Chin. His attempt failed and he was killed. The next line alludes to the song he sang before crossing the River I-shui: "The wind blows forlornly, the I-Shui water is cold; / a brave man, once he departs, never returns."

Charcoal-mute, disfigured, they emulated Yu Jang.
Singing a shallot song in tears they carried T'ien Heng.
Sincerity piercing the sun, why regret death?
Righteous minds destroyed the mountains, their lives insignificant.
The forty-six men yielded themselves equally to the sword.
Heaven's god cares little though they helped strengthen the loyal
sense.

Satō Naokata (1650–1719), in *On the Forty-Six Men.*

A Confucian scholar, Naokata distinguished himself as a student of the
Confucian scholar (and, later, Shintoist) Yamazaki Ansai (1618-82). But
he broke with his mentor as he became a proponent of a purist Chu Hsi
school.

Around two on the night of the fourteenth day of the twelfth
month, of the fifteenth year of Genroku, Asano Takuminokami's
retainers, Ōishi Kuranosuke and forty-five others, wearing helmets
and armor and carrying bows, arrows, and spears, assaulted Kira
Kōzukenosuke's house, killed or injured many of his retainers,
wounded his son Sahyōe, and beheaded Kōzukenosuke. On the
morning of the fifteenth, they retreated to Sengaku Temple in Shiba,
placed Kōzukenosuke's head in front of their lord, and stayed there.

Even as they were retreating from Kōzukenosuke's residence,
they dispatched Yoshida Chūzaemon and Tomimori Suke'emon to the
house of Inspector-General Sengoku Hisanao, Governor of Hōki, to
inform him of what they had done, provide him with a letter, and
announce that they would await an order from the shogun. The
shogun duly issued an order and placed the forty-six men in the
custody of Hosokawa Tsunatoshi, Governor of Etchū, Hisamatsu
(Matsudaira) Sadanao, Governor of Oki, Mizuno Kenmotsu, and
Mōri Tsunamoto, Governor of Kai. On the fourth day of the second
month, of the following year, an order was issued and the executions
of the men were carried out. The order said:

With respect to Asano Takuminokami, he was given the assignment of entertaining the imperial messengers. Nevertheless, he became
oblivious that he was in the palace and committed an intolerable act. As
a result, he was punished by death, while no measure was taken against
Kira Kōzukenosuke. On account of this, forty-six of Takuminokami's
retainers, vowing to avenge their master, banded together, broke

into Kōzukenosuke's house, carrying shooting equipment, and killed Kōzukenosuke. We deem that this act shows no respect for the authorities and that it is grave and intolerable. Accordingly, we order them to disembowel themselves.

The logic of this order is clear. That the shogun did not subject the men to a punishment reserved for felons but allowed them to disembowel themselves was an expression of shogunate compassion, and they should have considered themselves fortunate.

Nevertheless, worldly people, in their lightheaded clamor, assert that those forty-six men were loyal subjects and righteous men. Ignorant people are incapable of logical thinking, so we understand why they make such erroneous assertions. But even Mr. Hayashi, mourning their deaths, has composed a poem for them; comparing them with Yu Jang and T'ien Heng, he declared them to be righteous subjects. Furthermore, he has expressed his regrets over their deaths by writing, "They avenged their lord and revived righteousness." All scholars accordingly join in a lightheaded clamor, and many among them regret the deaths of those men.

Some even say that the government's decision was right and that the determination of the forty-six men was righteous. But if the government's decision was right, how could those men also be righteous? Such an argument is ludicrous because it errs in failing to clarify the logic. If someone who reads the books by sages and wise men utters a single word of logical thinking, worldly people regard him as their teacher. It is sad if he makes and spreads erroneous statements which confuse the minds of ordinary people. That the forty-six men should have regarded Kōzukenosuke as their master's enemy— quoting, as they did, "One doesn't live under the same heaven with the enemy of one's master or father"[20] — was a great mistake. Kōzukenosuke was not their enemy. He would have been if he had hurt Takuminokami.

Takuminokami struck at Kōzukenosuke out of personal resentment and anger, thereby going against the Great Law. Because of this the shogun condemned him to death. How can anyone think of

---

20. The written explanation prepared before the break-in contains this phrase. It is known that Horibe Yasubē (1670–1703), a member of the band and a noted swordsman, in drafting the explanation, asked Hosoi Hirosawa (1658–1735), a student of Confucianism and military strategy, if it was all right to change the original phrase and add "master." See note 14 of this section.

"avenging" such a man? When we consider his feelings, of course, his resentment and anger may be entirely understandable, but if he wanted to harm Kōzukenosuke, he should have done that after his assignment was over and choosing a more appropriate place. But he chose to violate the Great Law in the midst of the Great Imperial Rite of receiving the imperial messengers.

Worse, the way Takuminokami struck at Kōzukenosuke, it was such a hasty, immature, cowardly deed. He drew his short sword behind Kōzukenosuke who was discussing something with Kajikawa Yosobē, and slashed at him as he tried to run away. But the wounds were too shallow to bring death to the man, and he himself was captured by Kajikawa. With no courage and no skill, Takuminokami is merely a fellow to be laughed at. It's quite fitting that he should have been condemned to death, and his castle and other properties confiscated.

On his part, Kōzukenosuke wouldn't draw his short sword but simply fell in consternation, his face pale, prompting samurai throughout the land to laugh at him. His reaction was worse than death, an utter disgrace. Why should the shogun have punished him? Evidently he wasn't an enemy worthy of vengeance.

Nonetheless, those forty-six men, rather than sorrowing over the great crime of their master, decided to go against the shogunate will: They equipped themselves with weapons and used passwords and identification marks as in a battlefield to make the killing. That, too, was a great crime. Still, if, after they carried out their killing single-mindedly, preoccupied as they were with the thought of their deceased lord's fury—if, after that, they had reflected on the crime of having gone against the shogunate will and committed suicide at Sengaku Temple—while they wouldn't have acted in accordance with law, they would at least have deserved our pity.

Instead, they reported their act to Inspector-General Sengoku, saying that they would await a shogunate order. Also, in the letter they provided they said they respected shogunate authority, and to Sengoku himself the first thing they said was that they respected shogunate authority. What could these things have meant other than a scheme to win praise, escape death, and gain employment? Having violated the Great Law and gone against shogunate authority, they had nothing to report on, nothing for which to await an order. What they did was *not* what those prepared to die would do. These men rose out of the anger that they had been made masterless wanderers; they employed calculation and conspiracy to carry out their aim. They did what they did not mainly out of loyalty, not because of acute pain.

Someone who calls himself a samurai must think out things in detail and state his case clearly, so that he may relieve worldly people of their confusions. When you contemplate this question further, there certainly is good reason why people throughout the land agree, albeit in unthinking fashion, that those forty-six men were righteous subjects. Kōzukenosuke was born to be greedy, and he was detested by everyone for his arrogance, conceit, and evil mind. As a result, people didn't think of Takuminokami's crime but pitied his death instead, while hating Kōzukenosuke for continuing to live. So, when told that he was killed, all erupted with rejoicing and called the forty-six men righteous subjects.

Ah, because of the evil ways of Kōzukenosuke, so many people were killed, Edo was disturbed, and people became confused. Kōzukenosuke is the one to be hated.

An anonymous samurai, in *On the Forty-Six Men*
  Not Being Righteous Subjects.

Though I don't understand logic and other profundities that come from learning, if you look at it from the standpoint of the normal resolve of a samurai today, there isn't much you can't understand about it. About what happened to Asano and because of his action, people argue: "It was a quarrel," "No, it wasn't," "It was a vendetta," "No, it wasn't." But aside from such arguments . . . for a samurai to avenge his lord is quite natural. A samurai who can't is a coward. . . .

Some townsfolk, because of the way they feel, may think that those men did something that was hard to do, and so run around saying, "They're loyal subjects, they're righteous men." But if a samurai says, "Well, they surely did something that was hard to do," and goes on to praise them, that, to me, is incomprehensible. If a samurai goes further and composes poems and things in praise of them, thinking, They're godsends, I'd like to be a loyal and righteous samurai like them myself, that's being truly dumb. Anyone who doesn't have the resolve to avenge his master or father is no samurai at all, is what I think. Those samurai who praise these men to the skies, thinking they did something rare, do so because they have no resolve to speak of.

Scholars who argue this or that are also incomprehensible to me. If those men had killed their enemy when [as some scholars argue] he actually wasn't their enemy, they either were utterly brainless or did it for profit. If, on the other hand, they killed him because he surely was the enemy of their lord, there was nothing difficult or hard to do in what they did. Yet they say they were godsends for samurai, contrive to acquire swords and spears of the forty-six men, and visit their graves to pay their respects. What in the world they're thinking just beats me.

I would kill someone who's the enemy of my master or father anytime. I wouldn't even bother to be cautious and wear a body-protector or carry shooting equipment. . . .[21]

I can't speak for townsfolk. But why is it that unmistakable samurai are dithering so? If they really thought that avenging one's master or father was such a big deal, what's the point of working for their masters as they do? All this strikes me as funny.

Myself, I know no books or anything, I'm just a regular samurai. Scholars have investigated the matter deeply, I guess, and I'd like to hear what they have to say.

Asami Yasusada (1652–1711), in *On the Forty-Six Men.*

> Also known as Keisai, Yasusada, like Naokata, distinguished himself under the tutelage of Yamazaki Ansai. However, after criticizing his teacher, he severed his relationship with him.

The story of the vendetta by the men of Akō, Harima, is of course known throughout the land. But it appears that doubts are expressed from time to time: Even though there is no room for debate about what the forty-six men did for their master, some have said that in killing someone whom the government allowed to live in a state of grace, they proved themselves disloyal to the government. This argument has produced a variety of strained theories. From a number of places people have written to me to ask if this or that interpretation is right or wrong or better or worse. . . .

Kōzukenosuke, as chief officer for Great Imperial Rites and for the shogunate, appears not to have cared, because of his personal greed and willfulness, whether or not Takuminokami committed clumsy

---

21. The men who assaulted Kira's mansion are known to have worn *kusari-katabira*, jackets made of small iron rings strung together, and carried "shooting equipment," such as bows and arrows. Behind this statement is the notion that the moment he learns of the vengeance to carry out, a samurai must sally forth at once, without wasting his time on self-preserving precautions. See pp. 298–299.

errors, and made him disgrace himself in front of people in the Palace of Splendor. This infuriated Takuminokami and made him do what he did. Fundamentally, Kōzukenosuke's crime of taking advantage of shogunate authority and acting as he pleased was of the kind that should not have been allowed to stand without punishment by death. Even if Takuminokami had not struck at him first, he should not have escaped that crime. If the penalty did not go as far as death, he should have resigned his post; or he should have been stripped of his holdings.

On Takuminokami's part, that he was unable to bear personal anger and, becoming oblivious of the place of governance and the Great Imperial Rite, behaved impulsively, was his extraordinary fault. Nevertheless, he had not a speck, not a trace of ill will, against the government authority. Also, the government apart, it was not as if he had a tendency to forget himself. His fury had been building up for days, and when he was made to suffer another disgrace that day, he had no time to think of the past and future, but slashed at Kōzuke-nosuke. But the man ran, while at the same time Takuminokami himself was held back by someone else. Things happened so suddenly that he could not carry out his aim to the end.

Had Takuminokami been able to slash up the man to his heart's content, he would have killed himself on the spot. Or, if he had somehow been prevented from killing himself, he would of course have understood that he would receive a shogunate punishment of death.

From the viewpoint of the Great Law, the law to be applied was the one that holds that the two parties involved in a personal quarrel are equally punishable. If you say that Takuminokami had to be punished for having disturbed the place for a Great Imperial Rite, it must be pointed out that he did not do so for no reason, but that all that happened was because of Kōzukenosuke's personal willfulness. It follows that if Takuminokami was to be punished, as he was, then Kōzukenosuke should also have been punished. Yet, even though Takuminokami was put to death because of his crime of disturbing the place for a Great Imperial Rite, the other party, Kōzukenosuke, was let go without any kind of penalty. It follows – and let there be no room for further argument about this – that Takuminokami must be said to have been killed by Kōzukenosuke. In the circumstances, if those who considered themselves Takuminokami's subjects had not acted to kill Kōzukenosuke to carry out what their master had wanted to do with his sword, the Great Cause would never have been served.

It is evident, however, that all Ōishi did was to kill his master's enemy as the master had wanted to, and that he had not a speck, not a trace, of an intention to interfere with the shogunate. . . . Ōishi and his men did not kill themselves [after their aim was achieved], but left the disposition of their lives to the shogun. That shows they perfectly understood their master's loyalty to the shogun, the way he had always held him in highest respect. As these men's intentions gradually became clear, the government punished Kōzukenosuke's heir for disloyalty and treated the forty-six men with lenience; it did not condemn their relatives to death and even allowed the men to choose a place for their graves. . . .

Someone said: "Those men killed Kōzukenosuke because Takuminokami failed to kill him. But Kōzukenosuke never tried to kill Takuminokami. In the circumstances it was wrong for those men to call Kōzukenosuke their master's enemy."

. . . If your master failed to kill someone and he was killed as a result, who would you call your enemy if not that someone? Instances of reasoning of this nature are too numerous to list.

Someone said: "Takuminokami was poor at swordsmanship. His failure to carry out the killing is embarrassing. He would have been of no use to the shogun."[22]

This is also ridiculous. Even if he had been good at swordsmanship and killed the man instantly, what good would that have been? Aside from this, he was upset by the suddenness of it all; at the same time Kōzukenosuke ran away, and there was even someone who held him down. In similar circumstances there have been many instances in which the killing failed. If you say Takuminokami should have been punished as a useless fellow, how useful was the cowardly Kōzukenosuke who ran away? This type of argument is made not to fault the shogunate administrators' decision, but to pretend that it was all good. . . .[23]

There is also someone's theory, which is a particularly despicable argument. He says that the forty-six men couldn't gain employment anywhere, so they contrived this vendetta as part of their plan to seek stipends. If there ever has been an ugly thing said about this, this is it.

---

22. In a later period, General Nogi Maresuke (1849–1912) is known to have pointedly asked: "Why didn't he [Takuminokami] stab the man?" It is said that if the intent is to kill with a sword, the surest way is not to slash, as Takuminokami obviously did, but to stab. By asking the question, Nogi implied that Takuminokami didn't know how to handle a sword.

23. Sentences in this paragraph are somewhat shuffled in the translation.

From the very beginning to the end, these men, without exception, had given up their lives and even written their wills. Yet here's a man who says an ugly thing that a dealer in scrap iron might say. He must want to erase these men with his words.

Think of it: These forty-six men were going to break into a great mansion of a man of some stature with many of his retainers staying with him, along with prominent members of his family. How could any one of them hope to return alive?[24] How is it possible to say that they wanted to win stipends? It is an utterly unenlightened argument. . . .

Someone said: "The forty-six men formed a large group, equipped themselves with weapons, and used passwords and identification marks, as if fighting in a battlefield. That was a great crime. What do you say to that?"

I say: "If you put it that way, it may sound as if these men were acting to defy the shogunate authority. But even if you make it sound as if they formed an army, a small group of men were stealing into a mansion of a man of stature with the determination not to fail to kill the enemy of their lord, so they could not help making those preparations. They had no intention of defying government authority or disturbing it.

"Even when you try to kill your parent's enemy, you may end up creating a commotion, depending on your opponent or on the place, but that is not part of your intention. If this is the case, if you think only about government authority and fail to kill the enemy, you'll have to say that thoughts of your master or father are secondary to you.

"Further, the way these men had made their plans, they gave no trouble to the neighboring mansions and, once inside the targeted mansion, tried not to kill anyone who gave them no trouble. Also, as they left the house, they took care lest a fire break out by accident. If you accuse such men of defiance of the government simply because of their military outfit, you are deliberately ignoring what they truly wanted to do.

"On the whole, when it comes to a great accomplishment like this, you should see the true intent and forgive the few errors that may have been made, so that a loyal, righteous act may not be marred. Because it was during the night, without passwords confusion might have ensued. In case the enemy tried to escape over the fence, shoot-

---

24. Ōishi and his men killed sixteen men and wounded twenty-two.

ing equipment was needed. If you are wounded, you won't be able to kill the enemy, so they were right in wearing body-protectors.

"Suppose Ōishi and his son alone had stolen inside in ordinary garb and struck and killed Kōzukenosuke, would the shogun have said 'You have done nothing wrong,' and let them be?"

This may be a good place to look at the government's treatment of some of the relatives of those involved in the vendetta.

The forty-six men had a total of nineteen sons; four of these, who were fifteen years old or older, were exiled, but pardoned three years later. The others were also to be exiled as they reached fifteen years of age. But they all took Buddhist vows because this exempted them from exile. These treatments were considered very mild in an age when punishment by association was standard and the example of Fang Hsiao-ju (1357–1402) was often cited with approval. Fang, a scholar of the early Ming Dynasty, refused to falsify a statement for a usurping king. As a result, not only he himself but all his relatives, from closest to remotest, numbering several hundred, were hunted out and killed.

Kōzukenosuke's adopted son (actually grandson), Yoshichika, was seriously wounded during the fight, but he was stripped of his holdings on the ground that he did not fight to the death to protect his father. He then was placed in the custody of a local daimyo as a semi-criminal and died of his wounds four years later. Less unfortunate, Yoshichika's actual father, Tsunanori, who had been adopted out to inherit the Uesugi family, merely "retired" during the same year, though he was still in his early forties.

All of the forty-six men expressed the wish to be buried at Sengaku Temple, which had Takuminokami's grave. Their wish was honored by the government.

Dazai Shundai (1680–1747), in *On the Forty-Six Men of Akō*.

Shundai began studying with the Confucian scholar Ogyū Sorai (1666–1728) in 1711, almost a decade after the incident. Sorai had a great influence on Shogun Tsunayoshi through his friend, Administrator

Yanagizawa Yoshiyasu. It was he who recommended death by disembowelment for the forty-six men, which was adopted as the government's verdict. Shundai, in writing the following commentary some
years after Sorai's death, makes the point of noting, in a passage not
translated, that his view accorded with that of his teacher.

Interestingly, Shundai confesses that at first and for many years
later he was a great admirer of what the forty-six men did, but had a
change of heart when he developed the reasons given in the first
paragraphs translated below.

Shundai said: ". . . In life, you can't tell in the morning what
might happen in the evening.[25] Who could have known that Kira
would *not* die and therefore waited until the winter of the next year? If
Kira had died before the winter of the next year, how could the Akō
warriors have accomplished what they did? In the event, would they
have shaved their heads and become monks, escaped to islands in the
sea,[26] or dug up his grave and whipped his corpse in the manner of
Wu Tzu-hsu?[27]

". . . I hear that the law laid down by the Founder[28] says that
anyone who kills a person in Edo Castle is to be punished with death.
The lord of Akō merely wounded Kira. His crime did not deserve
death. But the government gave him death, an excessive punishment.
The subjects of the lord of Akō should have resented this fact, if
anything. But Ōishi and his men did not resent what they should
have, but resented Kira. What they resented was insignificant.

"In general, those who serve a local lord should obey him,
holding the national ruler in awe, as long as the national ruler
is courteous to their own lord. But if, unfortunately, the national
ruler is not courteous to their lord, they must resent the national ruler.
This is because for the subjects of a local lord he is the only one
who counts. . . .

"Also, for the warrior of Japan there is a way. The moment he
sees his lord's [wrongful] death, he is expected to become profoundly

---

25. "You can't tell," etc., is a remark quoted in "Duke Chao First Year [541 B.C.]" in
the *Tso Chuan*.

26. The followers of T'ien Heng. See note 18.

27. Wu Tzu-hsu, unable to find the whereabouts of King Chao, who was responsible for the killing of his father and brother, dug up the grave of King P'ing, who was
equally responsible, and "did not stop until he had whipped the corpse three hundred
times." See "The Biography of Wu Tzu-hsu," in Ssu-ma Ch'ien's *Shih Chi*.

28. I.e., of the Tokugawa government: Ieyasu (1542–1616).

disturbed and in that deranged state dash out straight to the enemy's place. [If he is killed as a result] the death itself is regarded as righteous. Whether the act is right or wrong is never asked. From the viewpoint of a man of humane wisdom such a death is bound to be wasteful, but this way has existed from the beginning of this nation. . . .

"Ōishi and his men did not resent what they should have, but resented Kira and, in their action, were content to hold the national ruler in awe. Not only did they *not* know the correct ruler-subject relationship, but they also lost sight of what the warriors of this nation hold as their way. All this is a great pity."

The guest asked: "In that case, what should the warriors of Akō have done?"

Shundai said: "Nothing could have been better for them than to die at Akō Castle. . . . They should have come out of the castle and engaged in battle with the government emissaries. Then, retreating into the castle, they should have set fire to it, and everyone should have killed himself. When their corpses had burned up with the castle, it could have been said that the Akō men had done all they could. . . .

"If for some reason it was not possible for them to die at Akō Castle, they should have gone to Edo at once and, with all the troops available, attacked Kira. If they won the engagement, they thereupon should have killed themselves; if they lost, the same. The unifying element should have been death. Through it they would have discharged their responsibility.

"Yet Ōishi and his men were unable to do either. Instead, they waited leisurely and, employing idle conspiracies and secrecy, tried to kill Kira. What they had in mind was to achieve their aim, establish their reputation, and thereby seek fame and fortune. How unurbane of them! In the circumstances, it was lucky for the Akō warriors that Kira hadn't died before their attack.

"Then, too, when Ōishi and his men killed Kira and offered his head to the grave of their lord, they had achieved their aim, they had discharged their responsibility. If an ordinary man kills a shogunate aide, he is accorded death for that crime. In the event, there at that temple, those forty-six men should have killed themselves. Why then did they await a government order?

"They were unable to kill themselves but surrendered themselves to the government because they must have thought: We have accomplished a difficult task. If, fortunately, we are not forced to die, we will not die; obtaining employment and rank should then be as easy as bending down and picking up dust from the ground. If, unfortunately, we are to die, we will die by law. It shouldn't be too late to die then. Why then should we kill ourselves now? If this kind of thinking doesn't make them men seeking fame and fortune, what does? How unurbane of them! . . ."

Yokoi Yayū (1702–83), in *A Hick's Talk.*

> A samurai and haiku poet, Yayū is especially known for a collection of *haibun*, called *Uzura-goromo* (Quail's Robe).[29]
>
> Born in the same year that the vendetta took place, Yayū is thought to have written this commentary when he was sixty or older. In the prologue, he tells us that Kusaku, his "urine collector," happened to go to Edo and pick up a pamphlet on the forty-six men by a scholar called Dazai Shundai. He was "flabbergasted" reading it, so brought it back for Yayū to take a look. The title of Yayū's piece shows his obvious pique at Shundai's condemnation of the presumed thinking and action of Ōishi and his men as "unurbane."

"In life, you can't tell in the morning what might happen in the evening. Who would have known that Kira would *not* die, and therefore waited until the winter of the next year? If Kira had died before the winter of the next year, how could the Akō warriors have accomplished what they did?" etc.

Then he [Dazai] went on to say, "If their enemy had died before the winter, would the forty-six warriors have shaved their heads and become monks or whipped his corpse? If they'd done anything like that, I'd say they'd have made themselves laughingstocks throughout the land."

What kind of thinking is this?

Sure, it's always true that you can't count on anybody living forever, but this "always" is part of the changeability of it all. So, once you start worrying about everything in advance, you can't lend anybody any money, you can't make a marriage promise. Of course, if it had been a vendetta that took five to seven years, you might accuse them of procrastination, but they merely waited until the winter of the

---

29. *Haibun* is a prose piece, typically brief and interspersed with haiku. Most often written by a haiku poet, it can be elaborately allusive.

next year, and that they did, seeking the right timing and working out the plot so they wouldn't fail in the killing.

In Mr. Dazai's way of thinking, he seems to think that they should have attacked regardless of everything and, win or lose, died on the spot, as he said further on. In the end he failed to grasp the true intent of the forty-six men.

After all, Lord Asano, unable to bear his resentment and anger, decided to kill Lord Kira and die himself, in the sure knowledge that that would bring down his own house, and caring for nothing else, struck, but failed to kill. As a result, he alone had to die and have his house destroyed, while his enemy went on living. The thought that mortification must be eating the marrow of his bones, that the anguish must be making him turn in his grave, was what his loyal subjects could not bear, and that's why they carried out the vendetta.

In the circumstances, if, following Mr. Dazai's way of thinking, they put forward only their momentary righteousness and behaved like a dog snapping at you, and if, as a result, they alone were again the ones to die, Lord Kira would have been able to sleep in even greater peace, with nothing to fear, while Lord Asano would have been left with a greater mortification to nurse under the grasses. That surely couldn't have been their true intent.

For example, suppose a general who was ordered to destroy an imperial enemy thought that he wouldn't be able to establish his reputation if the enemy died of illness; suppose, therefore, that even before lining up his army or setting up defenses, he alone hastily dashed into the enemy land, brandishing his sword, and was killed, would the emperor praise him as his loyal subject? No, that certainly would make him a laughingstock throughout the land.

Rather, he must first solidly line up his forces and work out a strategy that will not fail him; only then can he invade the enemy land so that he may take the enemy's head according to plan and thereby lay the imperial worries to rest. That, I think, is the way a loyal subject must behave. If the enemy dies of illness in the meantime, all that has to be done is to cancel the expedition, and that won't be any disgrace to the general at all. . . .

The forty-six warriors had no resentment whatever against Lord Kira. Their lord's death by disembowelment was caused by his own rashness, not by Lord Kira. What these men did was to carry out what their deceased lord had intended to do so that they might lay to rest his resentment in his grave. That's why after they showed Lord Kira's head to him in his grave at Sengaku Temple they placed it on a ceremonial tray and handed it over to the monk. And when Chikara in his youthful thoughtlessness said something foul to the head, [his father] Kuranosuke sternly admonished him that you shouldn't behave rudely to a nobleman even when he has been beheaded. They had no personal anger.

The way they upheld righteousness—how can anyone bring up the notion of whipping a corpse? Their basic thinking was fundamentally different from that of Wu Tzu-hsu. It was also very different from someone becoming envious of someone else's great reputation and speaking ill of him. All this is so embarrassing it makes my armpits perspire. . . .

PART FOUR

A Modern Retelling

"THE ABE FAMILY"
BY MORI ŌGAI

O N THE THIRTEENTH OF SEPTEMBER 1912, the day of Emperor Meiji's funeral, General Nogi Maresuke killed himself by disembowelment, taking his wife, Shizuko, with him. He said in his testimonial: "In committing suicide to follow His Majesty in death, I am aware, with regret, that my crime in doing so is by no means negligible. However, since I lost my flag during the civil war of the tenth year of Meiji [1877], I have been looking for an appropriate opportunity to die, to no avail. Instead, to this day I have continued to be showered with imperial special favors and treated with exceptional compassion. While I have grown infirm, with few days left to be useful, this grave event has filled me with such remorse that I hereby have made this decision."

The loss of a flag in a single battle was not the only cause of Nogi's remorse—and his sense of indebtedness that he went unpunished. He had created vast casualties in his assaults on Port Arthur during the Russo-Japanese War, and he most likely knew that he was not relieved of his post, as recommended by the chief of the army general staff, because of Meiji's intervention.

Nogi's action, which some of the younger generation dismissed as "anachronistic," affected a number of people. In the United States, for example, Harriet Monroe (1860–1936) wrote a poem entitled "Nogi" and published it in the second issue of the magazine she had just founded, *Poetry*:

> Great soldier of the fighting clan,
> Across Port Arthur's frowning face of stone
> You drew the battle sword of old Japan,
> And struck the White Tsar from his Asian throne.

Once more the samurai sword
Struck to the carved hilt in your loyal hand,
That not alone your heaven-descended lord
Should meanly wander in the spirit land.

Your own proud way, O eastern star,
Grandly at last you followed. Out it leads
To that high heaven where all the heroes are,
Lovers of death for causes and for creeds.

Among the Japanese writers deeply shaken was Mori Ōgai (1862–1922).[1] An army officer who studied military hygiene in Germany and quickly rose through the ranks to become surgeon general at age forty-five, Ōgai was at the same time an influential man of letters actively engaged in introducing Western literary and philosophical ideas to Japan. His friend Nogi's suicide gave him pause. The depth of his feeling was obvious: On September 18, a mere six days after Nogi's death and on the very day he attended his funeral, he submitted to his publisher the first of his stories drawing on Japan's recent past. Entitled "Okitsu Yagoemon's Testimonial," it began: "I die by disembowelment this month, today. This will strike some as abrupt, and they might say that I, Yagoemon, had become senile or that I had become deranged. But that is not at all the case." Yagoemon goes on to recount what had happened thirty years earlier.

Ōgai published "The Abe Family," translated below, the following January. It was his second "historical story." In this recounting, Hosokawa Tadatoshi (1586–1641) is a son of Tadaoki (Sansai, 1564–1645), a warlord famous for his accomplishments in court protocol, traditional verse, and the art of drinking tea. Indeed, Okitsu Yagoemon's killing of his colleague, for which he atoned through disembowelment, occurred while the two men were on assignment to buy tea utensils for Tadaoki.

In the spring of the eighteenth year of Kan'ei [1641], Hosokawa Tadatoshi, Junior Fourth Rank, Lower Grade, Minor Captain of the Inner Palace Guards, Left Division, and Governor of Etchū, was preparing to put himself at the center of a long procession splendid enough for

---

1. Another was Natsume Sōseki (1867–1916), whose *Kokoro* is linked to Nogi's suicide. The novella can be read in Edwin McClellen's elegant translation.

a daimyo of 540,000 koku and to leave the cherry blossoms of his fiefdom, Higo Province, which bloom earlier than elsewhere, so that he might travel along with the spring, from south to north, on his biannual pilgrimage to the shogunate, in Edo,[2] when unexpectedly he fell ill. The medicine prescribed by his doctor did not show any effect and his illness became graver each day. An express messenger was dispatched to Edo with the news of the delay of his arrival. The third Tokugawa shogun, Iemitsu, known as a distinguished ruler, expressed concern for Tadatoshi, who had done some important work in destroying Amakusa Shirō Tokisada, leader of the Shimabara rebels.[3] On the twentieth of the third month, he had Matsudaira, Governor of Izu, Abe, Governor of Bungo, and Abe, Governor of Tsushima, compose an official letter of inquiry bearing their names and also had a Kyoto acupuncturist by the name of Isaku start for Higo. On the twenty-second he had a samurai by the name of Soga Matazaemon dispatched as a shogunate messenger with the letter signed by the three administrators.

Such measures from shogun to daimyo were unusual. But ever since the Shimabara rebels had been pacified three years earlier, in the spring of the fifteenth year of Kan'ei, the shogun had gone out of his way to extend courtesies to Tadatoshi on every possible occasion—giving him extra acreage for his Edo mansion, presenting him with cranes for his falconry, and so forth. At the news of Tadatoshi's serious illness, the shogun naturally tried to convey as much concern as precedent allowed.

Yet, even before the shogun began making these arrangements, Tadatoshi's illness, in his Flower Field Mansion in Kumamoto, had quickened its pace, and on the seventeenth of the third month, about four in the afternoon, he died, at the age of fifty-six. His wife was a daughter of Ogasawara Hidemasa, Fifth Rank in the Ministry of Military Affairs, whom the shogun had adopted and married to Tadatoshi. Forty-five that year, she was commonly called Lady Osen. Tadatoshi's first son, Rokumaru, had performed his manhood rites six years before, when he was endowed by the shogun with part of his name,

---

2. For "biannual pilgrimage," see the Introduction, p. xxii.

3. The "Shimabara rebels" refer to the peasants in the Amakusa region, in Kyūshū, who revolted in the tenth month of 1637. The rebellion, led by a Christian youth by the name of Amakusa Shirō Tokisada, was quelled in the second month of the following year, with all the 37,000 participants killed. Tadatoshi was one of the daimyo who provided an army for the suppression of the revolt on the shogunate order. For an account of the swordsman Yagyū Munenori's involvement in the arrangement of the government forces, see *The Sword & the Mind*, pp. 9–11.

mitsu, and changed his name to Mitsusada; at the same time he was appointed Junior Fourth Rank, Lower Grade, Chamberlain, and Governor of Higo. He was now seventeen. At the time of Tadatoshi's death he was in Hamamatsu, Tōtōmi Province, on his way back from his biannual pilgrimage, but at the news of his father's death, he returned to Edo at once. Later he changed his name to Mitsuhisa.

Tadatoshi's second son, Tsuruchiyo, had been placed in the Taishō temple, on Mt. Tatta, since childhood. He had become a disciple of Priest Taien from Kyoto's Myōshin temple, and was now called Sōgen. Tadatoshi's third son, Matsunosuke, was being brought up by the Nagaoka, a family related to the Hosokawa from the old days. Tadatoshi's fourth son, Katsuchiyo, had been adopted by his retainer, Nanjō Daizen.

Tadatoshi had two daughters. The elder one, Princess Fuji, was the wife of Matsudaira Tadahiro, Governor of Suō. Princess Take, the younger one, was later to be married to Ariyoshi Tanomo Hidenaga.

Tadatoshi himself was Hosokawa Sansai's third son, and had three younger brothers: the fourth son, Tatsutaka, Fifth Rank in the Ministry of Central Affairs; the fifth son, Okitaka, of the Ministry of Justice; and the sixth son, Nagaoka Yoriyuki, of the Ministry of Ceremonial. His younger sisters were Princess Tara, married to Inaba Kazumichi, and Princess Man, married to Middle Counselor Karasumaru Mitsutaka. Princess Man's daughter, Princess Nene, would later become the wife of Mitsuhisa, Tadatoshi's first son. Of his older siblings, the two elder brothers had assumed the name of Nagaoka, and one of his two older sisters was married to Maeno, the other to Nagaoka. His retired father, Sansai Sōryū, was still alive, at seventy-nine. Of these people, some, like Mitsusada, were in Edo, and some in Kyoto and other distant provinces when Tadatoshi died. They grieved at the news that reached them belatedly, but their grief was not as immediate and acute as that of the people who were in his mansion in Kumamoto at his death. Two men, Musushima Shōkichi and Tsuda Rokuzaemon, departed for Edo as formal messengers.

On the twenty-fourth of the third month the Rite of the Seventh Day was performed. On the twenty-eighth of the fourth month the floor boards of the living room of Tadatoshi's mansion were removed and his coffin was dug out of the ground below, where it had been laid, and, following directions from Edo, the corpse was cremated at Shū'un-in, in Kasuga Village, Akita County, before being buried on the hill outside Kōrai Gate. In the winter of the following year, below this mausoleum, a temple called Gokokuzan Myōge was built, and Priest Keishitsu, who had studied with Priest Takuan, came from Tōkai Temple, in Shinagawa, Edo, to become the resident chief priest. Later, when Keishitsu retired to the Rinryū Hut within the temple compounds, Tadatoshi's second son, Sōgen, would inherit the temple, calling himself Priest Tengan. Tadatoshi's posthumous Buddhist name was Myōge-in-den Taiun Sōgo the Great Layman.

Tadatoshi's cremation at Shū'un-in was faithful to his will. Once when he was out moor-hen hunting, he had stopped at Shū'un-in to have some tea. There he noticed that the beard had grown under his chin, and asked the chief priest if he had a razor. The priest had a basin of water brought and offered it to him with a razor. While having a page shave his beard, Tadatoshi, in a good mood, asked the priest, "I guess you have shaved lots of dead men's heads with this razor, haven't you?" The priest didn't know how to respond, utterly lost as he was. After this Tadatoshi became good friends with him and decided that the temple would be the place of his cremation.

It happened in the middle of the cremation. Some of the retainers guarding the coffin shouted, "Look, our lord's hawks!" In the dull-blue patch of the sky blurred by the tall cedar trees in the temple compound, and above the cherry leaves hanging like an umbrella over the round frame of the well, two hawks were flying in circles. While people looked on in puzzlement, the hawks, so close to each other that one's beak almost touched the other's tail, swooped down and plunged into the well beneath the cherry tree. Two men broke out of the group of several people arguing something at the temple gate, ran to the well, and, hands on the stone well-curb, looked in. By then the hawks had sunk deep to the bottom, and the surface of the water fringed with fern was glistening like a mirror as before. The two men were Tadatoshi's falconers. The two hawks that had plunged into the well and died were Ariake and Akashi, hawks Tadatoshi had particularly loved. When this became known, people were heard to say, "So, even our lord's hawks have followed him in death!"

Such a response was to be expected: Between the day of Tadatoshi's passage into the other world and two days before his cremation, more than ten retainers had killed themselves to follow him in death. Indeed, two days before the cremation, as many as eight men had disemboweled themselves at once, and the day before yet another had done the same. As a result, there were no retainers who were not thinking of death. How the falconers had been so careless as to let the hawks loose and why the hawks had plunged into the well as if chasing an invisible prey wasn't known, but no one even bothered to speculate. That they were the hawks Tadatoshi had loved, and that they died on the very day of his cremation, in the well of Shū'un-in where the cremation was being performed, was enough for the people to conclude that the hawks deliberately followed their lord in death. There was no room in their minds to doubt this judgment and try to find out some other cause.

The Rite of the Forty-ninth Day was performed on the fifth of the fifth month. The priests who had performed the various rites up to that time included Sōgen and those from Kisei-dō, Konryō-dō, Tenju-an, Chōshō-in, and Fuji-an. Now the sixth of the fifth month came around, but still deaths by disembowelment occurred. Not to mention those who intended to follow Tadatoshi in death, their parents, siblings, wives, children, and even those unrelated to them thought only of death, while absent-mindedly welcoming the acupuncturist from Kyoto and formal messengers from Edo. They did not collect iris stalks to adorn their eaves for the annual celebration of Boys' Day. Even those who had newborn sons raised no streamers and kept quiet, as if trying to forget that sons had been born to them.

When and how it came about is not known, but an unstated rule governed a retainer's following his lord in death by disembowelment. The retainer's profound respect and love of his lord did not automatically entitle him to perform the act. Just as permission was needed for accompanying the lord on the biannual pilgrimage to Edo in peacetime, or to the battlefield in wartime, so was it absolutely necessary to accompany him across the River of Death. A death without permission was "a dog's death." And a samurai would not die a dog's death because good reputation was of the utmost value to him. To plunge into the enemy turf and get killed in battle would be praiseworthy, but it would not win a man any honor if he ignored the order, sneaked out to accomplish some exploits, and was killed. That would be a dog's death; in the same way, killing oneself by disembowelment without permission would serve no purpose.

At times, a retainer disemboweling himself to follow his lord in death without permission might not be thought to have died a dog's death. Such a case was possible where a tacit agreement had formed between the lord and the retainer he had especially favored—where the absence of permission did not mean anything. The teachings of the Great Vehicle were expounded after the Buddha entered nirvana even though the Buddha had not given permission to do so. But this was permissible, it is said, because the Buddha, omniscient of the past, the present, and the future, had allowed that such teachings would ensue. Some people could die for their lords without permission in the same way that the teachings of the Great Vehicle could be preached as if from the Buddha's own mouth.

How, then, was permission obtained? Among those who had already died for Tadatoshi, Naitō Chōjūrō Mototsugu provides a good example. Chōjūrō had worked for Tadatoshi in his study and won his special favor. After Tadatoshi fell ill, he never left his side. When Tadatoshi realized he would never recover, he told Chōjūrō that if his death became imminent, he, Chōjūrō, should hang in the alcove near his pillow the scroll with two large characters, *Fu-Ji*, "Incomparable."[4] On the seventeenth of the third month, when his condition gradually deteriorated, Tadatoshi said the time had come to hang the scroll. Chōjūrō did as he was told. Tadatoshi took one look at the scroll and closed his eyes for a while in meditation. Then he said his legs felt dull. Chōjūrō carefully pulled open the skirts of Tadatoshi's bedclothes and, as he massaged his legs, looked Tadatoshi directly in the eye. Tadatoshi returned the look.

"Sir, may I make a request?"

"What is it?"

"Your condition seems serious indeed, and I pray that you recover as soon as possible with the protection of the gods and the Buddha, as well as with the remarkable effect of good medicine. However, one must prepare for the worst. If the worst should happen, would you please kindly command me to accompany you?"

Chōjūrō gently held up Tadatoshi's foot and put his forehead on it. His eyes were full of tears.

"No, I will not do any such thing," said Tadatoshi and, though looking at Chōjūrō in the eye till then, he twisted his body to turn away.

"Please, do not say that, sir." Chōjūrō held up his lord's foot again.

"No, no." Tadatoshi kept his back turned to him. One of the retainers sitting in attendance in the same room said, "You're too

---

4. One of the two sets of Chinese characters applied to Mt. Fuji.

young to be that impudent. Restrain yourself." Chōjūrō was just seventeen years old that year.

"Please." Chōjūrō said as if choking, and kept his forehead on his lord's foot, which he held up for the third time and would not let go.

"You are stubborn," said Tadatoshi as if angered. But as he said this, he nodded twice.

"Sir!" Chōjūrō said and, with Tadatoshi's foot held in his hands, bowed down low near the bed and remained still. At that moment he felt himself fill with a sense of relaxation and calm as if he had passed some very difficult spot and reached the place he had to get to; other than that, nothing came to his consciousness, and he was even unaware of the tears he shed on the mat made in Bingo Province.

Chōjūrō was still quite young and had done nothing remarkable, but Tadatoshi had given him constant attention and kept him close. The young man liked drinking, and once committed a blunder for which another might have received a reprimand. But Tadatoshi said, "Not Chōjūrō but the sake did it," and dismissed it with a smile. Because of this Chōjūrō came to believe that he had to return this generosity and make up for his mistake. After Tadatoshi's illness became serious, this belief became the firm conviction that the only way to convey his apologies and compensate for the error was to follow his lord in death.

If you stepped into this young man's mind to look closely at it, though, you'd find that side by side with the thought that he would, by his own will, follow his lord in death, another thought existed with equal force: that he was obliged to die because other people expected him to do so—a sense of dependency on others for moving in the direction of death. In other words, he was worried that if he did not die, he would be subjected to horrible humiliation. This was his weakness, but he was not in the least afraid of death. And so nothing had interfered with his wish to ask his lord for permission to die, with that determination dominating his entire mind.

After a while Chōjūrō felt Tadatoshi tense his foot that he held with both hands and stretch it a little. He thought his lord felt it had become numb again, and began slowly to massage it as he had done at the outset. Then his old mother and his wife came to his mind. He reminded himself that the relatives of those who commit suicide to follow their lord receive preferential treatment from the lord's house. He thought that he now had placed his family in a safe position, that he could die peacefully. With the thought, his face brightened.

On the morning of the seventeenth of the fourth month, Chō-jūrō put on his formal attire, came to his mother, told her of his decision to follow his lord, and said some words of farewell. His mother showed no surprise. Though she had not said it to him, she had long known that this was the day for her son to disembowel himself. If he had told her that he would not do so, she would have been alarmed.

His mother called in his newlywed bride from the kitchen and asked if the preparations were made. The wife rose to her feet at once, and returned with a tray of sake, which she'd had ready since earlier that morning. Like the mother she, too, had long known that this was the day for her husband to disembowel himself. She had set her hair neatly and wore one of her better house kimonos. Both mother and wife appeared the same, looking formal and solemn, but the corners of the wife's eyes were red, revealing that she had wept in the kitchen. When the tray was set before him, Chōjūrō called in his brother, Saheiji.

The four drank from one cup by turns, silently. When the cup had made a round, the mother said, "Chōjūrō, I know you like drinking. Why don't you drink a little more than usual today?"

"Right, mother," Chōjūrō said, and he drank one cup after another with a smile on his face, obviously feeling good.

After a while, he said to his mother, "I have enjoyed the sake, and feel a little drunk. The sake has worked better than usual, per-haps because I've been worried about various matters for the last several days. May I excuse myself and rest a while?"

With that Chōjūrō rose to his feet and entered the living room, where he lay down in the middle of the room and soon began to snore. When his wife, who had followed him quietly, put a pillow under his head, he moaned and turned, but kept snoring. His wife gazed at his face for some time; then abruptly she rose and left the room. She knew she should not cry in his presence.

The entire household was quiet. Just as mother and wife had known the master's decision before being told, so had his retainers and handmaid. Nothing like laughter was heard either from the stable or the kitchen.

The mother stayed in her room, the wife in hers, and the brother in his, each in deep thought. The master snored away in the living room. In the window of the living room, which was left wide open, a bundle of *shinobu* fern, with a wind chime attached to it, hung under the eaves. The wind chime faintly tinkled from time to time, as if to remind itself of its job. Beneath it was a washbasin, a tall piece of rock with a hole dug in the top and filled with water. Perched on the wooden dipper placed across the basin face down, was a blue darner, wings drooping mountain-shape, motionless.

Two hours went by, and another two hours. Now it was past noon. The wife had told the handmaid to get lunch ready, but she was not sure her mother-in-law wanted it. She hesitated to go to her to ask because she was afraid that if she asked her about a meal, her mother-in-law might suspect that she was the only one who thought of eating at such a time.

At that juncture Seki Koheiji came, a man Chōjūrō had asked to be his second. The mother called the wife. The wife bowed to her and, her hands on the floor, remained silent to see what her wishes might be.

"Chōjūrō said he'd rest awhile," said the mother, "but it's some time since he excused himself. Here is Mr. Seki. I would think it's time to wake him."

"Yes, you're right. It mustn't be done too late," said the wife. She rose to her feet at once and left to wake her husband.

In the living room, the wife looked at her husband's face again, just as she had when she brought in the pillow. The thought that she was going to wake him to death made it difficult for her to speak for a while.

Though in profound sleep, he must have felt the bright light coming in the window; his back was turned toward the window, his face toward her.

"Come, my dear," the wife called out.

Chōjūrō did not wake.

The wife edged up to him on her knees and touched his shoulder that rose high. Chōjūrō yawned, stretched his elbows, opened his eyes, and sat up.

"You have rested very well," said his wife. "I woke you because Mother said it was getting late. Mr. Seki has come too."

"I see. It must be noon now. I thought I might take a little rest, but I was both drunk and tired and wasn't aware how time was passing. I think it's time to take rice with tea and go to Tōkō-in. Tell Mother I'm ready."

On a life-or-death occasion a samurai did not eat his fill. But he would not set out to do something important with an empty stomach, either. Chōjūrō had indeed intended to take a nap, but ended up having a much longer, though pleasant, sleep than he had expected, and found out it was already noon. That's why he offered to have a meal. So, though it was more a matter of formality, the four members of the family sat at table as they did at ordinary times, and had lunch.

Then Chōjūrō prepared himself calmly and went with Seki to his family temple, Tōkō-in, to disembowel himself.

Around the time Chōjūrō held Tadatoshi's foot in his hand to ask for his permission, some others among Tadatoshi's retainers who had enjoyed his special favors asked, each in his own fashion, permission to follow him in death, and those who did so, including Chōjūrō, numbered eighteen. All of them were samurai Tadatoshi trusted deeply. Therefore, Tadatoshi wished sincerely to leave these men behind him for the protection of his son, Mitsuhisa. Also, he was fully aware that it was cruel to have them die with him. But he gave each of them the word, "Granted," while feeling great pain in doing so, because the circumstances did not allow him to do otherwise.

Tadatoshi believed that the men he kept in such close employment would be glad to offer their lives for him. He also knew that killing themselves would not be a painful thing for them. If, however, he did not give them permission to follow him in death but made them survive him, what would happen? The other retainers would show no restraint in saying that these men had not died when they should have, that they had no sense of obligation, that they were cowards. If that were all, they might put up with it and wait for the chance to offer their lives to Mitsuhisa. But suppose someone went on to say that he, now the deceased lord, had kept such men in his employment without realizing that they had no sense of obligation and were in fact cowards, that would be more than they could bear—there would be no end to their regrets. When he thought this far, Tadatoshi could not but give his permission. That was why, even while feeling worse about it than about his own illness, he said, "Granted."

When the number of the retainers to whom he gave permission reached eighteen, Tadatoshi, who had lived through times of peace and disturbances for more than fifty years and was acquainted thoroughly with every shade of human affairs, thought in his illness and pain about his own death and the deaths of the eighteen samurai. No living thing can avoid death. Right next to an old tree that withers and dies, young trees sprout green leaves and flourish. From the

352 • LEGENDS OF THE SAMURAI

viewpoint of the young men surrounding his first son, Mitsuhisa, the old men whom he, Tadatoshi, had around him were no longer needed. They could even be obstacles. He wished they would survive him and provide Mitsuhisa with the kind of service they had provided him, but there were now enough new people who could do the same for his son, and they might be waiting for their turn impatiently. Some of his own appointees had probably garnered hatred—or at least, had become targets of jealousy—in carrying out their duties for such a long time. Seen this way, telling them to live longer might not be an entirely sagacious idea. Granting them permission to die may have been an act of mercy. So thinking, Tadatoshi felt some consolation.

The eighteen men who asked for and were granted permission to follow Tadatoshi in death were Teramoto Hachizaemon Naotsugu, Ōtsuka Kihē Tanetsugu, Naitō Chōjūrō Mototsugu, Ōta Kojūrō Masanobu, Harada Jūjirō Yukinao, Munakata Kahē Kagesada, Munakata Kichidayū Kageyoshi, Hashitani Ichizō Shigetsugu, Ihara Jūzaburō Yoshimasa, Tanaka Itoku, Honjō Kisuke Shigemasa, Itō Tazaemon Masataka, Migita Inaba Muneyasu, Noda Kihē Shigetsuna, Tsuzaki Gosuke Nagasue, Kobayashi Riemon Yukihide, Hayashi Yozaemon Masasada, and Miyanaga Katsuzaemon Munesuke.

Teramoto's direct ancestor was a man by the name of Teramoto Tarō, a resident of Teramoto, in the Province of Owari. Tarō's son, Naizen'noshō, served the Imagawa family. Naizen'noshō's son was Sahē, Sahē's son was Uemon'nosuke, and Uemon'nosuke's son was Yozaemon. In the Korean conquest[5] Yozaemon served Katō Yoshiaki's army and did some distinguished work. Yozaemon's son was Hachizaemon and during the siege of Osaka Castle once worked under Gotō Mototsugu.[6] After the Hosokawa family retained Hachizaemon, he was given 1,000 koku and was made head of a fifty-gun regiment. He disemboweled himself at the An'yō temple on the twenty-ninth of the fourth month. He was fifty-three years old. Fujimoto Izaemon seconded him. Ōtsuka was a superintendent of police who received

---

5. Toyotomi Hideyoshi (1537–98), the de facto ruler of Japan at the time, sent armies to Korea, in 1592 and 1597, with the ultimate purpose of subjugating China. Both campaigns failed.

6. Toward the end of 1614 and in the summer of 1615 Tokugawa Ieyasu (1542–1616), who had already founded the Tokugawa shogunate in Edo, laid siege to Osaka Castle where the Toyotomi clan and their followers were headquartered and destroyed them. Gotō Matabē Mototsugu (1570–1615) was a Toyotomi commander who was killed in battle during the second siege.

150 koku. He disemboweled himself on the twenty-sixth of the fourth month. Ikeda Yazaemon seconded him.

I have already talked about Naitō.

Ōta's grandfather, Denzaemon, served Katō Kiyomasa. When Tadahiro[7] was stripped of his fief, Denzaemon and his son, Genzaemon, became masterless drifters. Kojūrō was the second son of Genzaemon and had been retained as a page by Tadatoshi. He received 150 koku. The first man to follow Tadatoshi in death, he disemboweled himself on the seventeenth of the third month, at the Kasuga temple. He was eighteen. Moji Genbē seconded him. Harada, a recipient of 150 koku, served Tadatoshi at his side. He disemboweled himself on the twenty-sixth of the fourth month. Kamada Gendayū seconded him.

The Munakata brothers, Kahē and Kichidayū were the descendants of Middle Counselor Munakata Ujisada and their service with the Hosokawa began with their father, Seibē Kagenobu. Both brothers received 200 koku. On the second of the fifth month the older brother disemboweled himself at Ryūchō-in, and the younger brother at the Renshō temple. The older brother's second was Takata Jūbē, the younger brother's Murakami Ichiemon. Hashitani was from the Province of Izumo and was a distant offspring of the Amako clan. Retained by Tadatoshi when fourteen, he, a recipient of 100 koku, waited on Tadatoshi as a poison taster. When his illness became serious, Tadatoshi at times laid his head on Hashitani's lap and slept. On the twenty-sixth of the fourth month he disemboweled himself at the Seigan temple. As he was about to slash his abdomen, there was a faint sound of the hour drum at the castle. He told one of his retainers accompanying him to go out and ascertain the time. Upon his return, the man said, "I heard the last four, but I'm not sure what the total number of drumbeats was." This made Hashitani and others smile. Hashitani said, "Thanks for making me laugh in my last moments," gave the retainer the formal outer garment he wore, and disemboweled himself. Yoshimura Jintayū seconded him.

Ihara received ten koku and an allowance for three retainers. At the time of his disembowelment Hayashi Sahē, a retainer of Abe

---

7. The heir of Katō Kiyomasa (1562–1611), one of Hideyoshi's prominent generals. The way the Tokugawa stripped Tadahiro of his fief of 520,000 koku and banished him on the flimsiest of pretexts, in 1632, shows the ruthlessless with which the shogunate was trying to consolidate its power as late as seventeen years after the rival house, the Toyotomi, was destroyed.

Yaichiemon's,[8] seconded him. Tanaka was a grandson of Okiku, who has left us *Okiku's Story*,[9] and was a boyhood friend of Tadatoshi's since both went to study on Mt. Atago. Once during that period of study he quietly dissuaded the young Tadatoshi from entering the priesthood. Later a recipient of 200 koku, he served Tadatoshi as his personal attendant. He was quite good at mathematics, and was useful with that skill. As an old man he was allowed to sit cross-legged with his hood on in Tadatoshi's presence. He asked Mitsuhisa to permit him to follow Tadatoshi in death, but the permission was not granted. On the nineteenth of the sixth month, he stabbed his abdomen with a short sword, then sent a petition to Mitsuhisa, who finally gave him permission. Katō Yasudayū seconded him.

Honjō was from Tango Province. While a masterless drifter, he was retained as a servant by Honjō Kyūemon, a room attendant for Lord Sansai. After he arrested a burglar at Nakatsu, he was given fifteen koku and an allowance for five retainers. It was then that he assumed the name of Honjō. He disemboweled himself on the twenty-sixth of the fourth month.

Itō served as a senior accountant who received his stipend in rice. He disemboweled himself on the twenty-sixth of the fourth month. His second was Kawakita Hachisuke. Migita became masterless while with the Ōtomo family. Tadatoshi retained him with land worth 100 koku. On the twenty-seventh of the fourth month he disemboweled himself in his own house. He was sixty-four. Tahara Kanbē, a retainer of Matsuno Ukyō's, seconded him. Noda was a son of Noda Mino, the chief administrator of the Amakusa family, and was retained with a stipend in rice. On the twenty-sixth of the fourth month he disemboweled himself at the Genkaku temple. His second was Era Han'emon. About Tsuzaki Gosuke I will write later.

Kobayashi received ten koku and an allowance for two retainers. At his disembowelment Takano Kanbē seconded him. Hayashi was originally a peasant in Shimota Village, in Nangō. Tadatoshi picked him up; he gave him a stipend of fifteen koku and an allowance of ten retainers and appointed him gardener of his Flower Field Mansion. On the twenty-sixth of the fourth month he disemboweled himself at the Butsugan temple. His second was Nakamitsu Hansuke. Miya-

8. The first mention of the head of the family of this story.
9. A report on the fall of Osaka Castle, in 1615; it was published more than two hundred years later, in 1837.

naga, a kitchen officer who received ten koku with an allowance for two retainers, was the first man who asked Tadatoshi for permission to follow him in death. On the twenty-sixth of the fourth month he disemboweled himself at the Jōshō temple. His second was Yoshimura Yoshiemon. Some of these people were buried at their family temples, some close to Tadatoshi's mausoleum on the hill outside Kōrai Gate.

A surprisingly large proportion of these men were those who received their stipends directly in rice. Among them, Tsuzaki Gosuke has a particularly interesting story worth separate telling.

Gosuke, a recipient of six koku with an allowance for two retainers, was the keeper of Tadatoshi's dogs. He always accompanied Tadatoshi in falconing and was his favorite man during those field excursions. He begged, like a spoiled kid, for permission to follow his master in death, and got it, but the clan administrators all said to him, "The other retainers were granted high stipends and enjoyed some glory, but you were a mere dog keeper to our deceased lord. We understand very well that your sentiments are admirable, and it's a supreme honor that our lord should have given you permission. We think that should be enough. Will you please give up the thought of dying and serve our new lord?"

Gosuke would not listen. On the seventh of the fifth month he went to the Kōrin temple near the exercise ground with the dog he took whenever he accompanied Tadatoshi. His wife saw him off at the front gate and said, "You're a man, too. Try not to be lesser in glory than those in senior positions."

The Tsuzaki family's temple was Ōjō-in, but because it had some connections to Tadatoshi and so was inappropriate for someone like himself, Gosuke decided on the Kōrin temple as a place to die. As he entered the graveyard he saw Matsuno Nuinosuke, whom he had asked to second him, already waiting. He took down a light-green bag from his shoulder and pulled a lunch box out of it. He opened its lid and found two rice balls. He put them before the dog. The dog would not begin on them, but looked up at Gosuke, wagging his tail.

"You are a beast and may not realize it," Gosuke said to the dog as if he were speaking to a human being. "But your lord who caressed you on the head many times has already passed away. Many people who enjoyed his favors have already disemboweled themselves to accompany him. I'm a lowly retainer, but I'm no different from those of higher rank in having received a stipend to live from day to day. We're the same, too, in having enjoyed our lord's favors. That's why I'm going to die by cutting my stomach. Once I'm dead, you'll be a stray dog. I feel terribly sorry for you because of that. Our lord's hawks dived into the well of Shū'un-in and died. What d'you say? Don't you want to die with me? If you want to live even if you may become an abandoned dog, eat these rice balls. If you want to die, don't eat them."

Gosuke looked the dog in the eye; the dog kept looking Gosuke in the eye and would not eat the rice balls.

"So you'll die with me?" said Gosuke and gave the dog a sharp look. The dog barked once and shook his tail.

"All right, then. I pity you, but die for me." Gosuke held the dog close, unsheathed his sword, and stabbed him.

He put the dog's corpse to one side. Then he pulled out of his chest a piece of paper with something written on it, spread it on the ground before him, and put a stone on it as a weight. The paper was folded once—a formality he had picked up at someone's poetry meeting—and had this written like a regular tanka:

> Karō-shu wa tomare tomare to ouse aredo
> tomete tomaranu kono Gosuke kana

The administrators and all tell me to stop, stop it,
   but however they try to stop me, Gosuke can't be stopped

The paper was not signed. He simply thought that because the poem already had his name, he didn't have to duplicate it by writing it again. In this he was faithful to the tradition without knowing it.

Having decided that he hadn't left anything undone, Gosuke said, "Mr. Matsuno, now I must ask your help." He sat cross-legged on the ground and bared his chest and belly. He held the sword stained with the dog's blood upside down, and said aloud, "I wonder what the falconers have done. His dog keeper now follows him." He then laughed joyfully and slashed his abdomen crosswise. From behind him, Matsuno beheaded him.

Gosuke's status was low, but his widow was granted the same benefits accorded the other surviving families of those who followed Tadatoshi in death. This was because his only son had entered the priesthood as a child. His widow received a rice allowance for five retainers and was given a new house. She lived until the thirty-third anniversary of Tadatoshi's death. The son of Gosuke's nephew inherited his name, and after that, the Tsuzaki family served in the criers' unit for generations.

Other than these eighteen men who obtained permission from Tadatoshi and followed him in death, there was a man called Abe Yaichiemon Michinobu. He was originally from the Akashi clan, and his boyhood name was Inosuke. He began serving Tadatoshi very early and had now risen to the status of receiving more than 1,500 koku. During the Shimabara Conquest, three of his five sons rendered distinguished services and each received new land worth 200 koku. All his family expected Yaichiemon to follow Tadatoshi in death, while he himself made clear his wish to die every time his turn at night attendance came around. But no matter. Tadatoshi would not give consent.

"I'm pleased with your sentiments," Tadatoshi repeated. "But I'd rather you lived on and continued service with Mitsuhisa."

Tadatoshi had long had a habit of contradicting Yaichiemon. That went back to very early days; even when Yaichiemon was still a page, if he came to ask if he was ready for a meal, Tadatoshi would invariably say, "I'm not hungry yet." If another boy came to ask, Tadatoshi would say, "All right. Have the meal brought." There was something about Yaichiemon that tempted Tadatoshi to contradict him. Does this mean he was scolded often? No, that wasn't the case, either. No one else worked as hard, he noticed everything, and everything he did was faultless. Even if he, Tadatoshi, had a mind to scold him, he wouldn't have found a chance.

Yaichiemon would do on his own the kind of things other men would do only after being told to. He would do, without telling Tadatoshi, what other men would do only after telling their lord. And whatever he did was to the point and impeccable. It did not take long before Yaichiemon's attitudes as a servant stiffened.

At first Tadatoshi contradicted the man unthinkingly, but later when he knew that his mind had stiffened, he resented him. While resenting him, Tadatoshi was clear-headed enough to know how Yaichiemon had come to be what he was and realize that he himself was the cause. He wanted to change his habit of contradicting the man, and continued to want to do so, but as months and days passed and as he grew older, changing the habit became harder.

Everyone has someone he likes—and someone he wants to avoid—far above anyone else. When one looks closely for the reasons, one often can't find anything that can be pinpointed. Tadatoshi's dislike of Yaichiemon was such a case. Still, there must have been something about Yaichiemon that made it difficult for people to feel friendly to him. For one thing, this was clear from the fact that he had few close friends. Everyone respected him as an outstanding samurai. But no one would approach him in a relaxed manner. At times, an oddball would try to become close to him, but his perseverance would fail in a while and he would begin to stay away. When Yaichiemon was still called Inosuke and wore bangs, one of his seniors who had often talked to him and helped him in various ways finally gave up by saying, "You can't get a crack at him." When you think about such things, it is no mystery that Tadatoshi could not change his habit though he wanted to.

In any event, while Yaichiemon was unable to get his permission despite his repeated requests, Tadatoshi died. A little before Tadatoshi's death, Yaichiemon looked his master in the eye and said, "Sir, never have I asked you a favor. This is the first and only favor I ask in my whole life." Tadatoshi returned Yaichiemon's steady gaze and declared, "No, will you please continue service with Mitsuhisa?"

Yaichiemon thought hard about the situation and made up his mind. A hundred men out of a hundred would think it impossible for someone with my status not to follow his lord in death but to survive him and continue to face the retainers of the clan. In the event, the only thing left for such a man would be either to disembowel himself, knowing that would be a dog's death, or to leave Kumamoto masterless. But I am what I am. Let them think what they like. A samurai is no concubine. That I wasn't liked by my master doesn't mean the loss of my reason for being. That was what he thought, and he kept going to work every day as he had.

The seventh of the fifth month came and went. By then all of the eighteen men had followed Tadatoshi in death. Throughout Kumamoto people talked only about these men. There was no other talk than who said what at the moment of death, how so-and-so's manner of death was superior to everybody else's, and so on. Even before all this, Yaichiemon had had few who would talk to him except about work, but after the seventh of the fifth month he found himself far more isolated in his office at the castle. He knew his colleagues tried not to look him in the eye. He knew they looked at him only when he was looking away or when his back was turned. This was extremely unpleasant. But, he thought, I'm alive not because I hold my life dear. Even someone who thinks the worst of me couldn't possibly think I hold my life dear. If it was all right to die, I'd be glad to die right on this spot. So he continued to go to his office carrying his head high and leaving his office carrying his head high.

A few days later an outrageous rumor reached his ear. Who began it was unknown, but it went like this: "Abe stays alive, it appears, glad that he didn't get his permission. Even without it one could disembowel oneself if one wanted to. Abe's belly skin seems different from an ordinary man's. He should perhaps oil a gourd and cut his belly with it." To Yaichiemon this was unexpected. Anyone who wants to speak ill of me may say whatever he pleases, he thought. But how can anyone look at me, be it from straight ahead or from the side, and say I'm a man who holds his life dear? Someone who's determined to say something bad certainly can. All right. I'll oil a gourd and cut my belly with it to show them.

That day, as soon as he left his office, Yaichiemon sent urgent messengers to summon to his mansion in Yamazaki two of his younger sons who now lived independently. He had the furniture between the living and guest rooms taken away, and waited formally with three of his sons sitting beside him: the first son, Gonbē; the second son, Yagobē; and Shichinojō, the fifth son, who still wore bangs. Gonbē, whose boyhood name was Gonjūrō, rendered distinguished services during the Shimabara Conquest and received new land worth 200 koku. He was as remarkable a man as his father. About the recent situation, he had asked his father only once, "So you did not get your permission," to which the father had said, "No, I didn't." There was no further exchange on the subject between the two. They understood each other so completely that nothing more needed to be said.

Soon two lanterns came through the gate. The third son, Ichidayū, and the fourth son, Godayū, almost simultaneously arrived at the entrance, took off their raincoats, and came into the room. Humid rain had started the day after the forty-ninth day after Tadatoshi's death, and the heavy, dark sky of the fifth month hadn't had a chance to clear up. The sliding doors were all left open, but it was muggy and windless. Yet the candle flames on candlesticks were wavering. A single firefly passed by through the trees in the garden.

The master of the house looked around at those who had gathered, and opened his mouth.

"Gentlemen, I thank you for coming even though I sent for you in the dark. I heard the rumor is already known to all the retainers of this clan, so I think all of you have heard it, too. They say my belly is such that I can cut it only with an oiled gourd. So I'll cut it with an oiled gourd. Kindly witness how I do it."

Both Ichidayū and Godayū had set up separate households after each was granted new land worth 200 koku for his military exploits at Shimabara, but of the two Ichidayū, who had been assigned to the heir apparent early on, was among those who came to be envied as the rulers changed. He edged forward on his knees a little toward his father:

"I understand you perfectly, sir. Some of my colleagues said, 'We hear your father continues his service according to our deceased master's will. We'd like to express our congratulations that both fathers and sons can work together for our lord.' The way they said it made me gnash my teeth."

Yaichiemon, the father, laughed. "I know how you felt. Don't get involved with those nearsighted bastards. I'm not supposed to die but I will; they will then insult you after my death as the sons of the man who couldn't get his permission. It was part of your fate that you should have been born my sons. When you have to suffer shame, suffer it together. Avoid fighting among yourselves. Now, look how I cut my belly with an oiled gourd."

Having said this, Yaichiemon disemboweled himself right in front of his sons, then stabbed himself in the neck from left to right, and died. His five sons, who had been unable to fathom their father's mind, felt sorrow; but at the same time they felt they had stepped out of a precarious place and put down one of the burdens they had carried.

"Big brother," said the second son, Yagobē, to the first son. "Father told us not to fight among ourselves. No one would object to that. In Shimabara I wasn't in the right place and wasn't granted any land, so I'll have to depend upon you from now on. But whatever may happen, you have a reliable spear in your hand. You may count on that."

"We all know that. I don't know what's going to happen, but the land I get is your land," Gonbē said curtly, and folded his arms with a frown.

Abe Yaichiemon and his Sons

"Exactly," Godayū, the fourth son, said. "We can't be sure what will happen. There will be some who say disembowelment without permission isn't the same as following one's lord with his consent."

"That's too obvious. But whatever may happen," said Ichidayū, the third son, looking straight at Gonbē, "whatever may happen, let's not separately deal with our opponents but stay together all the time."

"We will," said Gonbē, but he didn't seem relaxed about it. He always thought of the good of his brothers, but he was one of those who are unable to express themselves with ease. Further, he tended to think and do things by himself. He seldom consulted others. That's why Yagobē and Ichidayū pinned him down this way.

"If they knew you, my big brothers, stood together, they wouldn't dare talk ill of our father," said Shichinojū, the son who still had bangs. His voice, thin as a girl's though it was, was weighted with such strong conviction that to everyone sitting there it was like a streak of light illuminating the darkness ahead.

"Now," Gonbē stood up, "I must go tell mother to ask the womenfolk to take leave of our father."

The succession ceremonies of Mitsuhisa, Junior Fourth Rank, Lower Grade, Chamberlain, and Governor of Higo, were completed. New lands or increased stipends were granted and assignments reshuffled for the retainers. All heirs of the eighteen samurai who followed Tadatoshi in death succeeded to their fathers' positions. As long as there was an heir, there was no exception. These men's widows and old parents were given allowances; houses and mansions were given to some, and even repairs were taken care of by the government. The eighteen were the men favored enough by the previous master to be allowed to accompany him on his way to death, so some in the fiefdom may have felt envious, but none jealous.

The treatment of the succession of Abe Yaichiemon's surviving family, however, was somewhat different. The heir, Gonbē, was not allowed to succeed to his father's position as it was. Yaichiemon's land, worth 1,500 koku, was splintered among the five brothers. The total of the family members' land holdings remained the same, but the status of Gonbē, who succeeded to the main house, was downgraded. Needless to say, Gonbē felt he'd shrunk in stature. His brothers didn't feel good, either. Each man's holdings increased, to be sure, but till then their main house with holdings of more than 1,000 koku had made them feel that they stood under a giant tree, whereas now they felt like acorns trying to see which is taller than the others, as the saying goes. As a result, they knew they ought to be grateful, but in fact felt put upon.

Government prompts no one to seek a scapegoat as long as things stay on a normal course. An inspector-general[10] at the time, who happened to enjoy the present ruler's favor and served very near him, was a man by the name of Hayashi Geki. Clever in small matters, he was suited to the role of companion that he had held when Mitsuhisa was the heir apparent; but he was somewhat lacking in the ability to see an overall picture and tended to get bogged down in details. He decided a line had to be drawn between Abe Yaichiemon, who chose death without the late lord's permission, and the other eighteen men who died true to form. Accordingly, he recommended that the Abe family's holdings be divided. Mitsuhisa, later a thoughtful daimyo, had little experience as yet. He gave little consideration to Yaichiemon and his heir Gonbē, whom he did not know. He adopted Geki's recommendation simply because he noted a point in it that indicated an increase in the holdings of Ichidayū, with whom he was familiar as he kept him in close employment.

When the eighteen men killed themselves to follow their lord, many of the retainers of the Hosokawa clan despised Yaichiemon because he had not done the same even though he had served near Tadatoshi. Now, only a few days later, Yaichiemon disemboweled himself with dignity. But, regardless of the right or wrong of the matter, contempt, once expressed, is hard to fade away: There was no one who would praise Yaichiemon now. In allowing the Abe to bury Yaichiemon alongside Tadatoshi's mausoleum, the government should have gone a step further and, instead of forcing a line to be drawn in succession matters, treated the family in the same way as those of the other eighteen men. Had it done so, the Abe family would have felt honored and competed among themselves in loyalty. As it was, however, by placing the family a step below the others, the government put an official stamp on the contempt the retainers felt for the Abe family. Yaichiemon's sons were gradually alienated from their colleagues, and they lived from day to day in great discontent.

The seventeenth of the third month of the nineteenth year of Kan'ei came around. It was the first anniversary of the death of the

---

10. *Ō-metsuke*, responsible for keeping an eye on the conduct of vassals. See "Forty-seven Samurai," p. 306, and elsewhere.

previous lord. The Myōge temple next to the mausoleum had yet to be built, but there was a hall called Kōyō-in built, where Tadatoshi's memorial tablet bearing his Buddhist name, Myōge-in-den, was kept and where a monk by the name of Kyōshuza resided as chief priest. Days before the anniversary, Priest Ten'yū arrived from the Daitoku temple, of Murasakino, Kyoto. Apparently the anniversary ceremonies were going to be a splendid affair; for about a month, the castle city of Kumamoto busied itself in preparations.

The day came. The weather was fine and warm, and the cherries alongside the mausoleum were in full bloom. A curtain was set up around the Kōyō-in and foot soldiers guarded it. Mitsuhisa came in person and first offered incense before his late father's tablet, then before the tablet of each of the nineteen men. Next, the men's relatives were allowed to do the same. They were also presented with ceremonial wear bearing the Hosokawa crest, as well as seasonal suits: *naga-kamishimo* for those of the rank of mounted escort and above and *han-gamishimo* for those of the rank of foot soldier. Those of lower rank received monetary gifts for services for the deceased.

The ritual proceeded free of trouble, except for one strange thing that happened. When Abe Gonbē, as a member of the surviving families of the deceased, went, in his turn, before Tadatoshi's memorial tablet, he unsheathed his dagger as soon as he finished offering incense, cut his topknot, and laid it in front of the tablet. Taken aback by this unexpected behavior, the samurai overseeing the services looked on a while in confusion. It was only when Gonbē walked back several steps with calm dignity as if nothing had happened that one samurai came to himself and ran up to Gonbē, shouting, "Mr. Abe, wait, sir!" and stopped him. A couple of others joined him, and they took Gonbē to another room.

When questioned by the overseers, Gonbē explained: You might think I've gone mad, but not at all. My father Yaichiemon served impeccably all his life. That's why he was ranked among the other honorable men even though he disemboweled himself without our deceased lord's permission. His service also enabled me, a mere surviving relative, to offer incense before our late lord's tablet in advance of some other people. And yet, the authorities seem to feel that I am incompetent and cannot serve as well as my father did; they divided up my father's land holdings and parceled them among my brothers. My being has become inexcusable to our deceased lord, our present lord, my late father, my relatives, and my colleagues. I've had this thought for quite a while. Today, when my turn came to offer incense before our late lord's tablet, I was suddenly overwhelmed and decided to abandon the samurai status. I'm more than willing to receive any punishment for lack of proper consideration for the occasion, but I haven't gone mad.

When he learned Gonbē's explanation, Mitsuhisa was displeased. First, he was displeased with what Gonbē had done, which was deliberately provocative. Second, he was displeased that he had accepted Geki's advice and had done what he shouldn't have in the first place. Mitsuhisa was still a youthful, impetuous ruler of twenty-four[11] who lacked the ability to control his emotions and restrain his desires. He had little sense of magnanimity of conferring favors in response to resentment. He had Gonbē jailed on the spot. At the news Yagobē and the other members of the Abe family closed their gates—to await further instructions from the lord, they said. At night, however, they gathered and conferred secretly about their future.

In the end the family decided to turn to Priest Ten'yū who had come down for the Buddhist ceremonies for the first anniversary of the previous lord and was still staying there. Ichidayū went to see him at his inn, told him the entire story, and asked him to plead with Mitsuhisa to reduce whatever penalty he might have in mind for Gonbē. The priest listened carefully and said: "What has happened to your family deserves a great deal of pity. But I am in no position to say meddlesome things about whatever measures Lord Mitsuhisa may devise. If, however, Gonbē were to be sentenced to death, I would certainly plead with the lord to save Gonbē's life. Especially now that Gonbē cut off his topknot, he's the same as a priest. I'll do everything I can when it comes to saving his life."

Feeling encouraged, Ichidayū went home. Upon hearing his message, the rest of the family thought they had now found an escape route.

Days passed, and the time for Priest Ten'yū to return to Kyoto drew near. Whenever he had a chance to talk to Mitsuhisa, Ten'yū tried to bring up the matter of leniency toward Abe Gonbē, but he was unable to find one. There was a good reason for this. Mitsuhisa knew the priest would plead for mercy if he condemned Gonbē to death during his stay. As a priest from a great temple, Ten'yū's words could

---

11. Mitsuhisa was born in 1619 and died in 1649. So his age, given as seventeen at the outset, is off the mark.

Legends of the Samurai

not have been ignored. Mitsuhisa simply waited for him to leave before disposing of the matter. Finally the priest left Kumamoto without accomplishing anything.

As soon as Ten'yū left, Mitsuhisa had Abe Gonbē taken out to Idenokuchi and hanged. The official reason given for the punishment was that Gonbē had behaved irreverently toward the previous lord's memorial tablet, that the behavior showed no fear of authorities.

Yagobē and the other members of the Abe family gathered and conferred. Granted Gonbē's act was disrespectful, their late father Yaichiemon was at least counted among those who followed Tadatoshi in death. Because Gonbē was the heir to such a man, they would have accepted a death sentence if it had come to that. They would not be complaining if he had been ordered to disembowel himself as a true samurai. But, instead, Gonbē had been hanged in broad daylight like a common thief. From that they could only conclude, argued the Abe, that they would not be left in peace. Even if Mitsuhisa made no further move against them, how could a family whose member was hanged continue in service, side by side with their colleagues, without embarrassment? There was no room for discussing the right or wrong of the matter now. Yaichiemon must have anticipated a time like this when he advised the brothers not to be separated from one another no matter what happened. There was no choice left but for the entire family to fight against the punitive force the government would send, and die together. There was not a single dissenting voice.

The Abe family gathered together their wives and children and shut themselves up in Gonbē's Yamazaki mansion.

News of this unpeaceful move of the Abe family reached the authorities. Secret police agents came to inspect. The Yamazaki mansion was quiet, the gates bolted. Ichidayū and Godayū's houses were empty.

Men were assigned for a punitive force. Takenouchi Kazuma Nagamasa, the head personal attendant, commanded the group in charge of the front gate; the squad leaders under him were Soejima Kuhē and Nomura Shōbē. Kazuma, who received 1,150 koku, headed a thirty-gun squad. Chief of retainers Shima Tokuemon, a hereditary retainer, accompanied him. Both Soejima and Nomura drew 100 koku at the time. The commander of the group in charge of the rear gate was another head personal attendant, Takami Gon'emon Shigemasa, who had land worth 500 koku. He, too, headed a thirty-gun squad. His squad leaders were Hata Jūdayū, an inspector, and Chiba Sakube, Kazuma's own squad leader who drew 100 koku at the time.

It was decided that the men would move against the Abe family on the twenty-first of the fourth month. On the preceding night, watchmen were deployed around the Yamazaki mansion. Late that night a masked samurai came over the fence, but Maruyama Sannojō, a foot soldier of the patrol group headed by Saburi Kazaemon, killed him. After this there was nothing of note until daybreak.

Sometime before, two official notices had been issued to the neighborhood. One was that even men on duty must stay home and be on the alert for fires. The other was that those not on the punitive force were strictly forbidden entrance to the Abe mansion, but that they should be free to kill any fugitives escaping the house.

The Abe family learned about the assault date the day before. First they cleaned the entire mansion and burned everything unsightly. Then all of them, young and old, had a banquet and drank. Then the old and the women killed themselves, and the children were stabbed to death. Then they dug a large hole in the garden and buried the corpses in it. What remained were only the young and tough men. Under the supervision of Yagobē, Ichidayū, Godayū, and Shichinojō, all the sliding doors and sliding screens were removed, and in that large space the retainers were made to gather and offer prayers loudly, striking gongs and drums, while they waited for the day to break. They explained this was done for the dead souls of the old, the wives and children, but in fact it was to prevent the servants from becoming frightened.

The mansion in which the Abe family shut themselves was where Saitō Kansuke was later to live. Across from it was Yamanaka Matazaemon's house. On its left and right lived Tsukamoto Matashichirō and Hirayama Saburō.

The Tsukamotos were one of the three families that made Amakusa County their domain, the other two being the Amakusa and the Shiki. While Konishi Yukinaga[12] ruled one half of Higo Province,

---

12. A merchant-turned-warlord (d. 1600) and a devout Christian with the baptized name of Agostino. Defeated in the battle of Sekigahara, and now a fugitive, he asked a passerby to capture him and take him to the enemy authorities because, as a Christian, he was unable to take his own life. After capture, he was beheaded. There is a book about him published in 1607 in Genoa.

Amakusa and Shiki committed crimes and were punished with death. Only Tsukamoto remained and served the Hosokawa family.

Matashichirō was on good terms with Abe Yaichiemon and his family. Not only the heads of the houses but also their wives and children often visited each other. Among them, Yaichiemon's second son, Yagobē, who believed he was a good spearman, and Matashichirō, who was also skilled with the same weapon, liked to boast good-naturedly to each other, saying such things as, "You may be a good spearman, but you'd never beat me" and "No, how could I get beaten by you?"

For this reason, ever since he had heard Yaichiemon failed to obtain permission to follow the previous lord in death, Matashichirō guessed how he must have felt, and was sorry for him. As the Abe family declined through the series of misfortunes that followed — Yaichiemon's disembowelment without permission, his heir Gonbē's behavior at Kōyō-in, his execution as a result, and the remaining family's shutting themselves up — the pain he felt for them was no less than what a relative might have felt.

Late one night, Matashichirō sent his wife to the Abe family to inquire after them. Because the Abe were acting like a besieged army in rebellion against the government, Matashichirō was unable to communicate openly with the male members of the family. But someone who knew, as he did, what had happened from the beginning would not be able to condemn the Abe men as evil. Furthermore, he, Matashichirō, had been on close terms with the family. A woman visiting them secretly to make inquiries, he thought, would be excused even if it was found out later. His wife was pleased to hear her husband's words and, taking with her whatever she thought the Abe might need, went to see them late at night. She too was a woman of spirit and was determined that should her visit ever be revealed, she would take the entire responsibility and not get her husband into trouble.

The Abe family were overjoyed to see her. When the world was full of flowers blooming and birds singing, they were forsaken by the gods and buddhas and by the people and had had to shut themselves up like this. Yet there was still one man considerate enough to send his wife to see them, and there she was, a wife willing to follow his words. The gratitude the Abe family felt was profound. The women, in tears, asked her to remember to offer prayers for them, now that they were condemned to such a death that no one else would care to do that. The children who had been forbidden to go outside clung to the gentle woman they loved, from right and left, and would hardly let her go.

The night before the punitive units were to head for the Abe mansion came. Tsukamoto Matashichirō gave deep thought to the situation. I'm on friendly terms with the Abe family. So, at the risk of possible future punishment I sent my wife to inquire after them. Still, next morning the government's punitive force will come to the Abe family. Sending out a punitive force is the same as starting a battle to subjugate rebels. The official notices urge care with fires and against interference, but it would be impossible for a samurai to stand by and watch. Compassion is compassion, justice justice; there's something I can do, too, Matashichirō thought. Late that night he went out of the rear entrance quietly into the semi-dark yard and cut all the ropes that tied together the bamboo fence separating the two houses. Then he went back into his house, changed his clothes, took down his short spear from the decorative crossbeam near the ceiling, drew it from a scabbard with a hawk feather crest, and waited for the day to break.

Takenouchi Kazuma, the leader of the punitive unit assigned to head for the front gate, was born to a family renowned for its military men. His ancestor was Shimamura Danjō Takanori, who won a reputation as a powerful archer under Hosokawa Takakuni. In the fourth year of Kyōroku [1531], when Takakuni was defeated at Amagasaki, in the Province of Settsu, Danjō plunged into the sea with two enemy soldiers held under his arms, and died. His son, Ichibē, served the Yasumi family of Kōchi and called himself Yasumi for a while. But when he had Takenouchi-goe as his domain, he changed his name to Takenouchi. Takenouchi Ichibē's son, Kichibē, served Konishi Yukinaga, and for his exploit at the flood attack on Ōta Castle in the Province of Kii, he was awarded by Toyotomi Hideyoshi a camp coat decorated with a scarlet sun drawn on white glossed silk. During the Korean Conquest he was confined in the Rhee Palace for three years as Konishi's hostage. After the Konishi family was destroyed, he was summoned by Katō Kiyomasa[13] to serve him for 1,000 koku; but he

---

13. Kiyomasa (1562–1611)—Konishi Yukinaga's rival during the Korean campaigns and in other matters—was given one half of the Province of Higo to rule, with the other half given to Konishi. Katō's Kumamoto Castle, one of the more aesthetically pleasing castles that remain to this day, may have been influenced by Konishi's, which was destroyed after his death; Katō transferred at least one donjon from his rival's castle before its destruction.

quarreled openly with his new lord and left the castle town of Kumamoto in broad daylight. As he did so, he had his retainers carry guns with their matchlocks ignited in case Katō sent a punitive force after him. Hosokawa Sansai, in Buzen, picked him up for 1,000 koku. At the time Kichibē had five sons. The first son, also called Kichibē, later had a Buddhist tonsure and called himself Yasumi Kenzan. The second son was called Shichirōemon, the third Jirōdayū, the fourth Yachibē, and the fifth Kazuma.

Kazuma served Tadatoshi as a page and was by his side during the Shimabara Conquest. On the twenty-fifth of the second month, in the fifteenth year of Kan'ei, when the Hosokawa soldiers mounted an assault to take over the enemy castle, Kazuma asked Tadatoshi to let him join the first attack force. Tadatoshi would not listen. But when the page repeated the request like a spoiled kid, he became angry and shouted, "You buster, just get out of my sight!" Kazuma was sixteen then. As the young man jumped out, however, Tadatoshi called out, "Don't get hurt!" Chief Shima Tokuemon, a sandal-bearer, and a spear-bearer followed him. With the master and his retainers added, there were four of them. The volleys of guns from the castle were such that Shima grabbed Kazuma's scarlet camp coat and tried to pull him back. Kazuma yanked himself away and climbed up the castle's stone wall. All Shima could do was to follow him up. Eventually they made an entry into the castle and fought but Kazuma was wounded. Tachibana Muneshige, of Yanagawa, who was governor of Hida, who had broken into the castle at the same spot, was a veteran warrior aged seventy-two. He witnessed the action and later said that three men— Watanabe Shin'ya, Nakamitsu Naizen, and Kazuma—distinguished themselves and he sent them testimonials signed by himself and others. After the castle fell, Tadatoshi gave Kazuma a sword made by Seki Kanemitsu and increased his stipend to 1,150 koku. The sword was one foot ten inches long, "directly tempered" and unsigned, with horizontal file markings, its fastener capped with three silver nine-star crests, while its scabbard was bronze-rimmed, lacquered gold. One of its two fastening holes was filled with lead. Tadatoshi treasured this sword and, even after he gave it to Kazuma, often borrowed it for visits to the castle.

Ordered by Mitsuhisa to lead a punitive force against the Abe, Kazuma returned to his office. There one of his colleagues whispered into his ear: "That bastard seems to have some merit, too. Mr. Hayashi has done well to put you in charge of the front gate."

Kazuma pricked up his ears. "Do you mean Geki recommended me for this assigment?"

"Exactly. Geki said to our lord, 'Our previous lord singled out Kazuma for promotion. Why not give him the job so he can requite that favor?' Isn't this a good opportunity?"

"Damn." Kazuma knitted his brow. "All right. I'll die in the fight," he declared and left the office abruptly.

When he heard about Kazuma's reaction, Mitsuhisa sent a man to Takenouchi's house with a message, "Try not to get wounded. Complete the mission successfully." Kazuma said, "Please inform our lord that I have received his kind words with gratitude."

Upon hearing from a colleague that he had been given this assignment because of Geki's recommendation, Kazuma decided to die. The decision was firm and unshakable. Geki had referred to requital of a favor, he was told. He didn't mean to hear it, and he didn't need to: Geki would have recommended Kazuma only by referring to that. The thought agitated Kazuma no end. Certainly, I had the honor of being promoted by our previous lord. But since my manhood ceremony I'd received no special favors among the personal attendants, of whom there were many. Receive favors everyone did, more or less. Why, then, should I be singled out for the requital of favors? The answer was obvious: I should have followed my lord in death, but I didn't; so I'm being sent to a place where I could risk my life. I'd be glad to give up my life any time, but I wouldn't want to die because I had failed to follow my previous lord in death. How could anyone suppose that someone like me, who wouldn't value his life now, would have valued it as long as the end of the Rite of the First Forty-ninth Day? There was no ground for that supposition. After all, there was no clear line between those who received enough of lordly favors to oblige them to die and those who did not. I've continued to live because there was no suggestion to die made to any of the young samurai who, like me, served near our previous lord. If it had been all right for me to follow him in death, I would have been the first to do so. I had assumed that that was obvious to everyone. But now I've been stamped as one who should have died long ago, and this is excruciating. The disgrace I've been sullied with is of the kind that can never be washed off. Only Geki could think of putting a man to such shame. Geki is such a man. But why did our lord accept such advice? One can endure being hurt by Geki, but one cannot endure abandonment by one's lord.

When I tried to climb into the castle in Shimabara, the previous lord tried to stop me, because he wanted to prevent a mounted escort from being conspicuously among the first attack force. The present lord sent him word not to get wounded, but what was meant was different: This time, the message was that I take care of my life which I valued so. How can I be grateful for that? It's like having an old wound whipped anew. I must die as soon as possible. Death will not wash away the disgrace, but I must die. It will be a dog's death, but I must die.

So thinking, Kazuma could not rest. He curtly told his wife that he was ordered to lead a punitive force against the Abe, and began his preparations alone. Those who followed their lord in death faced death with calm relief, but Kazuma hastened to death to escape pain. Except for Chief Shima Tokuemon, who understood the situation and made the same decision as his master, none of the members of his house fathomed what was in Kazuma's mind. His wife, who had married Kazuma—twenty-one this year—in the previous year, was still like a young girl and did not know what to do but wander around the house with their baby daughter in her arms.

On the night of the twentieth of the fourth month—the day before they were to break in—Kazuma washed himself with cold water, shaved the pate of his head, and perfumed his hair with a renowned incense, Hatsune, which Tadatoshi had given him. He put on a pure white garment, its sleeves tucked in with a white cord, and wore a white headband. He then had a jagged piece of paper attached to his shoulder for identification. The main sword he wore was a thirty-inch Masamori, which had been sent home as the keepsake of his ancestor after his death in battle at Amagasaki. He coupled it with the Kanemitsu granted him on his first participation in battle. At the gate his horse was neighing.

When he stepped down to the yard, holding a short spear, he tied the strings of his straw sandals masculine-style and cut off the extra ends with his dagger.

Takami Gon'emon, who was in charge of the rear gate of the Abe mansion, had originally the family name of Wada and was a descendant of Wada, Governor of Tajima, who lived in Wada, in the Province of Ōmi. At first, the Wada family followed Gamō Katahide, but in the generation of Wada Shōgorō they began serving the Hosokawa family. Shōgorō rendered distinguished service during the battles of Gifu and

Sekigahara.[14] He worked under Tadatoshi's older brother, Yoichirō Tadataka. When Tadataka incurred his father's anger—because the Maeda, from which his wife had come, had left the battlefield in Ōsaka too soon, in the fifth year of Keichō—and decided to wander around as Priest Kyūmu, Shōgorō accompanied him as far as Mt. Kōya and Kyoto. In the end Sansai summoned him to Kokura and, giving him the family name of Takami, made him head guard. The land he received was worth 500 koku. Gon'emon was his son. Gon'emon did some good work during the battles in Shimabara, but because he went against a military command, he was temporarily stripped of his position. Redeemed after a while, he was made a head personal attendant. On the day of the break-in, he wore a black silk garment bearing the family crest and took out and wore the Bizen Osafune sword he had long prized. He then stepped out carrying a three-pronged spear.

Just as Takenouchi Kazuma had Shima Tokuemon under him, Takami Gon'emon had a page with him. One summer day a few years before the Abe incident occurred, the page, who was off duty, was taking a nap in his room, when a colleague of his returned from some errand with his master. The latter stripped himself naked and picked up a bucket to go to the well, but when he saw this page sleeping in the room, he said, "Do I have to return from work with my master and find you sleeping around instead of getting me water?" and kicked the page's pillow away. The page leapt to his feet. "I'd surely have gotten you water if I'd been awake, but you didn't have to kick my pillow away. You can't get away with that," he said, drew his sword, and slashed him from the head down.

Then the page calmly stood astride the man, gave him the *coup de grâce*, went to the chief's hut, and gave him the details. "I would have killed myself on the spot, but I thought you'd have found the whole thing inexplicable," he said, and prepared to disembowel himself. The chief stopped him and went to Gon'emon to report to him what had happened. Gon'emon, just back from his office, had not changed his clothes yet. So he went straight to Tadatoshi's mansion and reported the incident. Tadatoshi said, "Your page's action is understandable. No need for disembowelment." The page had since pledged his life to Gon'emon.

---

14. Both battles took place in 1600, or the fifth year of Keichō. In Tokugawa Ieyasu's moves to control the country, the battle of Sekigahara, on the fifteenth of the ninth month of that year, proved decisive.

The page had a quiver on his back and a short bow in his hand as he stepped out beside his master.

The twenty-first day of the fourth month, in the nineteenth year of Kan'ei, was slightly cloudy, as often happens during wheat harvest time.

At daybreak, Takenouchi Kazuma and his men gathered before the front gate of the Yamazaki mansion where the Abe family had secluded themselves. Although the people inside had been making a good deal of noise with gongs and drums all throughout the night, now there was not a sound, as though the place were empty. The doors of the gate were closed. From the bottom leaves of the sweet oleander growing a few feet above the wood-board fence hung a cobweb adorned with dewdrops sparkling like pearls. A swallow appeared from somewhere and swooped inside the fence.

Kazuma dismounted and stood a while, sizing up the situation. Then he ordered, "Open the gate!" Two foot soldiers climbed over the fence. There was no enemy around the gate, so they destroyed the lock and took off the wooden bolt.

The next-door neighbor, Tsukamoto Matashichirō, hearing Kazuma's men open the gate, ran in over the bamboo fence whose ropes he had cut the night before. An almost daily visitor to the house, he knew its layout to the last detail. With his short spear poised, he sneaked in through the kitchen door. Of all the Abe men who had shut themselves in the main room with the doors closed so they could kill those who broke in one by one, Yagobē was the first to sense someone at the rear entrance. He came out to the kitchen, holding his short spear.

When the two men confronted one another, they were so close their spear blades almost touched. "You're Matashichirō!" Yagobē called out.

"It's me. You liked to boast. I thought to check out how you fight with a spear."

"You said it right. Come!"

They stepped back and fought for a while, but in handling the spear Matashichirō was much the better. He stabbed Yagobē deep in the chest. Yagobē threw his spear away and started back toward the main room.

"Coward! Don't run," Matashichirō shouted.

"No, I won't. I'll cut my stomach," Yagobē said and withdrew inside the main room.

That instant, there was a shout, "Uncle, fight me!" The young Shichinojō flew out like lightning and stabbed Matashichirō on the thigh. Having just delivered a serious wound to his close friend, Matashichirō had lost his alertness and became a victim of a boy. He threw his spear away and fell down.

Inside the gate, Kazuma deployed his men to every part of the compound. Then he went straight to the entrance. There he saw the front doors ajar. When he touched the doors to open them, Shima Tokuemon intervened and whispered agitated words into his ear: "Wait, sir. Today you're commander in chief. Let me go first." But no sooner did Tokuemon throw the doors open and jump in than Ichidayū, waiting for just that, stabbed him in the right eye with his spear. Tokuemon staggered back against Kazuma.

"Get out of my way!" Kazuma pushed him aside and stepped in. Instantly, Ichidayū and Godayū stabbed him through from both flanks.

Soejima Kuhē and Nomura Shōbē dashed in next. So did Tokuemon, despite his painful wound.

The same moment, Takami Gon'emon, who had broken in the rear gate and fought his way through the Abe retainers with his three-pronged spear, reached the main room. Chiba Sakubē stepped in right after him.

The two groups dashing in from front and rear attacked with shouts and cries. Although all the sliding doors and screens had been removed, the main room was merely a thirty-mat space. Just as the horrors of a street fight are much greater than those of a battlefield, so the men fighting there, like a hundred worms piled up on a plate devouring each other, were a horrible sight indeed.

While fighting with spears anybody who came in their way, Ichidayū and Godayū received countless wounds all over their bodies. But they wouldn't give up, but now, instead of spears, they were slashing with swords. Shichinojō had already fallen.

One of Takami's men saw Tsukamoto Matashichirō lying in the kitchen, his thigh stabbed, and said before going inside, "You were wounded. You've done excellent work. You should retreat as soon as you can."

"If I were able to walk to retreat, I'd go in and fight," said Matashichirō bitterly and gnashed his teeth. At that moment one of his own men who had come out of anxiety for his master ran in and carried him out on his shoulder.

Another of his men, a family retainer by the name of Amakusa Heikurō, guarded his master's exit by shooting at every enemy in sight with a short bow, but was killed.

Among Takenouchi Kazuma's men, first, Shima Tokuemon was killed, and then squad leader Soejima Kuhē.

While Takami Gon'emon fought, wielding his three-pronged spear, his page with his short bow stayed close to his unguarded side, shooting at the enemy. Later, he slashed with his sword. At one point he noticed a man aiming his gun at Gon'emon. "I'll get the bullet," he said and stepped before Gon'emon. The bullet hit him, and he died instantly. Chiba Sakubē, a squad leader who was taken from Takenouchi's group to join Takami, was badly wounded. He managed to go to the kitchen and gulp water from the water jug there, but could not move any more.

Among the Abe family, first Yagobē disemboweled himself, and then Ichidayū, Godayū, and Shichinojō expired from many deep wounds. Most of their retainers were killed in the fight.

Takami Gon'emon gathered the surviving men, both from the front and rear units, and had them break down the shack at the back of the Abe mansion and set fire to it. The smoke went straight up in the windless, cloudy sky and was visible from afar. Then they stamped out the fire, sprinkled water over it, and left. Chiba Sakubē, who was in the kitchen, and the other badly wounded men, followed, leaning on the shoulders of their retainers or comrades. It was just about two in the afternoon.

Mitsuhisa often went to visit his chief retainers in their houses. On the twenty-first of the fourth month, when he sent out a punitive force against the Abe family, he went to Matsuno Sakyō's mansion at daybreak.

Yamazaki was right across the Flower Garden where Mitsuhisa's mansion was located. When Mitsuhisa set out from his mansion, he heard a din in that direction. "They must have broken in now," he said as he settled in his palanquin.

When the palanquin had proceeded about a hundred yards a messenger came. It was then that Mitsuhisa learned Takenouchi Kazuma had been killed in battle.

When Takami Gon'emon led his men of the punitive force to the Matsuno mansion where Mitsuhisa was, he sent in a message that they had killed all the Abe family. Mitsuhisa offered to meet him right away and had him come round to the garden in front of the drawing room.

Gon'emon came in, pushing open the wicket attached to the fence overhung with deutzia flowers blooming pure white, and sat on the lawn, bowing low. Mitsuhisa saw him and said, "You seem to have been wounded. I appreciate your hard work." Gon'emon's black silk garment was smeared with blood, mottled, besides, with ashs and char that scattered when he and his men had stamped the fire out before leaving.

"No, sir, it's just a scratch." Gon'emon had received a hard spear thrust on the pit of his stomach, but the blade hit the mirror he had there and was deflected. The wound was no more serious than to stain a tissue paper.

Gon'emon reported each man's work in detail. He credited the Abe's neighbor Tsukamoto Matashichirō, who single-handedly had given Yagobē a fatal wound, with the most significant exploit.

"How did Kazuma do?"

"He ran in from the front gate a minute before me, and I did not have time to see him work."

"I see. Tell the others to come into the garden."

Gon'emon did. All, except those who were badly wounded and had already been taken home, came in and prostrated themselves on the lawn. Those who had worked really hard were sullied with blood, and those who had done nothing but help burn the shack were covered with ash. Among the latter was Hata Jūdayū.

"Jūdayū, how did you work?" Mitsuhisa asked him.

"Sir!" Jūdayū responded but did not dare raise his face. He was a big man, but very much a coward. He'd lingered outside the Abe mansion during the fight and came in reluctantly only after they had set fire to the shack before leaving the place. When he was assigned to the punitive force, the swordsman Shinmen Musashi,[15] seeing the man leave Mitsuhisa's chambers, slappped him on the back and said, "You're a lucky man! I expect you to do some good work." Jūdayū turned pale at this and tried to fasten his loose belt, but his hands trembling, he couldn't do the fastening—or so they say.

---

15. Another name of Miyamoto Musashi (1584–1645), for whom see pp. 254–272. Musashi became acquainted with Tadatoshi in 1640 and remained a Hosokawa guest for the rest of his life. Tadatoshi, an accomplished swordsman himself, is said to have urged Musashi to write down what he had learned through swordsmanship; *Gorin no Sho* was one result.

Mitsuhisa stood up from his seat. "I appreciate that you all worked so hard. Go home and rest."

The Takenouchi family was allowed to adopt a son so that the infant daughter could inherit the household,[16] but the family later died out. Takami Gon'emon received a stipend increase of 300 koku, and Chiba Sakubē and Nomura Shōbē, an increase of fifty koku each. Komeda Kenmotsu received an order and sent the group leader Tani Kuranosuke as a messenger to Tsukamoto Matashichirō with his compliments. When his relatives and friends came to congratulate him, Matashichirō laughed and said, "During the eras of Genki and Tenshō, attacking castles and fighting an army in the field were as routine as breakfast and supper. Destroying the Abe family was as easy as having a simple, damned simple breakfast tea." Two years later, in the first summer of Shōhō, when his wound was healed, Matashichirō was received in audience by Mitsuhisa. After putting him in charge of ten guns, Mitsuhisa said, "If you wish to go to a hot spring to heal your wound completely, you may. I'll also give you land for a villa outside the city; name a place you want." Thus, Matashichirō received a lot for building a house in Koike Village, in Mashiki. Behind the lot was a bamboo hill. When Mitsuhisa sent word that he could also have the hill if he wanted it, he declined the offer. Bamboos are not only useful during peace. Once a war breaks out, bundles of them are needed. So I'd feel uncomfortable owning the hill as my private property, he said. As a result, the hill was permanently entrusted to his family's care.

Hata Jūdayū was banished. Takenouchi Hachibē, Kazuma's older brother, had joined the punitive force on his own, but because he was not with Kazuma when the latter was killed, he was ordered to confine himself in his house for a period of time. A mounted escort's son and Mitsuhisa's personal attendant, who lived close to the Abe mansion, had been taken off duty, with the instruction to be on the alert for fires; so he and his father climbed on the roof of their house and put out the sparks. Later he realized that his action was contrary to Mitsuhisa's intentions in putting him off duty, and asked to be discharged from service. Mitsuhisa said, "No, that doesn't mean you are a coward. Be more careful in the future," and

---

16. So that the boy might marry the daughter and carry forward Takenouchi's family name.

kept him in service. When Mitsuhisa passed away, this attendant followed him in death.

The corpses of the Abe men were taken to Idenokuchi for inspection. When each man's wounds were washed in the Shira River, the one Yagobē had received when Tsukamoto Matashichirō's spear pierced his chest turned out to be superior to anybody else's, and that added to Matashichirō's reputation.

BIBLIOGRAPHY

THE LIST BELOW is limited to the basic Japanese texts used for translation and some of the more notable books consulted for commentary to prepare *Legends of the Samurai*, and to the books in English which either contain partial or complete translations of the tales, chronicles, etc., translated here or otherwise have direct bearing on this book. Poetic anthologies are not listed except for the *Man'yō Shū*. The Japanese section is cross-referenced.

I. IN JAPANESE

ARAI HAKUSEKI. *Oritaku Shiba no Ki* (Breaking and Burning Firewood). *Taion Ki; Oritaku Shiba no Ki; Rangaku Kotohajime*. Ed. Odaka Toshirō and Matsumura Akira. Iwanami Shoten, 1964. Hakuseki's autobiography.

Atsumori. Kōwakamai: 3. Ed. Araki Shigeru et al. Heibonsha, 1983.

Azuma Kagami (History of the East). Ed. and given in *kundoku* reading by Kishi Shōzō. 6 vols. Shin-Jimbutsu Ōrai Sha, 1976–79. This chronicle is originally written in *hentai kanbun*, bastardized Chinese. Vol. 6 is a glossary of terms, indexes, maps, etc.

Baishō Ron (On Plums and Pines). Ed. Yashiro Kazuo and Kami Hiroshi. Shinsen Shichō Sha, 1975. An account of the early years of the Ashikaga Shogunate. The title derives from the plum blossom as a metaphor for glory and the pine tree as a metaphor for longevity.

CHIBA TOKUJI. *Seppuku no Hanashi*. Kōdansha, 1972. An informal introduction to the history and custom of disembowelment.

Chūsei Seiji Shakai Shisō: Jō. Ed. Ishii Susumu et al. Iwanami Shoten, 1972. A selection of political and social documents from medieval

Japan, among them Asakura Takakage's "house law" and Hōjō Sōun's "21 articles."

Fudoki (Topographical Reports). Ed. Akimoto Kichirō. Iwanami Shoten, 1958.

Gikei Ki (The Life of Yoshitsune). Ed. Okami Masao. Iwanami Shoten, 1959.

Heike Monogatari (The Tale of the Heike). Ed. Ichiko Teiji. 2 vols. Shōgakukan, 1973–75.

——. Ed. Takagi Ichinosuke et al. 2 vols. Iwanami Shoten, 1959–60.

HIROSE TAKEO. *Hirose Takeo Zenshū.* Ed. Shimada Kinji et al. 2 vols. Kōdansha, 1983.

Hōgen Monogatari, Heiji Monogatari. Ed. Magazimu Yasuaki and Shimada Isao. Iwanami Shoten, 1961. Narratives of the disturbances of the Hōgen and Heiji eras.

INOUE MITSUSADA et al., ed. and comps. *Nihon no Rekishi* (A History of Japan). 26 vols. Chūō Kōron Sha, 1967–1973. I am greatly indebted to some of the individual volumes, such as the sixth, Takeuchi Rizō's *Bushi no Tōjō* (The Advent of the Samurai).

KAIONJI CHŌGORŌ. *Bushō Retsuden* (Biographies of Warrior-commanders). 6 vols. Bungei Shunjū, 1975.

——. *Shidan to Shiron: Jō.* Kōdansha, 1977. A collection of essays on historical writings.

KATSUBE MITAKE, ed. *Bushidō.* Kadokawa Shoten, 1971. The swordsman Yamaoka Tesshū's statements accompanied by Katsu Kaishū's commentary. Includes portions of Nakae Tōju's *Okina Mondō.*

Kinsei Buke Shisō. Ed. Ishii Shirō. Iwanami Shoten, 1974. Contains all the writings on the forty-seven samurai translated in *Legends of the Samurai.*

Kodai Seiji Shakai Shisō. Ed. Yamagishi Tokuhei et al. Iwanami Shoten, 1979. A selection of writings on political and social matters from ancient Japan, among them *Shōmon Ki* and *Mutsu Waki.*

Kojiki (Record of Ancient Matters). *Kojiki, Norito.* Ed. Kurano Kenji and Takeda Yūkichi. Iwanami Shoten, 1958.

Kokon Chomon Jū (A Collection of Ancient and Modern Tales that I've Heard). Ed. Nagazumi Yasuaki and Shimada Isao. Iwanami Shoten, 1966.

Konjaku Monogatari Shū (A Collection of Tales of Times Now Past). Ed. Sakamoto Atsuyoshi et al. 4 vols. Shinchōsha, 1978–84. The section of "secular tales from Japan."

——. Ed. Satō Kenzō. 2 vols. Kadokawa Shoten, 1954–55. The section of "secular tales from Japan."

——. Ed. Yamada Yoshio et al. 5 vols. Iwanami Shoten, 1959–63. Complete.

Kōwakamai. Ed. Araki Shigeru et al. 3 vols. Heibonsha. 1979–1983. Vol. 3 includes *Atsumori.*

Kōyō Gunkan (A Military History of the Great Men of Kai). Ed. and tr. into modern Japanese by Yoshida Yutaka. Tokuma Shoten, 1971. Excerpts.

KUWATA TADACHIKA. *Chosaku Shū* (Collected Works). 10 vols. Akita Shoten, 1979–80. Accounts of warlords, tea masters, women, etc., during Japan's "age of warring states."

——. *Nihon Bushō Retsuden* (Biographies of Japanese Warrior-commanders). 5 vols. Akita Soten, 1971.

Man'yō Shū (Collection of Ten Thousand Leaves). Ed. Kojima Noriyuki et al. 4 vols. Shōgakukan, 1971–75.

——. Ed. Takagi Ichinosuke et al. 4 vols. Iwanami Shoten, 1957–62.

MATSUNAGA TEITOKU. *Taion Ki* (Record of the People to Whom I Am Greatly Indebted). *Taion Ki; Oritaku Shiba no Ki; Rangaku Kotohajime.* Ed. Odaka Toshirō and Matsumura Akira. Iwanami Shoten, 1964. Teitoku's literary autobiography.

MIYAMOTO MUSASHI. *Gorin no Sho* (The Book of Five Elements). Ed. and tr. into modern Japanese by Kameda Shigeo. Kōdansha, 1986.

——. Ed. Watanabe Ichirō. Iwanami Shoten, 1985.

MORI ŌGAI. *Abe Ichizoku* (The Abe Family). *Mori Ōgai Shū.* Ed. Karaki Junzō. Chikuma Shobō, 1965.

MOROHASHI TETSUJI. *Rōshi no Kōgi* (Lectures on Lao Tzu). Daishūkan, 1973.

MURASAKI SHIKIBU. *Murasaki Shikibu Nikki* (Diary). *Makura no Sōshi, Murasaki Shikibu Nikki.* Ed. Ikeda Kikan et al. Iwanami Shoten, 1958.

Mutsu Waki (The Story of Mutsu). See *Kodai Seiji Shakai Shisō.*

Nihon Shoki (History of Japan). Ed. Sakamoto Tarō et al. 2 vols. Iwanami Shoten, 1965–67.

ŌTA GYŪICHI. *Shinchō-kō Ki* (Biography of Lord Nobunaga). Ed. Okuno Takahiro and Iwasawa Yoshihiko. Kadokawa Shoten, 1969.

Oze Hoan. *Shinchō Ki* (Biography of Nobunaga). 2 vols. Ed. Kangōri Amane. Gendai Shichō Sha, 1981. This edition contains Ōmura Yūko's *Sōken-in Dono Tsuizen Ki* (Record in Memorial to Lord Sōken-in).

RAI SAN'YŌ. *Nihon Gaishi* (An Unofficial History of Japan). Ed. and given in *yomikudashi* by Rai Seiichi and Rai Tsutomu. 3 vols. Iwanami Shoten, 1976–78.

Rongo (Confucian Analects). Ed. Yoshida Kenkō. Meiji Shoin, 1982.

Rōshi (Lao Tzu). *Rōshi, Sōshi* (Lao Tzu, Chuang Tzu). Ed. Abe Yoshio et al. Meiji Shoin, 1966.

SEI SHŌNAGON. *Makura no Sōshi* (The Pillow Book). *Makura no Sōshi, Murasaki Shikibu Nikki*. Ed. Ikeda Kikan et al. Iwanami Shoten, 1958).

——. *Makura no Sōshi*. Ed. Ishida Jōji. Kadokawa Shoten, 1980.

——. *Makura no Sōshi*. Ed. Kawase Kazuma. Kōdansha, 1987.

SHIBA RYŌTARŌ. *Junshi*. Bungei Shunju, 1978. A popular writer's affectionate portrait of General Nogi Maresuke.

SHIBASEN (Ssu-ma Ch'ien). *Shiki Retsuden* (Records of the Grand Historian: Biographies). Ed. and tr. into Japanese by Ogawa Tamaki et al. 5 vols. Iwanami Shoten, 1975.

Shōmon Ki (Biography of Masakado). Ed. and tr. into modern Japanese by Kajiwara Masaaki. 2 vols. Heibonsha, 1975–76.

Soga Monogatari (The Tale of the Soga Brothers). Ed. Ichiko Teiji and Ōshima Tatehiko. Iwanami Shoten, 1966.

Sonshi (Sun Tzu). Sonshi, Goshi. Ed. and tr. into Japanese by Amano Shizuo. Meiji Shoin, 1972. "The Art of War."

——. *Sonshi, Goshi*. Ed. and tr. into Japanese by Yamai Waku (Shūeisha, 1971).

Sōshi (Chuang Tzu). *Rōshi, Sōshi* (Lao Tzu, Chuang Tzu) and *Sōshi* (Chuang Tzu). Ed. Abe Yoshio *et al*. Meiji Shoin, 1966.

——. Ed. and tr. into Japanese by Mori Mikisaburō. 3 vols. Chūō Kōron Sha, 1974.

Shunjū Sa-shi Den (Tso Chuan). Ed. and tr. into Japanese by Kamata Tadashi. 4 vols. Meiji Shoin, 1971–81.

——. Tr. into Japanese by Takeuchi Teruo. Heibonsha, 1972.

Taiheiki (Chronicle of Great Peace). Ed. Gotō Tanji and Kamada Kisaburō. 3 vols. Iwanami Shoten, 1960–62.

TAKAHASHI TOMIO. *Bushidō no Rekishi* (History of Bushidō). 3 vols. Jinbutsu ōrai Sha, 1986.

——. *Yoshitsune Densetsu* (Legends of Yoshitsune). Chūō Kōron Sha, 1966.

Uji Shūi Monogatari (Tales Gleaned from Uji). Ed. Watanabe Tsunaya and Nishio Kōichi. Iwanami Shoten, 1960.

WATANABE JUN'ICHI. *Shijima no Koe*. 2 vols. Bungei Shunjū, 1988. A biography of Nogi Maresuke.

YAMAMOTO TSUNETOMO, *Hagakure* (Hidden in Leaves). *Mikawa Monogatari, Hagakure.* Ed. Saiki Kazuma et al. Iwanami Shoten, 1974.

II. IN ENGLISH

BOWRING, RICHARD JOHN. *Mori Ōgai and the Modernization of Japanese Culture.* Cambridge Univ. Press, 1982.

BRANDON, JAMES R., ed. *Chūshingura: Studies in Kabuki and the Puppet Theater.* Univ. of Hawaii Press, 1982. Includes a translation of a puppet-theater version of the forty-seven samurai.

CLAUSEWITZ, CARL VON. *On War.* Penguin, 1968. Col. J. J. Graham's translation.

CLAVELL, JAMES, tr. *Sun Tzu: The Art of War.* Delacorte Press, 1983. Retranslation of Lionel Giles's translation, published in 1910.

COGAN, THOMAS, JR., tr. *The Tale of the Soga Brothers.* Univ. of Tokyo Press, 1987. The most famous vendetta before the forty-seven samurai.

COOPER, MICHAEL, compiled and annotated. *They Came to Japan: An Anthology of European Reports on Japan, 1543–1640.* Univ. of California Press, 1965. Lively contemporary accounts of customs, castles, people, etc., of the period covered.

DALBY, LIZA CRIHFIELD. *Kimono: Fashioning Culture.* Yale University Press, 1993.

DILWORTH, DAVID, and RIMER, J. THOMAS, tr. *The Incident at Sakai and Other Stories by Mori Ogai.* Univ. of Hawaii Press, 1977. Includes a translation of "The Abe Family."

——. *Saiki Kōi and Other Stories by Mori Ogai.* Univ. of Hawaii Press, 1977.

FRIDAY, KARL F. *Hired Swords: The Rise of Private Warrior Power in Early Japan.* Stanford Univ. Press, 1992.

GRIFFITH, SAMUEL B., tr. *Sun Tzu: The Art of War.* Oxford Univ. Press, 1963. A U.S. brigadier general's translation of the famous Chinese tract.

KEEGAN, JOHN. *A History of Warfare.* Alfred Knopf, 1993. The famed British military historian points to the samurai as one of at least four notable warrior classes that have demonstrated the falsity of Clausewitz's well-known definition of war: "War is a mere continuation of policy by other means." The other three are the Polynesians of Easter Island, the Zulus, and the Mamelukes.

KEENE, DONALD, tr. *Chūshingura: The Treasury of Loyal Retainers*. Columbia Univ. Press, 1971. A translation of a puppet play based on the vendetta of the forty-seven samurai.

KITAWAGA, HIROSHI, AND TSUCHIDA, BRUCE T., tr. *The Tale of the Heike*. 2 vols. Univ. of Tokyo Press, 1975.

LIFTON, ROBERT JAY, et al. *Six Lives / Six Deaths: Portraits from Modern Japan*. Yale Univ. Pres, 1979. Includes savagely simplistic biographies of General Nogi Maresuke, Mori Ōgai, and Mishima Yukio.

McCULLOUGH, HELEN CRAIG, tr. *The Taikeiki*. Columbia Univ. Press, 1959; reprint by Greenwood Press, 1976. The first twelve chapters of the *Taiheiki*.

——, tr. *The Tale of the Heike*. Stanford Univ. Press, 1988.

——, tr. *Yoshitsune*. Stanford Univ. Press, 1971. A translation of *Gikei Ki*, a 15th-century account of Minamoto no Yoshitsune.

MILLS, D. E., tr. *Uji Shūi Monogatari. A Collection of Tales from Uji*. Cambridge Univ. Press, 1970.

MINEAR, RICHARD H., tr. *Requiem for Battleship Yamato*. Univ. of Washington Press, 1985. A translation of Yoshida Mitsuru's *Senkan Yamato no Saigo*, an account of the sinking of the largest battleship ever built. Yoshida was an ensign on board when the ship was sunk.

MORRIS, IVAN. *The Nobility of Failure: Tragic Heroes in the History of Japan*. Holt, Rinehart and Winston, 1975. A great account of nine mythological and historical figures and one group, the Kamikaze fighters, who have left an imprint on the Japanese psyche because they failed.

——, tr. *The Pillow Book of Sei Shōnagon*. 2 vols. Columbia Univ. Press, 1967. Translation of *Makura no Sōshi* with extended commentary and notes.

MURPHY, VINCENT, tr. *Build the Musashi: The Birth and Death of the World's Greatest Battleship*. Kodansha International, 1991. Translation of *Senkan Musashi*, an account of the Yamato's twin battleship written by Yoshimura Akira.

NITOBE, INAZO. *Bushidō, The Soul of Japan*. Now reprinted in *Bushido: The Warrior's Code*. Ohara Publications, 1979. The most famous account of bushidō by a Japanese versed in Western traditions.

PHILIPPI, DONALD L., tr. *Kojiki*. Princeton Univ. Press & Univ. of Tokyo Press, 1969. The most authentic English translation of the *Kojiki*.

POUND, EZRA, tr. *Confucius*. New Directions, 1969.

RABINOVITCH, JUDITH N., tr. *Shōmonki: The Story of Masakado's Rebellion.* Sophia Univ., 1986. The rise and fall of Taira no Masakado.

REISCHAUER, EDWIN O., and YAMAGIWA, JOSEPH K., tr. *Translations from Early Japanese Literature.* Harvard Univ. Press, 1951. Includes a partial translation of *Heiji Monogatari* (The Tale of the Heiji Era).

RIMER, J. THOMAS. *Mori Ogai.* Twayne Publishers, 1975.

ROSS, BILL D. *Iwo Jima: Legacy of Valor.* New York: The Vanguard Press, 1985.

RUCH, BARBARA. "Akashi no Kakuichi." *Journal of the Association of Teachers of Japanese,* Vol. 24, No. 1 (April 1990), pp. 35–48. A description of a minstrel who gave the final shape to the *Heike Monogatari.* Included in Yamamura's *Cambridge History,* for which see below.

SANSOM, GEORGE. *A History of Japan.* 3 vols. The Cresset Press, 1959; later imprint, Stanford Univ. Press. Old-fashioned and superbly entertaining history of Japan up to the middle of the nineteenth century.

SATO, HIROAKI, tr. *The Sword & the Mind.* The Overlook Press, 1984. Translations of Yagyū Munenori's tract on swordsmanship, *Heihō Kaden Sho,* and excerpts from Takuan's writings on Zen and swordsmanship.

SATO, HIROAKI, and WATSON, BURTON, tr. *From the Country of Eight Islands: An Anthology of Japanese Poetry.* Doubleday, 1981; reissued by Columbia Univ. Press, 1986.

SATOW, ERNEST MASON. *A Diplomat in Japan.* Seeley, Service & Co. Limited, London, 1921. An excellent book. The subtitle says it all: "The Inner History of the Critical Years in the Evolution of Japan When the Ports were Opened and the Monarchy Restored, Recorded by a Diplomatist who Took an Active Part in the Events of the Time, with an Account of his Personal Experiences during that Period."

TURNBULL, S. R. *The Samurai: A Military History.* George Philip, 1977.

TYLER, ROYALL, tr. *Japanese Tales.* Pantheon Books, 1987. An extensive selection of tales from a range of collections, including the *Konjaku Monogatari Shū.*

URY, MARIAN, tr. *Tales of Times Now Past.* Univ. of California Press, 1979. A selection of 62 stories from the *Konjaku Monogatari Shū.*

URY, MARIAN, and BORGEN, ROBERT, tr. *Kojiki: From Book II,* "The Yamato hero: The Story of Yamato-takeru, son of Emperor Keikō." *Journal of the Association of Teachers of Japanese,* Vol. 24, No.

1 (April 1990), pp. 89–97. Part of the "Readable Japanese Mythology" series.

WASHBURN, STANLEY. *Nogi*. Andrew Melrose, 1913. An American journalist's portrait of General Nogi Maresuke during the Russo-Japanese War.

WATSON, BURTON, tr. *The Complete Works of Chuang Tzu*. Columbia Univ. Press, 1968.

——, tr. *Meng Ch'iu: Famous Episodes from Chinese History and Legend*. Kodansha International, 1979.

——, tr. *Records of the Grand Historian of China*. 2 vols. Columbia Univ. Press, 1961. Translations from the *Shih Chi* of Ssu-ma Ch'ien.

——, tr. *The Tso Chuan: Selections from China's Oldest Narrative History*. Columbia Univ. Press, 1989.

WILSON, WILLIAM R., tr. *Hōgen monogatari: Tale of the Disorder of in Hōgen*. Sophia Univ., 1971.

WILSON, WILLIAM SCOTT, tr. *Hagakure: The Book of the Samurai*. Kodansha International, 1979. Excerpts from Yamamoto Tsunetomo's tract.

YAMAMURA, KOZO, ed. *The Cambridge History of Japan: Vol. 3, Medieval Japan* (Cambridge Univ. Press, 1990). Covers the Kamakura and Muromachi periods.

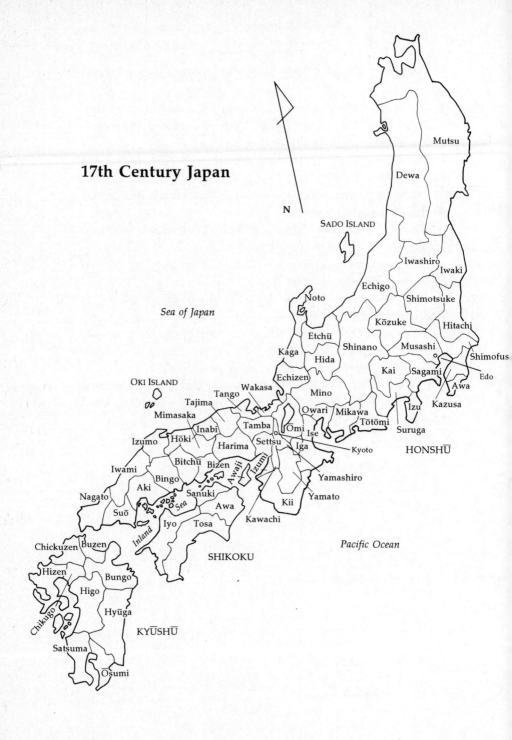

17th Century Japan

N

Sea of Japan

SADO ISLAND

OKI ISLAND

Mutsu

Dewa

Iwashiro

Iwaki

Echigo

Shimotsuke

Noto

Kōzuke

Hitachi

Etchū

Shinano

Musashi

Kaga

Hida

Kai

Sagami

Shimofus

Echizen

Wakasa

Mino

Edo

Tango

Tajima

Owari

Mikawa

Awa

Mimasaka

Tamba

Ōmi

Ise

Izu

Kazusa

Inabi

Tōtōmi

Izumo

Hōki

Harima

Settsu

Iga

Suruga

Iwami

Bitchū

Bizen

Kyoto

HONSHŪ

Nagato

Bingo

Awaji

Izumi

Yamashiro

Aki

Sanuki

Kii

Yamato

Suō

Sea

Awa

Iyo

Tosa

Kawachi

Inland

Pacific Ocean

Chickuzen

Buzen

SHIKOKU

Hizen

Bungo

Higo

Chikugo

Hyūga

Satsuma

KYŪSHŪ

Ōsumi

INDEX OF
IMPORTANT FIGURES

(ALL THE FIGURES IN "THE ABE FAMILY" ARE EXCLUDED)